Identity and Cultural Diversity

D1612150

Identity and Cultural Diversity examines immigration and its effect on diversity from a social psychological perspective. Immigration increases cultural diversity and raises difficult questions of belonging, adaptation, and the unity of societies: questions of identity may be felt by people struggling with the basic problem of who they are and where they fit in, and although cultural diversity can enrich communities and societies it also sometimes leads to a new tribalism, which threatens democracy and social cohesion.

The author Maykel Verkuyten considers how people give meaning to the fact that they belong to ethnic, racial, religious and national groups, and the implications this can have for social cohesion. The opening chapters consider the nature of social identity and group identification, and include discussions of identity development in adolescence, acculturation, and multiple and dual identities. Verkuyten then considers one of the most pernicious social problems: how conflict emerges from perceiving others as different. He examines when and why group distinctions grow into conflicts and considers the role of cultural diversity beliefs, such as multiculturalism and assimilation. The book concludes by exploring productive ways of managing cultural diversity.

Written in an engaging style, *Identity and Cultural Diversity* will be essential reading for undergraduate and postgraduate students of social and cultural psychology and other social sciences, and it also makes key themes in social psychology accessible to a wider audience outside academia.

Maykel Verkuyten is Professor at the Department of Migration and Ethnic Relations in the Faculty of Social and Behavioural Sciences at Utrecht University, The Netherlands. He is Academic Director of the European Research Centre on Migration and Ethnic Relations (ERCOMER).

Identity and Cultural Diversity

What social psychology can teach us

Maykel Verkuyten

Routledge
Taylor & Francis Group

LONDON AND NEW YORK

This edition published 2014
by Routledge
2 Park Square, Milton Park, Abingdon, Oxon, OX14 4RN

Simultaneously published in the USA and Canada
by Routledge
711 Third Avenue, New York, NY 10017

Routledge is an imprint of the Taylor & Francis Group, an informa business

British Library Cataloguing in Publication Data
A catalogue record for this book is available from the British Library

Library of Congress Cataloging-in-Publication Data
Verkuyten, M.
Identity and cultural diversity : what social psychology can teach us /
Maykel Verkuyten.
pages cm
Includes bibliographical references and index.
1. Cultural pluralism. 2. Multiculturalism. 3. Immigrants--Cultural
assimilation. 4. Nationalism. 5. Group identity. 6. Ethnicity.
7. Emigration and immigration--Social aspects. I. Title.
HM1271.V478 2014
305.8--dc23
2013004667

ISBN: 978-1-84872-120-3 (hbk)
ISBN: 978-1-84872-121-0 (pbk)
ISBN: 978-0-203-71014-2 (ebk)

Typeset in Times New Roman
by Saxon Graphics Ltd, Derby

Contents

List of figures

Acknowledgements

Over the years at our European Research Centre on Migration and Ethnic Relations (ERCOMER) at Utrecht University, I have had the pleasure of thinking and working with various people on questions of identity and cultural diversity. I am grateful for their support, suggestions, contributions, and many stimulating discussions. Several of them have been involved in particular studies as PhD students or colleagues, and others have provided invaluable comments and directions. So thank you, Jochem Thijs, Borja Martinovic, Ali Aslan Yildiz, Maike Gieling, Anouk Smeekes, Edwin Poppe, Marcel Coenders, Katerina Pouliasi, Caroline Ng Tseung-Wong, Willem Huijnk, Jellie Sierksma, Thomas de Vroome, Paul Hindriks, Fenella Fleischmann, Mieke Maliepaard, Anke Munniksma, and Jeroen Weesie. A special word of thanks goes to Louk Hagendoorn for his more than 20 years of support and interest in my work and for carefully reading a draft version of this book. Another word of thanks is for Anne-Linde Joki, who was involved in the first stages of preparing the manuscript. Finally, I would like to thank Christel, Wietse, and Ella for their continuous and indispensable warmth and trust in me.

1   The quest for identity and solidarity

The theme of identity is on the minds of a lot of people in our country. Not only among scholars and in political circles, but everywhere. It affects us all. Therefore it is important that the WRR has investigated this subject. A difficult job because there are so many dimensions to it. It has been seven years since I started my personal search for the Dutch identity. I received help from numerous experts. I had the privilege to meet many people, to see, hear and taste a lot from the Netherlands. It was a beautiful, rich experience for which I am enormously grateful. But *the* Dutch identity, no I did not find that. The Netherlands are: large windows without curtains so that everyone can look inside, but also valuing privacy and cosiness. The Netherlands are: only one cookie with coffee, but also enormous hospitality and warmth. The Netherlands are: sobriety and moderation, pragmatism, but also experiencing intense emotions together. So the Netherlands is much too many-sided to be captured in a single cliché. *The* Dutchman does not exist.

(Princess Maxima, 24 September 2007)

This quote is from a short speech given by the then Princess Maxima on occasion of the presentation of the report 'Identification with the Netherlands' of the Scientific Council of Government Policy (Wetenschappelijke Raad voor het Regeringsbeleid: WRR, 2007). The report discusses the meanings, causes, and correlates of Dutch national identification at a time of growing individualization, globalization, and migration. Being of Argentinian origin and having married the Dutch crown prince, the then future queen Maxima seemed the ideal person to give this speech. She is the most popular member of the royal family and a living example of successful immigrant integration. She learned the language quickly, visited all regions of the country, and is regularly seen participating enthusiastically in Dutch traditions and festivities. But reactions to her speech were not very favourable. In fact there was an outburst of public outrage and protest. The far right labelled her speech as 'well-intended politically correct claptrap', and some left-wing intellectuals considered her speech dangerous for social cohesion in society. They also accused her of being haughty because 'she was born in Buenos Aires, has lived in New York, and is landed now in Wassenaar (The Hague)'[1] and therefore would not understand that most people feel connected to one particular place. Others did not so much attack

Princes Maxima as the report of the WRR. For example, a prominent member of the Christian Democrats stated that 'The national identity definitely exists. The royal family itself is a good example of that. Of course there is pluralism, but we have a collective history and national symbols that bind the Dutch.'[2] Others pointed at 'the' Dutch values and norms that would define our national identity. The outrage and protests focused on the possibility that a Dutch identity did not exist, and the strength of the reaction indicates that a great deal was at stake.

For a long time it was problematic – and even more or less taboo – to discuss Dutch identity. The shadow of the nationalist excesses of World War II was responsible for this, but so was the on-going individualization of the society and the increasing economic prosperity that reduced the importance of national belonging. National identity was barely discussed, and when it was, an air of disapproval hung around it. The Dutch self-image was, rather, that we barely have an identity. Posing the question of what is typically Dutch created chiefly some innocent entertainment and was hardly taken seriously.

In the last ten years or so, however, defining Dutch identity has evolved into a serious matter. European unification, increased immigration, and the resulting cultural diversity may threaten Dutch national identity and the solidarity related to it (Lechner, 2008). Old certainties and ties are fading away, resulting in uncertainties and an increasing need for a clear idea of what the Netherlands is. Some do not believe in a Dutch identity or in any benefits from reviving it. Others, in turn, believe that Dutch identity urgently needs to be revitalized with a new content and *élan*. For them, being Dutch has increasingly become a question that requires a response, preferably one that is as clear and distinctive as possible. There is said to be confusion and uncertainty about who 'we' are and what 'we' stand for. There is also talk about a lack of self-knowledge and of self-confidence to publicly express and defend our own identity. This is considered problematic not only for the native Dutch, but also for newcomers. Without clarity one cannot expect immigrants to integrate, because it is not clear what they should integrate into. And without a clear Dutch identity we would not be able to support and embrace further European integration: we need a country to feel European in.

The debate about a Dutch identity is also a discussion about the proper sentiments and emotions attached to this. The call for pride in the Netherlands has been getting louder and more compelling and has even led to a new – although short-lived – political movement called '*Proud of the Netherlands*'. It calls for respect for Dutch culture and for pride in the Netherlands, without contempt and self-deprecation. A healthy form of patriotism is advocated. Anyone who refuses to share in whatever gives us a feeling of pride is quickly suspected of being a killjoy – someone with self-hatred and not truly Dutch at all. Respect from newcomers can be expected only if you yourself have respect for your own culture and identity. Others disagree and advocate, rather, a weak, open, relativistic vision of national identity.

Furthermore, the call today is not only for national pride but also for developing and showing emotional loyalty to the Netherlands, in order that a strong sense of 'us' comes about. Such a feeling would be necessary for social solidarity. Dutch identity should once again provide a warm feeling of security and unity, and that feeling should not be weakened by dual loyalties and multiple identities of minorities and immigrants. Immigration and cultural diversity put a strain on social cohesion, and diversity can lead to a lack of feelings of belonging together, considered a prerequisite for national solidarity, a unified society, and effective democracy. Politicians and the media claim that many immigrants have divided loyalties and a lack of attachment to Dutch society and therefore undermine a cohesive society (Lechner, 2008).

In other countries there have been similar struggles and debates concerning national identity. In many European countries there is a renewed emphasis on traditional national values, and immigrants – Muslims in particular – are scrutinized for their acceptance of a set of 'core values' and their loyalty to the host nation. France appointed a Minister for Immigration and National Identity, organized a national debate on national identity, and has advanced a plan for a 'House of the history of France' aimed at strengthening the national identity.[3] In Great Britain, schools are required to offer more history classes for the same purpose. In Germany, there has been talk of strengthening the national *Leitkultur*. Belgian identity is being threatened by the Flemish–Walloon rift. In Turkey lawsuits have been filed against those who insult or mock the Turkish identity, such as against the Nobel prize winner Orhan Pamuk. And in the United States Samuel Huntington has published *Who Are We? The Challenges to America's National Identity* (2004), while academic journals devote special issues to the subject of American identity.[4]

Immigrants are also expected to show the right national sentiments. In Great Britain, variants of the cricket test have been proposed. This refers to the conservative politician Norman Tebbit who, in 1990, in reference to an assumed lack of loyalty on the part of immigrants and their children, suggested that immigrants who support their native countries rather than England in the sport of cricket are not sufficiently integrated into British society. In France there was a national outcry when Arab French soccer fans booed the French anthem played at the start of a France–Tunisia game at, of all places, the Stade de France in Paris. There was a similar outrage in the Netherlands, when Moroccan Dutch fans disrupted a Dutch–Moroccan soccer match, and in Germany when a soccer match between Germany and Turkey was used by Turkish Germans to express their 'Turkishness'.

There has been a remarkable rise of interest in questions of national identity. Such interest has to do with individualization, globalization, and continuing international migration. Within Europe, on average, almost 11% of the population was born in a country other than the one in which they are currently living.[5] In the United States there is talk about a 'browning of America', and it is predicted that by 2040 immigrants will outnumber White European Americans. It has become difficult to think about national identity without taking immigrants and ethnic minorities into consideration. Ethnicity and cultural diversity are central elements of the national agenda. Worries are voiced about the loss of national feelings of togetherness, the lack of integration of immigrants, and, more generally, about minority cultural values and practices that are not compatible with the liberal values of Western societies. The resulting cultural misunderstandings and ethnic conflicts are considered to lead to a fragmentation of nations into parallel societies, such as the danger of a 'Londonistan' – a capital that is a haven for Islamic fundamentalists.

Questions of immigration and diversity are increasingly questions of religious diversity. Islam, in particular, has emerged as the focus of immigration and diversity debates in Europe (Zolberg & Long, 1999) and is also increasingly discussed in the United States. Muslims have been defined as an 'indigestible' minority (Huntington, 2004, p. 188), and Islam forms a 'bright boundary' separating immigrants from host societies (Alba, 2005). This is illustrated by headscarf controversies in European countries, the controversy about the Mohammed cartoons, and by national debates on the building of mosques and the establishment of Islamic schools and about the place of other Islamic institutions, practices, and claims within Western democracies (Helbig, 2012). However, in research on immigrants and ethnic minorities, religious identity has generally been disregarded (Chaudhury & Miller, 2008; Sirin & Fine, 2008). This is unfortunate, because religion is often of profound importance to people's lives, and religious groups are among the more salient buttresses of identity (Seul, 1999). Compared to identification with other social groups, religious group identification offers a distinctive 'sacred' and unfalsifiable worldview, moral guidance for practices and behavioural choices, and 'eternal' group membership (Ysseldyk *et al.*, 2010).

Living together

One of the most pernicious social problems is people's inability to get along with others whom they see as different from themselves. Sunni, Shia, and Alevi Muslims cannot get along in the Middle East, Turks and Kurds are involved in an intractable conflict in Turkey, Arab Moroccans look down upon Berber countrymen, Albanians are struggling for recognition in Macedonia, Korean Americans and African Americans are involved in conflicts in some American cities, and in many Western countries immigrants clash with natives and ethnic minority groups don't mix with each other.

Contacts between ethnic groups often lead to irritations, tensions, and conflicts. These are often considered natural reactions against threatening 'others', particular among the majority population. Some immigrants and ethnic minorities are also blamed for not really wanting to be part of the host society. There is mutual distrust, accusations, insults, and verbal abuses, there are subtle and less subtle forms of exclusion, and there is open hostility against minorities and against the host society. Cultures are labelled as inferior and backward or as decadent and superficial and, in any case, as incompatible, fostering conflict, not accommodation and adjustment. Stickers with the words 'Fuck the Netherlands' circulate, and some Muslim immigrants explicitly reject Western values, norms, and democratic principles. At the same time a report of the European Monitoring

Centre on Racism and Xenophobia (2006) signals a significant increase in Islamophobia, and European anti-immigrant political parties with slogans like '*Heimatliebe statt Marokkaner-Diebe*' (Austria). '*Our own people first*' (Flanders), and '*True Fins first*' (Finland) have the support of some 15–20% of the population. Such parties have become a significant factor in many countries, sometimes having a say in government policies, as has been the case in Denmark and the Netherlands.

But there are voices from the other side of the fence as well, on the part of those who believe in the positive effects of contact: that by spending more time together, different ethnic groups would develop more understanding and tolerance. People need time to get to know each other and, in time, harmony and social cohesion will follow, especially when there is support from authorities and institutions. In 2008, the European year of intercultural dialogue was launched, with the motto '*Together forever*', and in March 2013 there was a European Action Week against Racism, where the emphasis was on 'valuing diversity' and with the slogan, '*Who says we don't fit together?*' Furthermore, virtually every major city across Europe has a diversity policy, documented in reports with titles such as '*Strong Together*' and '*Unity Is Strength*'. In many European countries and schools, curricula and educational practices aimed at learning about cultural differences and combating racism and discrimination have been proposed and implemented. Diversity has also generated numerous consulting and training companies and has become a profit-making industry. Companies, health-care providers, officials, civil servants, and others spend large amounts of money on diversity training and consulting. These programmes try to promote tolerance and cultural understanding, sometimes trying to change people's attitudes by playing on shame and guilt ('only White people can be racists'), and sometimes by making people aware of their behaviour towards others. Many of the programmes try to change the attitudes of majority group members rather than trying to promote tolerance and cultural understanding among all ethnic groups, and to focus on what is involved in the actual living together.

Immigrants and minorities

Worries are voiced not only about national identity but also about the identity of immigrants and ethnic minorities. Crisis, conflict, confusion, uncertainty, fragmentation, loss, and deprivation are terms used to characterize their identities. Questions of minority identity are extensively discussed, not the least in Internet forums, blogs, and in the social media. Furthermore, in community centres, municipalities, newspapers, and on the radio and television, people express their views about what it means to be a Muslim in the Western world, how Kurds are different from Turks, what it means to be both Algerian and a French citizen, whether one can simultaneously be a Muslim and a German, and how one can integrate without losing one's identity. These views are expressed in debates that are organized around subjects such as '*Identity or Loyalty*', '*Identity and Citizenship*', '*Muslims and Identities*', and '*The Search for Identity*'.

People are drawn to identity issues, and there is clearly something the matter with 'identity'. The integration of newcomers has increasingly become a question of identity, where loyalty and the choice of a new country of residence has priority. Identity confusion or a spoiled identity are seen as responsible for a wide range of problematic outcomes, such as poor mental health, poor school performance, drop-out rates, vandalism, crime, and radicalization. For example, in the report *Resistance and Integration,* the Dutch Ministry of Immigration and Integration mentions that a lack of resilience has to do with the 'quest by young people for an identity in which they can find support and self-esteem' (2005, p. 17). In the report *Radicalism and Radicalisation* of the Dutch Ministry of Justice it is even stated that doubt or dissatisfaction with one's own identity is a necessary precondition for radicalization (2005). And in the *Action Plan Polarisation and Radicalisation* 2007–2010 of the Ministry of Home Affairs it is specified that 'the people who are susceptible to polarization and radicalization are mainly adolescents in search of their identity or vocation' (2005, p. 10).

Despite this diagnosis, the time for cultural recognition and multiculturalism has passed. In 2007, on the first anniversary of the London bombings, the headline in Britain's *Daily Mail* was 'Multiculturalism is dead'. Similar headlines and related articles have appeared in newspapers across Europe and beyond. It is no longer only the far right that criticizes multiculturalism but also mainstream politicians. In 2010, Angela Merkel, the German chancellor, declared that attempts to build a multicultural society in Germany had 'utterly failed', that the so-called '*multikulti*' concept did not work, and that immigrants needed to do more to integrate, including learning German. Similarly, the British prime minister, David Cameron, criticized 'state multiculturalism' in his speech on radicalization and the causes of terrorism in 2011. According to him, the solution is 'a stronger national identity to prevent people turning to all kinds of extremism'. Also in 2011, the then French president Nicolas Sarkozy declared in a nationally televised debate that multiculturalism was a failure and fostered extremism. He stated that, 'We have been too concerned about the identity of the person who was arriving and not enough about the identity of the country that was receiving him.' Spain's ex-premier Aznar, Berlusconi in Italy, Australian's ex-premier Howard and others, joined in consigning multiculturalism to the dustbin.

Multiculturalism is thought to be failing because it has nothing to offer to the majority population and emphasizes differences at the expense of a shared national identity. It results in minorities focusing on their cultural identities instead of on the host nation, and thereby it undermines a cohesive society. Furthermore, multiculturalism would stand in the way of the state's ability and legitimate power to stimulate a shared identity – for example, via the educational system and publicly funded media. Tolerance of diversity would lead to isolated communities and the acceptance of intolerant practices towards women, children, homosexuals, and apostates – especially of Muslim immigrants. The assumption seems to be that national solidarity and cultural diversity cannot co-exist, and the solution is sought in an emphasis on a core of cultural sameness. In the words of David Cameron, 'We need to re-assert faith in our shared British values which help guarantee stability, tolerance and civility.' Assimilation to the core national values is considered key; immigrants are monitored for their allegiance to these values (Kundnani, 2007), and their acceptance as fellow citizens is conditional on passing a national values test. Many countries have been trying to promote a set of shared values that make up the national identity.

In Europe the idea that multicultural policies have failed and have led to more rather than fewer problems has become widely accepted. Some, however, argue that the multiculturalist critique is largely off-target 'primarily because it misidentifies the nature and goals of the multiculturalism policies and programmes that have emerged over the past 40 years during the "rise" of multiculturalism' (Kymlicka, 2010, p. 40). Still others question whether multiculturalism was ever a leading policy paradigm to begin with (Vink, 2007). They point out that policies are hardly ever driven by a single coherent and consistent (multicultural) model but are, rather, the result of on-going struggles over rival practices and discourses on immigrant integration (Bertossi, 2011; Duyvendak & Scholten, in press). This would mean that multiculturalism cannot be blamed. Others argue that the rhetoric has changed but not the underlying perspective and policies. The term 'multiculturalism' might have become problematic across Europe, but many of the original ideas, proposals, practices, and measures continue to exist under labels of pluralism and diversity (Vertovec & Wessendorf, 2010). Despite the rhetoric about the end of multiculturalism, extensive use of notions of diversity as something to endorse and encourage indicates continuing support for immigrant and minority cultural differences.

Country differences

The similarity in developments across Europe does not mean that there are no important differences between European countries. It is obvious that there are many historical, economic, and political differences and that differences in institutional and structural arrangements have an impact on national debates and policies, and on the opportunities and constraints faced by immigrants and minorities. Furthermore, in some countries, such as in Great Britain and France, there are large migrant groups originating from former colonies, and in others, like Germany and Sweden, there are many migrant labourers. Compared to migrant labourers, people from former colonies tend to have a different moral position towards the host society – one expressed in the slogan, 'we are here because you were there'. Additionally, whereas most Muslims in Western Europe arrived there as immigrants, some Eastern and South-Eastern European countries are home to significant numbers of non-immigrant Muslims. Moreover whereas former colonial ties resulted in the settlement of Muslims in France, Britain, and Spain, the Muslim population in Germany, Belgium, and the Netherlands is the result of these countries' recruitment policies for manual labour.

These differences in national contexts and migrant groups are in many ways important but become somewhat less salient when a comparison is made with the United States or Canada. For example, the socioeconomic situation of Muslims in

Europe is quite different from the relatively favourable position of American Muslims. Also, whereas multiculturalism has been declared dead in Europe, it is alive in North America. Although contested, the concept of multicultural education is quite popular in North America. For many, multiculturalism and the accommodation of diversity is still, in the words of the former Secretary of State David Crombie, 'part of what it means to be Canadian'. Multiculturalism 'evolved as a powerful bonding agent for Canadians. It helps to unite us and identify us'.[6] Although there is a continuing debate about this national self-presentation, it tends to be endorsed quite widely.

The difference between settler countries such as Canada and the United States and many European countries might have to do with the fact that the former are founded more on the idea of immigration and civic integration, whereas the latter are 'older' nations, with an established native majority population. In these older nations there is often an implicit ethnic representation of the nation, which emphasizes ancestry and defines 'group ownership', to which linguistic representations of nationhood and of the native population correspond: Dutch typically means 'ethnic Dutch', and German means 'ethnic German'. For a German or a Dutch person their ethnic and national identities are one and the same. An ethnic representation also implies a rather static cultural view according to which cultural traditions and national symbols need to be protected against change. In such a representation, the legitimacy of national membership is more often denied to non-natives, making it difficult for immigrants to feel included and to develop a sense of national belonging. Such a representation also makes it more difficult to incorporate cultural change and diversity in the national self-image. Most European countries tend to think of themselves as rather homogeneous, and as such ethnic, cultural, and religious diversity are seen as undermining the shared national identity.

The differences between North America and European countries have to do with many factors, including migration and integration policies, legal and political arrangements, economic conditions, institutional provisions, ideological beliefs, and the type of minority and migrant groups. Some of these differences are reflected in the terms that are being used. For example, in continental Europe commonly used terms are 'ethnic minorities', 'migrants', 'immigrants', 'newcomers', or 'foreigners'. The term 'race' is not often used, and there is a tendency to talk about prejudice and discrimination rather than racism. In contrast, in the United States the concept of race is commonly discussed, and there is some debate about the distinction between ethnicity and race. Ethnicity is defined differently but in general refers to a group of people who see themselves as having a common ancestry, shared history, and shared traditions. The term 'race' is typically used to refer to a group of people believed to share physical characteristics, such as skin colour and facial features. Some American scholars argue for reclassifying ethnic groups as racial groups, others tend to see racial groups as subsets of ethnic groups. Still others use both terms and speak of ethnic–racial or racial–ethnic groups.

The distinction between the concepts of race and ethnicity is sometimes important and useful, for example because these concepts direct attention to possible differences in ethnic and racial identity content (e.g. ancestry or skin colour). Yet, for other purposes the distinction might be less relevant. Research has found, for example, that the impact of ethnic prejudice on Latino youth is similar to the impact of racial prejudice on African American youth (Altschul *et al.*, 2006). Other research has found that the strength of group identification is psychologically more important than if the group identity is based on cultural, ethnic, or racial labels (Fuligni *et al.*, 2005). Furthermore, self-identification as African American rather than as Black – or, historically Negro – represents a shift from race to ethnicity. This all suggests that race and ethnicity should not be treated as fundamentally different. The American Anthropological Association argued against this by stating the following.

> The historical evolution of these category types is largely ignored. For example, today's ethnicities are yesterday's races. In the early 20th century in the U.S., Italians, the Irish, and Jews were all thought to be racial (not ethnic) groups whose members where inherently and irredeemably distinct from the white population.[7]

This book is not about the context of the United States, or that of Europe, for that matter. My interest is in more general social psychological processes and how these relate to and fuel questions of identity and cultural diversity. For example, prejudice and discrimination against minority groups are well documented in many countries around the world, and similar coping processes seem to be operative among different minority groups in trying to deal with these negative circumstances. The terms used to identify minority groups vary between countries and academic disciplines, and all have their specific connotations and problems. A culturally diverse society is particularly sensitive to the way language is used. Labels are important and can be subject to strong disagreements. Words such as 'migrant', 'guest-worker', and 'foreigner' point to different characteristics and often reflect a certain standpoint. Thirty years ago 'guest-worker' was a common term in countries like Belgium, Germany, and the Netherlands, whereas today it has become more or less unacceptable. In this book I generally use the term 'ethnic minority', because it is closest to my argument. In addition, I use the terms 'immigrants' and 'migrant groups' to refer to people who have themselves moved to a new society *or* whose parents have done so. The term 'natives' or 'majority group' will be used to refer to the non-immigrant population of the receiving country.

Identity, culture, and community

The previous discussion might give the impression that identity, ethnicity, and community are concrete, real things that can be touched, looked at, and handled. But the on-going debate about national identity, as well as ethnic and racial identities, indicates that this is not the case at all. These identities are not set in stone – they are socially constructed. Concepts such as identity and ethnicity should be used for thinking about forms and aspects of social relationships that are the outcome of never-ending social processes.

The Huron Indians of Quebec are today a respected Canadian 'tribe' known as the Wendat. They played a leading role in the Indian movement in the 1960s and 1970s. This is somewhat surprising because they were very much assimilated to the Western way of life and had lost most of their original culture, such as their language, religion, and various traditions. When the Belgian anthropologist Roosens told fellow academics in Quebec that he wanted to study the Hurons, he was advised not to, since they were no longer 'real Indians'. Yet, at the end of the 1960s and the beginning of the 1970s, ethnic leaders started to define authentic 'Huronness' in order to create a collective identity and political cohesion. But most of it was unrelated to the original traditions. Roosens (1989, p. 47) concluded that

> When I compared the characteristics of this neo-Huron culture with the culture depicted in the historical records, most of the modern traits, virtually everything, were 'counterfeit': the folklore articles, the hair style, the moccasins, the 'Indian' parade costumes, the canoes, the pottery, the language, the music.

This example points at several related things.

First, it indicates that the concepts of ethnicity, identity, and culture should not be used interchangeably. Ethnic minority and integration research is often embedded in an ontology of the social world that assumes that ethnic groups are cultural groups and that people who belong to an ethnic group 'have' the culture of that group. However, anthropologists have convincingly shown that culture is not a very useful basis for the definition of ethnicity (Barth, 1969). An important reason is that such a definition leads to a static and reified notion of culture. For example, the notion of 'multicultural society' quickly leads to the idea that cultures are bounded entities, clear-cut wholes, clearly distinguishable from other entities that are linked to other groups. The consequence of this is that the differences and contrasts *between* groups are emphasized and that similarities and commonalities are neglected. Moreover, the similarities *within* groups are easily exaggerated and differences are forgotten. If people belong to the same group and each group has its own culture, then little attention is typically paid to differences within groups and to the possibilities and realities of cultural change, mixture and renewal.

Second, the Huron example shows that a sense of ethnic identity can remain even though, from a cultural point of view, numerous changes have taken place. Acculturation as the process of becoming more similar culturally does not have to imply a change of group membership and self-definition (Hutnik, 1991). People often hold on to their ethnic identity, to what they feel is a continuity with their ancestral past and a loyalty towards their community, although their culture changes and becomes intermingled with that of others. The anthropologist Herbert Gans (1979) coined the term 'symbolic ethnicity' to argue that processes of acculturation and assimilation among descendants of immigrants in the United

States are often accompanied by a renewed interest in their ethnic identity. This interest is not intense enough to lead to ethnic institutions and organizations, but it does give rise to ethnic symbolism. It involves a nostalgic allegiance to the ancestry culture that is expressed in, for example, ethnic consumer goods, festivals, and holidays. In a word, people who regard themselves as Irish Americans may have lost much of their Irishness, but they hold on to an Irish identity by celebrating St. Patrick's day or frequenting an Irish bar. Immigrants can adapt to the society of settlement culturally, but not in an ethnic sense. They can remain proud of their ethnic background and strongly define themselves as, for example, Mexican (in the US context), Pakistani (in Britain), or Turkish (in Germany). Contacts between ethnic groups almost always lead to exchange of cultural characteristics and mutual adjustments, but at the same time the contact can result in enhanced ethnic consciousness and stronger group differentiation in order to maintain a distinctive identity (Tajfel & Turner, 1979). Cultural content and ethnic identity are to an important degree functionally independent. But the Huron example also shows that meaningful ethnic distinctions cannot be maintained without (invented) cultural features that function as markers of identity. Culture is often central in people's everyday thinking and talking about ethnic differences. For example, the cultural forms and histories of Black Americans form the raw material for the creative process that defines what it means to be a Black American.

Third, the Huron example demonstrates that sharing an ethnic identity does not have to imply a community that is held together by close social ties and networks among its members. There often is '*Ethnicity without Groups*', to use the title of a well-known book (Brubaker, 2004). Ethnic distinctions might be relevant for politics and policies, but that does not have to mean that they structure everyday life. The terms 'Mexican', 'Pakistani', and 'Turkish' designate heterogeneous immigrant categories rather than homogeneous and united migrant groups. Migrants and refugees in Europe, America, and Australia are sometimes reluctant to associate along ethnic lines, and they avoid ethno-cultural associations. For example, localities such as neighbourhoods and cities are often more important for self-definition and everyday social relationships than ethnicity. A sort of 'neighbourhood nationalism' (Back, 1996) can exist whereby the non-ethnic distinction between the 'established' and the 'outsiders' predominates in how residents understand and organize their social world.

A fourth lesson to be learned from the Huron example is that ethnic groups should not be taken as self-evident units of observation. This tendency is stimulated by policy categories, the media, and also by research. It is further supported by strong notions of multiculturalism and by 'ethnic studies' such as 'Chicano studies' and 'Asian American studies' as separate fields. But the Huron example draws our attention to processes of 'ethnicization': to the social processes of defining and marking ethnic distinctions and developing forms of solidarity. Ethnicization involves the process 'by which a group of persons comes to see itself as a distinct group linked by bonds of kinship or their equivalents, by a shared history, and by cultural symbols that represent, in Schermerhorn's terms, the "epitome" of their peoplehood' (Cornell & Hartmann, 1998, p. 34). *Creating*

Ethnicity: The Process of Ethnogenesis' is the title of Roosens' book, and leadership is often very important in this process of creation. Despite the invention of a Huron culture, the leaders were very successful in establishing a sense of a distinctive and positive Huron identity among their followers. And the Huron were quite successful politically in getting special rights based on their recognition as a Nation in a treaty with the British in 1760. This shows that leaders can construct and present ethnic identities in particular ways and influence others into adopting it as part of their self-understanding. This forms an important subjective basis for feelings of belonging together and developing and maintaining social solidarity.

Empirical contributions

The public debate about identity and cultural diversity is in full swing. Politicians, opinion makers, commentators, stake-holders, journalists, and writers express their views and opinions, either for or against diversity. Progressive politically correct voices embrace the vitality and richness of cultural diversity and tend to deny the real challenges that it poses to social solidarity, while ethnocentric conservative voices are convinced that diversity leads to social problems and fragmentation. In-between these, the majority of people aren't sure what to think about diversity but increasingly seem to give the latter voices the benefit of the doubt.

An avalanche of opinions, beliefs, and ideas are expressed and spread in society like wildfire. It is not my intention to add yet another opinion – at least, not immediately, and not out of nothing. The discussion will be based on research findings, but this is less straightforward than it might seem. Questions of identity and cultural diversity are complex and multi-faceted and therefore it is no surprise that they are studied from very different theoretical perspectives and in many disciplines, such as political philosophy, history, political science, religious studies, anthropology, geography, economy, educational science, cultural studies, and in psychology. As a consequence there are many findings on numerous topics, collected via various research methods and in all kinds of contexts. For example, social scientists have collected and analysed all sorts of statistics about topics such as employment status, education, housing, leisure, social networks, political opinions, social attitudes, group stereotypes, radicalization, and ethnic, racial, national, and religious identities. The number of studies conducted is incalculable and a great deal is known about the positions, problems, and attitudes of various immigrant and minority groups, of people living in towns and cities, in Black and White neighbourhoods, attending segregated and de-segregated schools, among the young and old, men and women, first- and second-generation immigrants, the religious and non-religious, those with many years of education and those with just a few.

Interestingly enough, the contribution of social psychologists is relatively small, at least where it comes to public and policy debates. One reason might be that it is assumed that, for example, immigrants' identification with the host society is the last and least important step in the integration process (Gordon, 1964). National identification is thought to be restricted to private feelings and to mere symbolic actions, without any substantive social consequences. Yet, group identification has consequences for labour market outcomes (e.g., Nekby & Rödin, 2007), educational achievements (e.g., Altschul *et al.*, 2006), and for group relations and for unity and cohesion in society. So the fact that social psychologists tend to be relatively invisible in public and policy debates is unfortunate. Questions of identity and cultural differences are eminently issues that social psychologists are concerned with. Moreover, multicultural society is not an abstract entity that can be understood in terms of the Enlightenment, the separation of Church and State, freedom of speech, tolerance and democracy, the correct interpretation of the Koran, and the true nature of our culture or identity. These philosophical, political, historical, and theological reflections can often be heard in the media and are important, but most people do not occupy themselves with them. Rather, a multicultural society is created in and through the everyday actions of real people. It is in everyday life that one is exposed to foreign languages, that questions are posed about yourself and others, about cultural practices that are or are not unsettling and disturbing, about the relationships one chooses to enter into or not, about how successfully or poorly one is coping with cultural diversity, and so on (e.g., Newman *et al.*, in press). This means that it is necessary to have an idea about what people want, what they need, what they have a tendency to do, how they usually respond, and what they find difficult to handle.

Psychological citizen

In this book I take the perspective of the 'psychological citizen' (see Moghaddam, 2008). This sounds more complex than it is. What I mean to say by it is that I discuss and examine identities and ways of dealing with cultural diversity in relation to general human tendencies, motives, needs, and beliefs. The focus is on the implications of (social) psychological thinking and research for contemporary issues, dilemmas, and possible solutions in our diverse societies.

At first glance it is not easy to say something meaningful about this. After all, characteristic of human nature is its tremendous openness and flexibility, leading to enormously rich and diversified forms of social life. Human nature is designed for nurture. We are programmed in a such a way that we need culture to complete ourselves (Midgley, 1979). Very little is pre-wired and a great deal is possible, resulting in a huge variation in mental life and behaviour between individuals, groups, and cultures. But the variation is not unlimited. Differences are constructed around basic patterns that cannot be ignored or 'escaped'. For example, there are universal human needs that have to be met in one way or another if people are to thrive, and there are typical ways how people process information and make decisions. The quest for identity can go in very different directions and results in many answers, but the questions that arise, and the doubts and uncertainties associated with them, are quite similar, such as who am I, where do I belong, what is important for me, how am I perceived and valued, how do we differ from them.

These questions and doubts have to do with basic human needs and concerns that are shaped, triggered, and threatened by societal circumstances and developments. Globalization and individualization are complex social processes. They offer unprecedented chances and opportunities but also generate threats and uncertainties. Psychologically, at least two related developments are important. The first is the incredible speed with which technological, social, cultural, and other related changes come about. In many spheres of life there are numerous, sometimes quite drastic, new developments that can have a profound impact on everyday life. It is not easy to keep track of all this, let alone to successfully adapt to all these changes. The corresponding psychological adjustments in ways of thinking, feeling, and acting need time to take root. Answers to questions concerning identity must be convincing and emotionally satisfying, and they have to take shape in appropriate behaviours. But if those answers quickly become outdated, they cannot easily evolve into more stable and secure identities. You can think one day that you belong to one group and the next day to a completely different one, but those external adjustments and changes are not always accompanied by an inner change and conviction. And you can move to another country or become absorbed into the European Union, but it takes years to really feel at home in your new country or to naturally perceive yourself as European. As migrants sometimes say: 'I have left my country, but my country has not left me.' Research among indigenous people like the Inuit, Aboriginals, and Native Americans has shown clearly that people need sufficient time to adapt slowly to rapid changes. If this is not possible, the scope of the ensuing problems is considerable. The same is true for original inhabitants of old neighbourhoods who experience a rapid influx of newcomers and who feel alienated and at a loss because their streets have changed drastically within just a few years.

Second, there is the daily bombardment of alternative social realities. Through television, the Internet, and travel one has access to information about various ways of life, lifestyles, beliefs, ideas, and practices. And as a result of migration and increased cultural diversity one may have to deal with these alternatives on a day-to-day basis. Indirect or direct contact with people who look different, believe different things, and practise different things raises the question not only of who they are, but also of who we are. Diversity and increased contact often lead to an emphasis on differences and identity. Other people show where they come from, with whom they belong, to whom they feel connected, and how they perceive and judge the world. This raises questions about who you are, where you yourself come from, and what you stand for. One's own identity is no longer self-evident. The sheer number of alternatives also implies that people living in the same context tend to share the same experiences less and less, and they develop worldviews that become more and more varied. This makes it difficult to maintain local communities. Moreover, there is a constant flow not only of alternative information, but also of opinions, attitudes, and judgements. Everyone is expected to have an opinion on everything, and everyone claims the right to express their opinion. In addition, everyone feels they have the right to challenge the other to speak up, to explain him- or herself, or simply to offend those you do not agree with. A guiding and representative central body that provides a normative and moral compass is increasingly lacking. And not everyone is able to sail by their own compass in these matters.

These global and social developments are challenging and lay the ground for initiatives, renewal, and creativity. At the same time, many people feel lost, insecure, and alienated. There are clear trends that go against globalization and individualization. There is an increasing focus on the psychological importance of city, region, ethnicity, and country. People search for direction, a sense of security, and something to hold on to, which they find in smaller communities that they can relatively easily identify with and be proud of. This is found particularly in cultural and religious communities, as they are linked with important spheres of life and embody shared experiences. Rapidly succeeding changes and the enormous quantity and diversity of information and opinions make people insecure about who and what they are.

Ethnicity and social psychology

Migration, integration, assimilation, multiculturalism, and tolerance are not only political, policy, economic, philosophical, and sociological issues, they are directly related to social psychological questions. Social psychologists are interested in group identities and relationships between groups. They ask themselves why and when people classify themselves and others into social categories. They examine the consequences of these classifications. They want to know what the psychological mechanisms are behind positive and negative relationships between groups. They examine how far people are able to deal with multiple or dual identities and how such identities develop. They wonder how people react to stigmatization and exclusion. And they examine how cultural diversity and group differences can be managed. There is social psychological research on these issues that increasingly concerns national, ethnic, religious, and cultural groups. A social psychological perspective has a great deal to offer to questions of identity and cultural diversity.

However, social psychology is not a homogeneous field of study. The focus is on various topics, there are many theories, and different methods are used, ranging from experiments in the laboratory to the collection of everyday, natural conversation. It is therefore necessary to specify what my approach is and to indicate that I will have to limit myself.

The minority aspect

In relation to ethnic minorities, social psychologists tend to focus more on the 'minority' aspect than on the 'ethnic' aspect. The 'minority' aspect draws attention to the importance of numerical differences and social positions of power, status, and prestige. Identities and group differences are examined from a structural point of view. The unfavourable social position is seen as the defining principle of ethnic and racial minority groups, and as the central issue for understanding minority identity. Ethnic or racial minority identity are considered reactions or responses to status differences and the predicaments of negative stereotypes, discrimination, and forms of racism.

The emphasis on group status means that phenomena are attributed not to supposed cultural characteristics but, rather, to social circumstances. For example, there is a tendency to hold Islam responsible for almost every problem among European Muslims. However, many of these problems may have to do with learning to live as a religious minority in an environment that is not exactly enthusiastic about your presence. Most Muslims come from a country where they form the dominant majority, and now they find themselves in a minority position and to belong to a group that is held in low regard.[8]

Yet, ethnic identity is not composed simply of a minority status, and treating it as such limits the ability to examine and understand the richness of the meanings and experiences associated with this identity. In focusing on the 'minority' aspect of ethnic minorities, the 'ethnic' aspect tends to be ignored. Ethnic minority groups are treated like any low-status or powerless group to which the same social psychological processes are applied. But what about ethnicity: where does the ethnic aspect comes in?

The ethnic aspect

Ethnicity is often thought of as culture that is transmitted across generations, and research on the 'ethnic aspect' tends to focus on cultural content. Although in social psychology an interest in culture is growing, it is still limited. However, studying ethnic minorities and ethnic relations inevitably raises all kinds of cultural questions, related, for example, to the way culture is implicated in ethnicity, acculturation, group relations, and multiculturalism. The importance of culture for human psychology and everyday life is enormous. The Huron example shows that ethnicity and culture should not be equated, but this does not mean that both cannot be strongly connected. In people's mind ethnic identity is typically associated with culture and not only as an 'instrument' for drawing ethnic boundaries: 'ethnic relations cannot always be fully understood by way of analyses of competition and domination, but may also be regarded as "encounters between cultures"' (Eriksen, 1993, p. 136). Situations of intensive contact between ethnic groups show that cultural differences do exist and do matter. For instance, language, traditions, and practices are not only – arbitrary – means for marking ethnic distinctions, but also meaningful cultural aspects as such, both for one's ethnic group and for outsiders. Many people from ethnic minority groups, for example, have a cultural background that differs from that of native inhabitants. Immigrants from Turkey, Morocco, Sudan, Iran, and other places cannot simply choose to do away with their childhood and everything they learned culturally. When people from different origins live close to each other, the feeling that others have different customs, habits, and ideas is accentuated rather than moderated. After all, people see and experience first-hand that a number of supposed differences are not merely stereotypical but have actual implications, related, for example, to gender differences, socialization practices, and values, norms, and habits. Such differences are not imaginary, as the many misunderstandings and conflicts in intercultural communications show. Cultural differences are often difficult to verbalize, but that does not mean that they are not real. These differences are deduced from very subtle and unspoken signals that are communicated in interactions. Culture is tacit, lived, and physically felt rather than realized and verbalized. It is the unreflexive part of mundane everyday practices. Often people are quite sure of the existence of cultural differences, even though it is difficult to indicate exactly what those difference are.

However, it is also true that 'culture' is a readily accepted explanation that can obscure rather than improve our understanding. A focus on culture often means downplaying situational and material circumstances. In public debate, but also in research, it is quite common to attribute all kinds of problems and differences between ethnic groups to – assumed – cultural characteristics and deficits. The most diverse phenomena, such as educational performance, truancy, unemployment, vandalism, and crime, are explained by referring to culture. This sometimes leads to remarkable suggestions. An example is the proposal in the Netherlands to rebuke boys of Moroccan origin in a culturally appropriate way, such as giving a cuff on the ears or humiliating them in front of their own people.[9] In most cases, these cultural interpretations are nothing more than stereotypes and afford little or no insight into the actual processes that are important in everyday life. The reference to culture is not specific enough and often gets in the way of asking important questions. You do not meet any cultures but you meet real people who try to live their lives in diverse and often complex social, economic, and historical circumstances.

A crisis in social psychology

After the horrors of World War II, psychologists were puzzled about why and how such horrors could have happened. Which psychological forces were responsible for this? Surely, the psychological make-up of those involved in the atrocities should be responsible – that is, a pathological personality type that is the product of a family history of authoritarian upbringing. Others referred to general motivational or cognitive processes for understanding these atrocities, and prejudice and stereotypes more generally. For example, strong frustrations due to an economic decline might lead to aggression against scapegoats, and harmless, general cognitive principles might underlie stereotypes and prejudices in all people. For instance, although not leading to atrocities drawing a clear distinction between categories of people would inevitably lead to stereotypical thinking and prejudicial attitudes. The cognitive orientation in social psychology that became dominant in the 1970s has yielded a large quantity of findings. But there has also been discontent.

In the early 1970s there were extensive discussions concerning the crisis in social psychology. Scholars began to wonder where all this social psychological research had led (e.g., Elms, 1975; McGuire, 1973). The step from studying internal psychological mechanisms to the explanation of relationships and conflicts between real groups in real life was too great. In an attempt to understand important social phenomena, scholars were becoming more and more caught up in the details of mental life. Key points – that basic psychological processes can turn out very differently depending on social and cultural circumstances and that human thought and action always take place in a social context – were gradually forgotten. As a result, it was felt that much of social psychology had little to say about important social problems. The processes and factors that could be manipulated and systematically examined in experimental settings were often not the ones that really mattered in the outside world. The discontent in the 1970s led a number of researchers to start looking for an alternative (see Armistead, 1974). As social psychologists, they continued to be interested in psychological principles, but now in the context of structural and ideological characteristics of the social world. One of the core ideas was that knowledge of basic psychological processes and principles does not offer an adequate understanding of social reality. These researchers were very critical of approaches that simply tried to explain social phenomena on the basis of general psychological processes, such as group conflict being the result of human aggression or discrimination being the result of competition. This is like trying to analyse a football match starting from the idea that humans have an innate tendency to compete. But such a tendency says little or nothing about how the game is played, about the course of the match, how a team functions, and how the opposing team is perceived. To use a metaphor: it is of no use to try to explain a traffic jam by investigating what is happening under the hood of a car.

An analysis of basic psychological processes should not be confused with behavioural regularities in the real world. Psychological forces and processes need to be considered in their social context. For example, it is important to know that people strive for a positive group identity, but that tells us nothing about how this is achieved. As we will see, there are many ways in which one's own group can stand out positively, such as by being competitive or, rather, by being cooperative. And the fact that people look for a sense of certainty about who and what they are says nothing about when this search is particularly strong and what it is that gives a feeling of belonging and grounding. Sometimes people also seek uncertainty, and something to hold on to can be found in a rich and glorious past but also in dogmatic principles. There are general psychological processes, but in order to give explanations and to make predictions about actual human behaviour, it is necessary to consider specific circumstances and contents. The structural, cultural, and ideological features of the social world must be taken into account. Only then can we understand how psychological principles underlie human action. At the same time, psychology helps us to understand which features of society will affect what people think, feel, and do. It helps us to know what to look for in the social world and to understand why and how particular circumstances affect people's lives.

In this book I take a social psychological perspective, but not one that is predominantly concerned with abstract and general mental processes and tends to ignore cultural and ideological content. A social psychological understanding of ethnic minority identity needs to focus on both the relevant underlying processes for groups that differ in status and power, and on contextual cultural meanings. For understanding what it means to be a member of an ethnic group, we must consider not only basic needs and motives but also the cultural and ideological context within which identities are located and defined.

What do we know and how do we know?

A large amount of research has been conducted into various aspects of ethnic, national, and religious identities and questions of cultural diversity. Some understanding of the type of research that is being done provides a basis for making discerning judgements about research findings that are discussed in this book. Researchers can proceed in very different ways and take on quite different roles. They can describe social and psychological reality, take a picture of it, make a film about it, manipulate it, listen to it, and observe it.

Describing

There is much descriptive research in which all sorts of information is expressed in numbers. Any reasonably large city has a poll among its residents or conducts a 'Youth Monitor Survey', schools, organizations, and institutions keep records, and national institutes for statistics or social research produce regular reports on immigration, minorities, and integration. All this work is important because situations, developments, and problems are mapped, and this provides important input and starting points for policies. But what exactly those starting points are is not always clear. Apart from the fact that numbers are never just numbers because their collection and processing depends on all kinds of decisions about definitions and categorizations, there is also the question of interpretation. Descriptions provide answers to 'what' questions ('what is the state of affairs') but typically fail to answer 'how' and 'why' questions. The finding that only half of Dutch Moroccan youth in Amsterdam feel connected with the Netherlands leads to a call for new policies. But what exactly do you do? Without having an understanding of what is behind this finding, it is difficult to take appropriate measures. To explain this finding, some will point to a historical tradition of distrust among Moroccans, others to their experiences of discrimination or lack of schooling, and yet others to the collectivist culture in which loyalty to one's own community comes first. And in an attempt to get a further grip on the matter, a typology or taxonomy is proposed: the suspicious, the misunderstood, the frustrated, and the loyal youths.

At the descriptive level, such a typology may be useful because it provides a summary of some related attributes. But typologies only classify information; they do not provide an explanation. You can give a typology of phenomena or of different types of explanations, but you cannot give an explanatory typology. The reason is simple: there are many roads that lead to Rome. One and the same phenomenon may have different backgrounds. For example, individuals can be prejudiced due to ignorance, out of frustration, by feelings of threat, or because their own group expects it of them. Similarly, discrimination can have many reasons, such as racism, negative stereotypes, and lack of consideration. In addition, multiple reasons can play a role simultaneously: frustration and threat and group expectations. Stereotypes do not need to translate into discriminatory conduct. People may also be aware of their negative thoughts and feel guilty about them, they may not be in a position to exclude others, a strong group norm against discrimination may exist, and so on. It is the interplay between the various factors that ultimately determines what happens. An adequate explanation can only be based on a careful analysis of the psychological and social factors and processes that are involved. This not only requires a systematic way of thinking, but is also restricted by the boundaries of what is possible in research.

Taking a picture

Multicultural reality is complex, and the possibilities for research are limited. This also applies to large-scale, representative survey research in which opinions, attitudes, and behaviours among different ethnic groups and different segments of the native population are assessed. This type of research is conducted in many countries and provides a wealth of information that is analysed using increasingly complex statistical methods. It primarily examines whether ethnic groups differ on a range of outcomes: whether, for example, people of Pakistani, Indian, or Bangladeshi origin living in Great Britain differ in terms of socioeconomic position, health, and well-being, and in their attitudes towards society, themselves, and many other issues. This approach means that these ethnic groups are taken as self-evident units of observation and analysis. Individuals from the same country or with parents from these countries or who themselves have ticked the same 'ethnic' box in a questionnaire are taken together as a separate ethnic group that is then compared with other groups, including the natives.

   This procedure contains the danger of over-stating the concreteness of ethnic groups and of lumping together people who actually have a very diverse (sub) ethnic or cultural backgrounds. Furthermore, the description of group differences is frequently phrased in explanatory language in which ethnic group membership is a factor in an explanatory model. If it is found that Moroccan Dutch youth identify less strongly with the country than do their Surinamese Dutch peers, then it is typically implied that the 'ethnic variable' forms an important element of the explanation for this. This tendency is supported by the statistical language that is used with formulations like 'ethnicity explains the differences in national attitudes'. But the empirical observation of an association does not explain why that association exists. There must be something substantive, something meaningful that explains the group difference found. Furthermore, it might be the case that it is not ethnicity that is important for national identification but, rather, socioeconomic position, educational level, migration history, or locality, and these factors might differ between youth with a Moroccan or a Surinamese background. Identification with the country might be a matter of socioeconomic position rather than ethnicity, but this, again, raises the question of why exactly this position is important.

Research does try to examine whether other factors are more important than ethnicity. Some people identify more strongly with the host country than others. People also differ in many other characteristics, such as place of residence, age, ethnicity, religion, sex, political affiliation, income, education. These characteristics are also related to each other. Older people generally have a higher income than younger people, and on average men earn more than women. The statistical analysis can determine which of these characteristics is associated with the degree of national identification while controlling statistically for all the other factors. For example, when the individual differences in identification run parallel with differences in education, there is a statistical relationship: the lower the level of education, the stronger the identification.

But this statistical relationship is, again, not a substantive explanation. Why exactly is education related to national identification? What, precisely, is behind this link? Do the less educated feel more insecure about themselves, do they feel more easily threatened by newcomers, do they have more contacts with other ethnic groups and therefore a stronger tendency to differentiate themselves, or do they, rather, have less contact with other nationals and therefore a more ethnocentric worldview? Do they think in less sophisticated ways and therefore more in us-and-them terms? The observed statistical correlation is the beginning of the quest for an explanation, not the endpoint.

Another example is Robert Putnam's (2007) research on cultural diversity, which has caused quite a stir. Putnam presents the results of his extensive research among Americans from 40 different communities in the United States. It appears that trust in neighbours is lower wherever the ethnic diversity in the neighbourhood is higher. This applies not only to the trust in neighbours from different ethnic groups, but also to neighbours of one's own ethnic group. According to Putnam, with increased ethnic diversity, all people become like turtles. They withdraw and isolate themselves into their homes. But why this should be remains unclear. That people turn away from other ethnic groups in ethnically diverse communities is perhaps understandable, but it is more difficult to imagine why they also withdraw from their own ethnic group. Here too, the statistical relationship is a starting point for looking for an adequate explanation.

In this type of research, the researcher works like a photographer, taking a separate 'picture' of many individuals and examining whether some things go together. Perhaps it turns out that men more than women, or the old more than the young, wear typical national emblems. Furthermore, the researcher can also take a mental picture by asking in a questionnaire not only how strongly people identify with their nation, but also about their political beliefs, their trust in others, whether they feel insecure about themselves, and so on. These aspects might be related to each other and also to national identification. People with more right-wing beliefs and those who feel more insecure probably identify more strongly with their nation. In this case there are statistical associations between mental constructs, such as beliefs, attitudes, feelings, and identifications. This gives a further understanding of what could be behind national identification, but the meaning of these associations is not self-evident. Is it because people hold politically conservative beliefs that they are more nationalistic, or is it the other way around, or are both caused by something else – a 'third variable', such as feelings of insecurity? A third variable can also be responsible for the fact that no association is found between two things. A large-scale research survey conducted in more than 700 organizations in the United States examined the effectiveness of diversity-training programmes on the hiring of minority members in management. It was concluded that these programmes were ineffective (Kalev *et al.*, 2006). But it is possible, for example, that organizations that were unwilling to change their hiring practices implemented the training programmes to make it look as if they were pro-diversity.

Making a film

Questions of causality and disturbing third variables cannot be solved by complex statistical analyses. An adequate answer requires theoretical reasoning, additional studies, and a different research design. For example, to improve our understanding, other large-scale studies can be conducted to assess whether an observed relationship depends on specific factors and conditions. Putnam's findings might be specific to the United States but not hold true in the European context, or they might be specific to neighbourhoods and not apply to organizations and schools, or might depend on the index of ethnic diversity that is used. These kinds of questions help us to move in the direction of finding an explanation but still begs the question of what exactly is going on.

It is also possible to do longitudinal research over a longer time period, for example by asking the same people the same questions annually for five consecutive years. This means that the researcher is trying to make a film rather than to take a picture. A film with only five images is not very extensive, but it is better than a single picture. A film exists of separate images that show how a scene develops over time. It makes it possible to see whether people who are insecure at the beginning of the film are more nationalistic later on, or the other way around. So some understanding of possible causal relationships can be obtained, but causality itself cannot be determined. We are never certain that insecurity in the first year of the research actually caused nationalism two years later. Much happens in two years' time, and it is possible that something else in a person's life is responsible or involved. This is especially likely when more time has passed, suggesting that the time between two measurement points should be short. But identities, beliefs, feelings, and behaviours typically do not change overnight. It can take quite some time before feelings of national belonging take root, and the most appropriate time interval for measuring developments in national identification depends on theoretical reasoning.

Manipulating

Social psychologists often use an experimental research design that offers the best answers to questions of causality. The basic principle is straightforward: If I want to know whether additional light promotes the growth of tomato plants, I give one group of plants extra light and another identical group of plants not. After a while I can observe the result, and I know whether additional light indeed promotes the growth. The same principle is used in psychological research. An experimental group is subjected to some manipulation or 'treatment', and the control group is not. The manipulation serves as an operationalization of a theoretically assumed psychological process. On the basis of the difference in responses and reactions between the two groups, it is determined whether the manipulation or treatment does indeed have the expected effect. For example, if the proposition is that feelings of insecurity lead to stronger national identification, then such feelings are evoked within participants of the experimental group and not in the control group. Because this feeling is the only thing that differs between the two groups, differences in national identification can be attributed to the degree of feeling insecure.

This example shows the strengths but also limitations of this approach. Social psychological experiments are often about 'putting people in strange places where strange people ask strange questions'. Therefore the question is always how people will react outside an experimental setting in which many factors are relevant (Michell, 2012). Insecurity is an important factor, but how exactly this plays out depends on the everyday circumstances in which people find themselves, and on other psychological and social principles that come into play. Nevertheless, experiments are a useful and powerful means to investigate these principles. They make perfect sense as a way of advancing our understanding of psychological processes and consequences and therefore are an important tool and place to start – that is, if the experimental study is theoretically driven and focuses on understanding of the real world. Theoretical assumptions have to be made and the social context should be kept in mind. For example, there is not much sense in setting up experiments that do not correspond to what happens in the real world. These experiments can provide simple, elegant models that can be tested systematically, but this has little to do with everyday reality. They are 'experiments in a vacuum': experiments for the sake of the experiment. Relevance is thereby exchanged for formal precision. It is comparable to someone who has lost his keys in a dark part of the street and then starts looking for them under a lamppost because he can see better there. No matter how good the light, he will never find his keys.[10] Assumptions must be realistic, and the experiment must contribute to an understanding of social reality, not of a fictional world that only exists in a laboratory.

Field experiments can be very useful in this respect. For example, we can compare the hiring decisions of employees who are divided on a random basis into one group that did and another that did not take part in a diversity-training programme. With such a design we can see whether the training programme has an effect on the hiring of minorities in management. There is also field experimental research on labour market discrimination of immigrants and ethnic minorities. An example is a study in the Netherlands in which professional actors, with differing ethnic backgrounds, were trained to apply in the same way and with the same job-relevant characteristics for the same jobs. It turned out that ethnic minority job applicants were almost twice as likely to be rejected by temporary employment agencies (Andriessen *et al.*, 2012).

This book presents and discusses the results of different social psychological experiments. These experiments deal with identities and relations between groups and inevitably focus on small pieces of the larger puzzle. To complete the puzzle, no piece can be missed, but it is also important to realize that a particular piece never tells the whole story. Social psychologists doing research on a particular psychological principle or process often tend to forget that in all their enthusiasm. They start to explain complex social realities by a single principle, such as the need for self-esteem, or a lessening of uncertainty, or social dominance orientation. Or they assume that a simple sequence of cause and effect provides an adequate explanation, like frustration leading to aggression. But these one-sided explanations are, of course, rarely satisfactory, and moreover, they imply a limited understanding of human beings. Humans are not like helpless machines: they can image future realities, plan ahead, and debate and negotiate about the meaning of the world. Human behaviour and social life is not only about cause and effect or patterns of associations – it is also about imagination, anticipation, narratives, purpose, coincidence, and luck.

Listening

Experimental work is valuable, but it provides no final answers. Small-scale and intensive examination of a particular situation or a small group of people, can, for example, map in detail the relevant factors and processes and how they play out in everyday life. Not only does this provide a rich image of multicultural reality, but it is also useful for the further development of theoretical ideas. By showing in detail that a general assumption does not apply in a particular case, a theory can be falsified or at least improved with the necessary precision.

Experimental work and also questionnaire research are limited because they are not able to map the diverse and complex feelings and thoughts that people often have when it comes to questions of identity and cultural diversity. Many people are struggling with these issues, but most researchers tend to offer them very little opportunity for telling their own stories. People often want to explain how they feel and why they have certain views, but they are only asked to push computer keys or to indicate their level of agreement by ticking a box. People often also want to discuss topics and issues that occupy them, rather than only answering the questions that are of interest to the researcher. Listening to people, to what they have to say in their own words about their own experiences and feeling, is in social psychology but also in sociology, a greatly underestimated source of information for discovering regularities and generalities in the ways in which people understand and deal with issues of identity and cultural diversity.

Observing

Ethnic identity is not only about attitudes, beliefs, and feelings but also about verbal and non-verbal behaviour in social interactions. Furthermore, 'Studying social behaviour in real life contexts is essential, not only to return social psychology to its roots, but also to ensure that our contributions are both theoretically rich and socially valuable' (Bar-Tal, 2004, p. 677). It is in social interactions that identities, group differences, and belonging are enacted and talked about (Benwell & Stokoe, 2006). For example, ethnic identity can be seen as a situational accomplishment rather than as an inner sense of being a member of an ethnic group. This means that it is important to pay attention to the ways in which people craft and explain their identity in relation to specific others. This is a largely neglected but crucial aspect of the ways in which identities form and structure 'everyday life, as it happens'. It is in social interactions that people define social reality and negotiate who they are. Interaction is norm-oriented: the things individuals say and do imply a normative framework of accountability that supports or challenges their identity claims. The types of behaviours and discourses that are used to construct an ethnic identity and to provide an account provide an understanding of the ways in which people actually negotiate an acceptable ethnic identity in everyday life. For this book it means that I also consider types of social psychological research that focuses on analysing conversation as it happens in social interactions.

This book

This book is about social identities and group relationships as they arise and develop in multicultural contexts. It takes the perspective of the psychological citizen. The social psychological thinking and research that I discuss is geared towards a better understanding of multicultural societies. This understanding will not be looked for in detailed descriptions of concrete situations and circumstances, or in the very different meanings that ethnic and cultural groups have and that individuals attach to them. Such descriptions are important and informative and are regularly made, especially in anthropology and cultural studies. This book is about more general psychological principles and how these play out in everyday life. This is important for several reasons.

One reason is that in this way theoretical fragmentation can be prevented. There is a large number of ideas about the backgrounds of various developments and issues in relation to identities and cultural diversity. Most of these ideas point to similar psychological principles, such as feelings of insecurity, threat, alienation, and exclusion. By focusing on those principles, the number of theoretical concepts remains limited, and the underlying similarities and differences between phenomena can be investigated.

Another reason is that research on questions of cultural diversity is closely linked with public policy issues and public debates. This implies political sensitivities and heated debates about responsibilities and loyalties. In discussions about cultural diversity, putting the blame on one another is a favourite pastime. As a result, there are many different concepts in circulation for the same phenomenon (e.g., 'colour blindness' and 'assimilation') and the same concept (e.g., 'integration') is used in many different ways. Another consequence is that relatively little attention is paid to the underlying theoretical principles and processes that are at stake. This is unfortunate, because, as the saying goes: 'nothing is as practical as a good theory'.[11] For our understanding, and therefore also policy-wise, it is important to take an analytical and theoretical approach – one that examines how and why certain phenomena come about. This is far from easy, because many factors interact at various levels, and many researchers, including myself, have argued that different levels of analysis should be considered in order to understand the phenomena of group identities and cultural diversity (e.g., Deaux, 2006; Verkuyten, 2005c). Here I aim to show how social psychological knowledge can contribute to a better understanding of questions and problems related to identities and cultural diversity. Social psychology can make a modest but useful contribution to understanding the complexities involved and thereby provides food for thought as well as signposts for trying to develop adequate responses to questions of identity and cultural diversity.

How do people give meaning to the fact that they belong to ethnic, racial, religious, and national groups, and what are the implications for intergroup relations when people – alone or with others – act in terms of who or what they think they are? That is the key question. Chapter 2 deals with the concept of identity and group identification. Identity is a multi-faceted and confusing concept, and one that often leads to all kinds of misunderstandings and ambiguities. This chapter elaborates the idea that the scientific and policy relevance of the identity concept depends on conceptual clarity and an understanding of the various aspects of identity and underlying human needs. Chapter 3 discusses the issue of discrimination and the situational dependency of ethnic identity. Questions of identity development, particularly in adolescence, and of multiple and dual identities are addressed in chapter 4. Ethnic identity is, in principle, always 'one out of many', which raises the question of how this identity relates to other identities and whether so-called dual identities are possible. Us-and-them thinking relates to group identification and is often – implicitly or explicitly – linked to group tensions and conflicts. In chapter 5, it is shown that this is far from obvious. A simple relationship between group loyalty and group conflicts does not exist. It will be argued that it is necessary to determine when and why a distinction grows into a contradistinction or conflict. Chapter 6 is about valuing diversity. As a normative and policy model, multiculturalism does not seem to be the best response to cultural diversity. But that does not mean that there are not aspects that are useful, especially the idea of multicultural recognition in which group identities are approached in a positive manner. Chapter 7 investigates the proposition that societies need a common identity shared by all. But this raises the question how such a shared 'we feeling' can be realized and whether this always has a positive effect on the relations between ethnic groups. The chapter discusses different possibilities for trying to improve intergroup relations: what might work and what does not, and what needs special attention for ethnic relations to develop in a positive direction. In the concluding chapter 8 the book is brought to a close with a short retrospective of what has been discussed and a preview of what might be ahead of us.

Throughout the book, examples from different countries are used as evidence and to illustrate different ideas and claims. The examples are taken not only from Europe but also from North America and places like Japan, Turkey, Burma, and Mauritius. Yet, many of the empirical studies that are discussed have been conducted in the Netherlands. The main reason is that these studies have been conducted within the framework of ideas and the perspective that is presented in this book. Another reason is that one of the more ambitious and overt European attempts at multiculturalism was developed in this country, but the retreat of multiculturalism is also most evident here (Joppke, 2004).

Some 50 years ago, groups of immigrants started to come to the Netherlands, most of them originally from Turkey, Morocco, Surinam, or the Dutch Antilles. In the 1960s, the Netherlands was one of the European countries that recruited labour migrants from Morocco and Turkey. From the 1970s onwards, family reunification and formation led to a further increase in the Turkish and Moroccan immigrant population in the Netherlands. Currently there are around 800,000 people of Turkish or Moroccan origin in the Netherlands which accounts for approximately 5% of the population. The great majority of both migrant groups are Muslim; in terms of socioeconomic position and societal acceptance they are at the bottom of the ethnic hierarchy.

In 1951 a group of South Moluccans arrived in the Netherlands. They had served in the Royal Dutch Indian Army that had fought against the independence of Indonesia. Another colonial legacy is early immigration to the Netherlands from the former colony of Surinam in South America. Following the independence of Surinam in 1975, immigrants from diverse socioeconomic backgrounds came to the Netherlands. Like that of the Surinamese, the immigration of the Antilleans, which increased rapidly in the 1990s, concerned people with diverse socioeconomic backgrounds, including students, but also many underprivileged youth (labour migrants). Around 500,000 people with a Surinamese or Antillean background currently live in the Netherlands, which is around 3% of the population. The Surinamese and Antilleans have a better socioeconomic position than the Moroccans and Turks, and they are also more accepted by the native Dutch majority.

In the 1990s many refugees and asylum seekers who had fled from countries such as Iraq, Iran, Sudan, Ghana, Somalia, and Ethiopia sought refuge in the Netherlands; for example, in 2000 around 130,000 people came with the intention of settling in the Netherlands. In addition, there are new groups of 'labour migrants' from East European countries such as Poland and Bulgaria.

2   A jellyfish on the beach

About identity

On Monday, 17 January 2005, a woman stops her car at a pedestrian crossing in Amsterdam.[1] A young man takes this opportunity to steal the woman's handbag and escapes on the back of a friend's scooter. The woman responds by immediately reversing and starts a chase. She hits the scooter, and the purse snatcher is killed. In the debate in the days that follow, the background of the Moroccan purse snatcher plays a decisive role. For many Moroccan Dutch people, his death is proof that Moroccans run the risk of getting killed solely for stealing a handbag. Feelings of anger and the idea that Moroccans, as second-class citizens, are discriminated against and criminalized come to the surface. Many native Dutch have a different interpretation: the thief has himself to blame for his death, and the whole event is evidence of widespread Moroccan crime, the growing Islamic threat, and the failure of Dutch integration policy.

The following day family, friends, and acquaintances laid flowers, candles, and letters at the place of the 'accident'; it became a place of commemoration similar to those where an act of senseless violence has taken place. The following morning, it turned out that unidentified persons had removed the flowers and letters and replaced them with a racist drawing. New flowers were placed, and stickers of ladybugs were attached as a symbol of acts of senseless violence. That Wednesday it was announced that on the following Friday a silent march, another key symbol of senseless violence, would take place, from the central railway station to the place of the 'accident'. In consultation with the family and minority organizations, Mayor Cohen announced that he would not allow a silent march, but that a memorial procession could be held from the location to the local mosque. The organizers of the march, however, continued to speak of a silent march. On Friday night, after the march, which was attended by roughly 500 mostly Moroccan Dutch, Prime Minister Balkenende voiced his support for Cohen's decision: the place of commemoration, together with the term 'silent march', would wrongly make the deceased a victim of senseless violence.

The event itself and those that followed from the incident were interpreted differently. Yet there is no doubt that the distinction between 'us' and 'them' was paramount, and that most people were inclined to make interpretations and choose sides along these lines. Those directly involved responded to the situation as native Dutch or as Moroccan. Personal characteristics and individual circumstances hardly mattered. With the march Dutch Moroccans presented themselves as a self-confident group and with their definition of 'silent march' also as well integrated in Dutch society. With the term 'memorial procession', Cohen attempted to re-define the situation as a private matter for family, friends, and acquaintances who wanted to express their grief. Apparently there was much at stake, and it had everything to do with identities and group positions. But what sorts of identities were actually involved here?

About identity

Identity is a complex, multifaceted, and confusing concept. The Dutch historian Kossman once warned: 'Walk around it with caution, inspect it from all sides but do not step into it, simply treat it like a huge jellyfish on the beach' (Kossman, 1996). And social scientists have argued that 'identity is too ambiguous, too split between "hard" and "soft" meanings, essentialist connotations and constructive qualifiers to serve well the demand of social analysis' (Brubaker & Cooper, 2000, p. 2). But we cannot simply avoid the concept as easily as we can steer clear of a jellyfish. The concept is omnipresent and is used to describe and explain phenomena and processes that lend themselves to be defined and specified. Yet, the usefulness of the concept is subject to some clarity and precision. That seems obvious, but descriptions and definitions are sometimes rejected. It is argued that identities are fluid and characterized by fragmentation, contradiction, ambiguity, and variability. Depending on the circumstances and conditions, identities take different forms. Because definitions emphasize common characteristics, this diversity would be ignored or denied. Therefore, capturing meanings by definitions would imply fixing them and thus should be resisted and rejected. Unfortunately, this is an invitation to confusion and obscurantism. After all, the observation that identities are fragmented, ambivalent, and changing presupposes an idea of what the concept 'identity' implies. How else do we know that identities are at stake and not, for example, politics or the weather. Fragmentation and change can be understood only when it is clear what exactly is fragmented and subject to change. Definitions are rejected, yet it is inevitable that one falls back on an implicit notion of identity. It is much better to try to be clear.

I am ...

> There are twenty numbered blanks on the page below. Please write twenty answers to the simple question 'Who am I?' in the blanks. Just give twenty different answers to this question. Answer as if you were giving the answers to yourself, not to somebody else.

This is the instruction for the 'Twenty Statements Test' developed in 1954 by sociologists Manford Kuhn and Thomas McPartland. The test was meant as a more objective way – than the then popular intuitive, introspective methods – to study how someone perceives him- or herself. This test became quite popular and has been used in many countries and cultures (see, e.g., Cousins, 1989; Driver, 1969; Hurstfield, 1978). People tend to give different answers, such as their name, references to their appearance, personality traits, private feelings and desires, and social characteristics such as occupation, gender, religion, and ethnic background. All these answers tell us something about how they see themselves, but not in the same way. One's name is something different from private feelings and desires, which, in turn, differ from belonging to social categories and groups. Some answers refer to characteristics that are objectively identifiable and verifiable – what one is to others – while other responses relate to the subjective sense of self – what one is to oneself. And some answers refer to things that make someone unique, as one's name, while others refer to things that are shared with many others, such as gender and religion. Over the years, a variety of classification systems have been developed to try to bring order into the multitude of answers. The systems vary considerably, as do the interpretations of the responses (see Spitzer *et al.,* 1969).

   Your identity is who you are. It is as simple as that. But behind that simplicity hide more complex questions. That I am somebody, somebody who is distinguishable from others, is obvious, but who am I? Is my identity located in my deepest wishes and desires or, rather, in the fact that I live in a particular country or belong to a social class? What matters when it comes to knowing *who* I am and where is the limit with *what* I am, and *how* I am? The term 'identity' is used in all these different ways.[2]

Who am I?

It is quite common for people to respond to the Twenty Statements Test by first stating their name and sometimes their date of birth – that is, provided the research is confidential. By giving your name you are identifiable, no longer anonymous. It is then possible to find out everything that you have written down and how your answers differ from those given by others. It is no different in daily life. With your name you are identifiable as a distinct individual who can be addressed, as well as spoken about in your absence. The identity that is at stake here is simply who you are as an individual person, as stated on your ID card or in your passport – and, in the future, on your genetic blueprint. It is what makes you recognizably different from all other people in the world. It is an identity that is defined at birth, and there is nothing subjective to it. It usually does not lead to much uncertainty or misunderstanding either. Apart from cases due to mental illness, people know very well who they are (David Johnson, not Jesus Christ); mistaken identity can have dramatic consequences, as in cases of 'identity theft', where one person pretends to be someone else for an extended period of time, but often it is only a source of innocent fun and pleasure. Your personal identity is a given, one that can be objectively established, which makes it extremely important for all kinds of social contacts. Unambiguous recognition by the outside world is critical in many situations. The thrill of stories about spies, false passports, and the identity of victim and murderer are based on this. A good example is the movie trilogy

'*Bourne Identity*' about 'special agent' Jason Bourne, who has lost his memory and tries to find out who he actually is.

What am I?

In addition to one's name, almost everyone refers to various social categories in answer to the Twenty Statements Test. The Test appears largely to be answered with, 'a man', 'a Muslim', 'a citizen of London', 'a student', 'a British Indian', 'a teenager', 'an European', 'a bachelor', and so on.

When you think about who and what you are, you tend to place yourself in various social categories and groups. This is quite striking. If you ask someone to indicate who she is, she tends to place herself in social pigeon-holes. We define ourselves through the categories and groups we belong to. This no longer involves what makes you distinctive and different from any other person; rather, it has to do with the characteristics that are shared with others. The emphasis is not on you as a unique individual, but on you as a member of a larger category. Being recognizable different from all other people ('who you are') is not at stake here but, rather, similarity to others. The emphasis is not on individual uniqueness but on what is shared with others. Being a member of a particular category or group *is* your intended identity, and one that takes your individuality away. That membership is not superficial or meaningless; it says something about the kind of person you are. It is an identity that is shared with others. Through that membership you are bound and connected to others. It concerns features that place you socially, give you a position in the world, define your coordinates in time and space. In this way you are differentiated from people who do not possess that particular characteristic and are merged with those who share it with you. It indicates *what* you are in a certain respect (e.g., Mexican) and what you are not (e.g., not Cuban). Those sharing a certain attribute are considered to be different in the same way from those who do not possess that attribute.

Answers to the Twenty Statements Test show that there is a wide range of categories and groups according to which people classify themselves. Unlike with personal identity, answers to the 'what-am-I question' are always multiple. It is not about determining who a specific individual is but, rather, establishing categories of people and the defining characteristics of those categories. The information that is given is about social classifications and group memberships. If we know that someone is a German, or a male, or a resident of Berlin, then we are still not very close to finding the perpetrator of a crime. An individual always belongs to multiple categories. Some are shared with certain people and others with other people. This means that a particular feature gives only a 'partial identity', or a 'one-among-others identity', which is reflected in additions such as ethnic, religious, national, and gender identity. It does not make much sense to use the singular notion 'identity' for the totality of all your social identities. All those social memberships say something about what you are; their unique combination might say something about who you are as an individual person, in the previous sense of identity. If we know that the killer is a German person, a resident of

Berlin, male, a bachelor, an accountant, middle-aged, and lives in the Berlin district Kreuzberg, we are already a bit closer to tracking down the culprit. However, these different social identities do not in some mysterious way add up to a singular, overarching social identity.

An important question, however, is how the different social identities relate to each other. In most cases, belonging to different categories causes rarely any problems. The memberships are complementary and make life varied and rich. The social identities in question relate to different domains of life, for example (work, family), or are on different levels of abstraction (neighbourhood, city, country). But the social categories to which people belong may also be difficult to reconcile because they entail opposite meanings and conflicting demands. It is often not easy to be a good mother, a loving wife, and a successful career woman all at the same time. And it is not always easy to be both a devout Muslim and a Dutch or German citizen (see chapter 3).

Each partial identity provides only limited information about yourself or someone else. There is often a tendency to think that one knows quite a lot about a person on the basis of one particular social identity. For example, in studies on ethnic minorities, it is not uncommon to assume that ethnic identity is central or decisive for what people consider themselves or others to be. However, there are always more social identities that, depending on the circumstances, are psychologically salient and sociologically prominent. People are not one-dimensional creatures. By considering each single social identity as one among many, one avoids the risk of reducing people to one single feature that is assumed to dominate.

What can happen, however, is that one particular identity becomes central and highly absorbing. There can be circumstances in which a particular identity dominates your thoughts and actions and starts to play a role in almost every situation. The social identity at issue constantly plays a role, eclipses other social identities, and is communicated in all kinds of situations.

This can arise from the motivations, desires, and experiences of the individual – that is, compulsively from within. This is the case with the typical macho who exaggerates the importance of his masculinity in relation to other social identities and always tend to think in male/female terms, or with the notorious racist who can only see the world in black and white because a difference in skin colour or ethnic background determines his or her beliefs.

Specific social identities can also become overwhelming when society forces people to place a particular identity at the forefront of their minds and central to their behaviour. Although you speak fluent Dutch, you have a job, and were born in the Netherlands, you can still be seen by others as different and be labelled as a foreigner. Or, as one girl in one of our studies put it: 'With everything I do, the term foreigner can always come to the surface. You can always be placed somewhere, suddenly with one single word, with an angry or frightened look. Therefore it is very difficult to feel at home here, to feel a fully fledged Dutch person.'

Ethnicity and race can also develop into stigma identities, which provide a chronically salient distinction or a master status that cannot be ignored and serves to define the essential character of those classified. An example of this is the Roma identity in many East European countries. A person can be a doctor, an engineer, or a teacher, but as soon as she or he is known to be a Roma, this identity tends to become the definitive one. Other examples are a nation at war, when national identity takes precedence to almost all other ones, and a society in which race or ethnicity is used as the principal criterion for making social distinctions, like in apartheid South Africa. In that case skin colour or ethnic background is the first and predominant characteristic for determining (in)equal possibilities and opportunities.

With social identities we are dealing with classifications based on characteristics that are socially meaningful. What you personally make of it is something else. Identity in the sense of a social category or group to which you belong is not necessarily the same as the way you privately experience and feel about yourself. The meaning of an ethnic, national, or religious identity is historically, culturally, and politically contested and construed. A social identity provides a socially meaningful place in the world and can involve all sorts of psychological dynamics. Membership of a particular group can engage people strongly or not, touch them lightly or at a deep level, and give positive or negative self-feelings.

Identity as a social phenomenon – what one is socially or what one is to others – should not be confused with one's sense of identity – what one is to oneself. Yet, as a social phenomenon identity refers to social constructions, to the way in which classifications are socially created and provided with shared meanings, and these meanings become subjectively relevant when social identities are salient. With social memberships you are bound and connected to others, and you temporarily ignore part of your uniqueness and individuality. Social identities are associated with a minimum of normative expectations and precepts, and these fill your mind when the identities are operative.

Furthermore, with social identities what others think and say is critical, and your personal claim to a particular social identity must be lived up to in interactions and relationships with others. That does not mean that there is no leeway, and that you yourself have nothing to contribute. Psychologically you can go in many directions, and also from a social point of view you can choose to ignore certain social identities, to adapt and adjust the meaning of existing identities, or to try to find acceptance for new social identities. Although some individuals and groups have a wider range of choices than others, there are always ethnic options available (Song, 2003; Waters, 1990). Prevailing meanings and demands can be negotiated, adapted to one's situation, and questioned. Although their room for manoeuvre may be quite small, individuals are not passive victims of their circumstances. They negotiate about the interpretation of ideas and expectations that are attributed to a particular social identity. Choices are made and justified; some interpretations find social acceptance and become popular, others hardly or not at all.

How am I?

Personal identity and all sorts of social identities are about 'who and what you are to others'. Answers to the Twenty Statements Test also involve many references to psychological dispositions, such as personality traits, skills, beliefs, attitudes, and preferences. You are someone who loves good food and likes travelling, you are concerned about the environment, impatient and shy, and someone who feels insecure or, rather, over-confident. These answers all say something about *how* you are on the inside. The characteristics in question can be expressed in your behaviour, but they may also stay hidden in the depths of your mind. Each answer tells something about yourself, but in a different way than the previous two meanings. What is at stake is not so much who or what someone is from a social point of view, in the eyes of and in contact with others, but, rather, who someone is deep down inside to him- or herself. It is about your own mental life to which others never truly have access. The social environment does not provide you with an identity in this case but, more often, constitutes a threat to your individuality. The environment often determines that you can no longer be 'yourself', or that you lose your individuality. You feel fake, inauthentic, and no longer in touch with your true self. But it could also be that you feel an inner emptiness, as if there is no inner core that characterizes you and gives you direction – an emptiness that needs to be filled with, say, faith and spirituality or a hedonistic lifestyle. Knowing who you really are, being able to be yourself, provides inner peace, balance, and confidence.

The questions and possible problems that are at issue here differ from those with the previous two meanings of the term identity. It is not about social distinctiveness and shared behavioural expectations, but about an inner core – the real me – that one may or may not be aware of and that allows one to be really oneself. Identity in this sense coincides with the subjective experience and is by definition good and desirable. It is about finding yourself and remaining true to yourself. And in order to hear your own soul or to discover and get in touch with your basic, true self, you can take courses on silent retreats, meditative painting, contemplative dance, and so on.

There is also a more mundane version of this, in which it is not about being conscious of one's own special core or 'inner self' but of self-awareness, self-knowledge, and self-feeling. It still concerns your inner psychological life, but now, in terms of self-uncertainty, self-esteem and knowing what you desire, believe, and find important. This is the popular field of 'the self' and everything that is related and involved. In this field there is often little or no distinction between the concepts of 'identity' and 'self'. Both terms tend to be used indiscriminately, and the choice of one or the other seems accidental because their meaning would be the same. However, at the same time it is not concluded that the term identity (or self) does not have a separate meaning and therefore that one can do without it. Typically, there is still an implicit sense that both concepts, although they are in some way interconnected, refer to different things. This is particularly evident in cases where the word 'identity' is used to indicate that in one's sense of the self, or self-concept, also social roles, group memberships, discrimination, social adjustment, status, or whatever societal issues are involved. With the concept of self-awareness or self-feeling this is not adequately covered. In other cases, however, the two terms are used again interchangeably.

The use of the word 'identity' in the sense of self-consciousness and self-feeling is often unnecessary and confusing. If identity coincides with the self, it implies that an identity can only change if the self-perception, for whatever reason, changes, and vice versa. But it is, of course, not that easy or straightforward. People can start to see and feel themselves differently, while they are still being classified and approached in the same way from a social point of view. Similarly, a different social identity does not mean that one's self-understanding has changed. A certain identity can be imposed upon you and you are aware of this and accept it, but you may need time to internalize it and incorporate it into your self-concept. An example are the changes that occur when becoming an 'ex' – as, for example, when one becomes a former employee when retiring, becomes a former citizen of a country after emigration, and an ex-bachelor after marrying (Ebaugh, 1988). The sudden change in social position is associated with a gradual change in self-understanding. It takes time to get used to the new category into which you are placed and to forget the old meanings you used to live by.

Social identities

The 'who', 'what' and 'how' meanings of the term 'identity' indicate that the one identity is not similar to the other. The quest for identity indicates uncertainty about oneself: Who am I, what am I like, with whom and to what do I belong, and what does this mean? These are the questions that keep you busy. But those questions are not all the same and have different answers. Morris Rosenberg (1979, p. 16; italics in original) explains the difference between the sense of one's personal dispositions and social identities as follows:

> whereas dispositions may be felt as more of what we *truly* are, the identity elements tend to be experienced as more of what we *surely* are. The individual, for example, may feel that the social identity elements represent solely his social exterior whereas the 'real me' is expressed in his dispositions. The world, he feels, looks upon him as a lawyer, a black, an American, a Catholic, but the real self what he deep down truly and really is – is sensitive, poetic, gentle, and philosophical.

The question 'how am I like' refers to individual qualities, tendencies, preferences, and desires that are typical or characteristic of you as a unique person. It is about how you are internally, and an answer to that question gives the reassurance of a clear and secure sense of self. The answer to the question 'with whom do I belong' or 'where do I fit in' is not determined by how you are internally. What this brings to the fore are categorical classifications, groups, and social memberships. These place you in the social environment and bind you to others. Here the sense of security that an answer provides is the security you get from a sense of belonging and the related normative meanings that stipulate how you should act. You no longer have to hesitate about what you are, where you belong, and how you should act, because you know, for example, that you are a Muslim and follow the will of God, or that you are a Jew. After discovering that he was Jewish, the photographer Kaluzny said: 'Suddenly I had the sense of being connected to a world, a place in history, a people, that I have never experienced. To me Judaism is a culture, not just a religion, and it gives me a place to belong' (in Kessel, 2000, p. 96).

Social identities are not like private affairs or beliefs but depend on what goes on in public. They are the outcome of social processes that produce and maintain group boundaries based on certain criteria. There are, for example, so-called primary categories, classifications that are meaningful in almost every culture and era, such as gender, age, and skin colour. These features are plainly visible and recognizable and almost always meaningful in one way or another. In general, differences between men and women, young and old, Black and White are easy to spot and therefore readily applicable for categorization. *Observing* these differences quite quickly results in grouping people *based on* these differences. The term *visible minorities* indicates that the degree of visibility is important. Immigrants or ethnic groups that look 'different' in comparison to the majority population may find it harder to be accepted, just as it is harder for them not to be approached and assessed in terms of their ethnic background. If visible features are the basis for categorization, it takes outsiders relatively little effort to identify someone as belonging to that category. Certain features, such as skin colour but also distinctive clothing, are immediately noticeable. A single glance is enough to categorize people. With other cues – such as language and accent – it is a little more complicated, but after careful observing and listening the categorization is done quickly.

Classifying people into categories is, of course, strongly influenced by the cultural context. People are differentiated on the basis of a variety of attributes and characteristics. Some features are clearly visible, but other criteria are recognizable only to those familiar with local traditions and meanings. For a cultural outsider, the subtle ways in which social distinctions are sometimes made is difficult to understand. In addition, the same criteria can be interpreted in many different ways. There are no cultures in the world that do not make a clear distinction between men and women in their classification of things, in the way the two sexes are allowed to behave, and in what they are supposed to be like as human beings. Although the role differentiation is to a certain extent biologically given, there are extreme differences between cultures and historical periods in prescribed behaviour for the sexes. The same goes for age differences. Differences in ethnicity, nationality, religion, and skin colour also take on all kinds of social meanings that are subject to continuous change and continuing disputes and debates.

For a social classification to be a real 'social identity', it needs to have corresponding beliefs and – stereotypical – behavioural expectations. A categorization based on eye colour or ear length is usually superficial and meaningless. In daily life these attributes are simply irrelevant and are not accompanied by beliefs about differences between groups of people and expectations about how these people are and behave. But this can, of course, change, as with regard to eye colour as shown in the documentary *The Eye of the Storm* (see chapter 5) and for the ear length as was supposedly the case on Easter Island. In both cases, an apparently meaningless feature developed into real-life social identities: they were used to draw a group distinction that was associated with differential stereotypical expectations and behavioural consequences. And that is not all. They were also used as nouns to define people. Having blue or brown eyes or having long or short ears no longer concerned just physical features; it was used to typify different kinds of people: the blue-eyed and the brown-eyed, the long-eared and the short-eared. Social identities are expressed in the language of nouns. Someone is a Turk, a Mexican, a Basque. In using such words, no quantifiable qualities are defined, as with adjectives. Nouns reflect separate social types, with characteristics and boundaries that suggest a more than superficial difference. One group of people is deemed to be like this, the other like that. With that they become real social identities with real social and psychological consequences. On Easter Island, according to tradition, the long-eared were the dominant group, but eventually they lost their position in a revolt by the short-eared.

Social construction of identity

Social identities are socially constructed and therefore neither inevitable nor fixed. Although they often appear and feel solid and overwhelming, they are the contingent outcomes of social processes. Categorizations that appear to be self-evident and natural can become the subject of discord and lead to new or adjusted distinctions. This does not mean that change is easy or can come overnight. Like gender identity, ethnic, racial, national, and religious identities are typically embedded in institutional, cultural, social, and also economic and political arrangements, which make them difficult to ignore or to re-define. But distinctions that have for a long time seemed self-evident and natural can become the object of disputes and gradual change. Old distinctions and understandings may increasingly fail to make sense of new relationships and come to contradict new beliefs. Whereas for centuries the idea of inherent racial inferiority made sense to many White Americans and White South Africans, it does no longer for most of them. At the same time, new distinctions are introduced and can develop into real social identities for the people concerned.

Another example is political classifications that can lose their predominant legal status and start to function as categorizations in everyday social life, like the term *Hispanic* in the United States. Originally used for statistical and political reasons, it gradually evolved into a social identity for some of those categorized by it. There is also the usage of the term *West Indians* in Great Britain, which initially functioned as an ascribed label for people coming from diverse Caribbean islands like Trinidad, Jamaica, and Barbados. These people regarded themselves as members of different groups. Gradually, however, they started to regard themselves as West Indians. At first, this occurred mainly in contacts with the majority group, but very soon it also started to play a role in contacts between and within the groups involved. The same goes for *Asians* in the United States and in Britain, and for the anthropological term 'allochthonous' that predominates in the Netherlands and in Flanders to label non-Western immigrants (see chapter 4).

The introduction or change of a term is, of course, in itself not enough to accomplish a change in the thoughts and behaviour of people. In 1988, at a conference of Black leaders in Chicago, the president of the National Urban Coalition proposed the term African Americans to refer to Black Americans. Hence, an ethnic term was proposed to replace a racial one. Most leaders accepted the proposition, and the new name spread quickly. Nevertheless, identity formation needs the label to become the prevailing and functional term in everyday social life. It has to grow from idea, notion, and expectation into a social reality – that is, a term by which people define themselves and each other and interpret behaviour, one that is part of shared social beliefs and practices. This is not self-evident. For example, in academic circles in the 1970s the term *Afro-Americans* was used, but this term did not become the prevailing one among the population and was associated with a particular hairdo and racial differences. Another example, is the Dutch term *medelanders* ('fellow countrymen'), which was proposed as an alternative to 'allochthonous'. The term is a nice variation on the Dutch word for Dutchman (*'Nederlander'*), but it has not been socially adopted.

Clearly distinguishable behaviours can also be the starting point for identity formation. People can do particular things together and have reciprocal expectations. Recognizable shared activities are conducive to the development of a social identity. For instance, identification with certain musicians and music (such as rock and rap) is typically accompanied by characteristic behaviour and appearance. This can lead to a social categorization with the related identity definitions (rockers, rappers). The Rastafarian movement, with its typical hairdo, reggae music, and the use of green and yellow colours, is an example of identity formation on the part of certain categories of youngsters. In an interview Bob Marley was asked the question 'How important are the dreadlocks?' He answered with, 'This, this is my identity, man.'

Another obvious example is the language spoken. The observation that a number of people do the same thing in the same way or speak the same language easily leads to the conclusion that it is a distinguishable group the members of which differ in a certain way from other groups. But this observation is by no means self-evident. It is not enough to assert or claim an identity. The fact of doing things differently or of speaking a particular language has to be recognized and validated by the wider society: turned into a social identity.

Sense of social identity

Social reality is critically important, but social identities are not only about what goes on in public but also about what goes on in people's heads (Brubaker, 2004), and especially about the relationship between the two. Social identities are the outcome of social processes but become real for people by providing a meaningful place in the world. To have significance as a social or political force, ethnic, national, or any other social identity must be personally acknowledged as self-defining. Thus, it has to be real not only in the sense of having real social consequences for opportunities and rights, but also real and meaningful in a psychological sense. People must define and understand themselves in terms of their group memberships.

Social psychologists are particularly interested in the subjective sense of self that is derived from social categories and groups. This is what they usually refer to when they use the term 'social identity': the sense of self that is derived from group memberships and the meanings associated with that group membership. They are interested in when and why people define themselves as group members and what the consequences of these self-definitions are.

This focus on the subjective sense of social identities implies, for example, that the interpretation of a self-description on the Twenty Statements Test is not self-evident. On this test someone might respond with 'I am religious', but that does not necessarily indicate that she is categorizing herself into a particular category of religious people. This answer can refer to her personal beliefs and thereby be part of her personal self. Likewise, she may define herself as intelligent, shy, and athletic as characteristics that typify her personally or '*how* she is'. But these same terms might also be used to indicate social identities ('*what* she is') when she is thinking about her membership in the category of intellectuals, introverts, or athletes. Psychologically, the critical issue is whether people themselves understand these things as characteristics that provide the basis of a personal sense of self or whether they understand them to be social identities that connect them to others. Thus, she can describe herself as intelligent or athletic (adjectives) and see this as qualities that describes her personality, or she can say that she is an intellectual or an athlete (nouns), which make her part of a group with the related stereotypes and behavioural expectations. It is comparable to clothing that can be used to show that you are unique and different from others or, rather, that you belong to a certain group.

The distinction between these self-descriptive meanings is, of course, not always so clear-cut, but the central issue is whether and when your sense of self is bound up with your membership of certain social categories or groups. The sense of social identity represents the psychological reality of group life with the related meanings and behavioural expectations (Turner *et al.*, 1987). People are group members, not only socially but also psychologically. They define themselves as group members and act as group members, and the latter is possible because of the former. Self-understandings such as 'I am a Basque', 'I am a Muslim', 'I am a Mexican American' provide a meaningful place in the social world. But because social identities are socially constructed, the meaning of any of these memberships is not purely personal or idiosyncratic. What an ethnic, religious, or national identity means is a historical, cultural, and normative matter. With the act of defining oneself as a group member, these socially defined meanings become self-relevant. You start to understand yourself and thereby the world in terms of the social and cultural norms, values, and beliefs associated with that particular identity. Moreover, because it defines who you are and what counts for you, you start to behave on the basis of these group meanings. Thus, when a particular social identity is salient, your mind is socially structured: it is filled with socially defined and shared meanings that guide your perception and behaviour (Turner *et al.*, 1987).

It is when you see yourself as a group member that the mental and behavioural corollaries of group membership come to the surface. The deathly 'incident' in Amsterdam triggered the distinction between native Dutch and Moroccans, which led to different forms of behaviour. When in a particular situation I define myself as ethnic Dutch, I come to think of myself in terms of a membership that I share with other Dutch people, with the norms, values, and beliefs that are commonly associated with this social identity. This has far-reaching implications. It means that what counts in that situation is the fate and standing of my ethnic group as a whole and of me as a group member, rather than my own personal fate. I am concerned about the Dutch as a group, and my feelings of pride, shame, or threat do not relate to me personally, but to the achievements, standing, and interests of the Dutch. Psychologically, these feelings are just as real as personal beliefs and concerns, and sometimes even more real and important. In times of war and revolution, and among fundamentalist groups, individuals are sometimes prepared to sacrifice their lives in order to protect or advance the common good.

When individuals define themselves as members of a particular group, they will attribute the stereotypical traits and dispositions to themselves. Research on stereotype threat offers an example (see Quinn *et al.*, 2010). Stereotype threat occurs when people are in a situation where a negative identity-based stereotype can be applied to their performance. In such a situation you tend to be concerned about the fact that others might think that you will not succeed and therefore fear that you will confirm these beliefs. For instance, in an intellectual testing situation, African Americans may be concerned about the negative group stereotypes (African Americans as not being very intelligent), and this leads to decreased performance. This idea received empirical support in various experimental studies. In these studies, equally intelligent African American and European American students were given the same difficult test. Half of the students were told that the test is diagnostic of their intellectual abilities and the other half that it is not. In the diagnostic situation, African Americans performed worse than European Americans, whereas in the non-diagnostic situation both groups performed equally well. The phenomenon of stereotype threat has been demonstrated across gender, ethnic, and other minority groups. It has also been found that performance can be changed depending on which social identity is salient in a testing situation (Shih *et al.*, 1999). When Asian American women thought about themselves in terms of their Asian identity, they performed better on a mathematics test (stereotype of Asians being good at mathematics) than when it was their gender identity that was salient (stereotype of women not being good at mathematics).

The phenomenon of stereotype threat implies a situational threat. It is about a stereotype that is 'in the air' (Steele, 1997) and becomes self-relevant in a particular situation. The phenomenon depends on knowledge of the social stereotypes and on one's sense of identity. For example, it is when children get older and become more aware of racial stereotypes that these stereotypes can hamper their performance (McKown & Weinstein, 2003). And among Afro-Caribbeans in New York it has been shown that second-generation – but not first-generation – students underperformed in a stereotype threat situation (Deaux *et al.*, 2007). Both groups of students were aware of the negative stereotypes about African Americans, but only the second generation was incorporating an African American identity in their sense of self.

Groups and categories

There are many types of categories and groups that differ in many ways, such as in size, goals, structure, and history. Some of these are functional and indicate roles and positions, such as teacher–student and policemen–civilian. Others refer to intimate relationships, such as friends and family. Still other classifications seem particularly designed to distinguish and differentiate groups, such as youth sub-cultures. There are also groupings that have a long tradition and history, such as ethnic, national, and religious categories. And there are broad categories to which people belong, such as adolescents or the elderly. The number and diversity of these categories is considerable. It is obvious that all of these do not have the same meanings and implications. Belonging to a family is something different from membership in an organization or the category of immigrants. A common sociological distinction is between categories and groups. A category is a collection of people who share a particular characteristic but have hardly anything to do with each other, such as taxpayers or adults. A group is about social interactions and relationships that result in community life. This distinction is important because the normative expectations and consequences are different. For instance, it is more difficult to hold each other accountable within a category than within a group or community.

Social psychologists tend to define a group in a subjective sense – namely, as several people who share the same social identity. This does not mean that they find the distinction between categories and groups unimportant. Rather, the relevance of this distinction lies in the content and meaning of the social identity. Different categories and types of groups have different norms, values, and beliefs associated with it.

Research has examined whether people distinguish different types of categories and groups by asking them to cluster a large number of groupings and attributes (see Hamilton, 2007). The clearest distinction that people tend to make is between intimate groups (friends, family), working parties (committees, working groups), and social categories (women, ethnic minorities). People have been found to spontaneously apply this trichotomy when they process and store information about groups. Also, this division in three appears to be associated with different expectations about the needs that these groups fulfil, about typical characteristics of each of the three, and about associated norms and obligations. Intimate groups tend to fulfil the need for solidarity and mutual support, while the need for a distinctive and positive social identity is more central in social categories.

However, the tendency to distinguish between these groups says little about how actual groups are presented and understood in daily life. Social categories can, for example, be defined as intimate groups. This is what happens in the process of ethnicization in which a community defines itself in ethnic terms. The *idea* of shared ancestry and origin forms the core of ethnicity. In most cases, this idea of a shared origin is supported by other features, such as a separate language, cultural traditions, or a shared religion. Language, culture, and religion are the obvious and important markers of and for ethnic groups. However, those features are not necessary, and they can also lead to internal divisions. An example is the Karen in Burma (Kuroiwa & Verkuyten, 2008). For over 50 years, the Karen have been engaged in a violent struggle for recognition and (partial) autonomy with the government of Burma. For this struggle, one of the continuing challenges for the Karen is to be and remain united. This means finding a shared characteristic or common denomination. This is not easy, because the various sub-groups speak different languages (Sgaw, Pwo, and Pao), practise different religions (they are Baptists, Buddhists, and Animists), and originate from various geographical and cultural regions. A common Karen identity can therefore not be found on the basis of a common language, culture, or religion, but they do share a narrative about a common origin and migration from Mongolia. This is an important basis for the claim that they are '*a* people' despite their substantial internal differences.

Another example of the way in which categories can be understood is ethnicity and nationality that appeals to a (supposed) shared origin and kinship. The rhetoric about these groups is often peppered with terms such as 'fatherland', 'motherland', and 'brothers and sisters'. As Connor (1993, p. 373) points out, there is a 'near universality with which certain images and phrases appear – blood, family, brothers, sisters, mothers, forefathers, home'. The definition of where one's primary loyalties and closest bonds (ought to) lie is based on one's origin and kinship. The emotional ties with blood relatives and the familiarity with the social environment of childhood years are projected on the ethnic or national community. In his victory speech after the presidential election of 2012, President Obama said: 'We are an American family, and we rise or fall together as one nation and as one people.'

A further example of how a category can be presented as an intimate group is the Ummah as a global community. A good Muslim should stand in solidarity with brothers elsewhere. For some Muslims the idea of the Ummah as one big Islamic family is increasingly important. Especially some young Muslims in the West are drawn to this idea of the Ummah. Those who perceive the Ummah as a single Muslim family easily interpret an attack on other Muslims elsewhere in the world as an attack on themselves. A Muslim in London who sees Internet images of the struggles in Syria, Afghanistan, or Palestine feels the pain of his or her brothers and sisters there.

History

Ethnic and national identities do not only have normative implications but are also defined in historical terms that have political meanings. Political history is inseparably linked to what it means to be an American, French, German, or a Serb, and the memory of slavery plays an important role in the self-definition of many African Americans. Similarly, the period of the Crusades and the conflict in the Middle East affects the Muslim identity of some youths in Western Europe.

Having a colonial past or a history of labour migration has relevance for understanding issues of ethnic minority identity and ethnic relations. Collective representations about the past are not only shaped by the present but also influence present conditions, perceptions, and behaviour. An example is the South Moluccans in the Netherlands (see Verkuyten 2005c). In 1945, two days after the end of the Japanese occupation of what was then called Dutch-India, a group of nationalist leaders proclaimed the independent Republic of Indonesia. The Dutch sent troops in order to re-establish control over their colony. They also enlisted former military from the Royal Dutch Indian Army (KNIL) who had fought during the war. Among them were many soldiers from the Moluccan Islands. After Indonesia became independent in 1949, the Dutch government wanted to demobilize the KNIL. But the government had granted them the right to be demobilized in the place of their choice. The Moluccans wanted to go to East-Indonesia, but this was impossible due to the political situation. Because they were still in the service of the Dutch government and because of the delicate political situation, the Dutch government saw no other solution than to bring the Moluccan military and their families to the Netherlands. On arrival, the military were dismissed from the army, which made them feel they had been betrayed and left to their own devices by a government and country for which they had risked their lives and which had promised to take care of them. This history plays a central role in the way Moluccans define themselves and their relationship with the Dutch and other ethnic minority groups in the Netherlands. By stressing the historical relationship, a continuity with the Dutch and with the present situation in the Netherlands is defined. This historical discourse also implies rights and claims. After all, the Dutch bear great responsibility for the fate of the South Moluccans and the way they were treated in Indonesia and after their arrival in the Netherlands. As discussed in chapter 4, this ought to give the Moluccans a justified claim to a special position and treatment, in particular in comparison with other minority groups.

History gives meaning to ethnic and national identities. These meanings are enshrined in rituals, festivities, museums, monuments, heroes, documents, and narratives. People are storytellers *par excellence*. The writer E.M. Forster once gave the following example about the difference between two sentences: 'The king died and the queen died' and 'The king died and then the queen died of grief'. The second sentence is much more suggestive of a story and is therefore easier to remember. Moreover, the addition of an explanation makes the second event plausible, while in the former case there are many possible causes for the death of the queen. People are first and foremost storytellers. They live with and on the basis of stories. They also tell stories about themselves that are examined, for example, by narrative psychologists (see Crossley, 2000; McAdams, 1993). These stories may refer to yourself as a member of a group or community or to the history and characteristics of that group or community itself.

The story of 'me-as-a-group-member' can be very extensive and detailed, for example if you have a personal history of migration, deprivation, and struggle for advancement. It can also be relatively superficial if you belong to the dominant majority group and you have never really had to give much thought to your ethnic group membership. Sometimes the stories of the various groups you belong to are compatible and easy to combine; at other times this is much more difficult because of historical events (e.g. colonialism) and political tensions. For a Chinese Dutch person it is usually not too difficult to unite the two identities, but this can be different for a Palestinian Israeli, an Algerian Frenchman, or a Surinamese Dutch.

Stories at the group level are mainly concerned with events from the past that are often used to legitimize or question rights and entitlements, and for understanding existing group relationships more generally (Eidelson & Eidelson, 2003). A group of people can see themselves as the chosen ones and therefore morally superior. The Nazi ideology of the Aryan race being destined to rule over other people is a clear example. But self-glorifying myths or chosen glories (Volkan, 1999) are readily created in many situations and used to justify entitlement claims and to demonize other groups.

An injustice from the past can also function as a benchmark to determine what we are and what we are entitled to. Indigenous groups such as Aboriginals and Native Americans may claim land and resources taken away from them in the past, and some descendants of slaves may claim financial compensation for past mistreatments. Past periods of injustice, exploitation, and dramatic events might form the cornerstone of a group identity. They can function as chosen traumas (Volkan, 1999), which can be promoted by leaders to unify and mobilize people, as the following example illustrates.

Collective trauma and Alevi identity

Collective trauma 'occurs when members of a collective feel they have been subjected to a horrendous event that leaves indelible marks upon their group consciousness, marking their memories forever and changing their future identity in fundamental and irrevocable ways' (Alexander, 2004, p. 1). Trauma stories are animated and powerful and tend to evoke victim beliefs that sustain the perception of vulnerability and threat with the related fear about the continuity of one's group. The facts of traumatic events are seldom in dispute, but there are always different ways in which events can be presented and made sense of. It is not the event per se but, rather, the social representation of it that turns it into a collective trauma: calling an event or a series of events 'traumatic' requires interpretation. Most people do not experience the traumatic event personally but develop a sense of collective trauma through oral history, education, and the media. For example, it is not the personal experience of slavery but, rather, the collective representation of it as a cultural trauma that defines African American identity and can unite African Americans politically (Eyerman, 2004). Collective trauma always involves a 'meaning struggle', a grappling with an event that involves identifying the 'nature of the pain, the nature of the victim and the attribution of responsibility' (Eyerman, 2004, p. 62). In this struggle over meanings and interpretations interest groups, organizations, and leaders play a key role. They are involved in defining the nature of the traumatic event, and they can use their interpretation as political capital in trying to unify and mobilize others. Narratives about collective trauma that emphasize the innocence of 'us victims' are particularly useful for this. An example is the 'Sivas massacre' in 1993, in which the Hotel Madımak in the Turkish city of Sivas was set on fire and 37 Alevi intellectuals died in the flames (Yildiz & Verkuyten, 2011).

The Alevi face much discrimination in Turkey, but in the last 20 years they have become increasingly visible in Turkish public life. They have established associations, foundations, and prayer houses, held conferences, and published magazines and books (Vorhoff, 2003). However, they have not succeeded in creating a unified Alevi movement to address and challenge the different forms of oppression that they face. One reason is the political situation in Turkey, which makes it difficult to be politically active and which increases the importance of the Alevi diaspora in Europe. Another reason is the wide variety of beliefs and practices among those who call themselves Alevi. Alevi identity is defined in linguistic, cultural, political, and religious terms (Shindeldecker, 2001). Some people argue that Alevi identity is a cultural lifestyle that has its roots in pre-Islamic Anatolia and Mesopotamia. Others claim that Alevi identity is more of a political orientation in which secularism and democracy are central, as well as a history of rebellion and opposition towards the Turkish state. Still others argue that Alevi is the Turkish – or Kurdish – interpretation of Islam and thereby different from the Sunni belief that would represent the Arabic interpretation of Islam. Thus, in Turkey as well as within Alevi communities in Western Europe, there is a continuing and intense debate on the most appropriate way to define Alevi identity (Van Bruinessen, 1996). Some of these interpretations of Alevi identity gain prominence in relation to the Turkish state, others in relation to the Sunni majority, and still others in relation to Western audiences and their discourses of human rights.

This diversity in interpretations and audiences has implications for the unity of the Alevis and the political claims that they can make. For example, those who define Alevism as an Islamic faith demand religious support from the Turkish Directorate of Religious Affairs (*Diyanet*), whereas those who define Alevism outside Islam demand the abolition of the *Diyanet*. Plurality and diversity of beliefs and ideologies is the distinguishing feature of Alevis. Their lack of unity is a hindrance for the social and political claims that Alevis can make. It is difficult to unite and mobilize people and to make political claims when there is no shared sense of 'us'.

A collective trauma can function as political capital in creating a shared moral identity, an identity based on moral values and innocent victimhood. The largest

Alevi organization in Europe, the Confederation of European Alevi Unions, construes and uses the collective trauma of Madımak to define Alevi identity and an inclusive victimhood. The narrative of the massacre draws clear group boundaries, defines group relations, and creates a sense of inclusive victimhood with other aggrieved and oppressed groups in Turkey. The trauma defines who 'we' (Alevis) and 'they' (Sunni Turks) are, and what the nature of the relationship between 'us' and 'them' is. 'Their' oppressive and violent character is contrasted with 'our' virtuous nature that makes 'us' vulnerable. This vulnerability indicates the need to be united and strong. These identity constructions serve political purposes, and the Sivas massacre is vital political capital for the Alevi Confederation.

Thinking in terms of 'we'

This example highlights an important aspect of social identities. These identities do not only define one's place in the world ('I am a Basque', 'I am Alevi'), they also allow us to think and act in terms of 'we' ('we Basques', 'we Alevis'), as, for example, happened in the aftermath of the deadly pursuit in Amsterdam. This is critical for coordinating one's behaviour with others and thus for social collaboration. In the words of John Turner (1982, p. 21), 'Social identity is the cognitive mechanism that makes group behaviour possible.' A social identity allows people to refer to themselves and others as 'us', making group behaviour possible. Social identities serve to unite and shape the actions of those who consider themselves members of a particular category of group. A shared sense of 'us' transforms relationships because people see each other as belonging to the same group, and they start to act on the basis of the collective understandings, beliefs, and norms that define who 'we' are and what counts for 'us'. Thus, a shared sense of 'us' gives unity and direction and is therefore an important basis of social power. It can turn a disparate collection of separate individuals into a collaborative social force – a force that can try to achieve identity-related goals such as the recognition of Alevi minority rights or the recognition of the Moroccan Dutch thief as the victim of senseless violence.

This does not mean that those who identify with each other automatically agree. There is almost always dispute and disagreement within groups – for example, about whether being Muslim, or Jewish, or Alevi has an ethnic, cultural, religious, or political meaning. An alternative Alevi voice to the Confederation of European Alevi Unions is the Cem Foundation, which has close ties with the Turkish state and does not define Alevism in terms of oppression and victimhood. Accordingly, they interpret the Sivas massacre quite differently: not as a symbol of the continuing violent oppression of Alevis by Sunnis but, rather, the result of a political conflict that undermines the stability and unity of the Turkish state.

Social identities provide, however, an important basis for mutual influence (Turner, 1991). Experimental research has shown that when people are encouraged to think about themselves as belonging to the same national category, there is an expectation of agreement and a motivation to reach consensus on the meanings and implications of the national identity (e.g., Haslam *et al.*, 1999). A common identity means that you are similar in one way or another and belong together, and this leads group members to seek agreement and try to create consensus. In contrast, people tend to assume that they disagree with members of another group because they are not like 'us' and therefore do not share 'our' perspective. When in London a Pakistani immigrant and an Indian immigrant define themselves in terms of their ethnic identities, they will expect to have different views, beliefs, and goals. However, if they meet in a neighbourhood context to discuss neighbourhood matters, their shared local identity motivates them to find and develop common understandings and agreements.

Political implications

The quest for identity is never finished, and argument, negotiation, and persuasion will always exist. Each identity definition is always only a temporary bearing in an ever changing world. Identities are not fixed entities but open-ended issues in an on-going debate. Attempts to fixate or coin the content of a social identity are extremely difficult. For instance, the question 'What makes French people French?' or 'What makes Germans Germans?' has many answers, none of which will be endorsed by everyone. The search for *the* national identity is a quest without end. As the continuing debates about national identity show, there are different meanings with different messages and implications in circulation. What it means to be German, French, Dutch, or Spanish is not given or fixed but open to contention and change. It is socially constructed in and through arguments and the social practices associated with this.

Contention arises not only because of the multiple and sometimes contradictory meanings that social identities typically have, but also because social identities have important social and political implications. Social identities do not merely reflect the world as it is but are involved in trying to make the world the place one wants it to be. The fact that social identity definitions have behavioural consequences implies that different definitions encourage different forms of action. It is by defining a particular identity in a particular way that people can be mobilized and moved in a particular direction. For example, past injustices and collective traumas are powerful symbols and effective instruments for creating a sense of victimhood. Victim beliefs can stir intense emotions and instigate offensive and violent reactions, but they can also fuel attempts to achieve equality and positive social change, or to prevent possible future harm. And defining national identity in ethnic terms makes it difficult for immigrants to be accepted and feel included, whereas a definition in terms of citizenship and civic commitment offers more opportunities for immigrants to develop a sense of belonging to the host nation. Thus, identity representations and definitions are disputed not only because they have multiple meanings but also because these definitions have political and social consequences.

Take the example of Mauritius, a small island in the south-western Indian Ocean. Its cultural complexity is substantial because in an area of 1,860 square kilometres, various ethnic groups live together (e.g. Hindus, Tamils, Telegus, Marathis, Muslims, Creoles, Whites, and Chinese), some 15 languages are said to be spoken, and the four world religions rub shoulders. The central image of Mauritius is that of a diasporic nation, and the cultural politics of the state encourages the cultivation of 'ancestral cultures' (Eisenlohr, 2006). Mauritians are primarily conceived of as subjects with origins elsewhere and on-going commitments to authentic diasporic traditions. This means that the public enactment of ethnic identities in ethnic holidays, religious festivals, and ancestral languages is one of the ways in which full membership in a Mauritian nation is claimed and demonstrated. However, according to the Mauritian Constitution, the numerically relatively large group of Creoles, who are former slaves of African origin, are not a separate community and therefore cannot claim similar rights as the Muslims and Hindus. A movement for their official recognition has been led by a Creole Catholic priest: Father Jocelyn Gregoire is an enigmatic priest with numerous followers who has independently, but with the approval of the local church authority, argued for the recognition of the Creoles in the Mauritian Constitution and the betterment of the Creoles' status through his movement the 'Federation des Creoles Mauriciens'. By re-defining Creole identity from a one-sided victimhood position to a more confident and responsible self-understanding, as exemplified by himself, he tries to give the Creoles a new purpose and a new role in the Mauritian nation.

In Burma the Karen face a different challenge in mobilizing in-group members. The Burmese government as well as some international organizations define the Karen as 'secessionists' and 'violent terrorists' who perpetuate the conflict only because of their stubbornness and for self-interested reasons. Such negative labelling questions the legitimacy of the goals and acts of an ethno-political movement and can easily hamper mobilization processes, because people may be reluctant to identify with a stigmatized social movement or group. Hence, it is crucial for the leaders to produce and communicate, in narratives and symbols (e.g., Karen flag, anthem, Martyr Day), alternative understandings of the Karen insurgency. They do this in three ways (Kuroiwa & Verkuyten, 2008). First, their emphasis on the Karen's indigenousness positions them as 'freedom fighters' rather than as terrorists: the Karen revolution is about getting back what was has historically been theirs. Second, and in contrast to the claimed dishonesty and aggressiveness of the Burmese, the Karen are presented as inherently simple, honest, tranquil, and a peace-loving people. The Karen are forced to act in a way that goes against their moral nature. Third, the story of great endurance by their leaders creates an image of committed people fighting for a legitimate goal. The hardships and the duration of the conflicts become signs of the Karen's sincerity and commitment to the group and its cause.

The symbolic presentation of the Karen as a peace-loving, sincere, and committed people is important not only for mobilizing co-ethnics, but also for demobilizing outsider opposition. The possibility of support from, for example, international organizations, and for collaboration with foreign agencies and governments, crucially depends on the understandings held by these organization and agencies. Obtaining their support requires that the struggle is presented as legitimate and the claims as reasonable.

Identity and identification

The importance of the subjective sense of social identity for people's thinking, feeling, and acting directs us to the question of the extent of psychological investment in any particular social identity. This investment determines the behavioural corollaries of group memberships and is not the same for everyone. Some people can identify quite strongly with their ethnic group, whereas for others it is of marginal significance. Group identification is a critical issue in understanding why some are more inclined than others to think in terms of their social identity, build their life around a particular identity, and react more strongly when the value and welfare of their group is at stake. When you identify strongly with your ethnic background, you will more easily see the world in ethnic terms, practise behaviours that are considered an intrinsic part of your ethnic identity, and feel emotionally more involved and affected by the past, present, and future of your ethnic community.

> In order to approach the topic of ethnic diversity and national community in a more productive manner, the WRR suggests to adopt an approach in which various possibilities for identification with the Netherlands are central rather than focusing on strengthening national identity and describing precisely what it is or should be.

This quote is from the report *Identification with the Netherlands* by the Scientific Council for Government Policy (WRR, 2007, p. 31) referred to in chapter 1. The central proposal in the report is to focus on different processes of identification instead of giving a blueprint of the Dutch national identity. There is much to say in favour of this, and social scientists have made similar proposals (e.g. Brubaker & Cooper, 2000). Analytically as well as policy wise it is much more useful and interesting to investigate which are the circumstances in which people feel more or less connected with the Netherlands, when and why it is possible to identify simultaneously with one's ethnic background and the Dutch society, and when and under what circumstances group identification leads to processes of ex- or inclusion. These questions are more productive than endless attempts to define and describe the content of the national identity.

So there is much to say in favour of the approach of the Scientific Council. Yet, the Council dismisses the importance of a Dutch identity quite lightly and unfortunately is very vague about what exactly identification means. According to the Council, identity always involves multiple processes of identification, and identification is seen as a 'dynamic process of establishing, maintaining and breaking up of connections' (WRR, 2007, p. 32). Three dimensions of identification processes are distinguished: functional, emotional, and normative. In the explanation given, three very different issues seem to be concerned: making distinctions and evaluations in functional rather than ethnic terms; the opportunity to follow one's own values and ideas and bring them into the public domain; feelings of connectedness with others and with the Netherlands. Identification thus appears to signify quite different things. The persistent conceptual problems associated with the concept of identity as signalled and described by the Council are shifted to the concept of identification.

Identification

Identity and identification are concepts frequently used together. Usually no distinction is made between them. However, social identities refer to categories and groups that have a range of characteristics that are socially defined and – to some extent – socially shared. Identification, in contrast, refers to one's subjective relationship to a category or group. People can identify with anyone or anything they like, whereas social identities have a social reality that cannot simply be ignored or dismissed.

In psychology, the term 'identification' was introduced by Freud. He was particularly interested in the role of identification in child development. Identification is the earliest emotional bond between two people. Someone who identifies with another behaves as if he or she is that other person. A little girl who identifies with her mother puts on her mother's shoes, tries to walk in high heels, and imagines that she is her mother. According to Freud, identification is more than imitation, because the little girl does not only imitate her mother, but she also feels a sense of oneness with her mother, and thereby her mother's characteristics become her own. Identification is based upon perceived similarities and is pre-eminently an emotional process. The observed similarities are grounds for identification, just as observed differences may lead to detachment. A definition or sense of similarity often goes hand in hand with a tendency to become emotionally involved with those with whom one identifies, whereas difference tends to lead to dis-identification. Identification involves a – temporary – reorganization of one's emotional life whereby pride and shame are particularly important (Rosenberg, 1979). I can admire or disapprove of a particular person, but that does not mean that I am proud of that person or ashamed of him or her. The moment I identify with him or her, feelings of pride or shame come into play. I admire a stranger who performs exceptionally well, and I feel proud if that person is my son or daughter.

Identification is not limited to a specific person or to a certain age. Most of us identify with an ethnic or national community, and this can result in feelings of security, belonging, and pride. Identification involves sameness, whereby wanting to become one and the feeling of 'one-ness' (emotional fusion) is paramount. The success of the group with which one identifies becomes one's own success, of which one is proud, just as failures are felt as personal failures that one is ashamed of and tries to make excuses for. The group and the group members are experienced as an integral and inseparable part of the self which implies 'a sense of oneness with them and to feel personally affected by what happens to them. For the group identifier, the distinction between me and my group is unclear: the fate of the group is experienced as the fate of the self' (Rosenberg, 1979, p. 179).

Identification and membership

Group identification typically corresponds with group membership. This is, for example, the case if a Basque starts to identify with the Basque cause and everything else that is Basque, or if a Pakistani in the United Kingdom is very conscious of his Pakistani background and strongly identifies with the Pakistani culture. Both examples involve identification with a group to which one is assumed to belong. Identification and group membership correspond, and the extent of emotional investment can be stronger or weaker, depending on the circumstances and on individual characteristics.

But it is also possible that one does not identify with a community or group to which one belongs. In such a case one wants to have nothing to do with the membership and adopts an attitude of aloofness. Instead of identification, dis-identification occurs, and one distances oneself from the group and resists the expectations and requirements that are associated with group membership. Members of the community often object to this, as illustrated in the terms *bounty* and *coconut* (Black on the outside and White on the inside) and the accusation of *acting White* and *selling out,* which can be heard among African Americans.

It is also possible to identify with a group to which one does not belong. If the membership of that group is relatively open, such as 'youth cultures', then a person can try to adopt the criteria for belonging, and in that case it is also relatively easy to obtain the particular social identity in the eyes of others. The situation is different when the identity criteria are rather rigid and permanent, as is the case with skin colour or gender. In that case, you can 'pretend' but not convincingly 'be' one of them. You will always in some aspect be an outsider. I can identify with Aboriginals in Australia or with African Americans, but this does not make me an Aborigine or African American. In his book on the English adventurer Richard Burton, who wanted to be seen as an Indian, Trojanow (2008, p. 206) gives the opinion of an Indian guru: 'You can disguise yourself all you want, but you will never experience what it's like to be one of us. You can always remove your disguise, that last resort always exists. However, we are prisoners in our skin. Fasting is not the same as starving.'

The role of group identification

Group identification is important because it is when individuals see themselves as group members that they will think and act in terms of their social identity. There are various ways in which group identification can play a role in people's perceptions and behaviour. I can explain this with the findings of a research survey on Dutch natives' perceptions of national identity threat and support for ethnic minority rights (Verkuyten, 2009b). Group identification can be an antecedent to perceived identity threats, it can be a consequence of perceived threats, and it can influence the relationship between identity threats and support for minority rights. These three possibilities are shown in Figure 2.1.

The 'group identity lens' model argues that group identification is an antecedent of perceived identity threats and will indirectly affect support for multicultural recognition, via its association with threat. This model posits that when a particular social identity is salient, it provides a 'lens' through which the perceiver sees the world and makes sense of it. Group identification functions as a group lens that makes people sensitive to anything that concerns or could harm their group. Thus, stronger group identification will lead to higher threat perceptions, and these perceptions result in a particular response.

The 'group identity reaction' model is based on the idea that perceiving identity threat leads individuals to identify more strongly with their group and that stronger identification leads to more negative reactions towards other groups. The idea is that people cope with identity threats by adopting group-based strategies that increase group identification.

The 'group identity conditional' model argues that group identification influences the relationship between identity threat and support for minority rights. Perceived threat can have different effects depending on group identification because the motivational meanings of perceived threat are different. Compared to low identifiers, those with high group identification are more likely to be concerned about their group, especially if the position and value of the group identity is at stake.

The results of three studies among Dutch natives were similar and in line with the group identity lens model. Group identification was positively related to perceived identity threat, and threat was, in turn, negatively related to support for multiculturalism and minority rights. Thus, group identification seems to lead to greater threat perception, and once threat is perceived, it leads to less support for immigrants and ethnic minorities.

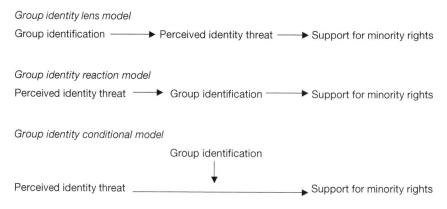

Figure 2.1 Three models for the role of group identification in the relationship between out-group threat and the support for minority rights

However, this research is of the 'take a picture' type, which does not allow one to draw causal conclusions. Furthermore, this empirical support for the group-lens model does not imply that the other models are not valid. The role that group identification plays depends on many things, including the situation in which people find themselves and the group to which they belong. There is, for example, among ethnic minority groups quite some evidence for the group identity reaction model. Longitudinal research (of the 'making a film' type) shows that identity threats in the form of perceptions of discrimination can lead to stronger group identification (Jasinskaja-Lahti *et al.*, 2009; Ramos *et al.*, 2012), and this, in turn, can lead to stronger support for minority rights.

Social identity dimensions

Group identification may be temporary and situational. In times of danger and uncertainty people will tend to identify more strongly with their national community than in times of peace and stability (Hogg, 2007). And in times of national achievements and glory (e.g., winning the World Cup or Olympic medals) people will feel national pride and a strong sense of belonging. Group identification varies depending on the circumstances. But given identical circumstances, there are also differences between people in the extent to which they identify with their group. For some individuals, identification can have a more sustained and permanent character, causing feelings of pride and belonging to become part of their sense of national identity. Self-identification *as* a member of an ethnic group ('I am a Basque', 'I am Dutch') is something other than the emotional meanings of identification *with* that group.

Most scholars agree that a sense of social identity encompasses cognitive, emotional, and behavioural components. However, ideas regarding the different identity aspects and dimensions vary a great deal (see Ashmore *et al.*, 2004; Leach *et al.*, 2008).[3] Typical behaviour that is seen by one scholar as an integral part of a sense of ethnic identity is considered by another a result or consequence of that identity. For example, is listening to Chinese music and having an interest in Chinese politics part of your Chinese identity, or, rather, a consequence of the fact that you are Chinese and you feel yourself Chinese? Someone who is not Chinese may have the same preferences and interests, but that doesn't make her Chinese, and another Chinese person may be completely Westernized in preferences and behaviour, but still considers herself Chinese. When is something part of your ethnic, religious, or national identity, and when is it not? And what about the difference between the importance that you attach to your ethnic identity and the emotional feelings you develop? Subjectively, your ethnic identity is not solely about which group you belong to, but also how important this is to you, what your feelings are about it, and what it all means to you. This should not be ignored or forgotten. For example when an immigrant finds his ethnic Turkish background important, natives often conclude that this is *the* most important identity, that he is proud to be Turkish, and that his primary loyalty is with the Turkish community. But the one does not necessarily follow from the other.

Following the distinction between cognitive, emotional, and behavioural components of social identity, I will focus upon self-categorization and importance (cognitive), value and belonging (affective), and appropriate conduct (behavioural).

Self-categorization

A sense of identity depends on categorizing yourself as a member of a specific group. In many cases, this happens without conscious thought, and there is hardly any doubt or uncertainty. You are what you are, and you categorize yourself in an appropriate manner. Depending on the context, one time that makes you a male, another time a student, and a next time a resident of Paris. Even though it may be rather straightforward in many situations, this does not mean that it is inconsequential. By placing yourself in a particular group or category, you indicate your position in the social world: what you are and where you belong. A group name or label has specific meanings, and changing labels entails different expectations. Or, as Foote (1951, p. 7) states, 'a person by another name will act according to that other name'. For example, it has been argued that Americans of Mexican origin who define themselves as 'Chicano' tend to act, think, and feel differently from those who describe themselves as Hispanic (Buriel, 1987). The former has a clear political connotation that points to exclusion and discrimination, whereas the latter is originally a policy term.

Because social identities refer to 'what you are to others', a self-definition is also a public statement. In the German or the Dutch context, to describe yourself as Turkish is not the same as referring to yourself as Turkish German or Turkish Dutch. The position that you adopt with these labels differs. In the first case you clearly place yourself at a greater distance from German or Dutch society than in the second one. Socially, however, the variation is not unlimited. Someone of Turkish origin living in Germany can hardly, or not at all, publicly describe himself as a Somali. If he nonetheless does so, this is typically not an identity claim but, rather, a political statement, for example in relation to the treatment of immigrants in German society or to express solidarity with other immigrant groups, just like President Kennedy's famous statement '*Ich bin ein Berliner*'. Self-definitions can also have a political meaning because of the policy implications of, for example, census data. The more people indicate that they identify as a member of a particular community, the more attention – and, sometimes, resources – go to that particular community.

Importance

A self-definition as such tells us little about how important it is for someone to belong to a particular ethnic group. For someone living in Great Britain, a self-definition as Bangladeshi may signify little more than a label that refers to one's place of origin, while for others it may be a central and essential part of how they see themselves. Someone may be Muslim among many other things, while for others it is the only thing that really matters. The psychological importance of social identities can be understood and examined in different ways. One is to simply ask people to indicate how important their ethnic, religious, or national identity is to them. As a rule, people will find all sorts of social memberships important. Such questions therefore say little about the importance of the various identities relative to each other. Yet, there may be a certain ranking according to which some identities take a more central position in one's self-understanding as the most important thing in one's life and the only identity that really matters. A particular identity can be like a coat that you never take off. When you think about yourself, for example, you think Muslim or White or Black before you think husband, teacher, American, or anything else. Therefore, people can also be asked to rank-order different social identities in terms of their importance. In addition, a particular social identity can be important without you really knowing it. It might be so self-evident or obvious that you do not think about it, even though on a deeper, unconscious level it directs your feelings and actions.

Value

You will most probably evaluate positively those social identities that you consider important. Living in the United States, you may find it important that you are a Mexican and you may also be proud of it. What you are and the related feelings are in agreement. But this is not necessarily the case. You can have a positive feeling about a certain identity without it necessarily playing a central part in how you perceive yourself. And you can find your Mexican identity important and at the same time be ashamed of it because of the social problems that some Mexicans cause. Or the stigmatization by society at large can make it difficult to be proud of your Mexican background; it may turn it into a spoiled identity. The lack of social recognition may have an impact on your ethnic self-feelings. And because your ethnic background evokes all sorts of negative feelings, it can actually dominate your consciousness, absorb your energy, and lead to forms of stigma management (Goffman, 1963; O'Brien, 2011).

Research shows that compared to self-categorization these positive or negative feelings are less dependent on the specific situation (Kinket & Verkuyten, 1997). That self-definitions quickly change depending on the circumstances does not mean that self-feelings are equally variable. Everyone can think of situations when a particular group membership is temporarily salient in your consciousness, and you feel disappointed and sad, or, conversely, proud and satisfied. This is the difference when your national soccer team wins or loses a World Cup match. At the same time most people will experience more permanent positive or negative feelings towards their national group memberships. In addition to situational variations there tends to be a more stable emotional baseline, similarly to the differences between the weather, which changes from day to day, and the climate. That emotional baseline also determines how someone feels in a concrete situation during a specific event. Hearing the national anthem will make those people who are generally proud of their nation emotional, while for others it will evoke little in the way of feelings.

Affective ties

Social identities involve not only self-categorization, importance, and value, but also *feelings of connectedness*. Belonging to an ethnic or religious community is often accompanied by a sense of inclusion and feeling part of something. Your own community is an extension of yourself, and it provides a framework that binds you to those who surround you. This is accompanied by feelings of loyalty and solidarity and a shared or common fate. The ethnic group is perceived as an integral and inseparable part of who you are. There is a sense of unity, and you are personally affected by what happens to people in your group and by what they experience. Such emotions do not develop overnight and also appear to differ relatively little across situations (Kinket & Verkuyten, 1997). Nor is it easy to experience them simultaneously with the same intensity for different ethnic or national communities. A self-definition in terms of Moroccan Dutch or Algerian French is relatively easy, but genuine feelings of dual loyalty and solidarity are psychologically much more complex, especially if the relationship between the two communities is rather tense.

Appropriate conduct

Social identities can be quite strongly connected to typical behaviours that function as group boundaries and define the meaning of the identity. You may, for instance, be of Moluccan or Chinese origin and consider yourself a Moluccan or a Chinese. But if you do not speak Malay or Chinese or do not practise any typical Moluccan or Chinese traditions and customs, you will easily be seen as not being a real Moluccan or Chinese, both by others and yourself. As a participant in one of our studies said, 'If you cannot speak Malay, you're not a real Moluccan.' And somebody else said, 'That's why I'm so Dutch and not really Chinese, because I barely speak Chinese and I cannot write in Chinese either.' An ethnic identity must be visible in ethnically appropriate behaviour, just as a religious identity is shown in religious acts. And Islam and Judaism, for example, are characterized by numerous behavioural prescriptions and proscriptions, making it sometimes difficult to feel a true Muslim if one does not participate in Ramadan or a true Jew if one does not eat kosher.

What exactly is appropriate behaviour can be quite clear at times, but it may also be subject to disagreement and debate. In any case, it involves behaviour that directly implicates what it means to belong to a particular group. The behaviour is part of the identity in question and therefore is *not an option or choice*. To consider yourself – and to be considered by others – a true Muslim or a true Jew, you need to observe the appropriate religious practices. Shortcomings in this area can lead to self-blame, such as I am not actually a Muslim or Jew, or I am not truly Chinese. The behaviour defines the identity in question. This is different from behavioural choices that you make as a result of feeling that you are a group member, such as preferring the cuisine of your ethnic group and listening to ethnic music or attending religious meetings and learning about the history of your religion. These behaviours are the outcomes of feelings of belonging and not intrinsic to what it means to be a group member.

Different dimensions

The fact that I discussed the different dimensions separately is, of course, not to suggest that they are not related to each other. But in order to examine and understand their relationships, it is important to first distinguish between them. After all, the psychological dynamics of self-definitions are different from processes of self-evaluations, feelings of solidarity, and identity behaviour. Research also shows that the various aspects cannot simply be reduced to each other and that sometimes there are obvious connections, but sometimes not (see Ashmore *et al.*, 2004). In threatening situations and for specific social identities (such as religious ones), the connection tends to be stronger than in more harmonious situations and for other identities (such as regional ones). In the former case it can be quite difficult for people themselves as well as for researchers to draw a meaningful empirical distinction between these dimensions because they are experienced as an integrated whole where high importance equals strong positive emotions, strong feelings of connectedness and shared fate, and specific behaviours.

However, in many other cases one cannot simply use the importance that is attached to ethnic identity for drawing conclusions about evaluations and emotions. People can feel emotionally attached to their group, even though that particular group membership is liable to evoke social disdain and disappointment. True sports fans will stay loyal and will not turn away from their club despite disastrous results. Similarly, a person can acknowledge and accept his or her ethnic group membership as self-defining ('that is me'), without having a feeling of solidarity towards that group and its members ('it does not evoke any emotions in me'). For example, you may know you are and define yourself as a senior citizen without identifying with the elderly. Research also shows that the different dimensions can have different behavioural consequences (see Ashmore *et al.*, 2004). Feelings of interconnectedness and shared fate are important for forms of collective action and social mobilization, whereas sentiments of pride make one feel good about oneself.

It is important to consider the differences between the dimensions, because research often focuses on a single aspect but subsequently draws conclusions about people's sense of identity in general. One example is the '*Annual Minority Reports*' of the Netherlands Institute for Social Research. These reports tend to gain much media and political attention. They are important and useful for a variety of reasons, but they are also in some parts quite superficial. For instance, ethnic identity is typically measured using only one question: 'Do you feel more Dutch or more Turkish (Moroccan, Surinamese, etc.)?' The response format has five possible options: fully Turkish, more Turkish than Dutch, equally Turkish as Dutch, more Dutch than Turkish, and fully Dutch. As so often, so here also the generality and broadness of a representative study comes at the expense of the necessary detail. But this does not stop researchers from computing statistical differences and correlations in order to formulate policy recommendations that then are extensively discussed in the media. It is, however, far from clear what an answer to that specific question indicates from a psychological point of view. For example, to what extent is the answer influenced by – political, cultural, situational – circumstances or, rather, reflects a more enduring internal reality? Moreover, the answer says nothing about the substantive meanings of these particular identities.

Ethnic identity motives

The different social identity dimensions that are part of one's sense of social identity are associated with basic motivational principles of identity. For example, the sense of belonging that an identity can give relates to the fundamental need for affective ties.

There are various theoretical ideas about the number and sorts of identity motives (see Vignoles, 2011), and the relevance of these motives will also depend on the type of social identity. Professional identities fulfil other needs than gender identities or than ethnic and national ones. Specific motivational principles can be more or less strong ingredients in specific identities. Our concern is with ethnic and related identities, and a great deal of theory and research supports the importance of four basic needs for human motivation. Human beings need and seek to have a sense of grip, of meaningful existence, of belonging, and of self-esteem (see, e.g., Baumeister, 2005; Williams, 2001). Each need is uniquely important, and when any one of them is lacking or threatened, people experience distress. A discussion of these needs helps us to understand the psychological dynamics behind ethnic and related identities and what happens when these motives are obstructed. Obstruction implies identity threat leading to mental and behavioural strategies to alleviate the threat. Before elaborating on the importance of these four needs in relation to ethnic identity, two other dynamics need to be briefly discussed.

The first is that social identities can serve group interests and are therefore sometimes fuelled by self-interested motives. For example, in utilitarian and rational choice theories, ethnicity is seen as an instrumental identity, and ethnic groups are treated as interest groups. A classic example is Cohen's (1969) work on urban ethnicity in Nigeria. He showed how kinship and cultural symbols were manipulated by Hausa traders seeking political gain. Ethnicity is considered a political resource for competing interests, and it is obvious that group interests often play a central and strategic role in ethnic identity processes. Moreover, when people have the idea that their group interests are threatened (they take away 'our' jobs), they will tend to react more negatively towards the assumed source of the threat (immigrants). This perspective of group interests is also successfully used in analysing processes of identity politics. An identity that is constructed around the idea of origin and kinship is, for example, used by minority and indigenous groups to claim compensations and rights, but also by extreme right-wing political groups with their 'Own people first' slogans.

Rational approaches are important, and in particular cases they provide adequate explanations. However, in these approaches self-interest seems to be the only motive or psychological reason for ethnic identification. This makes it difficult to account for those situations in which ethnic identification persist, even if, from an instrumental point of view, persistence brings disadvantages rather than advantages – as in the case of, for instance, certain groups of Roma, Native Americans, and ethnic separatists who are prepared to lose economically in exchange for autonomy and independence. Another limitation is that this account does not really address ethnicity per se. The focus is on non-ethnic circumstances and on political and economic interests. Ethnicity is regarded as a mere cipher for (class) interests and has no independent meaning or force in itself. It is seen as a manifestation or by-product of other more basic concerns. Ethnicity is viewed either as a screen that hides the real logic of people's position or an instrument that will disappear when no longer useful. Hence, ethnicity itself is not theorized or accounted for, and the specific meanings and emotions, sentiments, and experiences are neglected or dismissed as irrelevant. However, ethnicity often does have a distinctive meaning and emotional power in people's life. The meaning of ethnicity is not only rational– instrumental but also emotional and expressive.

The second point relates to group distinctiveness and having a distinctive social identity. Social identities provide a place in the world and delineate social positions; without group distinctiveness there is no clear social identity. What it means to be a German, or a Moroccan immigrant, or a Muslim depends on what distinguishes Germans from other nationalities, Moroccans from other immigrants, and Islam from other religions. Distinctiveness is an intrinsic, defining property of identity, and people use various strategies to preserve the distinctiveness of their social identities. Research has shown that when group distinctiveness is under threat, people try to differentiate themselves from other groups that are too similar, tend to define stricter group boundaries, perceive their group in more stereotypical terms, and try to express their identity in behaviour that symbolically affirms that identity (see Ellemers *et al.*, 1999). Research has also shown that people will typically identify more strongly with distinctive groups than with non-distinctive ones. And in research among Polish students it was even demonstrated that a distinctive national identity was considered more important than a positive one. The students emphasized distinctive negative national characteristics rather than positive traits that were shared with other European countries (Mlicki & Ellemers, 1996). For ethnic minority groups, distinctiveness threat often comes in the form of an emphasis on assimilation, which leads to a stronger emphasis on one's ethnic minority identity, especially for those who strongly identify with their group. A plea for assimilation easily turns into a threat to how you perceive yourself and how your ethnic group differs from other groups.

All this research indicates that group distinctiveness is an intrinsic aspect of social identity. Without it there is no clear social identity and therefore few possibilities to satisfy fundamental human needs. Distinctiveness is a prerequisite for social identities to provide a sense of grip, meaningfulness, belonging, and esteem.

Grip

One of the critical aspects of everyday life is to know how to go about things. People need to have the feeling that they are capable of acting on the world, that they have competence and control. Losing one's sense of grip, feeling helpless in dealing with things, is extremely unsettling. Most people find uncertainties stressful and they tend to prefer a dictatorship over complete chaos. What matters is that you have a sense of understanding the world and that you feel that you are not a victim of others or the circumstances, but have a choice in handling your own affairs.

A sense of grip can be sought and obtained in many different ways, such as by looking for information, listening to experts and authorities, and trying out new patterns of behaviour. Social categorization can also provide a sense of grip because it brings organization and structure to the complex and multifaceted social reality. Classifying the social world into categories provides order and something to hold on to. Not only as to know about who others are and what you can expect from them, but also for the question of what you are yourself and how you should act. Social identities function as orientation systems and frames of reference that provide order and stability. They give us direction with regard to what we have to think, feel, and do.

Furthermore, social identities provide us with a sense of being able to act upon the world. Social change becomes possible when people mobilize on the basis of a shared identity. A shared social identity implies that people act not separately as individuals but, rather, as a collective that can realize a particular vision of how the social world should be. Thus, a shared identity can empower people for trying to (re-)make the social world.

However, possessing a particular identity can also threaten one's sense of grip – for example, in case of a stigmatized minority identity. Stigmatization implies a heightened risk of becoming a victim of exclusion and discrimination, such as at school, when looking for work, and in your free time. This increased risk is in itself not without consequences. Every event or incident confronts people with the question of how this is to be explained. Successes and failures at school, at the workplace, or wherever can be attributed to different causes. In most cases it is not clear what exactly the cause is, because multiple interpretations are possible: 'What exactly is going on and why is someone saying or doing that?' These uncertainties hold true for everyone, but especially for stigmatized groups. For them, there is always the additional possibility of discrimination and with that comes doubt about the judgement and behaviour of the other: does he say that – the teacher, employer, neighbour, or policeman – because he really believes that or because he does not like Blacks. Is he sincere or prejudiced? Such a situation is stressful because uncertainty or ambiguity about why things happen to you is not a pleasant situation. It reduces your sense of grip.

A good understanding of the process of stigmatization can make you more confident and resilient. Developing sensitivity to the subtle and implicit signals of rejection is an essential step towards appropriate responses. It is also an important impetus for social change. If you are more aware of discrimination and stigmatization, you will be quicker to shield and protect yourself from it. Understanding and experiences with discrimination can lead to outrage and anger. This can initiate actions that result in real change. But, ultimately, this may also develop into mistrust and suspicion. Awareness and vigilance can become obsessive and lead to hypersensitivity. You become overly focused on the ever-present possibility of exclusion and discrimination. However, the attribution of negative experiences to discrimination implies that you place the control over important aspects of your life in someone else's hands: not you, but the one who discriminates against you determines what happens to you. With such an attribution, you define yourself as a victim who has little or no choice but to deal with the sense of helplessness that it involves. Ignoring discrimination, on the other hand, has a positive meaning for your sense of having a grip and control on your world. And this feeling is very important in order to lead your life in a pleasant and productive way.

Meaningful existence

People are aware of the vulnerability of their own existence and their mortality. As a result of this existential uncertainty there is a basic need for answers to questions about the meaning of the world and one's own presence within it. The search for meaningful existence is an essential feature of the human condition. People want to believe that their life has a more general meaning and purpose, and such a belief is a core component of psychological well-being. Anthropologists have argued that ethnicity can provide an answer to the 'perennial problems of life: the questions of origins, destiny and, ultimately, the meaning of life' (Cohen in Eriksen, 1993, p. 45). There are two related reasons for this. One has to do with the specific cultural worldview that ethnic groups can have and the other with the sense of continuity that an ethnic group gives.

First, cultural, religious, and nationalistic worldviews are belief systems that aspire to explain the significance and purpose of life. They explain why things are as they are and what, in the end, life is all about. These worldviews form a shared understanding of reality that imposes value and purpose on the world. They allow you to believe in explanations and principles that are not arbitrary and that go beyond your own personal interests, advantages, and pleasures, thereby making your existence meaningful. Research has shown that cultural worldviews buffer against existential terror and that people bolster their worldview when they are reminded of their mortality (Greenberg *et al.*, 1997). Furthermore, individuals or groups who challenge one's cultural worldview by thinking and behaving differently tend to be rejected and excluded. An assault on your cultural or religious worldview is very threatening, especially if your sense of meaningfulness is derived from it. Cultural disintegration and 'losing your culture' are threatening not only because they have negative impacts on your sense of grip but also because they undermine the meaningfulness of life. The result is psychological alienation whereby the available cultural convictions lose their self-evident importance and are no longer useful for making your life meaningful.

Second, the belief in origin, common descent, and shared traditions is what underlies the notion of being '*a* people'. As the anthropologist DeVos (1995, p. 25) writes: 'Ethnicity is, in its narrowest sense, a feeling of continuity with a real or imagined past, a feeling that is maintained as an essential part of one's self-definition.' Ethnicity provides a sense of historical continuity that extends beyond the self. Continuity is not the same as stability or the absence of change. There is always change within ethnic groups, but at the same time there is also a feeling of collective continuity, of being part of a particular ancestry and origin. A story about where 'we' come from gives an explanation and interpretation of one's own position in time and space. It makes one's existence meaningful because it gives a more general purpose that transcends self-interests and the 'here and now'. An ethnic group can afford a feeling of symbolic immortality because it makes you part of an entity that continues through generations. To pass on life and to be part of 'a people' that reaches back in time gives meaning to life.

Research shows that people attribute temporal endurance to the social groups to which they belong (Condor, 2006; Sani *et al.*, 2007) and that perception of group continuity provides existential security. The perception of your group as historically and culturally enduring is also associated with higher levels of group identification and more opposition against social change. Furthermore, people are more likely to show solidarity with their own group and opposition to other groups when they are faced with threats to the continued existence of their group. Such a threat triggers feelings of self-continuity that strengthen one's desire to protect one's group and to reject others (Smeekes & Verkuyten, 2013).

Affective ties and belonging

The question of who and what you are is also a question of where you belong. What do you feel connected to, and with whom do you feel at ease and at home? The anthropologist Goldschmidt (2006) speaks of 'affect hunger' to indicate that the desire for affective ties is just as strong as a full stomach. The need for affective ties forms a psychological basis for social contact and involvement with others and the environment. This need is directed to the outside world and connects people in a subjective manner to what they are surrounded by. People want to bind themselves to something or someone, to feel at home in their environment. If you succeed, the environment becomes emotionally part of you, and you feel included and connected. If it does not work out or does so only unsatisfactorily, feelings of isolation and 'not belonging' are the result.

Feelings of belonging also occur with ethnic, cultural, and religious communities. When people identify with such communities, these feelings come about naturally: the familiar affection provided by your own group, the confidence and warmth of being part of it, and the related claims on loyalty and solidarity. This is an important reason why one's primary affinity is usually with one's own ethnic community (Brewer, 2001; Yzerbyt *et al.*, 2000). It is from here, that warmth and support have been found since childhood. One's own community, with its culture, tradition, and religion, tends to be an important framework for bonding within which a sense of belonging and connectedness can be found. The emotional relationship with close relatives and the familiarity with the social environment of your childhood years are projected onto the ethnic group. This creates a sense of community and ethnic identity with the associated feelings of connectedness ('I am like them, one of them, that is where I belong'). Emotionally others are part of you, and you are a part of the social environment: there is a sense of belonging. Such feelings easily create a moral community in which loyalty, trust, and the obligation of mutual help and support are central. Others can rely on your help and support just as you can expect it back. Interdependencies are embedded in a community, and they are supported by a sense of community.

Affective ties come in all shapes and are formed in various areas or life: first and foremost with parents, family members, relatives, and friends, but also with the physical and spatial environment that people can make their own, can consider as a part of themselves, which they feel involved and responsible for and that they desire and miss when they leave 'home'. Feelings of loss, uprootedness, and displacement are typical for many immigrants. But above all people want to belong socially, to be included in groups and communities. Social exclusion hurts. It not only suggests that there is something wrong with you, but especially that you are not wanted or do not belong. There is neurological evidence that pain caused by social exclusion activates the same brain structures as physical pain (Eisenberg *et al.*, 2003). Moreover, social *ex*clusion generally evokes stronger emotional effects than social *in*clusion. Emotional 'numbness' is a typical first reaction to social rejection and exclusion (Baumeister *et al.*, 2007). People become indifferent, find it hard to empathize with others, and are less willing to adapt and to make a contribution. The chance of being rejected again outweighs the desire to belong. But there always continues to be a desire for relatedness.

Most immigrants and ethnic minority members want to belong not only to their ethnic group, but also to the host society. Exclusion and non-acceptance by the host majority is therefore threatening to their sense of belonging. A nationwide study of nearly 3,000 early adolescents showed, for example, that Turkish Dutch and Moroccan Dutch pupils in primary schools are more often the victim of ethnic name calling and exclusion compared to children of other groups (Verkuyten & Thijs, 2002). And because these children generally attach great importance to their ethnic identity, these experiences tend to have negative psychological consequences. Being excluded on ethnic grounds is painful. In addition, such forms of exclusion easily have the connotation of not really belonging in the Netherlands. Children of immigrants sometimes wonder if they will still be allowed to live in the Netherlands later on.

Esteem and recognition

Awareness of and the search for a place in the social world is always accompanied by the question of whether you are recognized and valued by others. When there is the slightest doubt or when the slightest provocation occurs, this question burst to the fore. This is a highly sensitive matter. This is reflected in the increasing emphasis on (the right to) respect and the time and energy put into trying to obtain, maintain, or restore the desired recognition and appreciation. Thomas Hobbes observed that 'men are brought to battle for any sign of under-value, either direct in their persons, or by reflection in their kindred, their friends, their nation, their profession, or their name' (in Rosenberg, 1979, p. 37).

Everyone has the need to be socially recognized and valued – not only for who you are as an individual, but also for what you are as a member of a group. This is especially the case when that group is very important for how you see yourself, such as is often the case with ethnic and religious groups. Stigmatization on these grounds is therefore threatening to one's feelings of self-worth. Low social esteem can lead to low self-esteem, and low social respect can lead to low self-respect. For this, people do not necessarily have to experience the stigmatization personally. Due to group identification, negative judgements about your group or fellow group members are felt as a personal matter. Thus, statements about the 'backwardness' of Islamic culture are seen and felt as a personal contempt and slander. The group cause becomes a personal cause: the insult directed to the group is felt as a personal attack. A native Dutch woman who converted to Islam 30 years ago, states it like this:

> Even though I belong here, I don't feel like an ordinary, normal person anymore. I have become an object, a species. The kind that you can lash out at. A part of my identity, my inner being is insulted every day.[4]

There is quite a large literature on the concept of recognition and the politics of recognition. These politics try to respond to people's desire to have their cultural characteristics acknowledged. The idea that acceptance and recognition of cultural diversity and cultural identity is crucial for feelings of self-esteem is, according to Burnet (1995), one of the key multiculturalist assumptions (see chapter 5). The public acceptance and recognition of one's group and culture are considered valuable as conditions for a positive group identity that sustains feelings of self-respect and self-esteem. For example, in his essay '*The Politics of Recognition*', the philosopher Taylor (1992, p. 26) argues that, 'misrecognition shows not just a lack of due respect. It can inflict a grievous wound, saddling its victim with a crippling self-hatred. Due recognition is not just a courtesy we owe people. It is a vital human need'. There is quite some research evidence showing that the public denial or misrecognition of one's group and culture facilitates an insecure group identity that undermines feelings of self-worth. And in the context of the United States it has been demonstrated that in interactions ethnic minorities seek to be respected, whereas Whites seek to be liked (Bergsieker *et al.*, 2010).

Recognition can first of all relate to having, or being entitled to, equal legal rights and obligations (Honneth, 1996). Equality in the legal domain indicates that minority groups are recognized by others as equal citizens and morally responsible members of society. Most democratic societies have this type of equality, at least for legal immigrants and groups that have settled in society. But recognition is also important in the sphere of social esteem where the social value of one's group is at stake. Individuals are judged and often want to be judged in terms of their ethnic origin and cultural beliefs, especially when they identify strongly with their ethnic group. Anticipating current debates and minority's 'world-wide push towards differentiation', Tajfel (1981, p. 317, italics in original) argued that

> the new claims of the minorities are based on their right to decide to be different (preserve their separateness) as defined *in their own terms* and not in terms implicitly adopted or explicitly dictated by the majorities . . . the wish to preserve their right to take their own decisions and keep their own 'identity'.

Minorities are struggling against denial of their identity and misrecognition more generally. Despite having legal citizenship, second- and third-generation immigrants are often not recognized as true citizens. When people think about who is 'really' Dutch, or German, or French, they implicitly think about the ethnic Dutch, the ethnic Germans, and the ethnic French. And even in an immigration country like the United States it has been demonstrated that there is an implicit association of American = White (Devos & Banaji, 2005).

Experiencing denial of recognition has a profound emotional impact on minority members. It is threatening to your feeling of positive self-regard when you hear that you are considered a problem, or that you come from a backward culture, or when your religion is mocked and belittled, or when you feel that you are a second-class citizen, or when under the pretext of integration you face strong pressures to assimilate. Minorities are often involved in a struggle for recognition. This is illustrated by the line 'All I am asking is for is a little respect' in the Aretha Franklin song that was popular in the US civil rights movements of the 1960s. The denial of recognition is likely to bolster 'segregated' minority identities and might even lead to politically motivated violence. In contrast, the experience of being recognized and valued implies that one feels accepted as a full member of society, which stimulates social and other forms of integration.

Multiple reasons

The needs discussed are uniquely important and cannot be reduced to each other. There is substantial evidence that when any of them is lacking or threatened, people show signs of distress and engage in coping strategies. These needs underlie many forms of social behaviour and are not exclusive to social identities. Furthermore, some play a more important role in some social identities than in others. For deriving a sense of continuity and meaningful existence, ethnic and religious identities are more appropriate than local or gender identities. And some social identities satisfy multiple needs, whereas others are more limited in this respect. Religion is an obvious example. Religions offer 'cosmologies, moral frameworks, institutions, rituals, traditions, and other identity-supporting content that answers to individuals' needs for psychological stability in the form of a predictable world, a sense of belonging, self-esteem, and even self-actualization' (Seul, 1999, p. 553).

This responsiveness to multiple needs makes religious groups attractive in times of uncertainties and threats. Yet, it is also something that makes 'extreme' groups attractive, such as sects, ultra-nationalists, and religious fundamentalists. These kinds of groups tend to be comprehensive and exclusive. They have clear rules and guidelines that one has to follow, and their moral righteousness provides a strong 'what to live for'. But the appeal of such groups and movements is more varied than that. A strong national, ethnic, or religious identity not only provides grip and meaning, but also comfort, warmth, and connectedness, and the proud feeling of having social value. All of this feeds into a self-conscious and self-assured attitude: you know what you are, what the right thing to do and to think is, where you belong, and what makes life meaningful. All the ingredients for a rich and happy life are there. But such identities can also evolve into a one-dimensional or black-and-white worldview: a sense of culturally or religiously founded moral superiority with the related actions to protect one's national, cultural, or religious purity. And if there are also feelings of humiliation, frustration, and relative deprivation involved, then the possibility of violence is never far away. Part of the mission of right-wing extremists or jihadist groups is to give people back their sense of grip and security, their feeling of belonging, and their dignity and pride.

3 Ethnic discrimination and social validation

In 1951, eight-year-old Linda Brown, of Topeka, Kansas, had to cross the railway track and walk 21 blocks every weekday to catch the bus to a Black school on the other side of town. She could not go to school in her own neighbourhood because it was a completely 'White' school. In those days, under the 'separate but equal' doctrine this was not allowed. Her father took legal action, which eventually led to the well-known case 'Brown vs. Board of Education' on which the US Supreme Court ruled in 1954. Based on 'modern authorities', school segregation was declared illegal. In the verdict the results of several studies were cited, including the famous doll studies of Kenneth and Mamie Clark (1947) on racial identification among Black children. In their research, they worked with Black and White dolls, and the children were asked to indicate, for instance, which doll resembled them, which doll was kind, and which one they preferred. The majority of Black children showed a preference for the White doll, considered that doll nicer, and also identified with it.

> some of the children who were free and relaxed in the beginning of the experiment broke down and cried or became somewhat negativistic during the latter part when they were required to make self-identifications. Indeed, two children ran out of the testing room, inconsolable, convulsed in tears.

> The child . . . cannot learn to what racial group he belongs without being involved in a larger pattern of emotions, conflicts and desires which are part of his growing knowledge of what society thinks about his race.

The first quote is from one of the articles in which the Clarks described their research and discuss the emotional reactions of some of the children (1947, p. 316). Interestingly, no differences between Black children in the highly segregated southern part of the United States and children in the north were found. Later, similar studies with similar results were carried out with children of minorities in Britain, Hong Kong, New Zealand, and the Netherlands (Brand *et al.*, 1974; Koot *et al.*, 1985; Milner, 1973). The conclusion the Clarks drew and that is summarized in the second quote (1947, p. 316) seems to have more general validity. Children develop a sense of their racial or ethnic identity in a social context in which their minority group is far from always being accepted, and that is not easy.

In this chapter I want to do two things. First I discuss the relationship between discrimination experiences and ethnic identification. Subsequently, I consider the everyday reality of ethnic identities by looking at their situational dependency, forms of identity enactment, and the importance of self-verification.

Discrimination and ethnic identification

Discrimination occurs when members of a group are treated unjustly on the basis of their group membership. Not hiring a woman because she is a female, an elderly person because he is relatively old, or an ethnic minority member because she is of Mexican origin are examples. These examples show that with discrimination social identities are at stake. People are treated unjustly on the basis of their group membership. Ethnic minorities can face different kinds of discrimination in various social settings and by different others, including co-ethnics. However, in general they are discriminated most often by the more powerful majority group. The discrimination can involve various spheres of life (e.g., labour market, housing) and can be situational and temporary or, conversely, more structural and systematic. Being the victim of discrimination implies that you are not in control, and it contains the message that you have lower status and do not belong here. It can give you the feeling that others decide about you, that you are not one of us, that there is something wrong with you, and that you might as well not have existed. In addition, discrimination can give you the idea that society itself is not just and worthwhile and that the government is not protecting you or is even making matters worse.

Ethnic discrimination implies that one's ethnic identity is involved. In chapter 2 I discussed three models of group identification: here I use two of these to explain the complex ways in which ethnic identity can be involved in perceptions of and experiences with discrimination.[1] First, ethnic identification can be an *antecedent* of perceived discrimination because group identification provides a framework or lens to interpret the social world (the 'group identity lens' model, chapter 2). Second, ethnic identification can be a *consequence* of discrimination because discrimination implicates one's ethnic self and therefore makes ethnic identity relevant and important (the 'group identity reaction' model, chapter 2).[2]

Group identity lens model

This model maintains that ethnic minority identity functions as a group lens that makes people sensitive to anything that concerns or could harm their group or themselves as members of that group, and thus, higher ethnic identification will lead to higher discrimination perceptions. Different studies have found supporting evidence for this model (see Major *et al.*, 2002). It is often assumed

that this association between ethnic identification and discrimination perceptions stems from an internal psychological process. People who identify more
strongly with their group are more concerned about things that affect their group
negatively and would therefore be more sensitive and vigilant about
discrimination, also in cases where there is no discrimination. In public debates,
accusations of ethnic minorities being over-sensitive, moaners, and exploiting
victimhood are frequently heard.

However, not everything is in the 'eye of the beholder'. There is a social reality
to represent, and veridical perceptions are possible and striven for. Human beings
are motivated to seek appropriate evidence for understanding their social world.
This implies a drive to understand and have a grip on the world and thus to create
adequate knowledge. Many studies have found that members of minority groups
perceive a higher level of discrimination directed at their group as a whole than at
themselves as individual members of that group. Taylor and colleagues (1990)
have labelled this phenomenon the personal/group discrimination discrepancy.
This discrepancy is a robust finding among an array of disadvantaged groups,
using differently phrased questions (see Taylor *et al.*, 1993). Several explanations
have been offered for this phenomenon, such as the minimization or underestimation
of personal discrimination and the exaggeration of discrimination directed at the
group as a whole. The former explanation has attracted the most interest, and the
minimization of personal discrimination can be the result of psychological and
social processes.

Psychologically, blaming outcomes on discrimination acknowledges that these
are under the control of prejudiced others. This means that the minimization or
underestimation of discrimination allows ethnic minority members to maintain a
sense of control. Thus, although an explanation in terms of discrimination
attributions might protect feelings of self-worth (e.g., 'that employer discriminates
against me, and therefore it is not my fault that I did not get the job'), it threatens
the belief in having control over personal outcomes in one's life (e.g., 'not me, but
the employer decides about my life'). The result is that ethnic minorities are
inclined to minimize and underestimate the extent to which they personally are
victims of discrimination, rather than to exaggerate discrimination experiences
(Ruggiero & Taylor, 1997).

Interpretations in terms of discrimination typically also imply accusations, and
the negative social costs related to these accusations can be another reason for the
minimization of discrimination. Experimental research has demonstrated that
individuals who report discrimination are perceived negatively by others (e.g.,
being 'moaners'), even when discrimination was the clear cause of the event
(Kaiser & Miller, 2001). In addition, it has been found that in the presence of
majority group members, ethnic minorities are relatively unwilling to report that
negative events in their lives are the result of discrimination (Stangor *et al.*, 2002).
Thus, minorities often tend to avoid blaming negative outcomes on discrimination
because they fear the social costs associated with making such claims. These
social costs do not relate only to the negative reactions of majority group members.
Co-ethnics also can react negatively towards individual group members – for

example, when they fear that they themselves or their entire ethnic group will be labelled as moaners who avoid responsibility for their lives (Garcia *et al.*, 2005). The social disapproval from co-ethnics is particularly painful because social support is typically expected from them.

The social costs involved may prevent discriminated people from reporting and confronting the discrimination they face in their daily lives. The costs further indicate that the perception of discrimination can stem from something external to minorities rather than from misperceptions and hypersensitivity. This might also be the case for the relationship between ethnic identification and perceived discrimination. Specifically, it is possible that majority group members react more negatively towards strongly identified ethnic minorities than towards those who identify only weakly with their minority group. As a result, the former group of minority members may actually face more discrimination than the latter. Native Dutch, French, or Belgian people, for example, might more often discriminate against Moroccan immigrants who identify relatively strongly with their own group than against Moroccans who feel less committed to their Moroccan culture and community. Compared to low identifiers, minority members who identify relatively strongly with their ethnic group will show or enact their identity more strongly in language, dress, posture, and so on. This 'doing of ethnicity' will elicit more easily negative and discriminatory reactions from the majority.

Cultural diversity is not only about dealing with differences but also about prevailing status arrangements in society. Majority members may assume that strongly identified minorities endorse status-legitimizing worldviews such as meritocracy and the belief in individual mobility to a lesser extent than do weakly identified minorities. Research has shown that these assumptions are not unfounded (Major *et al.*, 2002; Sellers & Shelton, 2003), and, thus, that there are reasons to expect that high ethnic minority identifiers challenge the status quo more strongly than low identifiers. For the majority group, discrimination is one way to deal with this challenge: making it more difficult for high minority identifiers to publicly show their identity and to enter the social system. Across six studies, Kaiser and Pratt-Hyatt (2009) found that majority group members expressed more negative reactions towards strongly identified ethnic minorities than towards weakly identified minorities. Thus, majority members actually tend to react more negatively towards the former than the latter group. This indicates that high identified minorities who claim to experience increased levels of discrimination are not oversensitive or moaners, or wallowing in victimhood. Rather, they do actually face more discrimination.

This is not to say that there is no strategic use of victimhood among ethnic minorities. There certainly is. Presenting oneself as a victim of discrimination and racism is valuable moral capital. It creates a sense of guilt within the majority, and the status of victim confers a feeling of entitlement and the right to remedies and compensations (Moscovici & Pérez, 2007). Victimhood can have strategic value because it offers the opportunity to make others feel guilty and responsible and thereby exculpate oneself.

Group identity reaction model

Research has convincingly demonstrated that recognizing discrimination against one's ethnic group and oneself as a member of that group has negative consequences for psychological well-being (see Pascoe & Richman, 2009). These consequences are particularly negative when the discrimination is pervasive and systematic. This raises the question how ethnic minority members cope with the pain of exclusion and discrimination. Group identification is one important means of coping. The 'group identity reaction' model (or 'rejection-identification' model) is based on the idea that being a target of discrimination leads individuals to identify more strongly with their ethnic minority group and that stronger identification is beneficial for psychological well-being. People can cope with threats like discrimination by adopting group-based strategies that increase identification with their minority group. Group identification, in turn, can attenuate the negative effects of discrimination on well-being. Some experimental and longitudinal evidence has shown that threats can indeed increase group identification or lead to greater emotional attachment to one's group (e.g., Jetten *et al.*, 2001). Further, research among ethnic minority groups shows that increased perceptions of discrimination predicts increased ethnic group identification. This has been found, for example, in three studies among Turkish Dutch people (Verkuyten & Yildiz, 2007), in a longitudinal study among immigrants in Finland (Jasinskaja-Lahti *et al.* 2009, 2012), and in a study among Latino students in the United States (Cronin *et al.*, in press).

Discrimination presents a threat to one's ethnic identity, causing minorities to turn increasingly towards their minority group. Strong attachment and emotional investments in one's group can be an important buffer to the negative psychological effects that exclusion typically implies. Minority group identification is associated with less depression and anxiety and more positive self-feelings and other forms of adjustment (Pascoe & Richman, 2009). Group identification supports well-being by providing security and a sense of belonging and acceptance. These feelings counter – to some extent - the psychological costs of feeling rejected and excluded by the majority population. Group identification also provides more opportunities for social support from co-ethnics.

Collective action

There is an additional benefit to turning towards one's ethnic minority group in response to discrimination. Group identification not only counters some of the psychological costs of discrimination but also offers a basis for collective action. Collective action is defined as any action that aims to improve the status, position, or influence of an entire group, rather than of oneself or of a few individuals (Wright *et al.*, 1990). This kind of action occurs when a person's behaviour is structured by a particular group membership with its shared values, norms, and goals. Group identification implies that individuals start to think and act on the basis of what the group defines and thereby think and act in concert with other group members. Discrimination and other forms of exclusion convey a negative social identity. Social identity theory (Tajfel & Turner, 1979) argues that group identification can lead to two broad strategies for constructing a positive social identity, despite threatening and discriminatory behaviour by the majority.

Social creativity is a first strategy. It is aimed at jointly creating a distinctive and positive social identity without changing the existing group relationships as such. There are three different forms of this process. The first is linked to redefining the content of one's minority identity. A classic example is the 'Black Is Beautiful' movement in the 1960s that fought not against the distinction between Blacks and Whites, but against the negative meanings and implications associated with this distinction. Typical of this movement was the slogan of the singer James Brown: 'Say it loud, I'm Black and I'm proud.' Another example is the growing interest in the Berber culture and the positive reinterpretation of being Amazigh (Berber) among some Moroccan youth in the Netherlands. The 'backward' Berber culture becomes transformed into a valuable tradition. This reinterpretation makes it possible to differentiate oneself positively from both native Dutch and Arab Moroccans.

Second, discrimination and stigmatization can be countered with positive attributes. There are always different dimensions on which groups can be compared with one another. One can emphasize characteristics on the basis of which one believes that one's own ethnic or religious community is superior, such as solidarity, respect, tradition, and faith. These features provide a positive distinction from the individualism, selfishness, and moral decadence of West Europeans, and thus offer a positive ethnic identity. But apart from the fact that this easily leads to caricatures and stereotypes about groups, the lack of appreciation of the majority group continues to rankle. For a positive identity, recognition and appreciation in one's own circle is all very well, but recognition and respect by others is even better – that is, if such a recognition is sincere. Finding dimensions of comparison where your group takes a favourable position is particularly beneficial if those dimensions are recognized by others, too, and are seen as important criteria for evaluation (Hornsey & Imani, 2004). There needs to be more to it than a sympathetic attitude towards folklore. It is about genuine social recognition of one's background, history, and culture: about the appreciation for being different.

Third, the comparison group can be adjusted. Upward social comparison, in which your own group sits relatively low in contrast to another, can be replaced by downward social comparison. Instead of comparing your position and status as Surinamese Dutch to the native Dutch, you can make a positive comparison with Turkish Dutch. And as Turkish Dutch you can feel superior to Turks in Turkey and to Moroccan Dutch because Turkish Dutch are more modern and more European. There is much research that shows that minority groups tend to compare themselves to other minority groups by making positive distinctions. This can lead to 'horizontal hostility', which involves looking down on other minorities (White & Langer, 1999; White *et al.*, 2006). Unity and solidarity among minority groups tend to be less common than the search for group differences.

Social competition is a second identity strategy for ethnic minorities facing discrimination and exclusion. They can act collectively to actually challenge and try to change the status quo. And because majority members may band together to resist change, forms of social conflict and open hostility can be the result. An example is the former Arab European League. The League attempted to give a political and democratic voice to those who had no voice. The *Black Power* and the *Red Power* movements in the United States served as their model, but the League did not support militant and radical strategies, such as is the case with groups of Salafists and Jihadists.

The strategy of democratic organization and confrontation is a direct way to address the stigmatized position. If you assert yourself as a group, you are no longer just a victim: you take matters into your own hands. Instead of being defined, judged, and positioned by others, you opt for *self*-definition and *self*-awareness. It is a shift from object to subject, from societal spectator to active player, from a group that is *spoken about* to a group that has to be *spoken with*. Empirical research has shown that group identification is an important predictor of willingness to engage in collective action on behalf of the group (see Simon, 2004). Group identification has been found to possess a unique mobilizing power over and above feelings of relative deprivation and cost–benefit calculations. This is particularly likely when there is a strongly developed and politicized sense of identification with a social movement (Simon & Klandermans, 2001).

Research has shown that people are more likely to take action if they feel that their group is being treated unjustly (see Zomeren *et al.*, 2008). But a subjective sense of injustice is not enough for collective action. It is also about whether you think the actions will have an effect, and if your group actually is able to bring about change. In a situation of 'learned helplessness' and dependency, a sense of injustice will not quickly turn into collective action. A sense of collective grip, of group efficacy, is needed. In addition, politicization of identity implies an identity definition whereby power inequality and the need for action have priority. Such an interpretation ties yourself to the fate of your group and gives a sense of inner obligation to participate in actions, or at least to support them. Your identity as a woman or homosexual can ensure that you are prepared to take actions for women or gays and to support them, and those actions can as a result strengthen your political awareness. But the willingness will be greater if you see yourself as a feminist or as someone that is part of the gay movement. Likewise, as a Muslim you can defend the interests of Muslims, but the sense of commitment to do so is much stronger in political Islam.

Individual mobility

In addition to forms of collective action, ethnic minority members can try to achieve a more positive social identity by following an individualistic social mobility path. They can dissociate themselves socially and psychologically from their devalued ethnic minority group (Wright *et al.*, 1990). As Tajfel and Turner (1979, p. 43) argue, 'individual mobility implies a disidentification with the erstwhile in-group' and, it can be added, an increased identification with the majority group and host society. You can try to distance yourself from your group and adapt to the majority as much as possible; to become as like them as possible and try to forget your own ethno-cultural background, or to limit yourself to symbolic ethnic behaviour (Gans, 1979). This strategy of assimilation can have personal benefits, and especially talented people may prefer this individual strategy to improve their personal standing. They compare their abilities and achievements with the majority population rather than their minority group, and they will seek affinity and personal improvement.

But this process often does not come without a struggle because it can lead to criticisms and accusations of co-ethnics and the loss of valuable co-ethnic friendships and group ties. Individual social mobility can bring respect and appreciation, but at the expense of valuable ties and traditional certainties. You might eventually find yourself alone, and it is not uncommon that to a certain extent people find themselves rootless, lonely, and insecure. What it means to be an ethnic group member and the warmth and acceptance of your ethnic community is no longer self-evident or may even be absent. In other words, the need to belong and to be recognized and respected can conflict with each other. The resulting conflict was already described in 1943 by Irvin Child in his study of second-generation Italian Americans.

An integration paradox

There is another aspect that complicates a strategy of individual mobility. The acceptance by the majority group is usually conditional – that is, you will need to become like them, which often gives the feeling that you still are not really or fully accepted. It is not easy to fit in. In the words of a well-educated Turkish Dutch person who says that he is planning to leave the Netherlands for Turkey: 'I was born and raised here… [but] whatever you do, even though you have graduated, you have a good background, you master the language, you just won't be accepted into this society.'[3]

This quote illustrates the so-called integration paradox: minority members who are relatively successful educationally and in the labour market are sensitive to ethnic acceptance and equality. Their structural integration and efforts to succeed make full recognition and inclusion by the majority group particularly meaningful and important. Experiences and perceptions of non-acceptance and discrimination despite successful integration into society lead to feelings of relative deprivation. These feelings arise when people themselves, or the group they belong to, do not get what they believe they deserve or should enjoy (Smith *et al.*, 2012). This would make them turn towards their own minority community and away from the host society – for example, by developing more negative attitudes towards the native population. Thus, the more successful ones would experience more discrimination and be more sensitive to ethnic acceptance and equality, which, in turn, would drive their reactions to the host majority. As some researchers put it (Buijs *et al.*, 2006, p. 208–209):

precisely minority group members who initially are the most strongly focused on social acceptance and mobility in the dominant society, explicitly turn away when they experience rejection and seek safety in a defensive, own group identity.

There is quite some empirical evidence for this 'integration paradox' in the context of the Netherlands. Among different ethnic minority groups it has been found that the higher- compared to lower-educated experience more discrimination and perceive more discrimination directed at their ethnic group (e.g., Ten Teije *et al.*, in press; van Doorn *et al.*, in press). These perceptions are related to a stronger ethnic group identification and a less positive attitude towards the Dutch and Dutch society. Thus, in agreement with the 'group identity reaction' model, the feeling that one's ethnic minority group is not accepted or discriminated in society is associated with higher ethnic group identification, which is, in turn, related to a less positive attitude towards the Dutch.

Furthermore, the perceived acceptance and treatment of one's ethnic group, rather than personal experiences with discrimination, were found to be important for the attitude of the higher educated (Ten Teije *et al.*, in press). This supports the idea that the more advantaged members of disadvantaged groups tend to engage in group comparisons and develop more negative attitudes towards the advantaged group. The better educated are more interested in the – often negatively framed – political and public debates on the integration of immigrants and minorities, and they tend to be more concerned about the vulnerable and relatively marginal position of immigrants. And when they perceive and experience ethnic discrimination, higher status minority members might be more assertive (Baumgartner, 1998).

It is likely that these processes are not specific only to the Dutch context but also operate in other societies (Cooney, 2009; Ogbu, 1993). Furthermore, there are reasons to expect that the integration paradox is not limited to attitudes towards the native population but also involves behaviour. A study showed that Moroccan Dutch youngsters who are in custody awaiting trial are much better integrated into Dutch society than their Moroccan Dutch non-criminal peers (Stevens *et al.*, 2009). Relative to the latter, the former more often speak the Dutch language fluently, have more contacts with Dutch people, and self-identify more often as Dutch. Their relatively strong orientation to Dutch society makes them extra-sensitive to inequalities and negative stereotypes. This increases the likelihood of feelings of relative deprivation, with the associated negative emotions of anger, resentment, and frustration that can lead to crime (Agnew, 2001; Smith *et al.*, 2012). Similarly, several studies in the United States have found relatively high levels of delinquency among ethnic minority youth who have a strong orientation to American society (Samaniego & Gonzales, 1999; Vega *et al.*, 1993).

Socio-structural context

The integration paradox indicates that the social context is critically important for understanding how ethnic minority members try to deal with their disadvantaged position. Psychological processes are always formed and played out in a social context. If we know that people strive for a positive identity, it does not say anything yet about how they try to achieve this in the particular circumstances where they find themselves. There are at least three social–structural features that, in combination, can influence people's responses to discrimination, and a disadvantaged status position more generally. These are beliefs about the stability and legitimacy of the status system and about the nature of the group boundaries. *Stability* refers to the extent to which group positions are considered to be changeable, and *legitimacy* refers to the extent to which the status structure is accepted as just. *Permeability* (or 'openness') refers to the extent to which individual group members can leave one group and join another. Together, perceived stability, legitimacy, and permeability influence the identity management strategies of ethnic minority members (Tajfel & Turner, 1979).

A strategy of individual mobility presupposes that group boundaries are seen as relatively permeable or open, indicating that membership in the high-status group can be achieved. Furthermore, this individual strategy is especially likely when the status differences are perceived as stable and legitimate. Under these conditions, collective strategies to achieve positive social identity are more difficult, making individual strategies more likely. There is empirical evidence for this reasoning (see Bettencourt *et al.*, 2001). For example, in a study among Turkish Dutch people it was found that when the ethnic relations were considered relatively stable and legitimate, perceived permeability was associated with lower Turkish identification and higher host nation identification (Verkuyten & Reijerse, 2008). Hence, in a stable and legitimate intergroup structure and when the Turkish Dutch participants saw opportunities to be accepted in the Dutch majority group, they tended to dissociate themselves more from their Turkish community and to associate themselves more with the Dutch. These results support the idea that in a stable and legitimate intergroup context with permeable group boundaries, ethnic minority group members tend to use not identity strategies of group identification and social competition, but, rather, group dis-identification and individual mobility (Tajfel & Turner, 1979). Increased group identification and collective actions are more likely when the boundaries are considered to be rather impermeable or closed (e.g., because of a 'colour line') such that ethnic minority members cannot improve their individual position. In addition, for collective action to occur, the intergroup structure has to be assessed as undeserved or illegitimate, and there should be a belief that the structure is not stable but can be changed.

The importance of perceived stability, legitimacy, and permeability indicates that identification processes do not take place in a social vacuum. The way in which minorities take up positions in society and orient themselves towards their ethnic community is often due not so much to their (alleged) cultural background, but, rather, to the societal conditions and existing group relations. Notions of unchallengeable group positions, unjust group differences, closed group boundaries, and feelings of threat and rejection lead to dissociation and withdrawal into one's own ethnic group, whereas a societal context that is seen as legitimate and open will stimulate a stronger orientation towards the host society and more successful integration.

Situational changes

In the academic literature there is quite a debate about the stability or variability of social identities. This debate is fairly heated at times, and it is not rare that people misunderstand each other because they talk about different things. It is especially popular to accuse opponents as wrongly seeing identities as stable, fixed, unchanging, or primordial, whereas in reality identities would be variable, flexible, changing, and situational. In this discussion it is not always clear what exactly is being argued or claimed – among other things, because the two dimensions of time and place are mixed up. In the case of variability, the focus is on situational changes in self-awareness and self-presentation. People tend to see and present themselves in a different way depending on the circumstances. The social categories that you use to place yourself and others in need to be appropriate for the situation. If in a given context Moroccan immigrants say one thing and Antilleans say another, then a division of Moroccans versus Antilleans is more likely, than, say, a distinction between men and women. The ethnic classification gives a meaningful distinction to what is being said. Furthermore, if Moroccans and Antilleans do and say things that are stereotypical for their respective groups, then this classification is even more obvious. In that context the ethnic classification helps you to get a grip on what is going on, whereas in another situation another group distinction makes more sense and is therefore more salient (Turner *et al.*, 1987).

However, there are not only the characteristics of the situation that matter for which social identity is salient. It also has to do with the importance that people themselves attach to their ethnic background and to ethnic group differences. Some have a stronger tendency or are more ready to perceive ethnic differences and to think in ethnic terms than others. The ethnic background can serve as a highly accessible framework or lens for interpreting and assessing the behaviour of others ('You say and do so only because I am a Mexican'), but also in the perception of who and what you are ('I am in first, second, and third place a Mexican'). There are individual differences in the extent to which ethnicity is considered important and these differences develop gradually over time in a process of socialization. Inner stability is about a longer time perspective.

Both perspectives focus on other phenomena and other questions and are complementary rather than contradictory. This is easy to see when you realize that individuals who gradually have developed a different understanding of their ethnic identity can act in very different ways in the same situation. Someone who attaches great importance to her ethnic identity will look at the world differently than someone for whom this is not the case. But it is equally true that the same person can feel quite differently about her ethnic background depending on the people with whom she is with at a particular moment and on other characteristics of the situation (e.g., presence of ethnic music, food, art). In the remainder of this chapter I focus on the situational perspective of ethnic and racial identity, while chapter 4 discusses the developmental perspective.

Everyday life

A drawback of a great deal of research is that it does not say much about the dynamics of daily life. The focus is typically on underlying factors and processes that are notoriously difficult to study in real life. A standardized, or at least controlled, situation is preferred. Additionally, researchers most often do not have the time or resources for continuous and long-term information gathering. It is therefore difficult to determine whether people are, for example, occasionally or more permanently aware of their ethnic background and which situations generate such awareness. Yet, it is not impossible to shed more light on this matter. For example, people can be asked to keep a diary in which they respond three or more times a day to specific questions about circumstances and feelings of that day. It is also possible to ask people to complete a short questionnaire on their mobile phones several times a day. Variations of this approach can be thought of, but the principal aim of such research is to systematically collect information about what people experience in a day.

Several researchers have used these kinds of techniques among White, Hispanic, Chinese, and African Americans (Downie *et al.*, 2006; Leach & Smith, 2006; Yip & Fuligni, 2002). The first notable finding is that White Americans are generally much less aware of their ethnic background than ethnic minorities. As a member of the dominant majority, being a White American is more normal and self-evident, while ethnic minorities are often 'the other' who stands out. The second finding is that the awareness of one's ethnic identity depends on the circumstances. For example, situations in which you are a numerical minority can result in stronger ethnic self-awareness, but it is also possible that you are very aware of your Chinese background when with family and Chinese friends. In some situations, you are seen as 'different' by others, or you opt for keeping a certain distance, while in other situations the emphasis is on what you share with each other. In any event, it is clear that one's ethnic background is not something that people are constantly aware of. This is well expressed by a Moroccan Dutch girl who said in one of our studies:

> It's really crazy. When I say that my Moroccan background is very important to me, then they immediately think that I feel Moroccan all day long.

Ethnic self-awareness depends on the presence of ethnically relevant cues. Moreover, the situation can have an effect on the meaning given to one's ethnic background. You can be very aware of your Chinese background in a classroom where you are the only Chinese student, but also among your Chinese family. Yet, what it means to be Chinese might differ considerably in these two situations. Similarly, there can be a difference in your thoughts and feelings about 'being a Mexican American' in a predominantly Mexican neighbourhood or in a neighbourhood where you are the only person with a Mexican background. These differences have a great deal to do with comparison processes.

Social comparisons

Social identities depend on comparisons and distinctions. People give meaning to who and what they are in comparison to others. This means that what is considered self-defining can vary depending on who the comparison is made with. For example, the meaning of being Scottish has been found to depend on whether a comparison is made with the English or with the Greeks (Hopkins *et al.*, 1997). Efficiency and diligence are seen as typical Scottish attributes in relation to Greeks, but not in relation to the English. When comparing themselves to the English, the Scottish judge themselves to be warm-hearted and socially sensitive. Furthermore, in a study among Chinese students living in the Netherlands participants were asked to rate themselves in comparison to Chinese or in comparison to the Dutch (Verkuyten & De Wolf, 2002). It was expected that self-descriptions would differ between the two conditions with the use of Chinese stereotypical traits being more common in comparison to the Dutch. It was found that the participants did indeed describe themselves as more 'emotionally controlled', more 'reserved', more 'obedient', and as more 'modest' in comparison to the Dutch than in comparison with other Chinese.

Further, in a study among Turkish Dutch people there was a large variation in how they describe themselves in social interactions (Verkuyten, 1997a) – not only by different people, but also by the same individual in different contexts of conversation. Compared with the native Dutch, the Turkish Dutch described themselves as more traditional, which was seen as something positive because it refers to a rich and valuable history. But a self-description in terms of tradition was not used in comparison to Turks in Turkey because in this context it meant old-fashioned and backward. The same goes for the description of being modern. In relation to native Dutch, the word 'modern' frequently had negative connotations because it referred to selfishness, neglect of family relationships, and moral decay. But the concept 'modern' was self-descriptively used by the Turkish Dutch in relation to Moroccan Dutch. People of Turkish origin would be 'more European' and thus more modern than Moroccans with their Arabic or Berber background.

Social identities are about group differences and relationships. When Turkish Dutch discuss the question of who and what Turks in the Netherlands are, they implicitly express who and what they are not. And by discussing the Dutch, they are implicitly speaking about themselves. This means that one's own identity is (partially) defined differently depending on the comparison that is made. There are several groups that may be meaningful for defining and characterizing one's own identity. In many cases, a comparison is made between majority and minority groups, or natives and immigrants, but that is not always so. Surinamese living in Amsterdam sometimes feel at a disadvantage compared to Moroccans and Turks, because they receive fewer subsidies. Chinese and Moluccans may feel that there is only attention for other minority groups who, on top of that, receive preferential treatment, and African Americans can feel that they are exploited by Korean Americans. The implicit assumption behind many social scientific approaches is that ethnic minorities define their identity in relation to the dominant majority group. Studies on ethnic relations are mainly concerned with minority–majority relationships and ignore relationships *between* minority groups. The majority group is implicitly assumed to be the only really significant other. However, in multi-ethnic societies there is a variety of groups in relation to whom people define their ethnic identity. South Moluccans define their identity not only in relation to the Dutch, but also in relation to what they define as 'foreigners', meaning people of Turkish and Moroccan background. Their self-definition very much involves a contrast with other ethnic minority groups. Similarly, for many Turkish people in the Netherlands a self-definition as Turkish often involves Moroccans living in the same area. In fact, many Turks are keen to differentiate themselves from the Moroccans who are said to be aggressive and criminal.

In addition, there are comparisons with the situation in the country of origin and within one's own ethnic community. Research among ethnic minorities has clearly shown that there is a preference for comparisons with co-ethnics over comparisons with other groups (e.g., Abbey, 2002; Leach & Smith, 2006). Differences and similarities within their own community get a great deal of attention in daily life and are much discussed. People make comparisons between subgroups within their community, such as between the first and second generation, between those with a darker and lighter skin colour, between integrating and assimilating individuals, and between orthodox and liberal Muslims; in addition, they also compare their current position with that of the past (Verkuyten, 1997a).

Very often, co-ethnics form the obvious frame of reference for comparison. The native majority group is often not very relevant, because natives are in a different position and have a different background. Those in the same position, who have a similar origin and share experiences, tend to form a more important framework for interpreting experiences and for what to think and how to act. It is mainly what people of your own ethnic community say and do that matters. They hold a mirror to your face which you are willing to look into, in order to know what you should feel, do and think.

Identity importance

The emphasis on situation and changing comparisons for understanding ethnic identity is critically important but does not mean that a more stable sense of self does not develop. In some situations, people are aware of their ethnic identity, but this awareness is stronger and more common among some individuals than others. Individual differences in the subjective tendency to view the social world in ethnic terms have social and psychological consequences. Using daily diaries, researchers have examined the everyday experience of ethnic identity among Chinese Americans (Yip, 2005; Yip & Fuligni, 2002). Chinese Americans appear to experience more pleasant and less unpleasant emotions on days when they feel more 'Chinese'. But this is only true for those who find their Chinese identity important. They are proud of their Chinese background, and being reminded of it is pleasant and forms a buffer against everyday tensions. However, 'being Chinese' may also occasionally prove to be an obstacle. For example, if you are Chinese, it is painful when you know that in a situation particular others – peers, teachers – have negative stereotypes about Chinese people. This can motivate you to make an extra effort in an attempt to prove the contrary, but more often those negative stereotypes are emotionally distractive and disruptive for social contacts. The research on situational 'stereotype threat' discussed in chapter 2 demonstrates this clearly. Particularly for those who feel strongly about their ethnic identity, negative stereotypes can lead to lower achievements and to avoiding situations in which these stereotypes are relevant and meaningful.

Social validation

Social identities are not like private beliefs but require social validation. People can live a life of outwardly fitting in but inwardly feeling a lack of belonging: they play their part but cannot be what they are. People can also feel that they do belong but experience that others do not recognize them as such. They can find out that their claim on a particular identity is not accepted or recognized by others. Operated transsexuals sometimes feel that the main problem is the environment 'that has to start seeing you as a woman because you already know who you are'.[4]

So the internal and the external do not have to match. A subjective sense of identity is something other than social validation. Your ethnic identity can be very present in your thoughts, but that identity must be lived up to in concrete circumstances and in relation to other people, both insiders and outsiders. After the terrorist attacks of 9/11 male Sikhs in the United States faced insults and hostilities. They were mistaken for Arab Muslims on account of their beards and turbans. Because of these visible features, their American-ness was increasingly questioned: 'they moved from a comfortable sense of belonging to an uneasy state of being an outsider and a threatening one at that' (Bhatia & Ram, 2009, p. 146). To inform the public about the difference with Islam and thus again be recognized as Sikhs, groups of Sikhs in New York and elsewhere in the country started a 'public relations' campaign.

Self-verification

Individuals want to confirm their view of themselves. Confirmation provides an emotional anchor and makes the world predictable and controllable. There is a desire to verify who you are, even if an identity is negative (Swann *et al.*, 2003). Various strategies in interaction with others are employed for creating a self-verification context. For example, ethnic minorities can choose to interact with co-ethnics who confirm their ethnic identity and avoid outsiders who do not. Selective interaction provides the social context for identity validation. People can also lay claim to an identity by displaying identity cues – for example, dressing or acting in a certain way or using a particular speech style. The choice of clothing, behaviour, accent, and posture are social prompts or interaction strategies that makes others validate and accept your group membership. These strategies are sometimes referred to as 'doing ethnicity' and 'doing race', or as 'identity performance or enactment'. The social recognition depends on the extent to which a social identity is expressed in appropriate verbal and non-verbal behaviour. With that behaviour, an identity classification can follow, and others behave towards you in a manner that confirms your identity (Burke & Stets, 2009).

In everyday situations, social classifications and identity claims are continuously being made and negotiated. There is a tradition of research that examines how people manage to get acceptance for a particular identity claim. The focus in this research is on types of verbal and non-verbal practices and the ways in which these function in social interaction, on how identities are adopted in daily conversations and interactions and how people manoeuvre themselves into certain positions or, conversely, reject being positioned by others. The interest is in the subtle behavioural and linguistic mechanisms that shape daily life. This work is close to what takes place in, for example, culturally diverse settings and is therefore of great importance if we want to understand what actually happens on the ground.

The audience

This work also shows that identity claims and enactment can differ depending on interaction with co-ethnics and outsiders (Klein *et al.*, 2007). People are engaged in actions that mark and implicate their ethnic identity. They perform behaviours relevant to the norms and values that are conventionally associated with a particular social identity, and this identity performance can differ depending on the audience. For instance, in a study among Portuguese Dutch, an experimental distinction was made between an anonymous and a non-anonymous situation (Barreto *et al.*, 2003). In a non-anonymous situation and facing a Portuguese audience, participants identified less strongly with the Portuguese and with Portuguese traditions, while in front of a Dutch audience they identified less strongly with the Netherlands and Dutch traditions and therefore more with the Portuguese and their traditions. In these public situations, others can weigh and assess identity claims, whereas in an anonymous situation one is free to embrace particular identities. Similarly, in a study among Swedish-speaking Finns and the group of Sorbs in Germany, it was found that minority language is used in private and semi-official domains of their own ethnic minority group, whereas the majority language communicates national belonging and is preferred in official domains (Broermann, 2008).

Another example is that of Muslim women who have been found to give different motives for their choice to wear a headscarf in discussions with Western women than with Muslim immigrant women (Roald, 2001). Involvement in religious practices communicates one's religious identity to co-believers and to outsiders. These practices symbolize group boundaries, and identity claims are likely to differ for interactions with these two groups. In-group acceptance, belonging, and identity authenticity (a 'real' Muslim) are critical issues in interactions with co-believers. It might be difficult to be accepted as a true Muslim when one does not participate in Ramadan, does not wear a headscarf, or drinks alcohol and practises premarital sex. One's claim on being a Muslim has to be negotiated in order to be recognized as a 'true' Muslim. People look to co-believers to verify their religious identity, and they can display other religious behaviours (praying, mosque attendance) that are recognized by co-believers and thereby confirm their identity.

A further example is a study on how African American youth use hip-hop culture, particularly rap music, to form and negotiate their Black identity in everyday interactions with other African Americans (Clay, 2003). It is shown how acceptance as authentically Black depends on one's ability to master the tools of hip-hop performance – that is, the right language, clothes, posture, attitude, and bodily gestures. And youths who are insecure about their acceptance and position in the group will want to confirm their group membership by enacting it even more strongly. These examples indicate that identity claims involve crucial issues of group acceptance and support as well as group obligations and pressures.

Whereas the question of identity authenticity is critical in interactions with, for example, co-ethnics, other issues can be more prominent in relations with outsiders. The intergroup sensitivity effect (Hornsey & Imani, 2004) indicates that criticism and negative views of majority members threaten the value of one's social identity and the ability to enact this identity in public life. In many Western countries, Muslims have to manage their religious identity in host countries that often portray Islam negatively, define Islam as a religion of intolerance and violence, and argue for the need for an 'Euro-Islam' or 'Europeanized Islam'. This means that in order to claim a morally acceptable identity, Muslims have to do some 'identity work' in relation to and in interactions with natives. For example, a Dutch Turkish Muslim states in an interview that she always deliberately speaks Dutch in supermarkets and makes sure that she is always smiling when she rides on a bus or tram even when she is not in a good mood. She wants to show that Muslims are normal friendly people. And Muslim organizations in Western Europe have been found to define a moral identity in contrast to Muslim terrorism (Yildiz & Verkuyten, 2013). Their moral identity is contrasted with 'what we are not'. The distancing from the terrorist label helps to construct a positive Muslim identity as well-adjusted and responsible citizens. When one's identity is called into question by an 'extreme not-us', like terrorists, this can actually serve one's cause because it raises public interest and gives ample opportunities to explain 'who we actually are and what we stand for'. After 9/11, sales of books about Islam increased and Islamic spokespersons and academics were frequent guests on talk shows providing a platform for Muslim voices in the Western world.

It also happens that minority members want to assimilate and become accepted and recognized as majority members, like a form of 'rite of passage'. But to be recognized as a real German, you need to show this in your words and deeds and give proof that you have abandoned the 'backward' culture of your original community. Natives need to treat you as a fellow group member, thereby confirming your identity claim. Yet one's different ethnic background makes full recognition and acceptance not easy. Disconfirming reactions from natives are likely, and these can lead to attempts to counteract this disconfirmation by 'over-adaptation'. You will try to live up to the identity claim even harder in everything that you say and do: you become more German than the Germans themselves.

Public domain

Many minority members and immigrants neither can nor want to give up their ethnic identity. You cannot simply shake off your cultural background and just put it aside, like you would do with a pair of glasses or a rucksack. Many of them want to merge their background with the country they live in. They want to perceive themselves as both Dutch and Turkish, Pakistani and British, or Algerian and French. These claims must be accepted by both the majority group as well as by one's own ethnic community. This is by no means easy, especially because it almost always involves adaptation and change. You want to be recognized and acknowledged as Turkish and as German, but in a different way than traditional Turks and unlike the individualistic Germans. Co-ethnics can blame you for 'becoming too German': Germans, on the other hand, can reject you for not adapting enough and for pretending and being insincere and opportunistic.

But it is also possible to display identity cues that try to create a context in which identities are verified in relation to insiders and outsiders. An example is President Obama, whose racial identity was at the centre of debate in his 2008 presidential campaign. He was criticized for being 'too Black' or not being 'Black enough'. Several Black critics argued that Obama was not really an African American because he had a Kenyan father and a White American mother and therefore lacked the heritage of the descendants of plantation slaves. And part of Obama's appeal for White Americans depended on him being seen as an American candidate rather than a Black one, and some implied that he was more 'Afro' than American. In his speeches, Obama responded to these challenges by making only implicit references to his racial identity and by depicting himself as the embodiment and personification of the cultural and social diversity of American society (see Augoustinos & De Garis, 2012).[5]

Another example is a Muslim woman who may decide to wear a headscarf in combination with Western clothing, by which she calls into question the accepted definitions of what it means to be a woman in the eyes of both the Western population and Muslim immigrants. Muslims girls who, together with a headscarf, have a Western dress style and a cosmetics and speech style, communicate that Muslim women can also be modern. The Western clothing signals a modern rather than traditional religious interpretation, and the headscarf symbolizes one's own form of emancipation. Especially among second-generation immigrants, female Islamic clothing includes a wide variety of styles and combinations of Western and religious clothing. The emergence of Islamic fashion has led to a focus on Western aesthetics, which simultaneously communicates being a Muslim. A concern with style is combined with the search for an 'authentic' Islam (Moors, 2009). Religiosity is an important motivation for wearing female Islamic clothing, but there are also social considerations. Women are concerned with upholding a religious, modest reputation and fear judgement from their religious community, and in relation to the Western public they cover themselves to visibly show their religious allegiance and represent Islam (Williams & Vashi, 2007).

Instrumental role

The display of identity cues in verbal or non-verbal ways communicates one's distinctive social identity: it tells others who you are, to which group you belong, and what this group membership means to you. But identity enactment not only has an expressive function but can also have an instrumental one. It can play a critical role in the achievement of collective goals related to the preservation or improvement of the standing of one's group. Minority members can engage in identity enactment to change the negative stereotypes and treatment of their group. The classic case is, of course, the 'Black Is Beautiful' movement; other examples are situations where 'inferior' or 'substandard' languages or dialects are put forward as symbols of group pride. Also, the wearing of a headscarf can become a political statement and form the basis for group coordination and organization. It can be used to claim group rights and to enhance the standing of Muslims in, for example, Western Europe. Furthermore, in Algeria covering the head served as a symbol of resistance against the French occupation (Moors, 2011), and in Turkey headscarves have become a political statement among university students. Young Turkish women claim the right to cover their heads and use the headscarf as a tool for emancipation and liberation (Lorasdagi, 2009). In addition, lower-middle-class women in Egypt started to wear headscarves in order to legitimize their presence in the public domain and to gain more freedom outside the home (Macleod, 1991).

A feedback loop

The previous discussion on identity validation and self-verification might give the impression of a one-way street: people trying to confirm socially what they already believe about themselves. But there is also a feedback loop because the way you enact your identity influences how you understand yourself. Social identities are communicated and negotiated in interactions, and the outcome of this can affect people's self-understandings. Identity enactment elicits reactions from others, and claims on, for example, identity authenticity can be questioned or rejected. The feedback given by others can make you unsure of what you are and where you belong or can, on the contrary, make you feel strong and confident. When you enact the right hip-hop language, clothes, posture, and bodily gestures, you are accepted and you feel truly Black. But it is not easy to feel a proper member of your ethnic group if language proficiency is an important ethnic marker and you do not speak the language. And for many Muslims, the communal aspects of rule-following ('orthopraxis'), and the public behavioural commitment to the rules of Islam are important to feel a real Muslim.

To summarize

The discussion on context, sense of identity, identity enactment, and feedback processes is summarized in Figure 3.1, which is taken from Klein and colleagues (2007).[6]

The left arrow indicates the importance of the social context, including specific experiences such as discrimination, in making ethnic (or any other) identity salient in your mind, including the different meanings that can be attached to it. The right arrow shows the enactment of the sense of identity, for expressive or instrumental reasons, and the related processes of self-verification and social validation. The top arrow indicates the feedback loop from enactment on the sense of identity. The arrow at the bottom running from 'ethnic enactment/behaviour' to 'social context' illustrates the idea discussed in chapter 2 that the social context is not given or static but formed by identity practices. These practices not only confirm the world as it is but can also be designed for changing the world in the direction that one wants it to be.

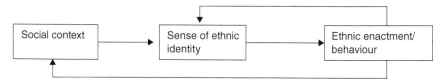

Figure 3.1 A model of the dynamics of ethnic identity

4 Identity development and duality

Csanad Szegedi was a prominent member of Hungary's far-right Jobbik Party. He served in the European Parliament in Brussels as one of the party's three representatives. He was also a founding member of the now forbidden Hungarian Guard, who wore black uniforms and had striped flags recalling a pro-Nazi party that briefly governed Hungary at the end of World War II. Szegedi was notorious for his incendiary comments on Jews, who, he claimed, were desecrating national symbols and taking over the country. When in 2010 he discovered that he himself was Jewish and that his grandmother had survived Auschwitz, things changed. Szegedi acknowledged his Jewish origins, was forced to resign from all party positions, and gave up his Jobbik membership.[1] He met with a Hungarian rabbi who afterwards said, 'Csanad Szegedi is in the middle of a difficult process of reparation, self-knowledge, re-evaluation and learning, which according to our hopes and interests, should conclude in a positive manner. Whether this will occur or not is first and foremost up to him.'

Szegedi's experience is not unique, because Holocaust survivors sometimes denied their own Jewish heritage, and Jewish children were adopted or placed in non-Jewish foster homes during the war and raised as Christians. Russian far-right Vladimir Zhirinovsky was anti-Semitic until he acknowledged that his father was Jewish. And many people were stunned when in 1997 *The Washington Post* published information that proved that the former Secretary of State, Madeleine Albright, had Jewish grandparents who had been killed by the Nazis. Albright was raised as a Roman Catholic and expressed shock at the news because she claimed absolutely no prior knowledge. There was a storm of emotional reactions, ranging from understanding and sympathy to scepticism and disbelief. Questions were also raised about the possible impact of Albright's Jewish roots on diplomatic relations and her efforts in the Israeli–Palestinian conflict.

The so-called crypto-Jews is another group of people who were raised as non-Jews and later discovered that they were of Jewish descent. Crypto-Jews are descendants of the fifteenth-century Jews of Spain and Portugal who, as victims of the Inquisition, were either forced to emigrate, to convert to Catholicism, or to be killed. Many converts chose to live overtly as Catholics but covertly as crypto-Jews and move to the Americas. Centuries later some people discovered their Jewish roots, and some of their stories and experiences, told in their own words, can be found in the book *Suddenly Jewish: Jews Raised as Gentiles Discover Their Jewish Roots*. The author of the book, Barbara Kessel, was intrigued by what happens when you find out that you are not what you thought you were – what happens to your sense of self when you discover your hidden roots. For most people this had a profound impact. They suddenly belonged to a different social category, a different ancestral community. Their idea about where they came from and where they fitted in changed, and this raised fundamental questions and created doubts and uncertainties. As Kessel writes (2000, p. 99), 'People who find out that they are of Jewish descent receive an information packet of tremendous import. They then have the task of assimilating that new information into their years-old image of self. Even to reject the information takes sizable psychic energy.' This information packet is not self-evident because there are ethnic, cultural, religious, and political definitions of what it means to be Jewish. It involves a large body of knowledge, beliefs, history, and behavioural rules. Finding out that one is Jewish raises questions about whether one should be circumcised, have a bar mitzvah, eat kosher food, and visit the synagogue, or, instead, feel Jewish without being observant or not feel Jewish at all. It also raises political questions, and some people said that they identified as Jews out of a feeling of responsibility and identification with the historical suffering of the Jews. It also raises questions of social recognition by gentiles and other Jews. As converted Jews, it is sometimes hard to be accepted by the Jewish community while it is difficult to be a Jew without others who share your beliefs.

Individual development

Kessel's book demonstrates that 'suddenly being Jewish' is an unsettling discovery that leads to diverse reactions ranging from lack of interest and considering it a non-issue to fully adopting Jewish culture and religion. For some it was traumatic because of anti-Semitic feelings they had, others struggled with trying to combine the Jewish heritage with their Christian upbringing, and still others enthusiastically embraced their Jewish identity. For almost all, becoming Jewish was a growing process that took time. It involved rethinking, exploration, and the development of new commitments and a new sense of self.

One of the adult interviewees who found out that she is of Jewish descent stated that 'her sense of self was already so fully formed that she regarded the discovery as peripheral, or, as she called it, a "non-issue"' (Kessel, 2000, p. 106). She found her heritage 'interesting' but not in any way defining of who she is today. Others, however, explained how the discovery of being Jewish profoundly changed something in them. They described it as a growing process in which they explored and gradually re-thought their view of themselves, transferred their commitments and loyalties, and changed their lifestyle. As one person said, 'At first, the idea of being Jewish didn't mean anything to me because I didn't know anything about it. Later, as I read Holocaust novels like Exodus and Mila 18, it became more and more meaningful' (2000, p. 81).

Finding out later in life that you are not what you thought you were is, of course, different from developing a sense of ethnic or racial identity from early on. Children and adolescents try to understand how the social world is composed and where they fit in. They ask themselves with whom they belong, what that means, and whether others recognize and value them. Through contacts with parents, family, friends, and the wider society youth develop an inner sense of their ethnic or racial background. There are many ways in which this can happen: there are several trajectories through which one comes to feel Turkish, Mexican, Dutch, or Chinese.

In the past 30 years, researchers have occupied themselves with the question of ethnic identity development. Most of this research has been conducted in the United States and among adolescents. Children younger than, say, 12 years of age are well aware of ethnic and racial group differences. They learn to label others as members of specific groups based on observable differences like skin colour, language, and clothing. In middle childhood they also make categorizations based on more intangible features (behaviours, heritage, traits), and they make social comparisons to interpret group differences. They gradually develop further (stereotypical) knowledge that they use to explain and understand behaviour, and they make distinctions in favour of their own group compared to other groups (Quintana, 1998; Rogers *et al.*, 2012).

Children are also able to label themselves as members of ethnic categories ('I am a Turk', 'I am Chinese') and at around five to seven years they internalize this membership and subjectively experience themselves as members of their group (Sani & Bennett, 2004). But when you ask a 10- or 12-year-old to tell you who she is, you will not hear a very elaborate or coherent story, especially not when you compare it to, say, a 20-year-old. Research on life stories clearly shows that an integral narrative of who you are develops for the first time in adolescence (e.g., Habermas & DeSilveira, 2008; McAdams *et al.*, 2006). It is in adolescence that a coherent sense of self gradually comes into existence. Adolescence is seen as the critical period for identity development, and research on ethnic and racial identity formation has focused on this period.

Bottom up

How do adolescents develop a sense of their ethnic or racial identity, and which factors are important? An answer to these questions can be sought in two ways. One possibility is to closely examine the specific circumstances and experiences of a particular group and use this information as a basis for a developmental model. This 'bottom-up' approach has, among other things, led to the well-known 'White identity' model of Janet Helms (1990) and the 'nigrescence' ('becoming Black') model of William Cross (1991). Cross was interested in racial identity during the heady days of the Civil Rights movement, and his original model is based on retrospective reflections of African Americans. The encounter with racism was thought to trigger a process of identity exploration and movement through different, increasingly advanced or matured stages of identity development towards a strong and healthy Black identity.

The model has been adapted and refined, and measurement instruments have been developed for assessing the assumed stages (see Cokley, 2007; Helms, 2007), but there are also limitations and criticism. The fact that the model provides a framework for examining the experiential, political, and cultural influences on African American identity is both its strength and a weakness. On the one hand, the model examines the qualitative aspects of racial identity development in detail. On the other hand, however, the model is specific to African Americans – that is, the model does not simply apply to other ethnic minority groups in the United States (Atkinson *et al.*, 1990), nor to other groups of Blacks outside this country (e.g. Wandert *et al.*, 2009). Furthermore, the qualitative differences between the stages are not very clear, and the stages say little about the underlying processes and the divergent trajectories of identity development. There is, for example, also the possibility of re-cycling, which involves the transition from higher to lower stages of identity development.

Top down

A second approach is the 'top-down' one, where a theoretically derived developmental model is used and tested empirically. In practice, this means that group- and culture-specific information is ignored in favour of a model that can be applied to different ethnic and racial minority groups in different settings. The idea is that adolescents have to deal with similar developmental challenges and that minority adolescents often face the task of dealing with cultural conflicts, negative stereotypes, and discrimination, or at least the fact that they are seen as different. The purpose of this approach is to look at common aspects of ethnic identity development that can be compared across ethnic groups. The best-known model is that of Jean Phinney (1989, 1992). Her model and the related measure that she developed is used in many studies, among different ethnic groups, and in various countries.[2] Phinney adapted Erik Erikson's (1968) work on ego-identity to the development of ethnic identity.

Erikson followed a psychoanalytic training with Anna Freud and emigrated to the United States in 1933. He was influenced by the anthropologists Margaret Mead and Ruth Benedict. He made journeys of exploration to the Sioux Indians in South Dakota and the Yurok Indians in Northern California. These travels convinced him of the importance of socio-cultural conditions for individual development. According to Erikson, the life cycle is made up of eight phases, and each phase is characterized by a core conflict or crisis. The more or less adequate resolution of a conflict determines future developments.

During adolescence the core conflict is between a secure sense of identity and identity confusion. At this age there are many physical and social changes that lead to doubts and uncertainties. It is a period of searching, experimenting, and selecting, which should ultimately lead to adolescents 'finding themselves' in a strong sense of identity. During this search or identity crisis there are several ways to keep them going, such as group formation with peers, which brings a sense of being valued and belonging, identification with idols and icons, and embracing an ideology or worldview that provides ready-made answers. How the identity crisis plays out depends on the opportunities and restrictions provided by the socio-cultural context.

Erikson (1966) also wrote about identity development among African Americans. According to him, the circumstances for this group are unfavourable for the development of a healthy identity. There typically would be identity confusion that could manifest itself in disdainful hostility towards that which is socially acceptable, and an emphasis on socially undesirable behaviour, as if many African Americans were saying, 'If I can only be slightly good, it is better to be really good at being bad.'

Ethnic identity development

Erikson's ideas about identity development were elaborated upon by Marcia (1966) in his work on identity statuses, and Phinney's model of ethnic identity is conceptually very close to Marcia's work. Like him, she distinguishes between exploration and commitment as the two key processes of identity formation. Exploration indicates the extent to which adolescents consider the various meanings that ethnicity has and can have in their lives. It involves efforts to learn about or gain an understanding of the history, culture, and social position of one's ethnic group and the implications of one's ethnic group membership. Commitment is the degree to which adolescents have made committed choices regarding the meaning of their ethnicity and the way they will live as an ethnic group member.

As shown in Figure 4.1 (page 92), four ethnic identity statuses are derived from the presence or absence of exploration and commitment. The least mature status is *identity diffusion*, which is characterized by little interest or understanding of your ethnicity (no exploration and no commitments). The status of *foreclosure* indicates commitment without first exploring the meaning of one's ethnic group membership for oneself (commitment without exploration). These adolescents adopt the ethnic attitudes, beliefs, and practices of their parents and family in particular more or less without thought. With age there can be increasing doubts about what had been taken for granted and increasing expectations about having to make up your own mind. This can lead to the status of *moratorium* in which the adolescent is in a state of active exploration about the different meanings of being an ethnic group member, but significant commitments are not yet made (exploration and no commitment). For a healthy ethnic identity development, this period of exploration should result in an *achieved* identity, characterized by commitment and a clear and secure sense of ethnic belonging (commitment after exploration).

Research evidence

There is a great deal of research examining Phinney's model. One question is whether these different statuses can be identified and ordered on a developmental continuum. Research among different ethnic and racial groups has revealed individual differences in adolescents' sense of ethnic self, and there is some

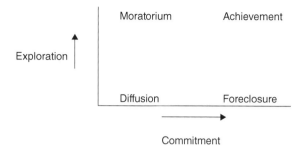

Figure 4.1 Four identity statuses resulting from the processes of exploration and commitment

evidence for the four statuses, although they cannot always be identified. Longitudinal research (the film-making approach) is necessary to know whether in adolescence there is a progressive change in the direction of an achieved identity. Several studies among ethnic and racial minority groups in the United States have examined this and shown that there is an increase in identity exploration from early to middle adolescence and that identity search becomes less strong in late adolescence (see Meeus, 2011; Quintana, 2007). The identity progression is gradual and subtle. Although ethnic–racial identity is less stable in early adolescence, there is no evidence of a dramatic identity crisis during adolescence. Rather, the findings demonstrate quite some stability with many individuals not changing their ethnic–racial identity status, or changing it very slowly and with only one status transition. The formation of an inner ethnic–racial sense of self seems to be less dramatic and dynamic than is often thought.

There is another interesting finding in most studies on ethnic identity development: a positive association between exploration and commitment. Adolescents with strong identity commitments are also involved in a great deal of identity exploration. This raises doubts about the idea that ethnic commitments or an achieved identity occurs *after* a period of exploration. Exploration does not have to be a precursor to commitment, which means that there is no developmental order between the two. It might be better to see the processes of exploration and commitment as two opposing forces with, on the one hand, attempts to develop and maintain a committed sense of self and, on the other hand, the questioning and rethinking of this sense of self (Meeus, 2011).

The positive association between ethnic commitment and exploration is further interesting and important because it suggests that the focus is more on ethnic identity maintenance than on identity formation. In general, adolescents do not begin the identity development process from a 'blank slate'. Especially, minority children know about ethnic–racial group differences and to which ethnic or racial group they belong. They have developed ethnic–racial self-feelings and forms of commitment. So-called dual-cycle models of identity development try to take these earlier commitments into account by arguing that there are two forms of exploration (Crocetti *et al.*, 2008; Luyckx *et al.*, 2005): The first is the reconsideration of previous commitments by comparing them to alternative ones and deciding whether one needs to change. The second is in-depth exploration, which involves the continuing monitoring, enriching, and strengthening of one's commitments. Adolescents can continue to reflect on their committed choices, look for new information, and talk with others about these choices. In other words, having developed strong ethnic–racial commitments is not the end of the story but, rather, can stimulate further exploration to maintain these commitments. A review of the existing research concludes that 'the present models of ethnic identity development indicate whether ethnic commitments are strong or not, and whether adolescents do more or less identity work in order to maintain them' (Meeus, 2011, p. 84).

The ethnic identity work of continuing exploration can be expected to differ between adolescents from ethnic minorities and majorities. One of the very few studies on identity statuses in different ethnic groups in Europe was conducted in the Netherlands (Crocetti *et al.*, 2008). In that study it was demonstrated that, compared to Dutch peers, early and middle adolescents from ethnic minorities were more often involved in exploring identity alternatives offered by their own ethnic group and Dutch society. More than their Dutch peers, they struggled with opposing expectations and cultural values, negative stereotypes, and the question of committing to the identity choices that Dutch society offers. Ethnic identity development is quite a task, especially for minority adolescents. Majority members are usually much less aware of their own ethnic background, which tends to act as an invisible norm and raises hardly any questions. In this research, more than 60% of the Dutch middle adolescents had not explored their identity (diffusion or foreclosure).

The role of racism and parents

There is empirical evidence that specific events and experiences can trigger ethnic identity exploration among minority adolescents. According to Cross's (1991) 'nigrescence' model, it is the encounter with racism that makes it difficult to ignore or deny any longer that discrimination influences one's life. Such an encounter experience may incite the process of racial identity search and exploration. Although Phinney's ethnic identity model does not specifically address the role of exposure to racism or discrimination for identity development, there is longitudinal research on this link. This research finds consistent support for the proposition that experiences with discrimination predict subsequent increases in racial and ethnic identity (see Quintana, 2007). Discrimination triggers the adolescent's ethnic identity development, which is in agreement with the group identity reaction model discussed in chapter 2. The evidence for ethnic identity increasing adolescents' vigilance and sensitivity to discrimination (the group identity lens model) is less consistent and strong.

Discrimination is not the only factor that plays a role in adolescents' ethnic–racial identity formation. Socialization within the family, at school, and in peer groups appears to be very important.[3] For example, warm and supportive parenting as well as family cohesion have been found to be associated with ethnic commitment and a more mature identity (e.g. Kiang *et al.*, 2010). The quality of the parent–child relationship is critical for the identity development of children across ethnic groups. Although children are remarkably resilient and can develop under the most depressing circumstances, the chances for healthy child development are higher when they have loving and caring relationships.

In addition to research on the quality of these relationships there is also much research on ethnic–racial socialization in minority families (see Hughes *et al.*, 2006). This research examines the mechanisms through which parents transmit specific knowledge, values, and perspectives to their children. Part of this work is concerned with the 'ethnic' aspect of ethnic minorities and focuses on the deliberate and implicit ways in which parents teach their children about their ethnic heritage and history. Cultural socialization can give children a sense of roots and belonging and stimulates feelings of ethnic pride. Another part of this work focuses on the 'minority' aspect and examines parents' efforts to promote their children's awareness of discrimination and to prepare them to cope with it.

Children's ethnic identity is the most investigated outcome of ethnic socialization. In general, the research shows that this type of socialization improves children's knowledge and ethnic pride (see Hughes *et al.*, 2006). Furthermore, among adolescents ethnic socialization is associated with identity exploration and more advanced stages of identity development. Promoting children's awareness of discrimination and preparing them to deal with it has also been found to be related to more advanced stages of ethnic identity development, but the evidence is quite limited. Moreover, it has also been found that children's increased awareness of discrimination can have negative psychological effects – for example, for an adequate grip on the social world (see Quintana, 2007). Being vigilant and prepared for discrimination is adaptive in social contexts in which discrimination is pervasive but can get in the way when discrimination is infrequent.

The research on ethnic socialization has predominantly been conducted in the United States and among African American families. There are only a few studies that have examined ethnic socialization across multiple ethnic groups, and there are not many studies that have focused on ethnic groups in other countries. Some of these studies suggest that across groups and countries there are remarkably similar developmental trajectories, also in comparison with majority-group children (e.g., Titzmann & Silbereisen, 2012; Updegraff *et al.*, 2012). Some of the identity challenges and tasks that adolescents face are quite similar in quite different contexts. Yet it is also true that aspects of ethnic socialization differ across groups or can have different meanings. For example, recent immigrants have been found to be more likely to socialize their children ethnically and to discuss discrimination than successive generations. Furthermore, there can be important ethnic socialization differences within ethnic minority groups, depending, for example, on parents' socioeconomic status, neighbourhood, and children's gender and age (see Hughes, 2006).

Outcomes

The importance of ethnic identity development is that it gives adolescents a clear and secure sense of their ethnic group membership, and this is associated with, for example, academic achievement, friendships, self-confidence, and psychological well-being. Many studies have found that a stronger or more mature ethnic identity goes together with positive outcomes. This has been observed across ethnic and racial groups, gender, and socioeconomic status (see Smith & Silva, 2011). These findings support the importance for adolescents of minority groups to develop a committed orientation to their ethnic group membership. However, most of these studies deal with associations at a particular moment in time (the 'picture-taking' approach) and therefore cannot tell us whether a more mature ethnic identity leads to better adjustment. A longitudinal design (the 'film-making' approach) is able to assess whether over time ethnic identity development is predictive of various outcomes. A few studies have used such a design. For example, in a two-year study among African American adolescents it was found that those with an achieved status had the highest levels of psychological well-being (Seaton *et al.*, 2006). In another study it was found that the self-esteem later in life was higher for American Indian youth who identified more strongly with their group (Whitesell *et al.*, 2006).

There is also research that demonstrates that ethnic identity commitment predicts better academic achievement. In one study that covered four years, ethnic identity was found to predict higher grade point average across subsequent years (Altschul *et al.*, 2006). In another study among Latino students, ethnic identity development predicted higher grade point average two years later, especially among students from lower socioeconomic backgrounds (Ong *et al.*, 2006). And in a study among African Americans, racial identity was found to predict later academic achievement (Chavous *et al.*, 2003).

These findings indicate that adolescents with a more mature identity not only have a positive social, academic, and psychological profile at a particular moment in time, but they are also more likely to do better in later years. A strong identity provides a sense of grounding, belonging, and pride, which forms a basis for self-confidence and the will to perform and achieve. It can also provide a buffer against threatening external influences, such as negative stereotypes and discrimination. One longitudinal study suggests that a strong and positive connection to one's ethnic group reduces the negative influence of perceived discrimination on mental health (Wong *et al.*, 2003, but see Seaton *et al.*, 2006).

Openness to others

Adolescents not only have to develop an inner sense of ethnic self, but they also have to learn to deal with cultural diversity. An assumption of ethnic–racial identity development models is that a more mature identity is associated with greater openness towards others. A common belief – also in social psychology – is that identification with your own group is associated with a rejection, or at least less positive evaluation of other groups. This is the classic ethnocentric reaction. Greater involvement with your own group would make you less open to others. In chapter 5 we will see that this reasoning is too simple and, moreover, ethnic–racial identity development models predict otherwise.

Developmental models distinguish between two types of commitment: with and without exploration. An achieved identity involves commitment and (in-depth) exploration. This is different from unreflectively choosing one's own community, such as is the case with a foreclosed ethnic identity. The different developmental models assume that changes in identity are accompanied by changes in attitudes towards one's own and other ethnic groups. First, if little consideration has been given to ethnic differences and your ethnic background, the attitude towards other groups will mainly be based on what significant others in the immediate environment tell you. This is followed by a period of broad exploration of the culture, history, and social position of one's group, which can lead to an idealization of one's minority community and to feelings of distrust and anger towards the dominant majority. Gradually this can give way to a more mature feeling about one's ethnic background, together with a stronger multicultural viewpoint. The security of an achieved ethnic identity forms the basis for approaching others in a confident and open manner. Such an identity reduces feelings of threat and has been found to go together with ethnic perspective-taking (Quintana *et al.*, 1999). A secure and confident sense of self as an ethnic group member can stimulate curiosity and the desire to come into contact with new people and ideas.

Unfortunately there is no research that has systematically and over time examined these ideas. Yet there is some initial evidence, such as research by Phinney and colleagues (2007) among several ethnic groups in the United States. Overall, their findings indicate that a secure ethnic identity is indeed associated with more positive attitudes towards other ethnic groups and more mature multicultural thinking. The results of two other survey studies conducted in the Netherlands provide further evidence.[4] One of these studies included adolescents of Turkish and Moroccan origin. It was found that those with a more achieved ethnic identity were more positive about cultural diversity than those in ethnic identity diffusion. The same was found in a study among adolescents with a Surinamese background. Among them, a more mature ethnic identity was associated with a more positive attitude towards native Dutch and the Dutch society. Thus, a more secure ethnic identity appears to be associated with higher openness and acceptance of cultural others. It provides the confident basis for meeting others, rather than being an uncertain inner bastion that constantly needs to be repaired and defended.

However, we should be careful in drawing firm conclusions because the number of studies is very limited and there is no research that monitors changes over time. Moreover, there can be mutual influences. Ethnic identity development might lead to a greater openness towards others, but others can choose not to go along with it or may even reject you. This can result in a reconsideration and further in-depth exploration of the question of what your ethnic–racial identity means to you.

Another qualification to this research is that individuals not only have an ethnic identity but are also part of various social groups that, separately or in combination with each other, are important for how they see themselves and react towards others. An example is religious identity, which is especially important among Muslim immigrants.

Muslim identity

Ethnic and religious identity have been found to be closely connected among adolescents from Latin American, Asian, and European backgrounds in the United States (Lopez *et al.*, 2011). The same has been found for Muslim immigrants. Studies among young Muslims in Sweden, Scotland, Denmark, and the United States (Saeed *et al.*, 1999; Schmidt, 2004) have shown that religious identity predominates, followed by ethnicity. And similarly as in the country of origin, what it means to be a Turk, Moroccan, Algerian, Afghan, Pakistani, or Arab is intimately linked to what it means to be a Muslim. For example, studies in the Netherlands among first and second generation Muslim minorities have demonstrated that those who identify more strongly with their religious group also identify more strongly with their ethnic group (Maliepaard *et al.*, 2010; Phalet *et al.*, 2008).

In general, religion can have an important and pervasive impact on adolescents and their development (Benson *et al.*, 1993). Longitudinal research has found that religious identity remains quite stable after middle adolescence, although religious participation tends to decline (Lopez *et al.*, 2011). Parents are considered the most influential socializing agent in children's development of religiosity. Research on the relationship between children's perception of their parents' religiosity and their own religiosity tends to show substantial relationships (e.g., Martin *et al.*, 2003). Research among Muslim youth in Western Europe has found that perceived religious instruction and parental role modelling, as reported by the child, are strongly related to religiosity in the second generation (Fleischmann, 2011). According to the Koran, Muslim parents have the religious duty to raise their children as good Muslims. Furthermore, there is an emphasis on childhood obedience and respect for parents that is only second to that for God (Mahtani-Stewart *et al.*, 2000). In addition, because of the anti-Muslim climate in most European countries, Muslim parents might emphasize the importance of religious transmission to preserve the continuity, integrity, and value of their Muslim identity. A strong Muslim identity might bolster children's resilience and effective coping with the pervasive negative stereotypes and discrimination. An interview study among Moroccan Dutch youth found that Islamic identity is very important and that emphasizing this identity is a way to feel in control and to feel a sense of belonging while living in a society in which they are considered outsiders (Buitelaar 1998; De Koning, 2008). Similarly, in an interview study among students in New York and in Colorado it was found that these students identify themselves as Muslims first and foremost and that their religious identity became even stronger after the September 11 attacks (Peek, 2005).

Several studies have found that the influence of parents on their children's religious development decreases during adolescence (e.g., Erickson, 1992; Francis & Brown, 1991). An interview study among Moroccan Dutch Muslims found that this is also experienced by adolescents themselves (Demant, 2006). Cultural broadening theory argues that with age, adolescents encounter more liberal and less traditional behaviours, beliefs, and attitudes than that of their parents (Hoge *et al.*, 1994). Cultural broadening may diminish the importance of religious group membership. In addition, adolescence is a time of autonomy seeking, and growing resistance to parental authority has been reported in various cultures, also among Muslim adolescents undergoing acculturation in Western societies (Fuligni, 1998; Mayall, 2001). Increased individual autonomy and greater influence of peers can mean that the influence of Muslim parents on their children's religious identity decreases with age, similar to the decreasing parental influence for ethnic socialization. Furthermore, a foreclosed identity in which the sense of ethnic belonging reflects the opinions of parents and other authority figures is more typical for young adolescents than for older adolescents who develop a sense of belonging based on their own process of exploration. In a study among Moroccan Dutch Muslim adolescents and their parents it was found that adolescents identified less strongly as Muslim than did their parents. Furthermore, for early adolescents, parent's religious identity was indeed strongly related to the religious identity of their children, whereas there was no association for middle adolescents (Verkuyten *et al.*, 2012).

Muslim identity development

As far as I know, Marcia's identity developmental model has not been systematically investigated in relation to Muslim identity of migrant youth. It has been applied, however, in an interview study among Muslim youth in Great Britain (Lewis, 2007).[5] Those with a *diffuse* Muslim identity believe in the core message of Islam but do not participate in religious rituals and practices. They have no real interest in their religion and do not feel any real commitment to it. They use Islam more as a cultural marker to reject assimilation pressures. A *foreclosed* Muslim identity is characterized by a lack of exploration and a rather unreflective choice for Islam as a set of unchanging and universal doctrines and rules. These adolescents see Islam as an eternal and perfect system that cannot be adjusted to the circumstances, and this leads to a gap between the Muslim community and the rest of society. One lives in multicultural Britain (a Muslim in Britain) but does not feel part of it (not a British Muslim). The vast majority of young people who participated in the study were engaged in the continuous exploration and interpretation of Islam in the context of their life in Britain (*moratorium*). They do see themselves as British Muslims, and they try to find a way in which their religion is meaningful in their lives without turning their backs on society. They are actively involved with the question of what it means to be a Muslim in contemporary Britain. They want to self-evidently express that they are Muslims living in a country where their future lies and where they try to feel at home. For them, being a Muslim is a fact, and their identity work is concerned with maintaining their religious identity in a non-Muslim society.

This identity work is never finished because there is in-depth exploration or the continuous monitoring of present understandings and commitments. This means that a more orthodox interpretation of the faith and one's Muslim identity can also gradually develop – not in a thoughtless and unexplored way as with a foreclosed identity, but by exploration in depth. There are indications that some older Muslim adolescents rediscover Islam and express their faith through following the rules of Islam closely. International political developments and the anti-Muslim climate in Western countries impels them to become more strongly defined by their faith and Muslim identity (see Voas & Fleischmann, 2012). There is a tendency to return to a 'pure' Islam and to use the Koran as the central guideline for one's life. In the words of a Dutch Muslim: 'I am also a fundamentalist . . . in the sense that I try to comply with the foundations of Islam. That is what every Muslim should do. In principle, every Muslim should be a fundamentalist. We should all return to the foundations of Islam.'[6] Orthodox belief implies the acceptance of the teachings of Islam and the belief that Islam contains the inerrant and unchanging truths about humanity and deity. Among Muslim immigrants this ideological dimension has been found to be an important aspect of their Muslim identity (Verkuyten & Yildiz, 2010a).

Orthodoxy

In Western societies there is the fear that the leaning towards a 'pure' Islam goes together with self-segregation, alienation, and a lack of commitment to the host society (e.g., Hasan, 2010). In addition, the emphasis on a 'pure' and orthodox Islam is often seen as threatening liberal democratic values. In all religions, orthodox belief can form a stepping stone towards radicalism and extremism, with severe social consequences (Appleby, 2000). The devastating effects of (violent) religious radicalism for people's lives and the functioning of society should never be underestimated.[7] However, for the great majority of Muslim migrants, religious orthodoxy probably does not lead to an antagonistic or radical attitude towards the host society.

In the Protestant Christian tradition, the religious orthodox join battle with modernization in the name of God. Orthodoxy represents an exclusive and absolute religious claim whereby people adhere to religious regulations and rules as closely as possible. The term 'orthodoxy' is also used for anti-modernist movements in Jewish and Islamic religious traditions. In the latter it is sometimes referred to as fundamentalism and Islamism (Herriot, 2009). These terms do not have the same meaning, and the literature distinguishes at least three types of 'Islamists'. Apart from the very small group of political–religious radicals who oppose democratic rights and liberties and sometimes favour violence, there are two main groups. One rejects the corrupt Western societies and seeks spiritual peace and salvation in a pure and apolitical Islam. The other is a political–religious movement in which religious dogma forms the foundation for a societal ideal that is to be achieved by democratic means. So, one group of Orthodox Muslims is characterized by withdrawal from the host society, whereas the other wants to be visible and tries to participate in the democratic process of that society.

In European countries there is the fear that the former group dominates. It may well be that religious radicalism and violence among Muslims is exceptional, but a substantial number of orthodox Muslims reject the host society and withdraw into their own religious community, so it is argued. For many Muslim youth, Islam gives a sense of belonging, meaning, value, and security. And they are often embedded in close-knit family and community networks that contribute to their religious beliefs, involvements, and commitments. The religious influence of the family and community is substantial and is maintained by very strong norms against apostasy and marrying a non-Muslim. At the same time, a growing majority of Muslims is born in European host societies. They see their future in these societies and are increasingly looking for ways to make a contribution and to feel part of society. Moreover, most Muslims strongly appreciate the freedom and opportunities to practise and propagate their faith (Buijs *et al.*, 2006; De Koning, 2008).

In a study on Turkish Dutch Muslims, orthodoxy did not appear to be incompatible with social and political integration (Verkuyten & Yildiz, 2010b). Those who more strongly accepted the teachings of Islam as the inerrant and unchanging truth about life and humanity were more strongly in favour of the rights and opportunities for Muslim to express their identity and for the democratic political organization of Dutch Muslims. These findings suggest that an orthodox interpretation of Islam can foster regular forms of political action, similar to Christian democratic parties.

Citizenship also implies that democratic rules and rights are consistently applied to issues or groups one disapproves of. Religion might be a reason for Muslims to apply democratic rules and rights selectively – for instance, when religious issues are at stake. Among Dutch Muslims and using an experimental questionnaire design, no evidence was found for religion being a specific reason for not supporting tolerant values (Phalet & Güngör, 2004). However, this study did not examine the role of religious orthodoxy. In another study (Verkuyten & Yildiz, 2010b), four political tolerance experiments were used in which Dutch Muslims were asked about different cases in which Islam was or was not involved, including the freedom to express offensive views, to burn the national flag, and the freedom to reject females for important administrative functions in religious organizations. For example the endorsement of free speech was examined by presenting the participants with either a religious or a non-religious issue ('Should it be allowed that a magazine uses drawings and words to make God and religion ridiculous?' versus 'Should it be allowed that racist groups express their views in the media?').[8] It turned out that the great majority of Muslims did not support the freedoms and rights in three of the four cases. They found it unacceptable to publicly express offensive views, to burn a national flag at a demonstration, and to reject female administrators. Importantly, however, the lack of support did not differ between the experimental conditions. Thus, the democratic rights were not applied selectively to Muslims. Furthermore, the more orthodox religious participants were not more politically intolerant. This suggests that there was no religiously motivated form of political (in)tolerance in which the freedoms and rights of Muslims are evaluated differently from those of other groups or religions. Furthermore, Dutch Muslims who more strongly endorsed a 'pure' Islam did not tend to apply democratic rules and rights more selectively.

These findings for the relationship between Muslim beliefs and democratic attitudes are not specific to the Netherlands. Several cross-national studies have shown that in general Muslims value democratic principles and see no contradiction between democratic values and religious principles (Esposito & Mogahed, 2007). One of these studies concluded that 'The most basic cultural fault line between the West and Islam does not concern democracy – it involves issues of gender equality and sexual liberalization' (Norris & Inglehart, 2004, p. 155).

Muslim diversity

Orthodoxy can go together with an emphasis on rights for Muslims and the importance attached to the political organization of Muslims *within* the host national democratic context. A return to the original sources of the faith can be a vehicle for cultural criticism as well as a basis for a societal ideal in which people stand up for the public recognition of Islam. Orthodox Muslims want to express and enact their faith in appearance and behaviour. In this way they confirm publicly how they see themselves and what they believe in. Furthermore, it can be important for orthodox Muslims to defend their interests in the host society by, for example, organizing themselves socially or politically. The endorsement of rights for Muslims and the attitudinal support for political organization is relatively high, especially among the more orthodox believers.

But we should be careful not to equate being Muslim with orthodoxy. There are many different Muslim groups (e.g., Sunni, Alevi) and many ways of being Muslim in Western Europe. Although Islam continues to be regulated by collective practices, some scholars argue that there is an emerging trend towards individualization and privatization of Islam (Roy, 2007). Research among West European Muslims has shown an increase in individualist interpretations of what it means to be a Muslim, alongside an interpretation in which a commitment to fellow Muslims and conformity to Islam as an ethics of public practices and rules is emphasized (Phalet *et al.*, 2008). For many Muslim immigrants, religious identity is about finding a way between individual meaning-making and conformist rule-following. In addition, there is a strong debate within West European Muslim communities about the ideological meaning of Islam. In this complex debate about beliefs there are more orthodox interpretations that emphasize that Islam is about fundamental, essential, and inerrant truths that should not be interpreted to fit in with the Western world. And there are more liberal or modern interpretations that focus on the development of an European Islam and prefer a belief that is adaptable to modern society.

It is clear that there is no single version of Muslim identity, just as there is no single version of Islam. The question of what it means to be a Muslim in England, or in Germany, or in France, or the Netherlands cannot be answered in any unambiguous and simple way. The native population in European countries, however, sometimes think that this is the case, and when they do they tend to have the traditional and fanatical believer in mind. That is the image that dominates the media and pushes the diversity within the Muslim population out of sight. But this is just like when someone who is unfamiliar with Christianity assumes that Christian fundamentalists are typical and the norm, or that you can only be Jewish if you follow the traditions of orthodox Judaism.

Acculturation

Some of the Jewish interviewees who were raised as Christians told Kessel about their struggle to combine their dual heritages, and one of them stated: 'I have feelings of being marginalized. I'm not part of either the Jewish community or the Christian community' (2000, p. 86). Suddenly being Jewish is not always easy and can imply a difficult process of acculturation.

Acculturation theory is concerned with the processes by which people of different cultural groups adapt to one another.[9] Acculturation implies mutual and reciprocal influences, but the main focus in thinking and research is on changes among migrants and minority members. After all, greater effort, initiatives, and change is typically needed and expected from their side. Cultural contact rarely takes place on an equal footing. The question is what happens to migrants and minorities when they try to adapt to the challenges posed by continuous first-hand contact with the people and culture of the host society. How do they adjust, and what does this mean for their feelings of belonging? Psychological acculturation refers to internal changes that may relate to cultural values, attitudes, behavioural preferences, and group identifications.

The concepts of ethnic identity and acculturation are often used interchangeably, but it seems better to consider the latter to be a broader construct that encompasses a wide range of changes (Liebkind, 2001). A changing sense of ethnic identity and a developing sense of host national identity can be considered central aspects of the acculturation process. It is not uncommon to assume that identification with one's ethnic community is inversely related to identification with the host society: Moving closer towards the one is considered to result in distancing from the other. Like communicating vessels: as people identify more with their own minority group, they distance themselves more from others. However, ethnic identification and identification as a member of the new society can be thought of as two dimensions that vary independently (Hutnik, 1991). For example, for many young Turks living in Germany it is often not a question of being Turkish or German but a question of the extent to which they feel Turkish as well as the extent to which they feel German.

The acculturation model shown in Figure 4.2 assumes two separate dimensions of identification that correspond with two distinct processes. A combination of

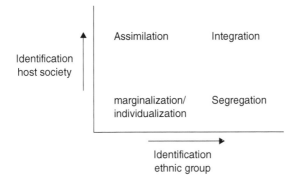

Figure 4.2 Four acculturation or identity positions

both dimensions provides a schematic model of four identity positions (Berry, 2001; Hutnik, 1991). Psychological *assimilation* focuses on identification with the host society. These are ethnic minority members who define themselves exclusively as German, and their main orientation is towards German society. With *segregation,* one sees oneself primarily in terms of one's own ethnic community and only feels, say, Turkish. This can be the result of a strong sense of commitment and involvement with one's community, but it might also be due to feelings of rejection by the majority population. Psychological *integration* refers to people identifying with both their own ethnic group and the host society. In this case, hyphenated self-definitions are used, such as Turkish-German, and terms such as dual and bicultural identity are also used for this. Finally, as opposed to integration, there is *marginalization* and *individualization.* In the case of marginalization, one does not feel a member of one's own ethnic community but also not of the host society. Someone with a Turkish background, for example, can feel neither Turkish nor German. While assimilation, segregation, and integration are all more or less the result of personal orientations and changes, this is generally not the case with marginalization. The Jewish person quoted at the beginning of this section argues that he had the feeling of *being* marginalized. Marginalization is usually not a choice but something that is the result of simultaneously not being fully accepted by one's ethnic community and by the host society. It is also possible, however, that a more individual or autonomous position is taken in which a self-definition in terms of one's ethnic group membership as well as the host society is rejected and other social identities or personal characteristics, qualities and goals are emphasized (I do not feel Turkish or German, but European or an individual) (Bourhis *et al.*, 1997).

Empirical findings

Several studies in different countries have examined self-definitions and group identifications among minority members of different ethnic groups and different ages. These studies show that the four forms of identification do exist, but not all to the same extent (e.g., Modood *et al.*, 1997; Verkuyten, 2005c) Defining oneself in terms of one's own ethnic group or in terms of a hyphenated position is more frequent, whereas adopting an assimilative and/or marginal position is rather exceptional.

There are important differences, however, between countries. For example, whereas in Canada and the United States compound labels such as Chinese Canadian and Mexican American are accepted and common, these are relatively exceptional in countries like Germany, the Netherlands, and Belgium. Cross-national research has shown that in Europe higher ethnic identification often goes together with weaker national identification, whereas in the United States both identifications tend to be separate (Phinney *et al.*, 2006). Thus, in settler countries, like the United States and Canada, immigrants typically are attached both to their own ethnic group and to the new homeland, but in non-settler European countries, some immigrants appear to put their ethnic or religious identity in contrast to their new homeland belonging. In 2012 in a large-scale study in the Netherlands it was found that only a minority of people of Turkish and Moroccan origin felt Dutch (28% and 37%, respectively) (Huijnk & Dagevos, 2012).

In addition to country differences, social scientists have shown that legal, structural, political, and social factors play a role in immigrant's national identification. For example, having citizenship, being of a later generation, length of stay in the country, higher education, better labour market position, higher language proficiency, and more social contacts with natives have all been found to be associated with stronger national identification (e.g., Heath & Roberts, 2008; Walters *et al.*, 2007; Zimmermann *et al.*, 2007). The list of factors and conditions is impressive, but the question is when and why exactly these factors contribute to national identification. Furthermore, there are also social psychological processes that are important such as perceived discrimination by the majority group which communicates that one is different and not a fully fledged national, but also perceived rejection from one's own ethnic community. For example, in a study among Latino immigrants in the United States it was found that perceived rejection from Americans was associated with stronger dis-identification with the United States, whereas perceived rejection from Latinos was related to lower ethnic identification and higher national identification (Wiley, in press). Similarly, in a study among Romanians and Moroccans in France it turned out that perceived rejection by, respectively, Romanians and Moroccans in the country of origin was associated with lower ethnic identification (Badea *et al.*, 2011).

Within migrant communities there are often normative pressures to maintain the ethnic culture and not to assimilate. In a study among Turkish Muslims in Germany and the Netherlands it turned out that higher discrimination as well as community pressures to maintain the ethnic culture were related to stronger religious identification and weaker national identification (Martinovic & Verkuyten, 2012). And in a study of daily acculturative hassles among Vietnamese Canadians, there was evidence for majority group hassles (e.g., perceptions of prejudice and discrimination) and ethnic hassles (e.g., feeling isolated from one's ethnic group, being perceived as too White), both having a significant negative impact on the acculturation process (Lay & Nguyen, 1998). Thus, immigrants and minority members might struggle with combining feelings of belonging and commitment to their ethnic community and the nation. The anticipation of loyalty conflicts, community pressures, incompatible values and practices, and perceived hostilities might undermine the development of a sense of host national belonging.

Outcomes

There are indications that from an adjustment point of view integration and segregation appear to be the most positive forms of acculturation (but see Rudmin, 2003). This suggests that preserving a tie to their own ethnic group and culture has a positive influence on the psychological and social adjustment of immigrant and minority members (see Nguyen & Benet-Martínez, 2013). The least favourable positions are the marginal and the assimilative ones. Both positions imply a kind of denial of the complex reality of living with two or more cultures, whereas acceptance of this is considered a prerequisite for effective coping. A marginal orientation is traditionally associated with psychological and behavioural problems and stress, and assimilation seems to be related to psychological costs such as cultural alienation, depression, fear, and loneliness (e.g., Arroyo & Zigler, 1995). Both forms of acculturation involve breaking off the emotional ties with one's own ethnic community. Several studies suggest that maintaining a relationship with one's community and culture has a positive influence on adjustment and well-being. People who distance themselves from their ethnic community must often pay for this with isolation, insecurity, and broken networks, while at the same time acceptance by the majority group is often partial, temporary, or conditional. In a Dutch study it was found, for example, that minority groups are at a much higher risk of developing schizophrenia than the native population (Selten *et al.*, 2007). The risk was even seven times higher among men of Moroccan descent. Moreover, the risk was higher for the second generation, who are less rooted in their community than the first generation. Schizophrenia was also more prevalent among those who live in neighbourhoods where there are few co-ethnics. It also appeared to be the case that those who do not identify with their ethnic community, or do so in a negative way, were five times more likely to develop schizophrenia than those with a strong ethnic identity. Against this background, a plea for assimilation or to 'let go of where you come from and unconditionally choose the Netherlands'[10] is outright asking for trouble.

Dimensions of integration

Psychological integration refers to identification with both the original ethnic group and the host society. This is not necessarily the same as cultural or social integration. The research literature distinguishes different aspects of integration, such as structural, cultural, social, and psychological integration (e.g., Esser, 2001; Gordon, 1964). It is often assumed that immigrants' identification with the host society is the last step in the integration process. According to acculturation theory, cultural integration is the combination of wanting to maintain one's minority culture together with trying to adapt to the host society. And social integration refers to social contacts with both members of one's own community and majority group members. The distinction between cultural, social, and psychological integration is important because these three dimensions of acculturation do not need to run parallel to each other (Schwartz *et al.*, 2010). This was demonstrated in a Belgian study among youths of Turkish and Moroccan origin (Snauwaert *et al.*, 2003). Around 80% of these youngsters were socially integrated (had ties within their own community as well as with the majority group), 40% in a cultural sense (cultural maintenance and cultural adaptation), and about 15% in psychological terms (identification with their own community and broader society). Roughly half of the youths favoured cultural segregation (only cultural maintenance), and 80% opted for psychological segregation (only identification with their own community). These results are important in three respects.

The first is that psychological adaptation and change appear to be more difficult than social and cultural adaptation. Even after cultural adaptations have been made, an ethnic self-definition may remain (e.g., Huron Indians as discussed in chapter 1). The second is that a unilateral identification with one's ethnic community does not necessarily mean that one does not culturally adapt or that one rejects ties with majority group members. Most immigrants and minority members are very keen to establish good relations with natives. But that is something different from developing a sense of unity with them or feeling emotionally connected to the host society. Cultural adaptations, developing social contacts and networks, and changes in one's sense of identity are different things. They may be related to each other, but the underlying factors and processes differ. Learning new customs, norms, and values calls on different skills and needs than establishing social relations and changing your sense of group belonging. It is probably easier to develop bicultural skills and form ethnically mixed networks, than to really feel emotionally connected with two communities.

There is a third issue that is important. Acculturation theory is about gradual changes from one position to another one. This sometimes gives the impression of rather fixed ethnic and national identities that are ready to be discovered rather than being appropriated in a creative manner. For some researchers the process of creative appropriation is critical and on-going, especially among youths. They sometimes go as far as to describe individuals as social chameleons, who change their identity at will. This is the image of going to a cafeteria in which a wide collection of identities is on offer and you choose a different ethnic meal each day. You are what you eat, or how you dress, or what music you listen to, or with whom you happen to interact with that day. The individual fabricates an identity using all kinds of information, particularly obtained via the Internet as a virtual laboratory where different identities are explored and combined. There are diverse and creative ways in which cultures are mixed, creating all kinds of hybrid forms of language, images, music, clothing, and ethnically ambiguous self-presentations. This process of fabrication can be challenging and enriching, but it can also lead to a dangerous game with radical and violent identities.

Yet, what exactly this mixing means in relation to social identities and everyday life is not always clear. Social identities should be lived up to and recognized by others. It is not just about what people choose to be behind their computer and in the virtual world, but also about how they are perceived and what they are simply expected to be in all kinds of social situations. Mixing different styles and trends does not provide a social identity just like that. Everyday life is full with expectations and obligations, and not all social identities are identical. One day you can eat Indonesian food and dress like a Chinese and the next day eat a kebab in a Tibetan ambiance, but *being* Indonesian, Chinese, or Tibetan thereby is not a commercially available option. These social identities are more than a superficial style or trend that can be arbitrarily adopted or dismissed. In one's mind and in the virtual world a great deal is possible, and people can combine all kinds of styles and trends, but emotions and loyalties are far less easy to ignore or combine. It is not enough to claim a social identity because it has to be recognized and acknowledged by others. The mixing of cultural meanings can, of course, lead to a new category with an associated label – a new mixture of cultural styles and trends that gets its own name that is used to identify and characterize its members, like, for example, the Tarkans and Yasminas.

Social identities are also embedded in social relationships. Changing relationships is not that simple, as they need to be formed and maintained. This requires investment in time and resources and brings with it expectations, commitments, and feelings of reciprocity and loyalty. Social identities cannot be reduced to personal taste and individual choice. The leeway for making choices is not unlimited and has to do with ancestry, visible differences, group boundaries, ideological beliefs, and structural positions that impose restrictions on who and what you can be. Moreover, the creativity game that youths play with identities is not representative for other age groups. With age, identity choices and commitments are being made, and more durable relationships are established.

Multiple identities

> The history of the American Negro is the history of his striving – this longing to attain self-conscious manhood, to merge his double self into a better and truer self. In his merging he wishes neither of the older selves to be lost. He would not Africanize America, for America has too much to teach the world and Africa. He would not bleach his Negro soul in a flood of white Americanism, for he knows that Negro blood has a message to the world. He simply wishes to make it possible for a man to be both a Negro and an American, without being cursed and spit upon by his fellows, without having the doors of opportunity closed roughly in his face.
>
> (DuBois, 1982, p. 4)

This quote is from W.E.B. DuBois' classic and seminal work, *The Souls of Black Folk,* which was originally published in 1903. The quote offers a very powerful statement of the wish to be both. A wish that is difficult to fulfil because of external threats and constraints. It is social reality that makes it (im)possible to be both. This critical role of reality is sometimes forgotten in present-day research that focuses on the sense of identity. In this research the wish to be both is examined in subjective terms with concepts such as dual identity, bicultural identification, hybridity, or hyphenated selves. These terms are not exactly the same and also are used in different ways.

Among other identities

Sometimes the term 'multiple identities' is used to refer to the simple fact that people belong simultaneously to several categories and groups. They have a range of social identities that become psychologically salient depending on the circumstances. You are French, a teacher, a socialist, a female, a mother, a Parisian, and so on, and, depending on the circumstances, one or the other identity is relevant. These identities go together because they refer to different domains of life or relate to different levels of abstraction. In her speech at the presentation of the WRR report, Princes Maxima stated, 'I have multiple loyalties. I am a cosmopolitan, a European, and Dutch.' Social identities are in principle always ones among others, which means that multidimensional human beings should not be reduced to one-dimensional creatures. But speaking about multiple identities in this way suggests that they coexist in parallel without no particular relationship to one another. Terms like dual identity and hybridity are used to challenge this assumption.

Dual identity

In acculturation theory the focus is on two identities that in principle exist in the same domain.[11] It has to do with potentially competing ethnic and national identities. According to Kay Deaux (2006, p. 119) this is 'the prototypical case for immigrants, an identity associated with the country of origin confronts the possibilities of a different American (or Canadian or French or other national) identity'. In acculturation research this duality is typically examined in terms of two separate identifications: with the country of origin and the host society. Dual identity would exist when both identifications are relatively strong – for example, I feel Dominican and I feel American. But it is not fully clear what these two separate feelings actually mean and whether this approach captures the subjective experience of a dual identity. Probably it does not, but whether this is true will depend on the interpretation of what a dual identity is. There are two main interpretations possible: identity alternation and blended identity.

The first is the more or less fluid movement or alternation between both identities depending on the social situation. Both identities are relatively independent, and the actual situation determines whether you feel Dominican or American. You feel Dominican when you are with Dominican people, and you feel American when your national identity is at stake. Furthermore, both identities can have a distinct set of elements associated with it. Being Dominican by origin does not have the same cultural meanings as possessing US nationality. The former can refer to ancestry, traditions, and heritage, and the latter to citizenship and the American Dream, and individuals can alternate between the two.

This process of alternating has also been described as cultural frame switching among biculturals (Hong *et al.*, 2000). We have examined how this works among Greek Dutch adolescents and adults (Verkuyten & Pouliasi, 2002, 2006). In our studies, there were always two mono-cultural groups involved: native Dutch and native Greeks in Greece. In addition, there were bicultural participants of Greek origin, living in the Netherlands. In an experimental design, the latter group was randomly divided into two groups: Greek Dutch and Dutch Greek. For the Greek Dutch group their Dutch cultural identity was made salient, and for the Dutch Greeks the same was done for their Greek cultural identity.[12] Among both adolescents and adults, the results showed that the two mono-cultural groups clearly differed from each other. For example, the native Dutch had a more individualistic cultural orientation, while the Greeks in Greece had a stronger collectivist or group-oriented orientation. Interestingly, and more importantly, the answers given by the bicultural Greek Dutch matched those of the native Dutch, while the bicultural Dutch Greeks gave similar answers as the Greeks in Greece. So, there was cultural frame switching: these bicultural people perceived the world differently depending on the cultural framework that was activated.

This form of cultural frame switching implies a sort of additive model in which both cultural identities coexist and are salient, depending on the circumstances. But both identities can also become integrated or, rather, be felt as oppositional and therefore difficult to integrate (Benet-Martinez *et al.*, 2002). In the former case, one feels at ease and at home in both cultures ('living *with* both cultures') and cultural 'frame switching' is relatively simple, as is the case for the bicultural Greek Dutch group. In the latter case, there is psychological tension and confusion ('living *between* two cultures') making it difficult to adequately switch between cultural frames.

Different identities can be incompatible or mutually exclusive because they imply conflicting loyalties, expectations and meanings. It is not always easy to be, for example, a Kurd and a Turk at the same time, or a Palestinian and Israeli, or a Dutch and Muslim because 'As a Muslim you have to give up your faith to participate in the Dutch society. To be allowed to participate. But then I would have to rip my heart out of my body.'[13] In a study in Germany and the Netherlands it was found that Turkish Muslims who perceive incompatibility between Western and Islamic ways of life identified more strongly as Muslims and less as host nationals (Martinovic & Verkuyten, 2012). It is not easy to live as a Muslim in a country that considers itself Christian or secular. In countries like the Netherlands and Germany few Muslims describe themselves as a Dutch or German Muslim. This is quite different in the United States, where practising Islam is consistent with and supportive of the religious diversity of the country. But the events of 9/11 and the concern for terrorism by Muslim extremists has also led in the United States to more negative views about Muslims.

Blended identity and mixed heritage

The second interpretation of duality is a so-called blended or fused identity that is distinct from either of the original categories: not 'I feel Dominican and I feel American', but 'I feel Dominican American', or 'Indian British', or 'French Canadian', and so on. This means that we are not talking about two separate strong identifications but, rather, a different category that is neither one nor the other but a blending or mixing of the two. Feeling French Canadian is something other than the combination of feeling French and feeling Canadian. It represents an unique cultural configuration, a set of meanings that cannot simply be deduced from knowledge of both separate identities. Another example is the Polish Tatars (Cieslik & Verkuyten, 2006). This is a relatively small community that has lived in Poland for over 600 years. They consider themselves a separate people and trace their ancestry to the Mongols of Genghis Kahn. They are also Muslims who live in a country where almost everyone is Catholic and the Catholic faith is an important part of the national identity. They describe themselves not as Poles or as Tatars but, rather, as Polish Tatars. They claim that they historically belong in Poland, and throughout history they have proven to be very loyal Poles. This distinguishes them from Tatars in other countries, whereas their Tatar origin and being part of the worldwide Muslim community distinguish them from the Catholic Poles.

A further example is that of children from ethnically and racially mixed marriages. In terms of origin these children – like Barack Obama – belong to two or more ethnic or racial groups. Another well-known example is the golfer Tiger Woods, who described himself as 'Cablinasian' a mixture of 'Caucasian, Black, Indian, and Asian'. Children of mixed parentage undermine the dichotomous scheme of belonging to one category or the other. What is a child born to a French father and an Egyptian mother, or a Turkish man and a Greek woman? The seemingly clear criteria for making ethnic or racial distinctions do not suffice in categorizing these children. This can lead to a blurring of group boundaries but can also be the impetus to demarcate group boundaries more strictly in order to stay 'pure', such as defining any person with 'one drop of Negro blood' as Black.[14]

Research is particularly interested in how children of ethnically or racially mixed marriages deal with their dual heritage. Psychologically the focus tends to be on questions of identity confusion, reduced psychological well-being, and problem behaviour, at least when there is a clear visible or group status difference between the parents involved. A marriage between a Dutch and an English person is less likely to be considered as ethnically mixed than a marriage between a Black man and White woman, or a Turk and a Dutchman. In the former case the emphasis is on the benefits of growing up with two cultures and languages, while in the later the focus tend to be on possible problems and conflicts. The latter children are thought to fall in-between, to not really belong to the ethnic or racial group of the father nor that of the mother. They would be caught up in an inner conflict, never feeling completely at home and remaining uncertain about their ethnic or racial identity. Feelings of isolation and identity diffusion are certainly possible, and in the clinical literature there are telling descriptions of this. Yet systematic research shows that many of these children are able to develop a positive identity and can avoid having to choose between one or the other (see Shih & Sanchez, 2005). The picture is not that negative, but also not that simple because many factors are involved, including family and neighbourhood characteristics.

Socially, there may be pressures to choose one of your backgrounds, or at least to prioritize one over the other. Mixed children often receive the implicit message that they should choose one of the two. Parents and family are also not always united in how they see the children and what they expect from them in terms of cultural orientations, preferences, and behaviour. The children may have to deal with questions, comments, and disapproval from the wider society, but also from their two ethnic or racial communities. This double minority position is described, for example, in the United States for children born to Caucasian and Asian parents ('AmerAsians') or Black and Latin American parents ('LatiNegras'), and also for so-called half-bloods among South Moluccans in the Netherlands (Verkuyten, 2005c).

Over time when these people identify with others who share the same mixed background, a distinctive social category with a distinctive identity label can gradually develop, such as with the Polish Tatars. Another example is in Central and South America, where the term 'mestizo' is used to express the mixed European and indigenous ancestry. In Canada the Métis are a recognized ethnic group of mixed White and native Canadian descent, and the Basters in Windhoek in Namibia are descendants of European settlers and Koisan groups.

Intersection

The concept of social identity complexity refers to individual differences in the way in which different group memberships are subjectively combined (Roccas & Brewer, 2002). An inclusive or complex identity structure implies that an individual accepts and acknowledges the distinctive memberships of his or her various groups. Alternatively, individuals with a relatively simplified structure perceive a strong overlap and interrelation among their identities. Social identity complexity 'involves understanding what people mean when they say that I am both "A" and "B"'. This description implies a construal of the self in which you feel a member of multiple groups. However, semantics make it difficult to know what the 'and' in this self-description actually refers to (Roccas & Brewer, 2002).

The notion of intersectionality as put forward by feminist and critical race theorists has similarities with the concept of social identity complexity. It is used to argue that social categories like race, gender, and social class often depend on one another for meaning (see Cole, 2009). In particular, members of groups holding multiple disadvantaged statuses would experience these social categories in close association and simultaneously. Identities that in principle refer to different domains of life (e.g., ethnicity, gender, locality) can interrelate in terms of defining experiences and forming social relations. Different social identities can become intertwined, because one classification influences the significance and meaning of the other. Racism is easily intertwined with nationalism and sexism: classifications based on skin colour become linked with classifications based on nationality and gender. Likewise, ethnicity can be understood in terms of gender differences in positions and responsibilities. For example, an emphasis on masculinity and a culture of *machismo* or *marianismo* is sometimes seen as a defining characteristic among some ethnic groups, particularly of Latin American origin (Diekman *et al.*, 2005).

In research conducted in the United States it was found that the intersected Black-woman identity was more important than the separate identities of being a woman and Black (Settles, 2006). And Deaux (2006) and her colleagues carried out a study among Dominican women living in New York. The women were asked to describe themselves as a woman, as a Dominican, and then as a Dominican woman. For each of the three, very different answers were given. Being a woman was described in terms of biological features and especially motherhood. The ethnicity question was answered by referring to cultural traditions, language, and pride in the country of origin. The combined category of Dominican woman elicited many positive descriptions, such as strength, intelligence, independence, and passion, which were rarely given for either single label. It was also noted that as Dominican women they had to deal with discrimination by White Americans and also by Dominican men. These findings clearly show that at the intersection of ethnicity and gender new meanings can emerge that differ from those of the two separate identities from which they derive.

The interplay between different identities that are affected by and affect each other can lead to new meanings, but it is also possible that one defines the other. One particular identity can dominate. For example, a person can describe himself as a Jewish doctor whereby he considers his professional identity primary and his Jewish background as describing what kind of doctor he is. Or, for an Indian lawyer, her Indian background can describe the type of lawyer that she is. But, of course, others do not have to recognize this and may predominantly consider him a Jew (or a doctor), and her as an Indian (or a lawyer). Furthermore, semantics make it difficult to know exactly what people mean when they use these kinds of self-descriptions. Some terms are easier to use as adjectives than others and therefore do not necessarily have to indicate a qualification of a particular identity. Terms like 'doctor Jew' or 'lawyer Indian' are not used in English, whereas an individual can in fact find his or her ethnic identity much more important than his or her professional one.

This problem of semantics can also make it difficult to know what hyphenated self-descriptions such as Turkish-German or Mexican-American actually refer to. The meaning of these descriptions can be quite different in North American and European countries, and also between European countries. Furthermore, there can be contextual differences. In Germany the ethnic term (Turk) is used to indicate what kind of a national (German) you are, but in Turkey the term German Turk is used to indicate the type of Turk that you are.

A concluding word

The example of 'suddenly being Jewish' shows the power of social identities. Discovering your true heritage means that you suddenly belong to a different social category with its baggage of cultural, religious, historical, and political meanings. This can have profound consequences for how you see yourself, for your loyalties and commitments, for your social relationships, your political views, your practices and behaviour. Social identities are social in origin, are socially defined and communicated, require social enactment and recognition, and serve various social functions. Although the psychological significance that they have for the people carrying them can be quite different and may be complicated and complex, in one way or another the relevance of these identities is bound to be great. Even if you have not been moulded by the identity expectations and behavioural patterns from an early age (which is usually the case), your thoughts, feelings, and behaviour are likely to be affected, and your freedom is restricted by the expectations of the social environment. And even if you do not derive your feelings of self-worth from your social identities (which again is usually the case), other people will make positive or negative judgements about you, whether you like it or not. But how, when, and why this happens and what the consequences are will depend on many things. You can be rejected or accepted in different situations and by various people for all kinds of reasons. And these experiences and events can affect the processes of exploration and commitment that are critical for the development of a mature inner sense of self and thereby for the importance you attach to a particular social identity and the ways in which you negotiate and try to combine different social identities. Your ethnic, national, or religious background needs to acquire a self-evident place in how you perceive yourself – a place together and in relation with other social identities, and with various individual characteristics, beliefs, and preferences. Only then is it a source of satisfaction and pride, of security and strength, and a confident basis for approaching others with an open, interested, and curious state of mind. But that does not have to mean that ethnic tensions and conflicts will not occur. Relationships between groups depend on the ways in which social identities are collectively defined and on the circumstances that elicit forms of 'us-or-them' thinking. Despite the important individual differences, there are many circumstances in which people think about themselves as 'we' Jews (or Muslims, natives, and so on), in contrast and sometimes in opposition to other ethnic or religious groups.

5   Blue and brown eyes

It is 1968, one day after the assassination of Martin Luther King. In the predominantly White town of Riceville, Iowa, Jane Elliott, a teacher, decides to make the children in her elementary-school class experience discrimination and racism. She comes up with a two-day exercise, which was later captured in the award-winning documentary *Eye of the Storm*. The documentary shows Elliot asking the class whether there is something that makes the children different from each other. One of the children suggests the colour of their eyes. Elliot adopts the idea and divides the class into children with blue eyes and children with brown eyes. For one day, the children with blue eyes are 'superior' and the children with brown eyes are 'inferior', and the next day it is the other way round. The 'superior' children are defined as being smarter and more honest, they get the best seats in the classroom, get a little more playtime, and at lunchtime are allowed to go for a second helping in the cafeteria. What happens next is well summarized by Elliot when she says, 'I watched what had been marvellous, cooperative, wonderful, thoughtful children turn into nasty, vicious, discriminating little third graders, within the space of 15 minutes.' The relationships in the classroom became determined by the meanings attached to eye colour. Children who had been friends suddenly found themselves on separate sides, or, as one student said: 'It seemed like Ms Elliott was taking our best friends away from us.' Children also made suggestions about enforcing the rules. One 'superior' child suggested that Elliot should inform the canteen staff about the rule that the 'inferior' children may not be given extra portions, and another child suggested that the teacher should keep her pointer on hand in case the 'inferior' children would be getting out of hand. During playtime, quarrels occurred when the 'superior' children started picking on others by calling them 'blue-eyed' (or 'brown-eyed'). During class, the answers given by the 'superior' children were interpreted in terms of intelligence and an ability to learn quickly, while the behaviour of the 'inferior' children was attributed to clumsiness and stupidity. The 'superior' children experienced the ease and pleasantness of being on top. They felt respected, valued, and strong and started acting in accordance to the position that they had. The 'inferior' children felt left out and unfairly treated and withdrew listlessly.

The classroom changed from a situation in which individual children interact with each other in various kinds of ways into a situation where two categories stand in opposition to each other. This is an example of what social psychologists call inter-group behaviour. People start to think, feel, and act in terms of the social category or group they belong to. From a situation where it involves 'you and I' it turns into a situation of 'us and them', with all its consequences.

But what exactly are these consequences? Elliot's exercise is regularly cited as an example of the inevitable tensions and conflicts that a group distinction would bring. The exercise is considered to demonstrate how easy it is to turn people against each other, simply by making two groups. But what is happening is more complicated and more interesting.

Teachers frequently make temporary distinctions between students for all kinds of functional reasons. In most cases, this has little impact on how children perceive themselves and others, and on the peer relations within the classroom. But there are also distinctions that go further and develop into real social identities. This happens when there is not only a categorical distinction to which normative expectations are linked, but the distinction is also used to characterize the nature of people. Elliot turns a physical feature (blue or brown eyes) into a separate category of people (the blue-eyed or brown-eyed). The children, in turn, use these nouns to explain the behaviour of fellow students ('she's a brown-eyed') and to insult ('stupid blue-eyed'). The insignificance of eye colour is transformed into a meaningful social identity. This way there is a great deal more at stake: what you are and represent, and what the other is and signifies. The children start to identify with the category that they belong to and distinguish themselves from the category to which they do not belong. The group identification makes the group distinction a personal matter. You feel respected and encouraged because you belong to a group that is in a privileged position, or you feel inferior and weak because your group is at the bottom of the social hierarchy.

Group identification has not only emotional meaning, but also normative implications. The group membership provides a shared perspective on social reality, and individual differences become less relevant than shared beliefs and expectations (see chapter 2). This means that the way in which a social identity is defined determines one's relation towards others. In her classroom, Elliot makes a specific distinction that is interpreted in a specific way. It is a distinction between 'superior' and 'inferior', coupled with expectations and rules for appropriate behaviour. The children start to behave in terms of how the situation is defined. And given the definition of the situation, their behaviour is reasonable. If there indeed are 'superior' and 'inferior' children, and being superior means that you have benefits and rights, it is almost logical that you behave in that way. But the specific interpretation that is given to the distinction implies that alternative interpretations are possible. The tensions and conflicts that arise in the classroom are not the inevitable consequences of creating a group distinction. Instead of 'superior' and 'inferior', Elliot could also have made a distinction in terms of 'being different' and 'being complementary'. If she wanted to teach the children something about cooperation and the positive aspects of diversity, such a classification would be appropriate. And the consequences for the relationships within the class would be dramatically different. But in the case of 'superior' and 'inferior', the situation can also still develop in various directions. 'Superior' can also mean that you are expected to help the 'inferior' children as much as possible and to be concerned about their ups and downs. Group norms can be pro-social, and Elliot could have introduced such a norm rather than define the group distinction in terms of unequal rights. Again, the consequences would have been different from those seen in the documentary. The 'superior' children can still feel valued and encouraged, but in this case because they belong to a group that does the morally right thing and helps others. The 'inferior' children will feel accepted and cared for.

The way in which the group distinction is defined determines how the children perceive themselves and others. Elliot uses eye colour, and because there are no social meanings associated with it, the distinction can be shaped in many different ways. In daily life historical, cultural and structural conditions limit the scope for giving variable meanings to social identities. Yet there is always leeway, as is illustrated in the many discussions concerning the meaning of ethnic and national identities. Often there are lively debates about the correct interpretation of particular identities. But the fact that there is some leeway does not imply that social identities are complete fabrications. They often refer to imagined communities but are not imaginary (Anderson, 1983; Vermeulen & Govers, 1997). Social identities are powerful because they are embedded in traditions, practices, and institutions, and because they regulate social reality in a meaningful and socially accepted way. Group memberships appear to say something about the nature of individuals: we are like this, and they are like that.

The identity meanings, however, should be made plausible or factual. For this, daily experiences, opinion makers, and authorities that propose and impose specific definitions and interpretations play an important role. In Elliot's classroom she is the authority, but her definition of the situation is not simply accepted by the children. At the beginning of the experiment, the children hardly identify with the meaningless groups of blue-eyed and brown-eyed. They are therefore extra sensitive to information that 'proves' that one group is actually better than the other group. Only when that information is convincing will their behaviour adapt to the definition of the situation. In the documentary it is shown that Elliot does quite a bit of work to make the distinction between blue eyes and brown eyes factual. At first, some children appear hesitant and resistant towards her statement that blue-eyed people are better than brown-eyed people. Therefore, she tries to present her definition as plausible – for example, by referring to the eye colour of George Washington and by presenting evidence from everyday life. In doing so, she stresses several times that it is indeed a fact that blue-eyed people are better than brown-eyed people. This provides the social identities the required reality, so that it becomes more than a game.

At summer camp

Social psychologists have also studied intergroup behaviour among children. One of the most famous studies is by Muzafer Sherif. He wanted to show that phenomena such as prejudice and discrimination must be understood at the level of relations between groups, and especially in terms of group interests. Together with his colleagues, he conducted the now famous 'summer camp studies' (Sherif *et al.*, 1961). A group of 12-year-old boys spent their summer holiday in a boys' camp. All the boys came from stable and relatively prosperous families and did not know each other beforehand. There were several stages in these field experiments. In the first stage, the children were divided into two groups. In two experiments, this took place after a few days of being at summer camp, and budding friendships were split up by placing friends into separate groups. In a third experiment, the boys were divided into two groups straight from the start – and the two groups camped in separate places and had their own activities.

In the second stage, the groups were brought together in competitive situations, such as tug-of-war and softball. The games could only be won by one group, and the winners received a prize whereas the losers received nothing. This stage brought a tremendous change in the behaviour of the boys. So far, they had mostly been indifferent to each other, but now two opposing parties emerged that were continuously measuring powers and calling each other names and even physically attacking each other. Friendships were almost exclusively developed within one's own group, and friends from the first stage who were placed into the opposing group were rejected just as strongly as other boys from that group.

In the third stage of the experiment, the two groups were confronted with tasks that could only be solved by joining forces. The idea was that the relationship between the groups would improve if the interests of both groups coincided and they were mutually dependent. This proved to be the case. The groups worked together on the common goals, and gradually the hostility reduced.

The results of these field experiments were later to a large extent confirmed in laboratory situations. They show again the significance of group memberships for human behaviour. As soon as people perceive themselves and others in terms of their group, a psychological shift occurs from 'I' to 'we'. The way in which 'we' is characterized influences the actions of the different group members. The result is increased uniformity in behaviour within the group and a distinction from the other group. Yet how this distinction takes form depends once again on how the intergroup situation is presented and interpreted. In a situation of competition people behave competitively, and in a situation of mutual dependence people seek contact and cooperation. The reactions are fairly predictable and show that differences and conflicts are not inevitable but do occur if there are conflicts of interest and especially if these are seen in zero-sum terms.

The evidence that many group differences and conflicts stem from conflicts over interests is overwhelming. But in some of Sherif's experiments it appeared that already in the first stage the own group was compared positively with the other one, and some boys spontaneously suggested challenging the other group. This indicates that opposing interests are a sufficient, but not a necessary condition for group opposition.

This has been further demonstrated and developed by Henri Tajfel, the founder of social identity theory. His personal life contributed greatly to his interest in groups and group identity. As a Polish Jew, in the 1930s, in order to be able to study at a university, he was obliged to leave his homeland. He went to France and began studying chemistry. At the start of World War II he served in the French army. He was captured, and from 1940 to 1945 he was imprisoned in German prison camps without his Jewish background coming to light. When he was released in 1945 and returned to France, virtually his entire family had been murdered. In the post-war years he worked in organizations that were concerned with the rehabilitation of war victims. He became increasingly interested in psychology and studied in Paris, Brussels, and London. From 1954 on he worked at several British universities, and particularly at Bristol, where, together with students and colleagues, he developed his ideas about social identity and intergroup relations.

Minimal groups

In a series of classic experiments, Tajfel and his colleagues examined whether simply belonging to an artificial group is sufficient to make you favour that group.[1] To this end he developed the so-called 'minimal group paradigm'. Individual participants – in the beginning this was English schoolboys – were divided into two groups based on fairly meaningless criteria such as estimating the number of dots on a projection screen or the preference for an abstract painting by Klee or Kandinsky. The participants had no contact with each other and only knew which of the two groups they belonged to. They then received a booklet containing a number of matrices. Using these matrices, they had to distribute points between two other unknown participants who were only identified by a number and their group membership, such as Klee number 4 and Kandinsky number 11. The participants were told that the points awarded would later be converted into money and be given to the others. It was in no way possible to award points to oneself individually. The results were surprising. The participants did not award an excessive number of points to either one of the two groups, but tried to be somewhat fair. Yet there also was a clear tendency to favour members of one's own group, not so much in absolute terms but, rather, in a relative way. The distribution behaviour was not geared towards the most rational strategy – namely, to maximize the returns of one's own group. The schoolboys were prepared to put up with a lower absolute profit if this meant that the *difference* between their own group and the other one was larger. This strategy of 'maximum differentiation' is a recurrent finding in the numerous experiments that have been conducted since then. The results have been confirmed in various age groups, in different countries and cultures, and with measurements other than the distribution of points.

Social identity theory

A surprising finding requires an explanation, which was gradually developed. Initially Tajfel suggested that a norm of competition was in play. It was also suggested that the findings were due to instrumental behaviour and group interdependence. Participants were said to assume that other members of their own group would also favour them, and members of the other group would disadvantage them. Another explanation was that the nature of the experimental manipulation – e.g., preference for a painting – suggests that one's own attitudes and feelings are shared with the group to which you belong (the *in-group*) and not with the other group (the *out-group*). This assumed similarity would be a reason to favour the in-group. Further research, in which participants were classified into groups by chance (flipping a coin), showed that this was not the case. Also in that situation it turned out that a strategy of 'maximum differentiation' was adopted.

Eventually, social identity theory was developed, and it provided a plausible explanation (Tajfel & Turner, 1979). People are not only unique individuals, but they also belong to many categories and groups. In all kinds of situations, they think of themselves in terms of those group memberships. The theory further suggests that people have a strong desire and need for a positive self-image. And because part of their self-image consists of group memberships, they have a tendency to understand their in-group in a positive way.

A positive in-group understanding can be achieved by making a favourable comparison with relevant out-groups. Belonging to a group that is better than another one gives a positive feeling, just as it is frustrating or painful when your in-group is worse off. When the national soccer team wins, it feels as if 'we' have won, and this makes you happy and proud. But when the team loses, you feel down and you tend to distance yourself from the team by arguing that 'they' have lost.

The minimal group experiments were deliberately designed so that all kinds of circumstances that may affect the task of allocating points had no influence. The participants only knew that there are two groups and that they themselves belong to one of them. That is the only information they could use to interpret the situation. In this anonymous and 'stripped' context, the group membership is the salient social identity. The only way to derive a positive feeling is by slightly favouring your in-group over the other one, There are no personal gains, and the comparison takes place at the level of groups.

The experiment is again an example of what social psychologists mean by intergroup behaviour. Their focus is on the psychological or subjective dimension: on what happens when people understand themselves as a member of a group and perceive the world in terms of their group membership. The capacity to think in terms of 'we' is the critical psychological foundation. This means that intergroup behaviour can also exist when you are alone in a room filling in a questionnaire or when you watch television in the evening or read a newspaper. What matters is that you assess the situation in terms of the group membership that is psychologically meaningful at that moment. The subjective side of intergroup behaviour and the mental processes involved are central. The importance of this lies in the psychological transformation that is at stake: from I to we (Turner & Reynolds, 2001).

Or, rather, maximum groups?

Social identity theory has had great influence on research on intergroup behaviour, not only in social psychology but also within political science, sociology, and anthropology. Researchers use the theory to explain phenomena such as ethnic conflicts, hostilities, and religious fundamentalism (e.g., Herriot, 2007; Horowitz, 2000). But, as so often, this popularity goes together with one-sided and selective interpretations of what the theory actually claims. For example, it is often assumed that according to the theory, ethnocentrism and prejudice are inevitable consequences of group distinctions, and that a stronger identification with one's in-group always involves a more negative evaluation of out-groups. Making distinctions would be virtually the same thing as formulating contradistinctions and evoking conflicts. But what exactly do these experiments show, and what precisely does the theory argue?

Stephen Reicher (2004) has claimed that it is possible to argue that maximum rather than minimal groups are formed in the experiments. Participants can, after all, only go by the categorization offered. There is simply no other information available, making the classification all-determining. Moreover, there is only one dimension of comparison: the distribution of points. But in daily life such a situation rarely exists, as there are almost always multiple categories and multiple dimensions of comparison. People make distinctions not only based on ethnicity, but also on grounds of religion, lifestyle, and nationality, for example. These classifications can complement, reinforce, or contradict each other and make the situation more complicated than in the case of a simple dichotomy. The important question is, when exactly or under which circumstances people judge and perceive themselves and others in terms of ethnicity, religion, or culture, and identify more or less strongly with these groups.

There are always several dimensions on which groups can be compared. Not all of these dimensions will be used to positively distinguish the in-group. This tends to occur on dimensions that are viewed as self-defining, and – as explained in chapter 3 – the self-defining dimensions do not need to be the same in comparison to different groups. There may be a situation of consensus rather than of opposition. Groups can agree on the characteristics on which they themselves are better and those on which other groups score higher: 'they' are more efficient but 'we' are more social. Many studies show that this is indeed often the case (e.g., Mummendey & Schreiber, 1983; Yzerbyt *et al.*, 2005).

Yet consensus is not always easy – for example, if different groups perceive the same features and dimensions as self-defining. A distinction is often made between the stereotypical dimensions of competence, warmth, and morality (Leach *et al.*, 2007). In general, morality appears to be the most important one when it comes to assessing one's in-group. The fact that 'we' may be less competent and less friendly is one thing, but it is quite another thing to accept that we may be less reliable, honest, and sincere. Cross-cultural research has shown that almost universally, moral traits are more strongly attributed to one's in-group than to out-groups. Other groups are sometimes seen as more efficient or friendly, but not as more reliable and honest. And if people identify very strongly with their in-group, they are also more inclined to attribute all kinds of moral qualities to their group. This applies not only to religious groups, but also to ethnic and national communities. For most people it is very important to see themselves as decent and moral. They want to live with a clear conscience and according to the moral norms and values for how others should be treated. If your group is responsible for all kinds of immoral acts and behaviours, this will also affect you. And that is very unpleasant.

In the minimal group experiments, the content of the two categories is unknown. Their characteristics and what they stand for remains unclear. There is no substantive information that participants can use to base the allocation of points on. Considerations of historical, cultural, and societal nature that are used in daily life to make distinctions and assign meanings are not available. But group norms and behavioural expectations are very important to take into account when trying to understand what happens. As noted in the example of Jane Elliot, group norms can also dictate pro-social behaviour. With self-defining pro-social norms, the tendency to place one's in-group in a positive light leads to showing that 'we' are kinder and more helpful than 'them'. Helping out-group members is a means of feeling good about yourself and can adjust negative images that others might have about your in-group (Hopkins *et al.*, 2007). Standing up for minorities and newcomers can serve to counterbalance the idea that your country is becoming an increasingly closed and inhospitable society. So, the search for positive group differentiation does not necessarily translate into exclusion or discrimination. A group norm can require cooperation and may put equality rather than self-interests in first place. As a result, people will have more positive attitudes towards others. For instance, in an experimental study, Tarrant and colleagues (2009) found that when an in-group norm of empathy for outsiders is salient, people report more positive out-group attitudes than when an in-group norm of detachment towards outsiders is highlighted.

The minimum group experiments convincingly demonstrate that solely making a group distinction is sufficient to elicit the tendency to make positive group differentiations. This is the underlying psychological dynamic. But how that translates into actual behaviour depends on many factors. Tajfel saw the experiments as a starting point, not as an end point. He was interested in how psychological processes take shape and develop in a social world filled with ideological, cultural, and structural characteristics. On the basis of the general need for a positive social identity, one cannot make behavioural interpretations and predictions. The psychological dynamic tells us *why* people seek positive group differentiation, but it does not tell us anything about *where and when* that happens, nor *how* such a distinction is made (Rubin & Hewstone, 2004). This is not difficult to understand when you compare it with eating behaviour. The fact that people need to eat and therefore will seek food is universal. But where, when, what, and how people eat is cultural and group-specific, and also tends to differ somewhat between individuals. Thus, from the fact that people need food, one cannot simply predict their actual eating behaviour. For this, all kinds of factors need to be taken into account.

Making distinctions

Social identity theory emphasizes the human need for a distinctive and positive social identity. People not only differ from each other as individuals, they also belong to all kinds of groups. Psychologically, these group memberships are just as important and play a substantial role in how you perceive and evaluate yourself. Research has provided numerous indications that people spontaneously and unconsciously have all kinds of positive connotations with their own group or community. Evolutionary psychologists explain this by arguing that humans have always depended on each other to survive. You share your genes with a small group of relatives, and therefore there is a preference to trust and help your relatives. Cooperation with those who partly share your genes contributes to the spreading of these genes. And that is what evolution is all about. Furthermore, on the basis of characteristics that signal or mark genetic relatedness (such as skin colour and facial features, but also language and appearance), the preference for your kin is extended to larger groups. Van den Berghe (1981, p. 43) states in this regard, 'Ethnic and racial sentiments are extensions of kinship sentiments.... There exists a general behavioural predisposition, in our species as in many others, to react favourably towards other organisms related to the actor. The closer the relationship is, the stronger the preferential behavior.'

In explaining behaviour, references to our evolutionary past are increasingly popular. But these so-called ultimate explanations say nothing about how that past is neurologically represented in the brain, and also nothing about the collective and individual meanings that always exist. These are different levels of explanation, which should not be mixed or confused. The fact that there is an evolutionary necessity to eat does not tell us anything about the related physiological processes, the different cultural and individuals meanings that food can have, or the actual eating behaviour. Another example is the tendency to be primarily involved in one's own community. This may be because humans find different forms of emotional support within their community. That is what they experience and what provides an explanation. Subsequently you might ask why emotional support is so satisfying and important to people. The answer is that this is just the way in which human beings are neurologically wired: they have a basic need to belong. The emotional support of others is pleasant because it goes together with chemical processes in our brains. Finally, there is the question of why the human species is biologically put together in that way, with the ultimate explanation of evolutionary benefits. The different levels of explanation show that the preference for one's own community cannot simply be attributed to our evolutionary past. The biological origin and neurological grammar of our feelings and emotions are important but say little about the variation in meanings and behaviours that always exist. The actual orientation to, and bonding with, one's community is also the result of cultural meanings and long-term associative learning (Buller, 2009; Confer *et al.*, 2010). Evolutionary and neurological accounts do not have the last word because they do not provide a detailed and nuanced understanding of actual human behaviour. There is always a social and cultural context that shapes people's thoughts and feelings. But this does not, of course, mean that brain images and other neural signatures are not informative. They certainly are, especially when they converge with more traditional indicators and measures and thereby cross-validate theoretical ideas (Fiske, 2012).

In any case, it is clear that there often exists a self-evident orientation towards one's own community. One example is a study in which it was investigated how people unconsciously react to words such as 'us' and 'them' (Perdue *et al.*, 1990). Within 55 milliseconds, these words were followed by terms that referred to either positive or negative traits. Compared with the negative traits, the positive ones were more quickly attributed to one's in-group. For the out-group there was no difference in the attribution of positive and negative traits. Other research shows that men are faster to classify the word 'he', while women are faster in classifying the word 'she' (Brewer & Brown, 1998). The unconscious mental activity is mainly due to the positive associations with one's in-group rather than negative associations with other groups. Various studies show that positive features and characteristics are unconsciously associated with the in-group. People respond more quickly to the combination of 'we–good' than the combination of 'we–bad'. The basic association seems to be '*what is known, is good*' rather than 'what is unknown, is bad'. The latter does occur, but is the result of circumstances that are not intrinsic to group classifications.

There is also neurobiological evidence for this interpretation. One study showed that different parts of the brain are active when people think about their in-group compared to an out-group (Van Bavel *et al.*, 2008). Another study showed that there are similar brain activation patterns when feeling sad as when observing in-group members feeling sad. In contrast, these same activation patterns were not observed for out-group members, and the less so the more prejudiced people were (Gutsell & Inzlicht, 2012). Further research showed that the neuropeptide oxytocin promotes trust and cooperation among individuals who belong to the same group (De Dreu *et al.*, 2011). This tendency to empathize and focus on the in-group does not mean, however, that the out-group is stigmatized or derogated. This only happens when the out-group is perceived as threatening the interests of the in-group. So oxytocin seems to lead to in-group favouritism rather than out-group derogation.

The numerous minimal group experiments typically yield a relative preference for one's in-group, and not a strong negative reaction to or rejection of others. There is a difference between intergroup differentiation based on in-group orientation or out-group rejection. In both cases there is a distinction in favour of the in-group, but the underlying dynamics differ. A preference for one's own group is not the same as an aversion to others. The fact that I prefer my own family and may think that we are nicer than other families does not mean that I dislike, reject, or even hate other families. And a negative reaction towards an out-group can be due to a variety of reasons: reasons of ignorance and a lack of contact differ from prejudice and racism. In the first case, there are various options for improving group relations such as getting to know each other, while in the second case more is required.

An unconscious preference and connection with one's own 'family' does not mean that other 'families' are rejected or devalued. The probability of rejection may be higher due to the lack of a genetic relationship or an in-group socialization process, but it is not self-evident. However, these unconscious positive associations with the in-group are not without implications. The tendency to choose for in-group members can have implications in daily life, especially when it comes to social interactions and the distribution of opportunities and positions. The principle of 'like attracts like' implies that in-group members are more likely to be helped in uncertain and ambiguous situations, more likely to be given the benefit of the doubt, less likely to be held responsible for things that go wrong, more likely to be given sympathy and to be trusted. In short, there are many subtle forms of distinction in favour of in-group members that can have an influence on the decisions that people make, for example, about relationships, friendships, and hiring and engaging people. Although one may be quite positive towards outsiders, the spontaneous tendency to favour in-group members can in practice mean unequal chances for out-group members.

Tensions and conflicts

The spontaneous orientation towards the in-group does not require a specific contrasting 'other'. With their reference to origin and ancestry, ethnic groups emphasize the historical continuity and similarity within their group. In principle, the focus is on what is passed-on and shared, and all that is required is an unspecified and undifferentiated reference to those who do not belong. It does not have to be a situation of 'us and them' but can be one of 'us and not-us'. The meanings attached to one's ethnic group are determined by internal standards and historical comparisons.

But there are many situations where dichotomies such as 'us and them' and also 'us *or* them' are involved. Group differences can develop into tensions and conflicts. Whether this happens and how it evolves depends on many political, economic, and historical factors. Social psychologists have been particularly concerned with the processes, causes, and correlates of prejudice, racism, and discrimination. Why is it that in some situations some groups are derogated and negatively treated, while in other situations and in relation to other groups this is hardly the case? Posing the question in this way means that individual differences are ignored: why is it that in the same situation some people are prejudiced while others are not? There is much research into individual differences in, for example, the dogmatism, conformism, authoritarianism, and social dominance orientation that underlie prejudice and discrimination (see Brown, 2010: Son Hing & Zanna, 2010). This research is important, especially to gain insight into the extremes of the uncompromising racist and the unconditional anti-racist. It is also important for understanding why under poor economic or threatening conditions some individuals are inclined to blame immigrants and others do not (e.g., Quillian, 1996), or why some individuals more than others tend to endorse diversity statements of political leaders (Sniderman & Hagendoorn, 2007).

But these studies do not explain why there are often important situational differences in the degree of prejudice and racism, why there tends to be broad social consensus on negative stereotypes, and why relatively rapid changes can take place in the extent of prejudice and discrimination. For this we must consider factors and conditions that have to do with intergroup relations. For example, whether people react negatively to minorities and immigrants will depend on the way in which the national identity and national interests are defined, and the extent to which newcomers are seen as threatening or, conversely, making a contribution to society. Similar reasoning can be applied to negative judgements that minority groups have of each other, or the dismissive attitude that they may have against the majority group and the host society. The majority, or other minorities, can be viewed as threats to one's cultural or religious minority identity, for example. Whether groups are perceived as threatening depends on the way in which they are understood but also on the understanding of one's own group. Stereotypes, prejudices, and discrimination have not only to do with how we see 'them' and the impact that 'they' have on 'us' but, importantly, also with how 'we' understand ourselves.

Perceiving groups

People attribute different characteristics and properties to different groups. Some groups appear more like real groups in which members are very similar, and in other groups the members seem to differ strongly from each other. The characteristics attributed to a group have implications for the extent to which people identify with it and how they respond to others. Three aspects are important here: the perception of differences, of entity, and of an underlying essence.

Group differences

Differences between people – such as in skin colour, age, and in attitudes and opinions – are more often continuous or gradual rather than dichotomous or absolute. Nevertheless, dichotomies are never far away. Think of the opposing categories 'foreign/indigenous', 'established/outsider' or 'friend/enemy'. It is tempting to think in dichotomies, and this has consequences.

Suppose you are shown eight vertical lines, and you are asked to estimate the length of each one. The eight lines differ by about one centimetre each time. This is a relatively simple task, and your estimates will probably be fairly accurate. But what happens when additional information is given by indicating a letter A or B? Above the four shortest lines, there is a letter A, and above the other four the letter B. This additional information has a striking effect. You will probably estimate the difference between the longest line A and the shortest line B to be larger (about 2 centimetres). There is also a tendency to estimate the differences among the four A lines to be smaller than they are, just as the differences among the four B lines. This simple experiment by Tajfel and Wilkes (1963) has been extended and repeated by other researchers, yielding similar results. The categorization of information leads to category differentiation: the perceived differences *between* categories are exaggerated, while the differences *within* categories are reduced. Introducing a categorization has a biasing effect on perception. This is also true for social perception.

A group of primary school children were given a list of 24 characteristics that they were asked to attribute to unknown peers, depicted in six photographs (Doise *et al.*, 1978). One group of children was told beforehand that the first three photographs would be of boys and the last three of girls: a gender distinction was introduced. The other children were not given this information in advance and just started with the assessment of the boys. The results showed a striking difference between the two groups of children. Compared to the second group, the first one used more gender-specific characteristics: more male-specific features for boys and more female features for girls. The distinction between the sexes was emphasized. Simultaneously, the same characteristics were used to describe the boys (or girls). The perceived differences within the sexes were reduced.

General cognitive processes play a role when it comes to perceiving differences and similarities between categories. Categorization is associated with differentiation and thereby forms the basis for stereotyping. But that does not mean that stereotyping is inevitable and that the content of stereotypes is fixed. The tendency to make cognitive differentiations plays a role, but always together with numerous social and cultural factors. Furthermore, also on a purely cognitive level the situation quickly gets more complicated because a simple dichotomy often does not suffice to get an accurate picture of what is going on. When spontaneously assessing situations, one will quickly consider multiple dimensions, making the process of cognitive differentiation more complex.

Research on the development of prejudice shows that children as young as six years have negative implicit (unconscious) attitudes towards ethnic out-groups and that these attitudes do not change much during adolescence (e.g., Baron & Banaji, 2006; Rutland *et al.*, 2005). Degner and Wentura (2010) point out, however, that in this research children are forced to categorize peers into only two different ethnicities.[2] In contrast, in their own research they assessed children's implicit prejudice with a task that examined children's spontaneous categorization processes. Using this task, they found that implicit prejudice was absent until the age of 12 to 13, and thereafter increased gradually. In other words, their research indicates that for younger children the category of ethnicity was not spontaneously activated and used in evaluating peers.

In one of our own studies, we presented a group of Dutch and immigrant children (10–12 years) with eight photographs of unfamiliar peers (Verkuyten *et al.*, 1995). The pictures differed by gender, skin colour, and facial expression (smiling or looking serious). First, the children were asked to categorize the pictures in as many ways as they wanted to: 70% made four pairs, 10% made a three-way division, and only 18% made a split into two groups. So the vast majority of children did not make a simple division into two, but made use of different features simultaneously. Moreover, there was little agreement among the children on the features that were used: the pairs formed by the children differed significantly.

Something else was found in this study – namely that the Dutch children saw fewer differences between the coloured peers than among the native peers. There was a tendency to think, 'they all look alike, while we differ from one other'. However, this was not the case among the coloured immigrant children. As far as they were concerned, it seemed, rather, to be a case of 'we are all alike, and they are different'. This result is not an isolated finding and shows the importance of group positions (see Mullen & Hu, 1989; Simon & Brown, 1987). A major difference between social categorization and the categorization of non-social information, such as the length of lines, is that the perceiver him- or herself belongs to one of the categories. The results of our research, as well as those of others, show that although out-group homogeneity ('they are alike and we are different') happens frequently, it is not an inevitable consequence of cognitive differentiation. In-group homogeneity ('we are alike and they are very different') is also possible, just like both groups being seen as equally homogeneous. The latter occurs, for example when an explicit comparison is made in terms of typical characteristics of one group and typical characteristics of the other group (Simon, 1992). Men generalize the characteristics attributed to women, and women accentuate the similarities between men. Such findings are important because they indicate that the perceived difference not only depends on the fact that you are more familiar with your in-group than the out-group, or that one group is numerically smaller and is therefore seen as less diverse.

The perception of in-group homogeneity occurs particularly at the level of those characteristics and dimensions that give meaning to one's own identity. 'We' are generally more tolerant than 'them', because tolerance is what characterizes 'us' Dutch. Or 'we' are generally more hospitable, because hospitality is something that is part of being Turkish. Perceiving the in-group as relatively homogeneous at the level of group defining features contributes to a positively distinctive identity. But this does not explain the fact that ethnic minorities tend to show stronger in-group homogeneity. Research shows that this is related to their numerical size and social status (see Simon, 2004). Members of a group that is numerically or socially in a minority position, will more likely feel that the group's distinctiveness is under pressure or being threatened by the majority. Experiencing the in-group as relatively homogeneous is one way of closing the ranks psychologically, which helps to protect the cohesion and integrity of the in-group.

Entity

Not every collection of people is perceived as a group, and some are considered more 'group-like' than others. Why is this the case, or what do people base their perception on? Donald Campbell (1958) asked this question in a classic article. He used the term 'entitativity' to indicate the extent to which a collection of people has the character of an entity: being thing-like or a real existing phenomenon.

Some groups form clear and cohesive units, while others are more like social categories and consist of a collection of rather separate, independent individuals. According to Campbell, the perception of entitativity mainly depends on the proximity of the group members, their similarity and shared destiny. When people live close together, behave in a similar manner and are all immigrants, they will easily be perceived as a real group. Other researchers have added further criteria such as social interactions, shared goals and group size (see Hamilton, 2007). In any case, it is clear that groups differ in the extent to which they are considered a real group.

In a national representative study among more than 2,000 native Dutch, almost 80% agreed that Turkish immigrants – and Moroccan immigrants – share the same values and form a coherent and well-organized group.[3] Such group perceptions are important, because they have an impact on the way in which information is processed. If an ethnic group is seen as a cohesive unit, people will more rapidly make use of stereotypes, behaviours and events will be more easily attributed to personality traits and less to circumstances, and group members will more quickly be held accountable for the deviant behaviour of other group members. Because ethnic minorities are typically perceived more as a real group than the native majority, they more often face stereotyping, personal accusations, and are held more often accountable for the negative behaviour of co-ethnics, such as adolescent boys causing trouble. In the Dutch national study it turned out that a stronger perception of immigrants forming an entitative group was associated with seeing them as less honest and law-abiding, and as more selfish, intrusive, violent, and politically untrustworthy.

Groups not only differ in their degree of similarity and interdependence, but also have different (political) goals and means. Some groups are better organized than others, and some groups can be perceived as having their own agenda that they might be able to realize. Thus it has been claimed that Muslims are aiming to Islamize European societies and turn them into Eurabia. The following quote[4] is from Pim Fortuyn, the popular right-wing Dutch politician who was assassinated in 2002, a few days before the national election. In the election his party 'List Pim Fortuyn' won no less than 26 of the 150 seats in parliament and subsequently became part of the coalition government.

> We are running out of time. Not just in the Netherlands, but in Europe. Is that what you want? I stand for this country that has been built in five or six centuries. What we are facing really is a fifth, I'll just be frank now, a fifth column! Of people that want to destroy our country. I will not tolerate that! I say: you can stay here but you will adapt. They'll tell me: Allah is great and you are a Christian pig.

Muslims are presented as a fifth column, an enemy behind our defence lines, with transnational contacts and foreign aid providing them with the means to set up the necessary organization and coordination for achieving their goal of an Islamic Europe – a fifth column under the influence of Riad, Ankara, or Rabat, with

Internet and satellite dishes as their ears attached to the facades of the houses. These fifth column beliefs have not gone away since 2002. In a national survey in 2012 we found that no less than 50% of the native Dutch agreed that Muslims are politically untrustworthy because they are more loyal to their country of origin than to Dutch society, and would want to turn the Netherlands into an Islamic country if given the chance (Hindriks *et al.*, 2013a).

These kinds of beliefs about immigrants and minority groups do not contribute to mutual trust and acceptance. On the contrary, the more minorities are seen as a real group, the more likely they are to be perceived as a threat to social cohesion and national identity. This makes it easier to argue that in order to face up to that threat, under no circumstances should there be policies that support cultural diversity and minority rights.[5] Among the native Dutch there was a significant negative relationship between supporting minority rights and the perceived entitativity of ethnic minorities. The more Turks, Moroccans, and Surinamese were perceived as real groups, the less such rights were favoured.

Essentialism

Groups differ not only in their 'thing-like' character, but they can also be seen as having an underlying essence that makes them inherently different. Psychological essentialism refers to the idea that groups are natural or inherently different kinds. Research shows that people distinguish between 'natural types' and 'artificial categories'. In contrast to the latter, which are manufactured (such as different types of cars, houses and lamps), natural types are categories that are discovered and have something deep down inside that distinguishes them, such as men differing from women, and homosexuals from heterosexuals. The visible differences and similarities are the surface features that are determined by the true nature or inherent structure that makes members of a category similar and inherently different from members of other categories. Biological racism is a clear example of this. Differences in skin colour are treated as more than 'skin-deep' because they would represent genetic differences that supposedly determine people's psychological make-up and behaviour.

In biological racism out-groups are not seen as inherently different but also as inferior and less human. Dehumanization refers to the process in which humanness is attributed more to the in-group than an out-group. In violent conflicts or situations of oppression (e.g., colonialism, slavery) this is evident in, for example, Jews being called 'rats' by the Nazis, the Tutsis being called 'cockroaches' around the time of the Rwanda genocide, and Blacks being called apes. A recent study showed that these metaphorical depictions can survive for a long time (Goff *et al.*, 2008). It was found that White Americans tend to associate Blacks more with ape images than with other wild animals, and that these images were more frequently used when describing Black compared to White criminals convicted for capital crimes. This research indicates that dehumanization can be quite common and is not limited to situations of violence, cruelty, and strong oppression. There is clear research evidence for this in studies with different groups, in different contexts and nations, and even among children (see Vaes *et al.*, 2012). For example, people believe that emotions such as hope, regret, and remorse are more typical of their in-group than the out-group. These emotions are a key aspect of what it means to be human, and therefore this bias attributes humanness more to the in-group than the out-group. Furthermore, research has shown that people tend to rate stereotypical traits of their in-group as more human than when the same traits are considered typical of an out-group.

Not only the concept of race but also that of ethnicity easily triggers essentialist beliefs (Gil-White, 2001). Ethnic nationalism, for example, considers national belonging to be something immutable that goes beyond local circumstances. It is seen as a kind of eternal natural thing – 'in the blood' – that comes down to a quasi-biological bond. The most profound and inexpressible ties would be with your ethnic group into which you are born and not, for example, with the country you migrate to and choose to live in. Blood is thicker than water, and you are and will always remain Turkish, Moroccan, Algerian, Iraqi, German, or Dutch.

Psychological essentialism implies the tendency to make all kinds of assumptions and to draw conclusions about the members of a natural category. The deep-rooted correspondence makes the category very 'informative'. The ethnic reference to origin and ancestry allows people to explain complex behaviours with a simple statement, 'Well, what do you expect, it is a Mexican (or Kurd, Moroccan, and so on)'. It also implies that you cannot forget your underlying nature. This makes it impossible to belong to another essentialized group: once a Moroccan, always a Moroccan.

These ideas are reflected in modern forms of cultural determinism. As discussed in chapter 1, ethnicity is often and self-evidently equated with culture. Different ethnic groups are considered to have different cultural characteristics, and culture deficits are thought to explain all kinds of phenomena, ranging from poor educational performance to criminality of ethnic minority groups: it 'simply is their culture' or 'that's simply part of their culture'. Cultural essentialism emphasizes the impossibility of forgetting your culture because culture determines who you are. You cannot deny your 'roots', as it were, unless you deny yourself and ignore who you are. A reference to culture says something quite stable about people and is therefore an important locus for interpretation. Culture is a concept with a large inductive potential. If we perceive someone as being from another culture, then we expect him or her to differ from us in a number of fundamental ways. This is quickly linked with the belief that cultural differences are rather clear-cut and incompatible. Cultures are set in opposition to each other and presented as unchangeable and as determining thoughts, emotions, and actions. However, this says nothing yet about how such an essentialized representation turns out in daily life.

A reference to profound and inherent cultural differences is typical of a cultural racist discourse in which immigrants and minorities are defined as subordinate, backward, or inferior, and one's own culture as needing protection. Through this, others are portrayed as unwanted and excluded, and initiatives to preserve one's cultural purity are legitimized. But a cultural essentialist discourse can also be found among minority groups and proponents of diversity and a multicultural society. They can emphasize the importance and meaning of genuine cultural differences and the need to recognize these differences. For example, some African Americans have suggested that due to deep cultural differences, Black and White children should receive racially segregated education. They argue that African Americans have their own style of learning in which verbal interaction and cooperation are especially important.

Furthermore, essentialist interpretations of one's own culture are employed by ethnic activists and leaders to legitimize their group claims (Verkuyten, 2003). A focus on internal (subcultural) differences and on processes of cultural mixing and change is not very useful for claiming the right to a cultural identity and the recognition of cultural group differences. Rather, multicultural approaches tend to equate ethnicity with culture and emphasize authentic cultural differences that should be recognized and respected. Ideas about the importance of cultural identity and minority rights are more relevant when groups are perceived in essentialist terms. Hence, for ethnic minority groups, higher in-group essentialism can be expected to go together with stronger endorsement of multiculturalism. In contrast, for the majority group, the perception of essentialist minority groups is more threatening. This perception may easily lead to a pattern of cultural racism in which different cultures are assumed to be incompatible and their existence as inherently problematic, leading to the rejection of multiculturalism. In a study among native majority and ethnic minority adolescents we found clear evidence for this reasoning (Verkuyten & Brug, 2004). When ethnic minority groups were perceived more in essentialist terms, the native Dutch participants were less in favour of multiculturalism. In contrast, for the minority group participants, ethnic minority essentialism was positively related to multiculturalism (see also Bastian & Haslam, 2008).

Cultural essentialism is an important political tool for ethnic minority groups (Hodgson, 2002; Morin & Saladin d'Anglure, 1997). It can be used by them to argue for multiculturalism and for challenging assimilationist ideas. For this, a discourse not only about in-group essentialism but also about majority essentialism can be useful. For example, an ethnic understanding of the majority group with the related cultural essentialism is useful for justifying exclusion of immigrants, but less so for arguing for assimilation (Verkuyten, 2003). For assimilation to be a realistic demand and a feasible option, a more open notion of belonging is needed in which ancestry is not a criterion and culture does not determine people's being completely. This also means, however, that immigrants and minority groups may dismiss the possibility of assimilation by defining the host community in ethnic and cultural essentialist terms. Thus, 'essentializing the other' is not only useful for majority groups to exclude immigrants and minorities, but also for minority groups to argue against the demand for assimilation (see Yildiz & Verkuyten, 2012).

But these essentialist beliefs also make it more difficult to define yourself as a member of several communities at the same time. It is not easy to understand yourself as Turkish Dutch if being Dutch is ethnically defined, and even less so if this is also the case for your Turkish identity. And it is almost impossible to perceive yourself as a Chinese Dutch if a White interpretation of what it means to be Dutch prevails. Entitative and essentialist groups are seen as coherent, exclusive, and unchanging, which makes it difficult for an outsider to become a 'true' member and for combining this membership with belonging to another group that is also understood in these terms. Research among immigrants in Australia showed that people who held essentialist beliefs were less likely to adopt Australian identity in their acculturation process (Bastian & Haslam, 2008).

Our national character

Groups can feel superior to other groups. They consider themselves, for example, chosen and predestined to lead the world, as possessing the ultimate truth, as morally pure and superior, or as having an enlightened and modern culture. Internally, this leads to rejection and the suppression of dissidents and deserters. The so-called 'black sheep effect' implies that in-group dissenters or deviant members are more negatively evaluated than analogous out-group members (see Marques *et al.*, 2001). Thus, when someone of my own group deviates from our group norm, I am inclined to view him more negatively compared to when a member of another group deviates from the norm of that group. A 'bad apple' in my own basket is more troublesome than a 'bad apple' in someone's else basket. This effect occurs even when individuals have a strong overall preference for their in-group, and the effect is larger when the status of one's group is threatened or insecure and for individuals who identify with their group.

The assumed group superiority can be manifested in missionary work and actions to convert others, but also in stigmatization and exclusion, and in acts of violence and purging. The way in which group members see themselves has implications for how they act towards others. Many religious movements urge their believers to be loyal to co-believers, and their claim to exclusive moral rightness easily evokes disapproval and dislike of others. But, as noted in the example of Miss Elliot and her class of blue-eyed and brown-eyed children, it is in principle possible that 'being superior' is translated into a caring attitude and providing assistance to the less fortunate. Identification with a religious group does not necessarily lead to the denunciation of other faiths but can also be associated with openness and reconciliation. Whether the former or the latter occurs depends on how religious identity is defined and the normative meaning that emanates from it. Prosocial behaviour, such as charity and helpfulness, may also be a consequence of how a religious community perceives itself. Religious group identification can go together with harmonious intergroup relations, even in times of threat (Anisman *et al.*, 2012).

An example of the importance of how religion is understood is our study of two groups of Turkish Dutch Muslims: Sunnis and Alevis (Verkuyten & Yildiz, 2009). The beliefs and religious practices of Alevis differ greatly from those of Sunnis. Alevi Muslims interpret Islam and the Koran in a spiritual, mystical, and humanistic manner, and not in terms of strict rules and regulations. For most of them, the love for God and other people comes first, regardless of their faith. What matters is how you approach and treat others, and whether you are behaving in a responsible and caring manner. In our study, 55% of Sunnis were explicitly negative about non-believers and only 22% were positive. For the Alevi Muslims the rates were 11% and 70%, respectively – a huge difference, which shows that there are different interpretations of being Muslim, resulting in a difference in the acceptance of outsiders.

Another example is national identity. There are many beliefs and ideas about the criteria that define national belonging and the content of the national identity. These definitions have profound implications because they define the boundaries of belonging with the related rights and responsibilities. In Europe, several commentators and politicians have argued that Islam seriously threatens the Judeo-Christian roots of European societies and cultures. Increasing numbers of Islamic schools, mosques, veiled women, and other visible signs of Islam would undermine the traditional ways of life. Consequently, in several countries it has been proposed to include in the constitution that the Christian tradition defines the nation. According to Zolberg and Long (1999), the focus on Islam in political debates in Europe is related to the fact that the European identity, despite national variations, remains deeply embedded in the Christian tradition in relation to which Muslim immigrants constitute a visible 'other' and Islam a 'bright boundary' (Alba, 2005). Research has shown that Christianity is more salient to national identity in European countries with larger Muslim populations (Kunovich, 2006). In three experimental studies we found that encouraging people to think about Dutch national identity as rooted in Christianity did indeed result in stronger opposition towards Muslim expressive rights (e.g., wearing of a headscarf, celebrating Islamic holidays) (Smeekes *et al.*, 2011).

A common distinction is one between ethnic and civic conceptions of the nation. Although this distinction has been criticized (e.g., Nieguth, 1999; Shulman, 2002), it offers a useful heuristic device that is widely used in the literature, and more importantly also in everyday life (Koning, 2011; Reeskens & Hooghe, 2010). Ethnic and civic nationalism are not only academic concepts but are also used by lay people and political activists to argue about belonging (e.g., Every & Augoustinos, 2008; Janmaat, 2006). An ethnic conception defines the nation in terms of supposed shared ancestry and an essentialist traditional culture. A civic conception, on the other hand, uses citizenship as well as institutional commitments and participation as criteria for national belonging. National identities in Germany and the Netherlands are typically defined through reference to the ethnicity of the dominant majority group: Dutch tends to mean ethnic Dutch, and German means ethnic German. In contrast, in France and the United States a more civic definition of national belonging predominates.

These two concepts of 'ethnic' and 'civic' are not mutually exclusive, but the emphasis may be different, and there are different implications for attitudes towards newcomers. In an ethnic definition, clear boundaries are drawn that make it difficult for minorities and immigrants to really belong, while this is much easier when applying a civic definition. There are several studies that confirm this. For example, an ethnic interpretation of national identity has been found to be associated with more negative attitudes towards newcomers and with tendencies to take action against them (Pehrson *et al.*, 2009a). This has been established at the country level as well. In a comparative study of 31 countries it was found that national identity is more strongly associated with prejudice against immigrants in countries where an ethnic interpretation of the national identity predominates in comparison with countries where a civic interpretation is more common (Pehrson *et al.*, 2009b).

Further evidence comes from a longitudinal study in Belgium (Meeus *et al.*, 2010). It was found that, over time, Flemish high school students who identified relatively strongly with their Flemish in-group, endorsed more strongly an ethnic understanding of what it means to be Flemish. And this stronger endorsement was related to greater prejudice against Moroccan immigrants. Another example is experimental research conducted in Scotland (Wakefield *et al.*, 2011). In three studies among ethnic Scots it was found that when an civic compared to an ethnic definition of national belonging was salient, a person of Chinese heritage was judged as more Scottish, his criticism of Scotland was more accepted, and he received more help because he was considered more Scottish.

These findings indicate that national identification is not necessarily linked to anti-immigration attitudes or prejudices towards minorities. Depending on how the national identity is presented and defined, it can also go together with more acceptance of newcomers and minority groups. For example, it has been argued that due to its self-understanding of having a unique history of colonialism, Portugal has developed a strong anti-racist norm. The ideology of *Luso-Tropicalism* is thought to make Portugal more open to immigrants (Vala, 2008).

Reicher and colleagues (2006) present an analysis of Bulgarian resistance against the deportation of Jews in World War II. Bulgaria was certainly not anti-German. Nevertheless, most Jews living in Bulgaria survived the war, and towards the end of World War II there were more Jews living there than there had been at the beginning. The result of a series of petitions, protests, and public demonstrations against anti-Semitic measures was that the Bulgarian Jews were not deported. Reicher and colleagues focus on identity definitions and present an analysis of the arguments for saving the Jews. There seem have been three aspects that came together in the following quote from a letter to King Boris in which opinion leaders responded to the evacuation and internment of Jews in Sofia in 1943.

> In subjecting our innocent fellow citizens to this cruel and pitiless measures, not only are we squandering a vast moral capital of which our generous and tolerant people had every right to be proud, we are also harming Bulgaria's reputation in the eyes of the world and compromising its future national interests.
>
> (Reicher *et al.*, 2006, p. 67)

Three arguments can be seen here. First, Jews were consistently referred to as Bulgarians – as equal citizens, just like everyone else. The Jews were part of the in-group, Bulgarians through and through, 'one of us' who you should stand up for. In this way, all Bulgarian citizens were addressed and urged to protest. But the Jews were helped not only because they were 'one of us', but also because 'we are the kind of people who help others'. Bulgarians were described as a historically and traditionally generous and tolerant people – that is the Bulgarian national character, with the corresponding moral implications. Anti-Semitic measures go against the national character; it is something 'we simply do not do'. Finally it was argued that the measures threatened Bulgarian interests. The international reputation of a civilized country is incompatible with anti-Semitic measures that therefore go against the national interest.

This example shows that a clear definition of what the nation stands for can have inclusive consequences for minority groups. A further example is the former Dutch Prime Minister Jan Peter Balkenende who, in 2008, stated:.

> The Netherlands is characterized by a tradition of religious tolerance, respect and responsibility. The needless offending of certain convictions and communities does not belong to this.... The Dutch government will honor this tradition and issues an appeal to everyone to do the same.

Balkenende made this statement during a press conference about the anti-Islam movie 'Fitna' that was released in the Netherlands by the far-right member of parliament Geert Wilders. Balkenende invokes a representation of Dutch national history as one of tolerance and respect in order to argue for acceptance of cultural and religious diversity in the present. In public debates in Western Europe, Islam and Muslims are often presented as undermining national identity and culture (Gijsberts & Lubbers, 2009), and many West Europeans perceive their way of life and that of Muslims as incompatible (Pew Research Center, 2005). However, Balkenende argues that Dutch nationals should accept Muslim immigrants because this is in agreement with 'our' history of religious tolerance. We are a traditionally tolerant country and therefore we ought to show respect for that which is important to others.

As discussed in chapter 2, people who identify closely with an in-group are more likely to act in accordance with in-group norms and beliefs. This means that when historical norms and beliefs prescribe tolerance of immigrants, especially highly identified group members should behave accordingly. This prediction is interesting and important because it goes against the common finding that higher national identifiers tend to be more concerned about their nation and therefore display more negative attitudes towards immigrants (see Wagner *et al.*, 2010).

In three studies (Smeekes *et al.*, 2012) we found that when a representation of historical tolerance was salient, native Dutch participants who identified relatively strongly with the Netherlands indicated more support for Muslim expressive rights. The reason for this was that these individuals experienced less incompatibility between the Dutch and Muslim ways of life and were therefore less worried that the continuity of their national identity is undermined. The presence and acceptance of Muslims is in line with the history of religious tolerance that defines our nation.

These findings indicate that high levels of national belonging do not inevitably lead to the rejection of immigrants but can actually go together with acceptance. A study conducted in the United States confirms this interpretation (Butz *et al.*, 2007). This study showed that highly nationalistic individuals became more positive towards Arabs and Muslims when egalitarian national values were made salient, whereas this manipulation did not influence attitudes of low nationalistic participants. Moreover, this study observed that whereas high nationalistic individuals generally had more negative attitudes towards Arabs and Muslims than low nationalists, the activation of egalitarian national values resulted in similar attitudes among both groups of participants.

These findings indicate that highly identified nationals are not only more likely to act in accordance with salient group norms than low identifiers, but are also more inclined to display prejudice against immigrant out-groups as a means of protecting positive distinctiveness (Tajfel & Turner, 1979). Yet, when the meaning of national identity is shared, national in-group members act in accordance with this category definition, and this reduces the differences between high and low identifiers' prejudices. Thus, while high national identifiers may generally be less positive about Muslims than low identifiers, when a representation of national historical tolerance is salient, this results in similar levels of acceptance of Muslims among both groups of identifiers.

These examples show that 'our' reaction towards newcomers is closely linked to how 'we' understand ourselves. It is not just the alleged characteristics of the newcomers that determine our feelings and behaviour, but also the perception that we have of ourselves. At the same time, newcomer characteristics do, of course, matter. Whether one reacts negatively or more positively towards immigrants and minority groups is related to the perceived nature of these groups.

The perceived nature of immigrants

Above I discussed the importance for intergroup relations of perceiving a group as an entity and of essentialist group representations. But these characteristics are not the only ones that matter. The way in which natives, but also minority groups, react to immigrants further depends on who these immigrants are and why they have come to the country.

People migrate for all kinds of reasons – making a living, improving their family's quality of life and life prospects, family reunification, and fleeing from oppression. For millions these reasons are strong enough to move to another country, sometimes risking their lives in a small boat at sea, or crammed into containers and trucks. Some migrants are well educated and highly skilled, whereas others have had little education in their country of origin. And some people migrate to a country the language and culture of which they know quite well, and others end up in very unfamiliar places. Also, people sometimes freely decide to migrate, or they may be more or less forced to leave their country for political, economic, and ecological reasons. All these factors can have an influence on the ways in which immigrants try to adapt to the host society. Furthermore, these factors might affect how the host society responds to immigrants. Skilled immigrants might be seen as hardworking and not challenging the social order, whereas poorly educated immigrants can be considered a drain on social services and a threat to the established order. In order to meet future demographic and economic needs, many Western nations seek to attract skilled workers and try, at the same time, to prevent the inflow of unskilled immigrants. Also, some countries make a distinction between categories of immigrants that are culturally less or more similar to the native majority, like Western and non-Western immigrants. It is maintained that forms of selective immigration are necessary, also because it conveys a sense of government control that reassures the public and works against prejudice and discrimination.

Among a representative sample of the native Dutch, Sniderman and Hagendoorn (2007) conducted a 'fitting-in' experiment. Participants were presented with one of four descriptions of a group of new immigrants. The first two conditions focused on economic prospects by making a distinction between highly educated immigrants who are well suited for well-paying jobs and not highly educated ones who are only suited for unskilled jobs. The third and fourth conditions focused on cultural fit, whereby the group of immigrants was characterized as speaking Dutch fluently and having a very good chance of fitting in smoothly with the Dutch culture, or as not being fluent speakers and not having a good chance to fit in smoothly. When problems of economic or cultural integration were made salient, people were more negative towards these new immigrants being allowed in. Groups that might pose problems are not as welcome as groups who do not. In addition, it was found that problems of cultural fitting in elicited more negative reactions than those of economic integration. Cultural 'deficits' of new immigrants seemed to matter more than economic 'deficits'.[6]

Stereotypes

The way in which immigrants are presented and understood matters for how people react to them. This means that different immigrant groups can be perceived and evaluated differently. When people encounter an unfamiliar group such as a new group of immigrants, they want to know at least two things. One is whether these others have good intentions and are trustworthy, friendly, or warm overall. The other is whether these others are competent and skilled and can produce outcomes that matter. Research in many different countries has found that these two dimensions of warmth (including morality) and competence underlie out-group stereotypes. Groups can be perceived as warm and competent (typically one's in-group and allies), cold and incompetent (the rich, elite), a mixture of high on warmth and low on competence (the elderly, disabled), and low warmth and high competence (the poor, homeless).

Immigrants are the quintessential 'other' and are often stereotyped as out-groups that rate low on both warmth and competence (e.g., Brambilla *et al.*, 2012). They are often considered untrustworthy and exploiting social services, health care, and the educational system. However, there can be important differences between immigrant groups, as is demonstrated in a study in the United States (Lee & Fiske, 2006). It was found that undocumented immigrants and Mexicans fitted the typical immigrant profile of low competence and low warmth. Asian immigrants, however, were perceived as low in warmth but high in competence because they were considered as highly competitive and having relatively high status. In contrast, Irish and Italian immigrants were seen as less competitive and having lower status and therefore as relatively more warm and less competent.

These findings show that there can be different images about different immigrant groups. These images are important because of the emotions and behaviours they trigger (Cuddy *et al.*, 2008). Immigrants who are considered nice but not very successful can trigger feelings of pity and empathy, with the associated intention to offer help. This is especially likely for refugee groups that had to flee their country. Being perceived as untrustworthy and unfriendly but at the same time as competent and successful can lead to envy and anger. Under stable societal conditions this leads to a grudging acceptance, but under societal breakdown this can turn into active attack and mass violence. Examples are violent attacks on Chinese shopkeepers and businesses in Malaysia and Indonesia, and on Muslims in India. Immigrant groups who are perceived as low on warmth and low on competence typically elicit feelings of contempt and disgust, with the related tendencies to dehumanize and exclude them. So-called 'bogus refugees' and 'fortune-seekers' are examples of this.

Voluntary and involuntary

The distinction between 'bogus' and 'real' refugees is based on the question of whether their displacement is primarily due to their own choice or to external circumstances. Responsibilities are related to choices, and rights and duties to responsibilities. If people make a free choice, they are responsible for their situation and can less easily make all kinds of claims on others. In his book *Multicultural Citizenship* (1995), the political philosopher Kymlicka distinguishes between voluntary and involuntary minorities. According to him, not all minority groups have equal moral claims. Cultural recognition and rights are considered adequate demands for domestic groups that were the original inhabitants, such as Indians, native Hawaiians, and the Inuit, or that have been historically wronged, such as descendants of African slaves. Immigrants, however, are at the other end of the moral spectrum, having waived their demands and rights by voluntarily leaving their country of origin.

Self-determination implies a personal responsibility for one's situation and position. Choosing to leave involves a responsibility to integrate into the new society, which is also in one's own interest. This reasoning supposes a clear difference between personal choice and lack of choice, which is often difficult to make. Yet, the distinction between voluntary and involuntary is not uncommon and is also used in scientific analyses (e.g., Ogbu, 1993). There are also social implications involved. Individualistic interpretations that stress people's own choice and responsibility or more situational interpretations that emphasize people's lack of choice are two common discourses used to define categories of 'deserving' and 'undeserving' in welfare debates, and to account for health and illness, unemployment, and poverty. Deservingness is also a critical factor underlying opposition to racial policy decisions, like affirmative action in the United States (Reyna *et al.*, 2006). Furthermore, in the context of Germany it was found that immigrant groups that were judged as more responsible for their need for public assistance were perceived to be less deserving of public support (Appelbaum, 2002). Likewise, a study showed that attributions of personal responsibility are linked to less support for affirmative action in relation to visible minorities in Canada (Quinn *et al.*, 2001).

This distinction between voluntary and involuntary is not only used to define categories of refugees – such as 'real refugees' vs. 'fortune-seekers' – but has also figured in talk about labour migrants who have been coming to Western Europe since the 1960s. For example, the idea of 'personal choice' has been used in the Netherlands to make Turkish and Moroccan immigrants assume responsibility for their situation and to argue for the need for assimilation. In contrast, an emphasis on Dutch industry and society recruiting these people as cheap labour migrants defines responsibilities for the majority group and provides moral grounds for cultural diversity and minority rights. This type of reasoning can be found among native Dutch people, as is illustrated in the following quote taken from our research in two districts of Rotterdam (Verkuyten, 1997b).

> I draw the line at the founding of Turkish schools; last year there was also a current affairs programme on television in which they discussed maternity clinics for Muslim women, especially for Muslim women, that sort of thing really makes me wonder what people are playing at. Why should we have to adapt ourselves to them when they come to the Netherlands voluntarily? In my opinion, if we go to another country out of free choice we have to adapt, just as they should have to adapt to us.

But the emphasis on 'free choice' is also noticeable when listening to South Moluccans distinguishing themselves from 'foreigners'. As explained in chapter 2, the Moluccans were brought to the Netherlands by the Dutch government in the 1950s after they had fought alongside the Dutch in Indonesia's war of independence at the end of the 1940s.[7]

> Moluccans are treated as any other foreigners. Almost all Moluccans will say, 'we're not foreigners, we're no immigrants', for if you look back properly, if you read the history books, you will see that the Moluccans didn't come here to work or anything like that. They didn't come here of their own accord. On the contrary, they were brought here by the Dutch government. Well, that's the difference between them and the foreigners. The foreigners came here to work and they all came here of their own free will.

In this quote, there is a clear rejection of a self-definition in terms of foreigners that incorporates all other immigrant groups. Foreigners have made a choice to come to the Netherlands, and as a consequence they should adjust and adapt. The interpretation of 'free choice' places the responsibility with the foreigners themselves and justifies the demand for adaptation. In contrast, the Dutch government brought the Moluccans to the Netherlands. They came 'on command', 'following instruction', and 'on political grounds'. It was the decision of the government to bring them to the Netherlands, and therefore the Dutch have a moral responsibility and obligation towards the Moluccans.

We have conducted four studies in which we experimentally investigated the importance of the way in which categories of immigrants are described (Gieling *et al.*, 2010; Verkuyten, 2004a, 2005b). Young adults, adolescents, and older children were asked to what extent the native Dutch should accept cultural diversity and rights for Turkish and Moroccan immigrants. In one condition, the emphasis was on the personal choice and responsibility of Turks and Moroccans in deciding themselves to come to the Netherlands as 'guest workers'. In the other condition the emphasis was on the recruitment by – and thus the responsibility of – Dutch industry and society. In a third condition, no explanation for the presence of these groups was given. The findings were the same in all four studies. Figure 5.1 shows the results of one of these studies.

An emphasis on the responsibility of Dutch industry and society in recruiting labour migrants leads to greater endorsement of cultural rights for Turkish and Moroccan immigrants. As shown in Figure 5.1, the approval is similar in the other two conditions, which suggests that the general and unspoken opinion is that Turks and Moroccans are themselves responsible for coming to the Netherlands. This indicates that perceived voluntariness of migration has a negative impact on the endorsement of cultural rights of immigrants. This interpretation is even more convincing when a similar effect is found for Dutch emigrants. In one study we found this to be the case. It was accepted less that after migration, voluntary compared to involuntary Dutch emigrants should be able to maintain their Dutch culture as much as possible (Gieling *et al.*, 2010).

In addition, we found that emotions play an important role in the evaluation of categories of immigrants and refugees. Political refugees, for example, will more

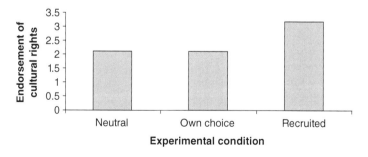

Figure 5.1 Endorsement of cultural rights by reason for immigration

quickly evoke feelings of sympathy and compassion, while 'fortune-seekers' will be more likely to cause irritation and anger. Feelings of sympathy tend to translate into supporting and helping behaviours towards others, while irritation and anger are more likely to lead to rejection. In two studies, we examined the role of these emotions on the extent to which people agree with policies on aid and support of immigrants (Verkuyten, 2004a). We focused on the reactions of native Dutch people to two different categories: political refugees and voluntary economic migrants. Towards political refugees, feelings of sympathy turned out to lead to support of the policies. In contrast, economic refugees evoked feelings of irritation and anger. Furthermore, results revealed that people who identify strongly with the Netherlands were less likely to support the policies, because they felt more irritation and anger towards economic refugees.

The importance of these and other findings (e.g., Augoustinos & Quinn, 2003) is that they show that the way in which the presence of minorities is presented influences what is considered reasonable and acceptable. This suggests that distinctions made in the media, in policies and by politicians, between, for example, 'real refugees' and 'fortune-seekers', can have important implications for intergroup relations in culturally diverse societies. Therefore, it should not come as a surprise that politicians tend to manipulate these categories, for example, to gain public support in elections.

The previous discussion has shown that intergroup relations depend on how 'we' and 'they' are construed and understood. But there is also the meaning of 'them' for 'us'. Newcomers might be very different from 'us' and therefore have quite a profound impact on 'our' way of life, or there might be competition over scarce resources, or conflicting expectations about the ways in which immigrants and minority groups should adapt. These are all important reasons why group differences can turn into tensions and group conflicts.

Small and large differences

We generally tend to like people who are similar to us. Small differences give the impression that there are similarities in values and beliefs, which is a basis for mutual acceptance and cooperation and leads to attraction. The so-called 'homophily principle' states that people have the tendency to associate with others who have similar backgrounds (McPherson *et al.*, 2001). This means that it can be expected that large differences between groups stand in the way of positive intergroup relations, while more similar groups get along more easily. When there is a large difference between groups, this gives the impression that 'we' do not share anything with 'them'. Clear differences highlight the group boundaries, making it easy to define one's own identity and making group differentiation more likely: after all, they are actually really different. There is empirical evidence for this, but the results are not unequivocal (see Jetten *et al.*, 2004).

It is also possible that not large but, rather, small differences lead to reactions in which a strong group contrast is made. Freud wrote about the 'narcissism of small differences'. As groups start to become more and more alike, there is a danger that one's distinctive identity is lost. Small differences may threaten the need for distinctiveness and thereby encourage people to mark their group boundaries more strongly. The differences between natives and minority group members who are increasingly becoming more integrated can become less and less. This can lead to stronger attempts to mark one's own identity. Both ethnic minorities and natives start to emphasize their identity. There is empirical evidence for this argument, but also evidence that is not supportive of this reasoning (see Jetten *et al.,* 2004).

If the empirical evidence is equivocal, this usually indicates that there are important intervening factors and conditions. Depending on the content of the identity in question, on the relationships between groups (e.g., competitive or not), and on the broader societal context, the group differences may lead to weaker or stronger intergroup differentiation. Moreover, differentiation can take various forms, such as in terms of evaluations and actual behaviour. Behaviour is particularly suitable for highlighting and marking distinctions when the differences become smaller. Muslim women who are well integrated can start wearing a headscarf, and as minorities continue to integrate, natives can increasingly mark their national identity with 'authentic' customs and traditions.

According to social identity theory (Tajfel & Turner, 1979), the degree of group identification is one of the important factors for understanding what exactly will happen. People who identify strongly with their in-group will easily perceive small differences as threatening. The group membership is important to them, and a lack of distinctiveness makes it difficult to have a clear and positive in-group identity. Therefore, they tend to highlight their distinctiveness, particularly through visible markers and behaviour. People who barely or only weakly identify with their group are less sensitive to group threat and have less need to clearly define and mark their group identity. They will focus more on the actual differences, and if these are greater, they will also view the group boundaries as more difficult to cross. Empirical results are consistent with these interpretations (Jetten *et al.*, 2004). In situations with small differences, people who identify strongly with their group tend to visibly highlight their group's distinctiveness. And large existing differences between groups lead to differentiation that is reflective of these differences by those who do not identify very strongly with their in-group.

Conflicting material interests

Life is full of opportunities and challenges, but also threats and dangers. You can be turned down, you can get laughed at, you can lose your job, you can have an accident, and you become ill and die. Moreover, there are many threats that do not concern you personally but, rather, have to do with the group to which you belong. Immigrants put 'our' facilities and services under strain, take 'our' jobs, and threaten 'our' way of living. Additionally, the European unification threatens our national identity, culture, and sovereignty, and terrorists threaten our security, democracy, and liberal lifestyle. These group threats can be very real for people, and the experience of feeling threatened is of particular importance.

Threat implies the possibility of losing something valuable. People care about many different things and can therefore feel threatened for many different reasons. In intergroup research, different forms of threat have been identified, and different responses in coping with these threats have been examined. Even though people might have little reason in their personal life to complain, they are worried about what will happen to 'us' and want something to be done about it. If people feel threatened, they try to defend themselves and they are inclined to address or remove the cause of the threat. It is hard to feel sympathy for people who are believed to take away 'our' jobs or are slowly taking over 'our' neighbourhood. Negative feelings are not surprising in these cases, and there is clear experimental and longitudinal evidence that feelings of out-group threat lead to out-group derogation and hostility.

As demonstrated by Sherif's summer camp experiments, group competition is an important factor in promoting hostility and conflict (Esses *et al.,* 2010). Yet the relationship between perceived group threats and prejudice or hostility can also work in the other direction. Prejudice does not only need to be a consequence of perceived threat but can also be the underlying source of it. A negative attitude distorts perception, and prejudice can lead to seeing out-group members as a threat to the in-group. Prejudice can function as a group lens that causes people to be over-sensitive and biased. As a result they are more likely to make interpretations in terms of group threats that justify their negative reactions. In a study using representative samples in 21 European countries it was found that prejudiced natives showed more opposition to immigration and to the naturalization of immigrants because they were inclined to perceive economic and security threats from immigrants (Pereira *et al.*, 2010). Prejudice is usually suppressed by anti-prejudice norms and personal moral standards. This means that its expression in behaviour and in the opposition to policies that benefit immigrants depends on a justification that makes it acceptable and understandable. The perception of realistic threats is a powerful justification because of the common-sense notion that people who are in danger have the right to defend themselves.

So-called 'realistic threats' refer to the possible loss of safety and material resources. Ethnic minority groups can be perceived as a safety threat, and conflicts between groups and negative group reactions are often rooted in a competition over scarce commodities: a zero-sum game in which 'they' take away 'our' jobs and houses. Realistic threats can eliminate the effect of a pro-social group norm that prescribes acceptance or anti-discrimination. When there is a feeling of competition over scarce resources, these group norms do not appear to lead to tolerance of immigrants (Falomir-Pichastor *et al.*, 2004).

There also may be feelings of physical threat, caused, for example, by experiences or media reports on criminality and terrorism. After 9/11 and the bombings in London and Madrid, part of the media in various European countries tended to picture Muslim immigrants as being a threat to the native population. There was a clear conflation of representations of terrorism with Muslims, creating an important impetus and justification for anti-Islam attitudes and for support for policies that limit the civil liberties of Muslim immigrants. This Muslim–terrorist discourse also seems to have affected the minds of White Americans. In an experimental study using a shooter paradigm, it was found that making White Americans think about Muslims and Arabs led to faster shooting of targets with ambiguous ethnicity and religion (Mange *et al.*, 2012). In another study it was demonstrated that Muslim appearance increased the speed of shooting responses (Unkelbach *et al.*, 2008).

Conflicting ways of life

In the 1970s, the fear that foreign cultures would swarm over England and override the British way of life was a main argument to oppose immigration and immigrants (Barker, 1981). Later studies in European countries found a similar public discourse of cultural threat to oppose immigration and minority rights. So-called symbolic threats are based on perceived group differences in values, norms, and beliefs. Out-groups that have different worldviews may be seen as threatening the cultural identity of the in-group and thereby its sense of grip and meaningful existence.[8] Many studies have shown that perceived threats to in-group values on the part of immigrants and minorities predict more negative attitudes towards these groups (e.g., Sniderman & Hagendoorn, 2007; Ward & Masgoret, 2006). Studying 17 European countries, McLaren (2003), for example, found that the belief that immigrants challenge or undermine national values was a predictor of negative attitudes towards immigrants.

Symbolic threat is based on perceived cultural differences. Other values and norms can be seen as incompatible or contradictory to what we stand for or believe in. There is a fear that an assumed Islamization and a 'tsunami' of Muslims would undermine our way of life. Similarly, the increasing demand for assimilation threatens the cultural identity of Muslims and other minorities. People tend to be negative towards those who might undermine the possibility of living in one's own culture and practising one's identity.

Feelings of threat that arise from perceived group differences in values, norms, and behaviours are not entirely imaginary. They can be quite real, like the difference in values and practices of conservative Muslims and liberal Dutch. This is especially the case when it comes to family values, equality between men and women, and sexual issues. A nationwide study showed that 50% of the native Dutch and 50% of Dutch Muslims believe that Western and Islamic ways of life are incompatible (Gijsberts, 2005).

Natives for whom their national identity is central often have a tendency to perceive ethnic minorities as a threat to the national culture. As a result, those feelings of threat lead them to be less in favour of minority rights (Verkuyten, 2009b). Perceived threat increases the emphasis on the obligations of newcomers. The national identity and culture that is thought to be under siege should not be further compromised by an endorsement of cultural diversity but should, rather, be strengthened by making clear cultural demands on newcomers. In the last 20 years there has been in many European countries a turning away from providing rights, services, and facilities for minorities and immigrants, to increasing demands of cultural adaptation and assimilation.

For minorities, it is the other way round. If they feel threatened in their culture and distinctiveness, they will make stronger identity claims and signal the infringement of existing facilities and rights. In situations of change and uncertainty, minority members prioritize rights, while the majority tend to emphasize duties (Moghaddam, 2008). This has nothing to do with cultural differences, but with differences in positions and interests.

The implication of realistic and symbolic threats for prejudice, hostility, and conflict is dependent on many factors. Some researchers try to argue that symbolic or, rather, more tangible realistic threats are more important for intergroup relations. But this is a rather useless either-or way of thinking. In some situations there is competition over scarce material resources, whereas in other situations the main concern is about culture and identity, and in still others the two forms of threat are closely interrelated. It seems obvious that the sense of economic threat will not be as strong in times of a booming economy than in times of economic downturn. Similarly, extensive media attention on crime and terrorist attacks nurtures feelings of danger and insecurity and thereby a negative attitude towards immigrants and minorities. In some situations, forms of realistic threat are the underlying cause of prejudice, in other situations it is, rather, symbolic threat that plays the key role, and sometimes it is both.

In the last ten years, the main concern in many European countries has been about feelings of cultural threat. Especially, the idea that the national identity is being undermined has led to negative reactions. A study of more than 1,200 native Dutch youths shows that feelings of symbolic rather than realistic threat are associated with prejudice against Muslims (Velasco Gónzalez, *et al.*, 2008). In recent years, public debate has mainly been concerned with cultural difference and identity, and this is reflected in how people respond to minorities. In European countries, perceived symbolic threat appears to be the main driver of the negative attitudes towards minorities and newcomers (McLaren, 2003). But it is very likely that with an economic crisis, there is a move in the direction of feelings of competition over scarce resources, leading to negative reactions towards immigrants and minority groups.

Additionally, not everyone reacts in the same way to out-group threats. There are individual differences in one's sensitivity to competition over scarce resources versus more symbolic issues. These individual differences have to do with social status and position (e.g., education, income), but also with the level of authoritarianism, social dominance orientation, and in-group identification. Perceived threat may have different effects depending, for example, on national identification, because the motivational meanings of perceived threat are different. Compared to low identifiers, those with high in-group identification are more likely to be concerned about their group, especially when the position and value of the group identity is at stake. For example, high identifiers have been found to react more negatively towards out-groups under threat than do low identifiers (e.g., Branscombe & Wann, 1994). Furthermore, Bizman and Yinon (2001) found that, among Israeli citizens, realistic threat to the in-group, but not symbolic threat, was a more important predictor of attitudes towards immigrants for high than for low identifiers. And in two studies in the context of Northern Ireland, it was found that symbolic threat, but not realistic threat, predicts out-group attitudes and trust for high identifiers only (Tausch *et al.*, 2007). These divergent findings regarding the two types of threat are due to the relative importance of realistic and symbolic threats in the context of Israel and Northern Ireland, respectively. The level of identification makes a difference for threats that are actually relevant in a given context.

Conflicting acculturation preferences

In chapter 4, I discussed acculturation processes that refer to changes resulting from cultural contact. It is not only minority group members who have a preference for one of the four strategies of segregation, integration, assimilation, and marginalization. The native majority also has an idea of what minorities should be doing. This means that a difference in opinion may arise: for example, immigrants strive for integration, whereas the majority group expects and demands assimilation.

Research in several European countries has shown that whereas immigrants tend to prefer integration or segregation, natives prefer assimilation and integration (see Brown & Zagefka, 2011). So immigrants and also ethnic minority members want to keep themselves somewhat apart, or at least partially retain their culture. The majority group, however, wants newcomers and minorities to adopt the majority culture, or at least take an active part in society. It is not fully clear why these preferences exist and how people decide on them. Research has examined the role of various factors, such as age and education, but this provides little insight into what exactly are the underlying perceptions and concerns. In any case, there often tends to be a group difference in the emphasis placed on the preferred acculturation strategy. Immigrants and minorities are more in favour of cultural maintenance, while the native majority leans towards adaptation. The agreement is partial at best.

Moreover, although substantial proportions of both groups may be in favour of integration, this does not mean that they have the same understanding of what this implies. In public life, minorities may have a preference for the combination of cultural maintenance and adaptation (integration), but privately cultural maintenance (segregation) can have priority. The majority, in contrast, may wish for change and adaptation in all domains of life, including the family sphere and in private life – that is what they consider 'real' integration or assimilation.

Furthermore, the preference for acculturation strategies might differ by acculturation dimension. In the previous chapter I discussed a study among Belgian adolescents of Turkish and Moroccan origin (Snauwaert *et al.*, 2003). Those youths were mostly in favour of social integration, followed by cultural and psychological integration. Natives may have a tendency to put these forms of integration in reverse order. Priority might be given to psychological integration, followed by cultural integration, and then social integration. They might believe that people who come to live in the country should be loyal and committed to it and wholeheartedly choose it – that is something that can be expected from immigrants and is necessary for a strong and unified country. Newcomers should also adapt culturally. The prevailing norms and values should be adopted and internalized, but some elements of the original culture can be maintained. Finally, newcomers should also integrate socially. However, if this means that they start moving into my street and neighbourhood, going to the same school and sports clubs as my daughter or son, it quickly becomes a different story. The demand for social integration often dies down when it involves one's own network or private life. So, whereas immigrants might find social integration easiest and struggle with psychological integration, the native majority might emphasize the importance of psychological integration and be reluctant when it comes to integration within their own social networks.[9]

According to Richard Bourhis and colleagues (1997), the degree of concordance or fit in preferred acculturation strategy is important for intergroup relations. Majority and minority groups can agree (e.g., both have a preference for integration or for assimilation of minority groups). But the discrepancy or mismatch can also be problematic – for example, if the one emphasizes the need for assimilation and the other integration. Furthermore, a conflict might arise when the minority wants to remain separate or when the majority group wants to keep them separate (segregation). Others have argued that it is important to distinguish between discordance over the issue of cultural maintenance of minority groups and over the issue of cultural adaptation and contact (Piontkowski *et al.*, 2002). A problematic situation would be the result of a mismatch on one of these two aspects, while a mismatch for both aspects would lead to conflict. In general, it appears that a greater discrepancy in preferred acculturation strategy is associated with more intergroup tensions, less positive attitudes, and more discrimination (Zagefka & Brown, 2002).

However, these negative outcomes might depend not so much on the mismatch between the actual acculturation preferences of majority and minority groups but, rather, on the perception of what the other group wants. Research has shown that immigrants are typically in favour of integration, while the native majority *believes* that immigrants opt for segregation. And immigrants might think that the majority wants them to assimilate, whereas in fact majority members may prefer integration. Differences in perception can lead to misunderstandings and conflicts. Research has shown that a greater discrepancy between one's own preference and the perceived acculturation preference of the out-group leads to worse intergroup outcomes (Brown & Zagefka, 2011).

It can be expected that the way in which majority members react to immigrants depends on the acculturation preferences of those immigrants. Immigrants who prefer assimilation or integration can be expected to be evaluated more positively than those who keep themselves separate. Assimilation and integration involve the adoption of the host culture, whereas separation does not. Cultural adoption indicates that the host culture is valued, and feeling valued by immigrants can be expected to lead to more positive attitudes towards immigrant groups. In addition, cultural adoption implies increased similarity between natives and immigrants, and a perception of similarity is one factor that can lead to a sense of shared belonging. Furthermore, assimilating immigrants who adopt the host culture without wanting to maintain their ethnic culture might be evaluated more positively than integrating immigrants. After all, assimilation implies that immigrants shed their previous markers of group identity and fully adopt those of the host society. This means that in comparison to integration, they can be perceived as more exclusively valuing the host culture and as becoming more similar to 'us' and thereby 'one of us'.

Several studies in different countries among adolescents and adults have found evidence for these different expectations (Maisonneuve & Teste, 2007; Van Oudenhoven et al., 1998; Zagefka *et al.*, 2012). Some of these studies have used an experimental design in which participants are presented with excerpts from a text in which a fictitious immigrant is described in such a way the he/she exemplifies an acculturation strategy of integration, separation, assimilation, or marginalization. Overall, assimilation tends to be valued most by majority members, followed by integration and then separation/marginalization. Majority members prefer immigrants to (exclusively) value and adopt the host culture.

These findings do not necessarily mean, however, that immigrants and minorities who want to assimilate to the mainstream are fully accepted. As argued earlier, assimilation can also be construed as threatening the distinctiveness of the majority identity and as undermining the dominant position of the majority group. Those in the majority who support group-based dominance and inequality can become more prejudiced and politically right-wing-oriented in a context of assimilation than in one of integration (Guimond *et al.,* 2010; Thomsen *et al.,* 2008). When immigrants lose their cultural heritage and try to become similar to the rest of 'us' (assimilation), the blurring of intergroup boundaries can pose a threat to the existing group-based social hierarchy in which the natives are on top. In contrast, immigrants who adopt the mainstream culture but without giving up their own ethnic culture (integration) are in a sense confirming the existing social hierarchy. Thus, majority members can be negative and rejecting if assimilation implies that their dominant position is undermined. This is particularly likely if it involves political participation. After all, politics is about power and can directly challenge existing group positions.

In research among a national sample of native Dutch we used excerpts from a fictitious interview with a Muslim immigrant. First, he briefly introduced himself by saying that he was 30 years old, was born in Turkey, and had been living in the Netherlands for 20 years. Subsequently the interviewer asked whether he had a good understanding of Dutch politics, and he answered affirmatively. In the control condition no further text was given. In the three other conditions he was asked whether he found it important that Muslims are politically active in the Netherlands. His answer was either 'Yes, certainly. They should try to have as much influence as possible with their own Islamic political party', or 'Yes, certainly. They should try to have as much influence as possible within the existing political parties', or 'No, they should keep out of politics as much as possible.' The first two answers indicate a preference to have contacts and to participate in the Dutch political system, either with a separate political party (integration) or within one of the mainstream parties (assimilation). The third answer expresses no desire for political participation (separation/marginalization). The participants were asked to indicate their feelings towards the fictitious person. As shown in Figure 5.2, they evaluated political segregation significantly more positively than political assimilation, which, in turn, was evaluated more positively than political integration. In other words, the situation in which Muslims want to participate politically with a Muslim party was rejected most strongly, probably because it is more threatening to the dominant position of the native majority than either participating in established political parties or keeping separate from the political process. Thus, in contrast to the existing acculturation research that finds a preference for assimilation and integration in the cultural domain, segregation was favoured most in the political domain. In the same research only 12% of the native Dutch agreed with the statement that Islam, like other religions, should have its own voice in societal and political issues.

Differences in power and entitlements

Power struggles are often at the heart of conflicts and hostilities between groups. Earlier I discussed the political and intergroup implications of fifth column beliefs. Increasing immigration can raise questions about the extent to which the majority group is able to keep on determining the 'rules of the game' and to impose its priorities and way of life upon newcomers. The fear that 'they' become co-deciders and thus become influential and may change 'us' rings alarm bells.

People experience safety in numbers and they often make inferences about the relative power of a group based on the group's size. Majority members can feel that their power position is threatened when the size of immigrants or minority groups is large or increasing. Research in Europe, the former Soviet Union, and the United States has demonstrated that both an actual and a perceived increase in the number of non-natives is related to feelings that one's majority group

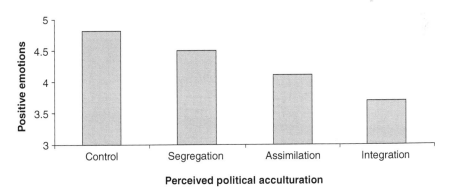

Figure 5.2 Positive emotions towards Muslims as a function of their political acculturation orientation

position is threatened (e.g., Minescu, 2011). Additionally, experimental research has shown that anticipated future ethnic demographic changes affect feelings of threat (Outten *et al.*, 2011). White Americans and White Canadians who were encouraged to think about a future in which Whites were a numerical minority were angrier towards and fearful of ethnic minorities and more sympathetic towards their in-group than Whites in a control condition. The perception of being outnumbered arouses feelings of vulnerability and danger. Within the context of Sri Lanka, the Singalese are the numerical majority and the Tamil the minority. In the broader region of south Asia the situation is reversed. In an experimental study, Singalese participants were found to describe Tamils as especially hostile, aggressive and supportive of terrorism in the context of south Asia compared to the context of Sri Lanka (Schaller & Abeysinghe, 2006).

Demographic changes signal a threat to the relatively advantaged position of the majority group. Discrimination and exclusion are means to protect one's interests and powerful position. In defining a sense of group position, proprietary claims to certain areas, privileges, and advantages are an important aspect (Blumer, 1958; Bobo, 1999). It is when out-groups are getting 'out of their place' and threaten what is considered rightfully 'ours', that conflict and hostility are likely. Ownership implies entitlements and justifies defending ourselves against others who aim to alter the status quo.

In 1965 the sociologists Elias and Scotson published a classic book entitled *The Established and the Outsiders*. The book is based on their research on intergroup relations in Winston Parva, a suburb of an industrial city in England's Midlands (actually South Wigston, Leicester). Winston Parva had fewer than 5,000 inhabitants and was situated between two railways, making it a distinct community with own factories, schools, churches, shops, and associations. There was also a sharp social boundary between the inhabitants of the three neighbourhoods – or 'zones', as Elias and Scotson called them. On the one hand, there was the relatively old working-class neighbourhood ('the village') and a middle-class neighbourhood; there was also a newer working-class area. Thus, the boundary did not follow the social class distinction that – certainly in those days – predominated in English society but was, rather, between the established who had lived the longest in Winston Parva and the 'newcoming' outsiders. The established were relatively cohesive, proud of the area, considered themselves superior, and made it clear that the outsiders did not belong. They had lived in the area the longest and considered themselves the rightful owners of Winston Parva. Their older presence was perceived as something valuable, which gave a sense of satisfaction and pride. The sense of ownership was a separate force that produced group cohesion, collective identification, and shared norms. The established were there first, claimed ownership, and had the dominant position that they tried to maintain by social control of (deviant) in-group members and by stigmatization and exclusion of the outsiders.

The sense of 'we were here first' with the related ownership claim is not specific to Winston Parva. A similar discourse can be heard among native inhabitants of other urban residential areas: 'we were here first and now our neighbourhood is taken over by "them"' (Verkuyten, 1997b). This type of discourse becomes more common if newcomers gain the upper hand and one's dominant position is threatened.

Belonging is typically rooted in place. Anthropologists use the term 'autochthonous' for groups who consider themselves primo-occupants of a given area and believe that their resources and power are threatened by newcomers. Autochthony claims turn up 'at highly different moments and places, without a clear link, yet assuming everywhere the same aura of self-evidence' (Geschiere, 2009, p. 2). The belief of 'we were here first' triggers self-evident notions of ownership and entitlements and thereby has consequences for intergroup relations: autochthony has an 'implicit call for excluding strangers ("allochthons"), whoever they may be' (Ceuppens & Geschiere, 2005, p. 386). For example, in parts of Africa, the claim of autochthony has become a political slogan for excluding supposed ethnic strangers and for unmasking 'fake' autochthons (Geschiere, 2009). The past 20 years have witnessed an upsurge of autochthony in West European countries, such as the Netherlands, Belgium, Austria, and Denmark. In these countries arguments about 'having been there first' are increasingly evoked to exclude immigrants from full participation in the receiving society. Autochthony has become a key notion in discussions about immigration and multiculturalism among the right wing Lega Nord in Italy, the British National Party in the United Kingdom, and Flemish nationalists in Belgium. Furthermore, in Flemish Belgium and the Netherlands the distinction between natives and non-natives is made most often by using the terms 'autochthones' and 'allochthones' that were introduced by the Dutch government in 1989 and adopted by Flemish policymakers in the 1990s. The terms draw a strong contrast between those who were here first and those who came later from elsewhere.

In two large-scale survey studies in the Netherlands we found that higher national identifiers expressed stronger claims to autochthony, and these claims were, in turn, associated with greater prejudice against migrant groups. This association with prejudice was especially strong for those participants who felt that immigrants were 'getting out of place' (Martinovic & Verkuyten, 2013b).

We are good, and they are bad

I have tried to show that intergroup relations depend on the way in which 'we', 'they', and the relationship between 'us' and 'them' is construed. These constructions are not self-evident, but topics of returning debates. The boundaries and content of 'our' national identity, the nature of immigrant groups, and the meaning that immigration and immigrants have for society and the host majority are regularly defined, challenged, and redefined. There is a great deal at stake, making for quite fierce and polarized debates. So far I have discussed the different elements separately, but in reality they typically go together, for example when it involves the stigmatization of and discrimination against minority and immigrant groups. Arguing for discrimination of 'them' requires a careful representation of 'us' and the impact that 'they' have on 'us'. This can be illustrated with the case of Geert Wilders.

Wilders is the undisputed leader of the far-right Party for Freedom (PVV) which was established in the Netherlands in early 2006. The party has no official members other than himself, and Wilders is known for his fiercely negative position on Islam. In Parliament, he has proposed several motions asking the government to put a stop to all immigration from Islamic countries, prohibit the building of new mosques, close Islamic schools, ban the Koran legally, tax the wearing of a headscarf, deport criminal Muslims when necessary after denaturalization, and require ethnic registration. These proposals have been included in the election programme of the PVV, and commentators from across the political spectrum have argued that they are discriminatory and go against the constitutional rights of equal treatment and freedom of religion. In 2009, the Amsterdam Court of Appeal decided that Wilders was to be prosecuted for inciting hatred and discrimination against Muslims, but after a rather long trial he was acquitted. Despite the controversy, Wilders has been quite successful in gathering public support. For a long time he dominated the political debate and became an important political factor in the Netherlands. In the 2010 national election the PVV won no fewer than 24 seats, making it the third-largest party of the ten political parties in the Dutch parliament. In October 2010, a minority government was installed with the support of the PVV. In the most recent national election (12 September 2012), the PVV won 15 seats.

I analysed Wilder's contributions to Parliamentary debates and national newspapers by focusing on the identity-defining processes through which his discriminatory proposals are made acceptable and right (Verkuyten, in press).[10] Wilders' rhetoric is a celebration of the Netherlands and the Western world as a cultural and moral community. This is contrasted with a violent and barbaric Islam. Islam is defined as being incompatible with our virtuous way of life and thereby placed outside our social and moral order. Moreover, Islam is presented as being against 'us' and aiming to take things over and to destroy us. This makes a strong solution to 'the Islam question' a form of self-defence and thereby acceptable and legitimate. Similarly to political speeches of George Bush and Tony Blair after the 9/11 attacks (Lazar & Lazar, 2004), Wilders uses the metaphor of war to present a confrontational view of the relationship, in which Islam is the hideous attacker responsible for the fight and 'our way of life' is attacked giving us the right to defend ourselves. However, in trying not to antagonize Muslim allies in their 'war on terror', Bush and Blair defined Islam as a religion of peace, tolerance, and progress that is perverted by Muslim extremists (Lazar & Lazar, 2004). In contrast – and similarly to the British National Party (Wood & Finlay, 2008) – Wilders works up a reified and intrinsically violent image of Islam. His political project is not an international coalition against Muslim terrorism but, rather, a battle against the alleged Islamization of the Netherlands, and of the West more generally. For this, a representation of Islam that would seek the violent destruction of the Western world is more useful. Furthermore, Wilders consistently defines Islam as being an ideology rather than a religion. One important political implication of this labelling is that the constitutional rights of freedom of religion and religious education do not apply, and therefore his proposals would not be discriminatory. In addition, the threat from Islam and the urgency and need for drastic measures is further strengthened by Wilders' consistent use of the term 'Islamization'. This term depicts an on-going empirical process that turns the future into a doomsday scenario that requires immediate and firm measures to stop it from happening.

According to Wilders, Islam is an ideology similar to fascism and communism. Lumping it together with these historically well-known ideologies of oppression further emphasizes how evil Islam is. It is an ideology that contradicts and threatens 'our' self-defining virtues of freedom, peace, and tolerance. Our culture represents the good that is threatened by a barbaric Islam. In this representation, discriminatory measures become not only acceptable but morally necessary: a fight of good against evil. In this battle, and in order to preserve our liberal values, we sometimes are forced to act in ways that go against our peace-loving and tolerant nature. Furthermore, in this moral universe, leaders like Wilders, who dare to speak up and defend our virtues, have moral strength, whereas those leaders who don't are traitors and cowards.

In Wilders' discourse, our virtues are threatened by Islamic ideology rather than by Muslims as a group of people. This distinction between ideology and people is an interesting type of rhetorical work that mitigates against accusations of prejudice. A focus on Islam draws attention away from human groups, and this makes Wilders' proposals to limit and proscribe Islamic schools, mosques, the Koran, and other visible signs of this religion understandable. Criticizing a system of belief is more acceptable than stereotyping or rejecting a group of people and is part of what is expected of a politician. In addition, defining a system of belief as being unequal to our norms and values is more acceptable than labelling a group of people inferior. Notions of equality depend on similarity, and, Wilders argues, because Islam is unequal to 'us', it is not discriminatory to treat Islam in a different way. Some things are simply more equal than others, making differential treatment not discriminatory.

Justification of discrimination is a rhetorically complex accomplishment that involves not only how others are defined but also how 'we' define ourselves and the meaning of 'them' for 'us'. It is this combination of category constructions that makes Wilders' policy proposals more acceptable and even morally necessary.

Our impact on them

I have discussed the importance for intergroup relations of how in-group and out-groups are represented and defined. But there is an additional issue. Earlier I showed that there is a tendency to consider minority rights and multiculturalism more acceptable in cases when 'we' have recruited labour migrants and are therefore (in part) responsible for their presence. This indicates that there is also the question of 'our' impact on 'them' and how we feel about that.

I can feel responsible and experience a sense of guilt and shame when someone of my group does something wrong, although I had nothing to do with it personally. Like basking in reflected glory, there can also be feelings of vicarious shame and collective guilt (see Branscombe & Doosje, 2004). Such emotions provoke specific behaviours, like guilt inciting the tendency to remedy things and to compensate for the damage done. Admitting guilt implies taking responsibility and, consequently, feeling the need to make amends, in one way or another. It is therefore not surprising that governments are not eager to acknowledge responsibility for historical wrong-doings, such as slavery, colonialism, genocide, and war crimes. Such recognition would mean collective guilt. Rather than excuses, ratification, or compensation, reputation management is often the main concern: taking care of the national image rather than of the disadvantaged or victimized group. It was not easy to digest the news in early 2008 in a report of the Council of Europe that appeared to show that in the Netherlands Islamophobia had risen sharply. Politicians were very quick to dismiss the report as unreliable and biased and tried to proceed to the order of the day.

It is also not surprising that sometimes it pays for minorities to present themselves as victims. Victims are not responsible; they evoke sympathy and generate feelings of guilt in others. Guilt places the victim into the spotlight and justifies aid and rehabilitation. Some speak of a modern culture of victimhood in which minority groups claim to be victims and demand concessions or compensation (Moscovici & Pérez, 2007). Members of the majority group tend to challenge this claim by pointing to the groups' own responsibility and the existing chances and opportunities in society.

But in-group responsibility cannot always be denied so easily. Because of the Nazi atrocities, it is still difficult to feel – or at least publicly state – that one is proud to be a German. These feelings and statements are problematic. Several studies have demonstrated the importance of collective guilt in group relations. It has been found that among White Americans a sense of guilt regarding slavery in the past leads to support of compensation programmes for African Americans (Swim & Miller, 1999). In Australia, a sense of shared guilt is associated with government willingness to officially apologize to the Aborigines (Leach *et al.*, 2006). In Chile, collective guilt is an underlying factor that drives the desire for compensation for the native Mapuche Indians (Brown *et al.*, 2008).

In the Netherlands, feelings of collective guilt have been examined in relation to the end of the colonial period in Indonesia (Doosje *et al.*, 1998). In one study, three experimental conditions were used. In one condition official documents and facts about the positive role of the Dutch in Indonesia (building infrastructure, education system) were highlighted; in a second condition, the emphasis was on the negative aspects (exploitation, murder); and in the third condition, a mixed message was given. The most collective guilt was experienced in the negative condition, and this led to greater support of compensation. Furthermore, there was an interesting pattern to the degree of national identification. In the two factual conditions, in which the emphasis was on either the positive or negative aspects, there was no difference between people with low or high Dutch identification in collective guilt and the endorsement for compensation. The reality of the situation was the decisive factor here. In the mixed condition, however, there was a difference. Low identifiers were more willing to acknowledge collective guilt and to give compensation, while high identifiers tended to whitewash the national consciousness. In another study it was found that high identifiers tended to avert or selectively interpret threatening historical information. For example, compared to low identifiers, those who identify strongly with their country were less likely to remember events such as national violence and aggression compared to low identifiers, while there was little difference in remembering good deeds (Sahdra & Ross, 2007).

The finding that the presented reality of the situation was decisive in both factual conditions is interesting. This means, for example, that people who generally do not attach much value to their national identity may be persuaded by the 'facts' or 'reality' of matters. This partly explains the success of far-right political parties. These parties – like the PVV of Wilders – tend to present themselves as the 'new realists' who, in relation to immigration, not only 'know how it is' but also dare to 'say it like it is' (Prins, 2002). This is in contrast to the political correctness of the 'leftist establishment', who are considered as blind to the facts or as turning a blind eye. The 'realism' discourse means that anyone who tries to put things into perspective is accused of being naïve or scared and a weakling.

The new realism evokes a sense of drama and urgency among the public, whereby the unity and identity of society is at stake. Even people who usually do not care much about their national identity can be convinced by it. As a result, the number of followers of far-right parties and related movements can grow considerably. Compared to lower identifiers, those with higher levels of in-group identification are more likely to be concerned about their group. However, lower identifiers may be brought 'on board' when there are 'real' problems and 'real' threats to society. For example, a study in the context of New Zealand used extracts adapted from political speeches to experimentally manipulate negation (versus recognition) of the historical basis of claims for reparation for past injustices suffered by the Maoris (Sibley et al., 2008). A comparison was made between liberal and conservative voters, and the former have, in general, lower national identification than the latter. It was found that the liberal voters expressed lower levels of opposition towards pro-bicultural policy in the control and historical recognition condition. However, in the historical negation condition they had increased levels of opposition comparable to those of conservative voters. Furthermore, in a representative survey in the Netherlands it was found that lower national identifiers were equally as supportive of immigration restrictions as higher identifiers when their national identity was made salient. This means that 'bringing considerations of collective identity to the fore enlarges the coalition opposed to immigration – above and beyond those already predisposed to oppose it' (Sniderman & Hagendoorn, 2007, p. 120).

A final word

There is a documentary that shows how Jane Elliot's students look back on the class experiment (brown-eyed vs. blue-eyed), some 20 years later. Some cannot remember very much, but for others it was an important experience that they took with them throughout their lives. They had personally experienced that there are profound consequences when people are divided into categories. But, as I have argued, it is quite difficult to say in advance what exactly those consequences will be. There are psychological processes, such as striving for a distinctive and positive identity, but there are also status differences between groups, there are various meanings given to group differences, there are all kinds of situational and contextual factors, and there are always mutual influences that develop over time. If natives mistrust immigrants and fear that they undermine or threaten their culture, they can demand strict assimilation measures and a stop to immigration; this can, in turn, fuel further alienation, bitterness, and anger towards the society on the part of immigrants – and so on, into a negative spiral.

A simple relationship between group commitment and group conflict does not exist. Making a distinction is different from formulating oppositions, the primacy of the in-group does not have to mean a preoccupation with other groups, and a preference for one's own ethnic community is not the same as derogation or hostility towards others. Group identification is important, as are differences in social status and prevailing historical and ideological notions about the way in which ethnic and cultural diversity should be handled. Differences between ethnic groups are closely related to differences in societal positions. Those positions inform the way in which the world is perceived and evaluated, especially by those who identify strongly with their community. And ethnic relations develop in an ideological climate in which either more or less space is offered to cultural diversity. The way in which people interpret and evaluate these relations is influenced by societal debates. Ethnic relations are not immune to a climate in which the emphasis is either on the importance of assimilation or, conversely, on cultural diversity and multiculturalism.

6   Multicultural recognition

The 'headscarf affair of the city of Creil' in 1989 attracted a great deal of attention from the French media. It led to a political controversy and was eventually dealt with in the Supreme Court. Originally, the controversy was about the wearing of headscarves in public educational institutions, but quickly it became a debate on the integration of ethnic minorities.[1] The affair began in September at the start of the new school year, when two girls of Moroccan origin and a Tunisian girl refused to take off their headscarves in class. The principal of the school saw the wearing of the headscarf as an ostentatious act of religious expression that could not be countenanced in a public school. On 21 September, after the parents had refused to accept the decision of the school, the children were expelled from the school. Two weeks later a compromise was reached. The girls were allowed to wear their headscarves at school, but not in class. Yet two weeks later, after the intervention of the *Federation Nationale des Musulmans de France*, the girls again refused to remove their headscarves in class. They were sent to the school library, and the principal wrote a letter to the Minister of Education requesting a clear decision.

The commotion was due to the fact that French public schools are religiously neutral and do not even offer classes in religion. Public education is seen as one of the symbols of the victory of the state against the clergy. The neutral position of schools represents the national values of universalism and equality. For the opponents, the headscarf symbolized the denial of individual freedom and, by the same token, the values of the Enlightenment, and was thereby considered a threat to the French identity. For them, wearing a headscarf represented fanaticism and lack of integration. Moreover, feminists argued that the headscarf symbolized oppression and the assumed inferiority of women. The headscarf was believed to be an obstacle to emancipation and to be incompatible with individual development and human rights.

For the proponents of wearing the headscarf, there were very different symbolic meanings at stake. Public schools were supposed to embody the equality and freedom of all ethnic and religious groups. Banning the headscarf would in fact go against the French values of liberty and equality. Moreover, the wearing of a headscarf would symbolize the acceptance and rights of Muslims and minority groups in a more general sense. The acceptance of the headscarf was seen as a recognition of minority identities and thus as a necessary step in the integration process. And for some Muslim women wearing the headscarf was an expression of their independence and autonomy.

Symbols are powerful, because they transfer complex and abstract contents in a simple and strong manner. And as the commotion surrounding the headscarf illustrates, symbols almost always have multiple meanings. As a consequence, symbolism can lead to a sharpening of group boundaries and differences. The headscarf gives visible form to the group differences in beliefs and values. In this way symbols mark group boundaries in a clearly identifiable and particularly profound manner. The headscarf embodies that which 'we' (do not) stand for, what 'we' attribute (no) value to and what 'we' are (not). The difference in symbolic meaning that is given to the same object leads to discussions that are bogged down in disagreement about the true symbolic meaning ('The headscarf stands for women's oppression by Muslim men', versus 'The headscarf stands for women's freedom of choice'). The symbol embodies and highlights the difference in conceptions and the lack of commonality. Contradistinctions are magnified and strengthened. Being convinced of one's own right excludes another's claim to the same. Recent examples are not hard to find in European countries. The debate about the headscarf is being held in many of these countries, together with debates about Muslim public servants and teachers not wanting to shake hands with a person of the opposite sex, and Muslim girls swimming in a 'boerkini'. These examples are seen by some as an attack on the national identity and an expression of the oppression of women. For others, on the contrary, they represent cultural identity, freedom, and independence. For some people, these are the final proof of the failure of multiculturalism; for others, it is a question of reasonable accommodation of differing cultural practices. The discussion about diversity and how to best go about it is being carried on at all levels, concerning not only ethnicity, but also religion. Islam, in particular, has taken the central position in European debates on immigration, along with the shortcomings of multiculturalism as a societal model.

Cultural diversity

> I do not want my house to be walled in on all sides and my windows to be stuffed. I want the cultures of all lands to be blown about my house as freely as possible. But I refuse to be blown off my feet by any.

This famous quote of Mahatma Gandhi stresses the importance of cultural diversity and cultural freedom. It is a plea for openness and interest in other cultures and a statement against fearful retreat into one's own closed circle. It portrays cultural diversity as a refreshing breeze that should not blow you off your feet. But Gandhi also warned of the danger of a one-sided emphasis on cultural diversity for the development of a shared national community. He called this the 'vivisection' of a nation – cultural diversity as a means to learn and grow in freedom, but not as an end in itself.

In 2002, Otto Schily, the then German minister of Internal Affairs, stated that the 'best form of integration is assimilation'. This statement reflects the *Zeitgeist* concerning the integration of immigrants. A decade after the Dutch intellectual Paul Scheffer published his newspaper article on '*The Multicultural Drama*' (2000), European politicians queued to announce the 'death of multiculturalism' (see chapter 1). Their declarations symbolize the 'assimilationist turn' at the beginning of the new millennium in Europe (Kundnani, 2007; Vasta, 2007). The previous policies were mostly based on some form of recognition of 'differences', which allowed the maintenance of ethnic and religious minority identities and cultures. Public funds were made available to support the foundation of places of worship, minority media, and educational initiatives. For example, in some countries lessons in the mother tongue were introduced at the beginning of the 1980s to encourage minorities to preserve their language and culture, and in several countries Muslims were allowed to open Muslim schools.

Starting in the 1990s, multicultural policies were criticized for diverting attention from immigrants' socioeconomic disparities – high unemployment, underachievement in education, and poor housing (see Joppke, 2004; Vertovec & Wessendorf, 2010). At the beginning of the new millennium, the criticisms focused more on social and cultural aspects, holding multicultural policies responsible for social fragmentation and the segregation of immigrant communities. Instead of creating a common vision of belonging to a shared society, these policies, it was maintained, emphasized cultural group differences that were leading to social cleavages. It was argued that a nation could only be held together by a core set of cultural values. The focus in countries like the Netherlands, the United Kingdom, Belgium, Denmark, and Germany was increasingly on immigrants and on minorities having to adopt the assumed national *Leitkultur*. European discussions on citizenship tried to reinvigorate theories of assimilation by emphasizing the importance of defining, preserving, and adopting the national culture.

For many, multiculturalism is an outdated notion that has produced a series of tragicomic setbacks, at most good for a scornful laugh about the silly old days. We had better let bygones be bygones. Multiculturalism can lead to many undesirable things, such as considerable confusion at best and social problems and parallel societies at worst. It has become clear that multiculturalism is not *the* normative and policy inspiring model that provides an unproblematic answer to the existing cultural diversity. Therefore, in many countries the emphasis is no longer on multiculturalism, but on integration and assimilation.

But we can ask ourselves whether the baby does not too easily get thrown out with the bathwater. If something is not working always or fully, that does not mean that it does not work ever or at all. The goal of assimilation is to make differences disappear and to transform members of minorities into 'ordinary' nationals. And although there are numerous definitions of integration, here also little attention is paid to the cultural identity of minority groups. It is clear that there are problematic issues with multiculturalism. But there may be aspects that are useful, especially the idea of cultural diversity and multicultural recognition in which group identities are approached in a positive manner. For example, minorities appear to be more focused on attaining success than avoiding failure and are also more motivated to perform well in organizations and educational settings that recognize and value their group identity (e.g., Derks, *et al.*, 2007). Furthermore, there is quite some evidence that diversity has positive outcomes on productivity, creativity, innovation, and the learning potential of work groups in the workplace (Ely & Thomas, 2001). On the other hand, there is also quite a large amount of evidence that cultural diversity is related to reduced social cohesion and more conflict in work groups and to lower organizational commitment (e.g., Milliken & Martins, 1996; Watson *et al.*, 1998).

'Multicultural' and 'multiculturalism' are ubiquitous terms. They are heard in political debates, in the language of ethnic group leaders, in local government strategies and budgets, in educational settings, in health care, in popular media, in commercial marketing, and in scientific publications. There are several dozen books, readers, and articles with these terms in the title, ranging from 'Multicultural psychology' (Mio *et al.*, 2006) to 'Multicultural public relations' (Banks, 1995), and 'Multicultural mathematics' (Nelson *et al.*, 1993). Issues of multiculturalism are studied by scholars from various disciplines, such as philosophy, political science, anthropology, sociology, communication studies, and (social) psychology. Given the wide range of actors, contexts, interpretations, and usages of these terms, it is apparent that no single view or strategy is implied. Multiculturalism can mean many things and can refer to practices, policies, attitudes, beliefs, and ideologies. The different definitions and interpretations have led to the use of adjectives to distinguish between forms of multiculturalism, such as critical and difference multiculturalism (Turner, 1993), 'cosmopolitan and pluralist' multiculturalism (Hollinger, 2000), and 'liberal and illiberal' multiculturalism (Appiah, 2005).

There are also large differences between countries. In Canada, in the early 1970s, multiculturalism developed into an explicit political strategy that was formalized with the Multiculturalism Act in the 1980s. The idea spread to other immigration countries such as Australia and the United States. In Australia, multiculturalism was directed against the assimilation ideal of the former 'White Australian Policy'. In the United States, the debate on multiculturalism was influenced by the civil rights movement, the 'cultural wars' in universities and in education, and by 'identity politics' and 'politics of recognition' of minority groups.

Canada, Australia, and the United States are traditional immigration countries. They are largely shaped by immigrants, and cultural diversity is more or less part of the national self-image. Particularly in Canada and Australia, there have been attempts to equate the national with the multicultural: 'It had to be made clear that one was not closer to the heart of the Canadian identity if one was called Jones than if one's name was Kowalski or Minelli' (Taylor, 2012, p. 417; for Australia, see Moran, 2011). In most European countries the situation is different. In those countries there exists historically a large native majority group, and questions concerning integration and cultural diversity are relatively new. Although migration to countries such as the Netherlands, Belgium, France, and Germany is certainly not a recent phenomenon (Obdeijn & Schrover, 2008), immigration is a minor feature in the national self-image. European multiculturalism is mostly seen as an accommodating gesture towards immigrants and ethnic minorities, not as something that concerns the whole of society.

But there are also relevant differences between European countries. In France there is very little room for multiculturalism, due to the republican ideal that puts the emphasis on individual citizenship and the need to turn newcomers into French. Historically, countries like Great Britain and the Netherlands have taken a more sympathetic attitude towards cultural diversity. Already in 1968, the British Home Secretary, Roy Jenkins, gave a famous speech in which he endorsed an integration model, 'not as a flattening process of uniformity but of cultural diversity, coupled with equal opportunity in an atmosphere of mutual tolerance' (in Vertovec, 1998, p. 29). This led to the development of a governmental 'race relations' industry, supported by anti-discrimination measures and an emphasis on racial equality.

One of the most extensive European policies in multiculturalism was in the Netherlands. In the 1980s the acknowledgement that most migrant workers would not return to their country of origin led to the official policy of 'integration with preservation of one's own identity'. Newcomers were perceived and assessed on the basis of their ethnic background rather than as individuals. The Dutch tradition to institutionalize cultural pluralism gave space to immigrants, such as granting local voting rights to non-Dutch residents, a range of subsidies for cultural activities, and public funding of Islamic schools. Since the 1980s, a great deal has changed. The idea of multiculturalism has been replaced by a policy of common citizenship and social integration, and many see cultural assimilation as the only realistic option (Vasta, 2007). Nevertheless, the Netherlands is still a country that makes allowances in numerous ways for the culture and religion of minority groups.

The retreat from multiculturalism in discourse, and to lesser extent in deed (Vertovec & Wessendorf, 2010), is not limited to the Netherlands. It has occurred in most Western countries and also at the level of political theory (Joppke, 2004). In several countries – including Canada and Australia – the practical necessity of another model of a diverse society is discussed. A strong liberal critique of multiculturalism has been developed, and political philosophers are questioning the principles and assumptions of multiculturalism (e.g., Barry, 2001). Several of these principles and assumptions are of a socio-psychological nature. Multi-culturalism is, after all, about groups and group identities.

Social psychological assumptions

In the first half of last century, newcomers often tried to downplay standing out from the population and endeavoured to become part of society as quickly as possible, for example by anglicizing their name: think, for example, of the Eastern Europeans who moved to the United States and the Dutch Frisians who emigrated to Canada, Australia, and New Zealand. In the 1960s, this changed in the United States with the rise of the civil rights movement and ethnic revival, which also occurred in countries such as Canada. Ethnic differences were rediscovered, emphasized, and propagated. The emphasis shifted more and more away from adaptation and commonalities in the direction of group differences and identity. Minorities claimed the right to be different and to maintain their self-determined identity.

The notion of multiculturalism sometimes went one step further. Not only was the possibility of preserving one's own identity emphasized, but this was also supposed to be a necessary factor if one was to integrate and to relate to others in an open and tolerant manner. Multiculturalism as the positive recognition and valuing of cultural differences would, it was argued, contribute to strong and positive identities and thereby to more harmonious ethnic relations. This assumption has been studied particularly by social psychologists. It involves multiculturalism in a form of multicultural recognition according to which cultural diversity is seen in a positive way, with minority groups getting the recognition they psychologically need and deserve (Parekh, 2000; Taylor, 1992). It is this assumption that I wish to investigate more closely in this chapter. To this end, I look first at attitudes towards multiculturalism from minority and majority group perspectives. Then I discuss the notion that multiculturalism is favourable for identity development, particularly among minorities. Subsequently, I examine the idea that multicultural recognition can contribute to positive group relations and mutual tolerance. Finally, I discuss some limitations and problems of multiculturalism.

Majority and minority differences

People strive for a distinctive and positive ethnic identity. This provides a sense of grip, meaning, belonging, and pride. It is therefore understandable that you want your ethnic group to be socially acknowledged, accepted, and appreciated. Moreover, such recognition can lead to a range of substantial benefits in the form of subsidies, facilities, and rights. For minority groups, multiculturalism offers the possibility of maintaining their own culture and gaining a higher social status in society. Therefore it is likely that minority groups will be in favour of multiculturalism rather than assimilation whereby they slowly merge into the larger whole.

The situation of the majority group is different. By supporting multiculturalism, they give space to the identities and needs of minority groups. They may see ethnic minorities and their desire to maintain their own culture as a threat to cultural dominance, group identity, and status position. In most European countries, especially, multiculturalism is seen as something for minorities only. It supports the position and cultural identity of minority groups and threatens the identity and social position of the majority. The majority group will therefore be more likely to argue for assimilation rather than for multiculturalism.

There is quite a great deal of research that examines the endorsement of multiculturalism using general statements (e.g., 'Migrants should be supported in their attempts to preserve their own cultural heritage'; 'Migrants should adapt and forget their culture as much as possible'). This research shows that among the majority, support for multiculturalism is indeed not very high.[2] Apart from Canada, where multiculturalism is generally favoured, surveys indicate that in, for example, Australia, the United States, Germany, Switzerland, Slovakia, and the Netherlands, this is not the case.[3] Majority group members appear to have a tendency to lean in favour of assimilation, while minority members are stronger supporters of multiculturalism. In eight studies conducted among native Dutch and Turkish immigrants, this difference was evident (see Verkuyten, 2006). The same difference between majority and minority members has been found in 20 other European countries (Schalk-Soekar, 2007).

Apart from status differences, there are other possible explanations for this group difference in the endorsement of multiculturalism or, rather, assimilation. One is that cultural characteristics might be involved. For example, Turkish immigrants may endorse multiculturalism more strongly than the native Dutch because the group-thinking that underlies it is in line with their more collectivist values and worldview. And assimilation, with its emphasis on individual citizens, may be more compatible with the typical individualistic values of the native Dutch. This interpretation cannot explain, however, why individualistic minority groups (e.g. African Americans) also tend to endorse multiculturalism more than the majority.

Another explanation is that resistance towards cultural change underlies the differential preference for multiculturalism and assimilation among both majority and minority groups. For the majority group, multiculturalism implies change to accommodate other groups, whereas assimilation means that minorities must change. Change in and of itself can be considered threatening, leading to a desire to avoid it. Thus, the same resistance to change might explain why majorities tend to favour assimilation and ethnic minorities favour multiculturalism. Zárate and colleagues have examined this idea in terms of 'cultural inertia'. Among Latinos in the United States they found supporting experimental evidence for it, especially among high identifiers (Quezada *et al.*, 2012; Zárate *et al.*, 2012). For example, when participants were encouraged to believe that their culture will have to change, high Latino identifiers expressed stronger political advocacy for Latino culture.

Cultural change can be resisted because, for example, it undermines one's sense of grip on the social world or threatens the distinctiveness and value of the in-group identity. It can also be resisted because it goes against status positions and group interests. Groups can endorse ideologies of multiculturalism or assimilation because it legitimizes their status position. In order to examine this latter possibility, we performed the following study (Verkuyten & Yildiz, 2006). Two different groups of Turkish Dutch participants took part in the research: with a Turkish and with a Kurdish background. There were two conditions. In one condition, attention was drawn to the situation in the Netherlands; in the other condition participants were asked to focus on the situation in Turkey. In the Netherlands, both the Turks and the Kurds are minority groups, whereas in

Turkey, the Turks are the majority, while the Kurds form a minority. In both conditions, participants reported how strongly they agreed with the same questions regarding multiculturalism and minority rights. Following the idea about the importance of group status, the expectation was that both the Turks and Kurds presented with the Dutch context, but only the Kurds in the Turkish context would be in favour of minority rights. In each of these settings, they form a minority. But the Turks in Turkey are the majority group and will therefore be less in favour of such rights. The results indeed confirmed these hypotheses, as can be seen in Figure 6.1.

In the Dutch context, no difference was found between Turks and Kurds, while in the Turkish context the Kurds were much more strongly in favour of minority rights than the Turks. The Turks also scored lower in the Turkish context, where they form the majority, in comparison to the Dutch context, in which they are a minority. The Kurds are a minority in both settings, whereas their status is significantly worse in Turkey than in the Netherlands. In Turkey they have been the target of a harsh assimilation policy for a long period of time. It was not, for example, until 2003 that the Kurds were officially given the right to use Kurdish names, broadcast programmes in the Kurdish language, and set up private language courses. It therefore stands to reason that the Kurdish participants were more in favour of minority rights in the Turkish context in comparison to the Dutch context.

So it appears that group status plays an important role in where one stands in relation to multiculturalism. Compared to majority members, minorities have more to gain from multiculturalism and therefore tend to support it more strongly. The results of these studies support social psychological theories, such as social identity theory (Tajfel & Turner, 1979) and social dominance theory (Sidanius & Pratto, 1999), that emphasize the importance of status differences and group interests. However, it does not follow from these theories that multiculturalism is by definition less relevant for majorities than for minorities. Majority members can be expected to endorse multiculturalism more strongly when it serves their group interest. Morrison and Chung (2011) focused on multiculturalism in relation to the way majority members think about themselves. They asked majority members to mark their race/ethnicity as either 'White' or 'European American' before answering questions about their ethnic attitudes. Multiculturalism tends

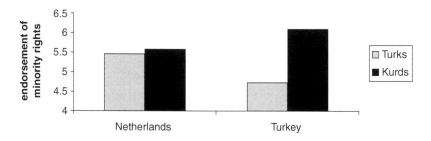

Figure 6.1 The endorsement of minority rights by national context and ethnic group

to be framed as pertaining to minority groups, and the 'White' label suggests that the majority lacks a meaningful ethnic identity. Therefore self-identifying as White, compared to European American, may cause majority members to feel more distant from ethnic minorities and to be less supportive of multiculturalism. The findings of their two studies supported this reasoning.

In another experimental study the question was whether seeing multiculturalism as self-relevant makes majority group members more supportive of cultural diversity (Stevens *et al.*, 2008). As predicted, majority members were less favourable towards multiculturalism after being presented with an ideology of acknowledgement and respect for minority identities than after being told that diversity is relevant to majorities as well as minorities (see also Plaut *et al.*, 2011). Thus, making multiculturalism relevant to majority members increases their support for diversity policies.

The fact that multiculturalism is not by definition less relevant for the group interests of majorities than of minorities can also be illustrated by looking at the difference between the national and the local level. For example, in the United States Whites constitute the majority and Blacks a minority at the national level, whereas this can be the other way around in neighbourhoods and at universities. One study showed that at the national level Whites endorsed assimilation more than Blacks, who were more in favour of multiculturalism. However, at the university level, when in a minority position, both Whites and Blacks endorsed multiculturalism more (Hehman *et al.*, 2012).

The importance of group status and group interests for the endorsement of multiculturalism is also evident by looking at different countries. Take the example of Mauritius (briefly introduced in chapter 2), which is viewed as a strong candidate of the 'truly successful polyethnic societies' (Eriksen, 2004, p. 79). Despite the representation of the nation as a complex multicultural mosaic, status differences exist between the ethnic groups. However, in contrast to studies in Europe and North America, the dominant group of Hindus does not endorse multiculturalism less strongly than the minority group of Creoles (Ng Tseung-Wong & Verkuyten, 2010). This counter-example is explained by the official image of Mauritius as being a diasporic nation and the related multicultural politics of the state that encourage the cultivation of 'ancestral cultures'. Diversity is based on the recognition of the culture of groups that have clear ancestral origins, like the Hindus, who are powerful in politics and the public sector. In contrast, the term 'Creoles' is used for a rather diverse population of descendants of African and Malagasy slaves. They do not have a recognized claim on an ancestral culture and ancestral language with an origin outside Mauritius. As a consequence, the diasporic ancestral culture policy justifies the position of the Hindus and has exclusionist implications for the low status Creoles (Eisenlohr, 2006).

Another example is Japan. Some researchers have argued that the Japanese maintain their privileged position by essentializing cultural differences in the name of multiculturalism. The endorsement of multiculturalism would be compatible with a strong ethnic-national identity because it enables the dominant majority to draw strict boundaries between ethnic minorities and themselves. In a large-scale study, a positive association between ethno-national identity and the endorsement of multiculturalism was found (Nagayoshi, 2011). Those who demand cultural homogeneity within Japan tend to approve of multiculturalism because it emphasizes the 'otherness' of ethnic minorities and justifies the right to maintain the original Japanese culture. This is quite similar to some of the arguments of extreme right-wing groups in Europe. For example, Alain de Benoist of the French National Front has said that they feel a strong bond with Taylor's (1992) multicultural politics of recognition, and he has claimed their '*droit de difference*'. Similarly, the supporters of the former apartheid in South Africa argued that communities should live separately from one another. This, it was argued, was not to prevent certain groups from participating in economic and political life or to make them a target of racism and discrimination, but to give every single cultural identity ample space to grow and to prosper.

These examples show that multiculturalism can serve the interest of majority members and therefore be relevant to them. As a result, majorities can endorse multiculturalism more strongly than minority groups, and this endorsement can lead to more negative intergroup relations. More generally, these findings support a functional interpretation of people's preference for different cultural diversity models. Groups tend to endorse the model that supports the maintenance of their cultural identity and group position in society.

Ethnic identification

Multiculturalism and minority rights are about groups and group identities. Those who identify more strongly with their group are also those who have more to gain, or lose. The difference between majority and minority members in their support of multiculturalism can therefore be expected to be related to the degree of group identification. The stronger minority group members identify with their ethnic group, the more importance they will attach to their identity and culture being recognized and respected. In contrast, among the majority group a strong national identity will be associated with a greater emphasis on assimilation. Several studies in the Netherlands confirm this idea (see Verkuyten, 2006). Minorities who identify strongly with their ethnic group, are more in favour of multiculturalism, while group identification within the majority is associated with a rejection of multiculturalism and an emphasis on assimilation. It also appears that among Turks in the context of the Netherlands and among Kurds in the context of the Netherlands and Turkey, a stronger ethnic identification is associated with greater endorsement of minority rights (Verkuyten & Yildiz, 2006). However, among Turks who are the majority group in the Turkish context, a stronger national identification is associated with rejection of minority rights.

But, once again, it is not just a question of the degree of identification, independent of the content of the national identity. In traditional immigration countries such as Canada and Australia, cultural diversity is to some extent part of the national self-image. This means that high national identification will be more easily associated with a positive attitude towards multiculturalism. If you are proud that you are Canadian and Canada is a country of cultural diversity, then you are more likely to accept multiculturalism. In Mauritius, this appears to be the case also. For both Hindus and Creoles, higher national identification tends to go together with a more positive attitude towards cultural diversity. However, in most European countries the situation is different, because there exists a traditional majority group, and multiculturalism is predominantly seen as something for immigrants and ethnic minorities. In these countries the debate about multiculturalism and assimilation involves opposing group identities which has a special bearing for those who identify with their group. For example, those who have weak group affiliations tend to have other reasons to agree with multiculturalism or assimilation, such as considerations of social equity and social cohesion.

Equality and cohesion

Group status and group identifications are important factors when it comes to understanding why people are either more or less in favour of multicultural recognition and minority rights. However, this is obviously not the whole story. There are additional considerations and arguments that need to be taken into account.

The multicultural society is a difficult and controversial topic. It leads to much confusion, ambivalence and disagreement. For example, research in Australia has shown that multiculturalism is considered to be beneficial for the economy of the country and as a means to combat social inequality, but that people also point at disadvantages, such as the threat to social unity and national stability (Ginges & Cairns, 2000). And research among Dutch natives indicates that many struggle with weighing the pros and cons of multiculturalism (Breugelmans & Van de Vijver, 2004). All kinds of principal and pragmatic arguments are put forward when it comes to the debate on multicultural society. Three key arguments can be identified (Vermeulen & Slijper, 2003). The first is the importance and value of cultural diversity and identity per se. The second refers to equal opportunities and the third to social cohesion. All three factors are consistent with those emphasized in social identity theory (Tajfel & Turner, 1979): group identification, and the legitimacy and stability of group relations. I will first discuss the last two.

Equality

In the early 1970s, the term 'multiculturalism' was predominantly used in relation to equality before the law and equal opportunities. Multiculturalism was seen as a strategy to combat domination, prejudice, and discrimination. Later the emphasis was placed more on the recognition of differences and cultural diversity. Common to most notions of multiculturalism is that they seek to go beyond equal civil and political rights for all citizens, to some level of public recognition and support of ethnic, cultural, and religious identities. Yet the notion of equality and equal opportunities has remained an important part of discussions around multiculturalism and minority rights. According to the political philosopher Charles Taylor (1992), two interpretations of equality are at stake: 'equal dignity' and 'equal respect'. The former refers to the shared humanity and shared citizenship of everyone. All citizens should be treated in the same way, and therefore policies need to be colour blind and set anti-discrimination measures, where necessary. The latter focuses on that which distinguishes people from one another. Equality can also mean that groups should be treated differently because meaningful differences should not be ignored. Taking cultural differences seriously sometimes implies that culturally sensitive interpretations of general rules and rights are necessary, and sometimes that differential treatment and special facilities are required, not as a means of creating a new inequality, but in ensuring justice to each and everyone. The equal right to express one's religion can mean that some practices are allowed for one religious community and not for others. Allowing the ritual slaughter of animals by Muslims and Jews is in some European countries an exemption from ordinary law. Sometimes special facilities are required, such as a place to pray at work. And the general right to practise your own religion can mean for the one celebrating Christmas and for the other not having to work to celebrate the end of Ramadan. Critics, however, point out that equality and cultural identity are not always easily reconcilable. In their opinion, equal rights should be based on the uniform idea of individual citizenship and not on (alleged) group differences, as the latter would only give rise to new inequalities (Barry, 2001).

In everyday life multiculturalism is also associated with the notion of equality. The emphasis on cultural differences and minority rights is seen as a means to tackle inequality and structural discrimination. Those who more often perceive structural discrimination against minorities will endorse multiculturalism more strongly. The injustice that results from discrimination leads people to stand up for the rights of minority groups. This applies to both majority and minority group members, as was found in four different studies (see Verkuyten, 2006). The recognition of ethnic inequality and unfair treatment is a clear reason for supporting forms of multicultural recognition. Moreover, there is a belief that multiculturalism creates a more open and accepting attitude towards others, which prevents discrimination.

But the argument of equality and equal opportunities can also unfold in quite a different direction. It can be used for opposing the idea of multiculturalism. Some natives view multiculturalism, with its special facilities and arrangements for immigrant groups, as an example of unequal treatment in which they end up with the short end of the stick. In their opinion, multiculturalism is not about differentiated treatment that allows minorities to have the same opportunities as the majority group, but they see it as discrimination against natives. They believe that multiculturalism only benefits newcomers and minorities, leaving natives out in the cold ('what about us?'), or even places them at a disadvantage. There sometimes is a grain of truth to this, and this sentiment is certainly not always or only due to resentment and prejudice (Verkuyten, 1997b).

Social cohesion and stability

The concept of multiculturalism almost always raises questions about social cohesion and national unity. It is not easy to create and maintain a sense of solidarity across ethnic and cultural boundaries. Proponents of multiculturalism claim that recognizing and embracing cultural differences is actually a prerequisite for the development of social cohesion and unity. It is only when people feel accepted and appreciated for what they are that they come to identify with the wider society in which they live. The integration and national identification of immigrants and minorities would require cultural recognition. In contrast, assimilation, with its emphasis on the culture and identity of the majority group, will only lead to minority members rejecting the society.

Critics, however, point to the divisive consequences of multiculturalism: what Gandhi called the vivisection of the nation. They maintain that the emphasis on cultural diversity leads to ethnic segregation and fragmentation, and that the recognition of cultural diversity and minority rights leads to intergroup problems and conflicts that undermine the stability and unity of society.

Majority and minority members do not give equal weight to these arguments. Research has shown that, compared to minority groups, majority members tend to place greater emphasis on the importance of stability and unity. And the stronger this emphasis, the less they are in favour of multiculturalism and minority rights, and the more strongly they endorse assimilation (see Verkuyten, 2006). But this difference in emphasis does not mean that minorities do not place any importance on national unity and cohesion. In fact, they do, but they expect a kind of unity in which there is room for their own identity as well. Proponents of multiculturalism argue that unity and a common national identity are equally as important as the recognition of difference (Modood, 2007; Parekh, 2000). A well-functioning society needs a sense of commitment and common belonging, making it important to foster a spirit of shared national identity. Without this, a society would degenerate into a collection of segregated cultural groups. It is argued that a dual identity is needed in which group distinctiveness is affirmed within a context of national unity and common belonging.[4]

Ethnic identity and self-feelings

> National unity, if it is to mean anything in the deeply personal sense, must be founded on confidence in one's own identity; out of this can grow respect for others and a willingness to share ideas, attitudes and assumptions.
>
> (Pierre Trudeau, 1971)

> Multiculturalism ensures that all citizens can keep their identities, can take pride in their ancestry and have a sense of belonging. Acceptance gives Canadians a feeling of security and self-confidence making them open to and accepting of diverse cultures.
>
> (Department of Canadian Heritage)

In the first quote, the former Canadian Prime Minister Trudeau articulates why multiculturalism is necessary for his country. The first part of the quote is consistent with the idea that recognition of cultural identity is important for national unity. The second part is about what social psychologists sometimes call the 'multiculturalism hypothesis'. Multiculturalism is expected to contribute to a strong identity and thereby to positive relations between groups. The second quote expresses the same idea but in a slightly different way. Thus, one part of the multiculturalism hypothesis concerns identity and self-feelings, and the other part is about acceptance, openness, and tolerance.

In most countries, multiculturalism supports the identity and culture of minority groups. The different versions of multiculturalism reject the idea of assimilation and stress that all groups have the right to maintain and express their distinctive identities. As Margalit and Halbertal say (1994, p. 491), 'Human beings have a right to culture – not just any culture, but their own.' But why exactly would this be? The reasoning is that culture inevitably and fundamentally shapes people in how they are. This is not meant to say that people are helpless victims of their culture, but that enculturation is crucial for the development into a competent, independent, and self-aware individual. Culture provides a worldview, a meaningful space that is necessary for making meaningful choices in life. The culture individuals grown up in moulds them in a profound and deep way. Multiculturalism, therefore, would not be about superficial or voluntary group memberships, but, rather, about profound ways of being. Proponents of multiculturalism tend to have a communitarian perspective: an individual's personality and sense of self would be primarily shaped by their own cultural community. Assimilation would therefore be an impossible demand, as it would mean turning your back on that which shaped how you are. Research shows that assimilation often involves social stress, anxiety, depression, and an increased risk of schizophrenia (e.g., Selten *et al.*, 2007; Veling *et al.*, 2008). Multicultural recognition, on the other hand, would allow minority members to develop a strong and positive identity that goes together with feelings of confidence and self-esteem. Respecting another person would not be possible without recognizing his or her cultural background. Or, as the British political philosopher Parekh (2000, p. 8) states, 'We appreciate better than before that culture deeply matters to people, that their self-esteem depends on others' recognition and respect.'

The idea that multiculturalism *leads* to a stronger identity and positive self-feelings is not easy to investigate. Experimental research can give some insight into the assumed causality, for example by comparing (temporary) group identification in a context where the emphasis is on multiculturalism or, conversely, on assimilation. I have used this approach in two studies among Dutch and Turkish Dutch participants (Verkuyten, 2005a). The main question was whether the experimental – and thereby situational – salience of multiculturalism has an effect on how strongly people identify with their ethnic group. In both studies, the same results were found. Native Dutch participants were more positive about their Dutch identity in the assimilation condition, whereas Turkish Dutch participants were more proud of their Turkish background in the multicultural condition. A social environment in which the identity of minorities is highlighted (multiculturalism) results in stronger group identification among minority members, while this is the case for natives in a context where the identity of the majority is highlighted (assimilation). In short, recognition and positive attention for one's own identity appear to lead to stronger group identification in both majority and minority group members.

In a context in which people are recognized and acknowledged in their cultural background, they will be able to develop positive feelings about their ethnic identity. Another way to demonstrate this is by comparing a variety of different situations, such as school classes. Schools differ both in the extent to which, as well as the way in which, they pay attention to cultural diversity. In one school multicultural efforts are made to promote and highlight diversity in a positive manner, while in another school the emphasis may, rather, lie on colour blindness in which 'children are children' (see chapter 7). By comparing a large number of classes, one can examine whether school differences make a difference for students' sense of ethnic identity. In a study carried out in 182 classes from 82 primary schools situated across the Netherlands, it turned out that multicultural education contributes to a more positive ethnic identity (Verkuyten & Thijs, 2004). In schools where ethnic differences are recognized and valued, students have more positive feeling about their ethnic background. This was the case for Dutch as well as for Turkish Dutch, Moroccan Dutch, and Surinamese Dutch students.

A further possibility to examine the influence of cultural recognition on self-feelings is to conduct experimental research. One can try to determine whether a situation in which cultural diversity is (temporarily) endorsed has an effect on how people feel about themselves. In one study among both Dutch and Turkish Dutch participants there were two experimental conditions: one focused on the recognition and appreciation of cultural groups and group differences (group context), the other emphasized individual characteristics and individual differences (colour blind or individual context) (Verkuyten, 2009a; see also Verkuyten, 2010). In addition, the degree of ethnic group identification was considered. Acceptance and recognition of cultural diversity is particularly important for those who identify with their ethnic group. They will derive their self-feelings from their group membership, and it is therefore important for them that their group is recognized. In contrast, situations where the emphasis is on cultural groups and group differences are not favourable for people who place little importance on their ethnic background and want to be recognized and valued for who they are as an individual person. For them, an individual context can be expected to contribute more to positive self-feelings. In both studies, and for both groups of participants, the results were identical. As shown in Figure 6.2 (page 172), a positive cultural group context is favourable for the self-feelings of participants who identify relatively strongly with their ethnic background, while an individual context is more favourable for participants who do not identify so strongly with this background. In short, the positive emphasis on cultural diversity is psychologically beneficial if your ethnic identity plays an important part in how you perceive

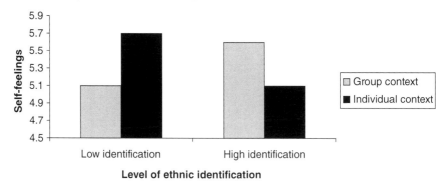

Figure 6.2 Self-feelings and ethnic identification for two experimental conditions (group and individual context)

yourself, but it is not so advantageous for people who take pride in their personal characteristics and accomplishments, and do not identify strongly with their ethnic community. The findings were similar for the Dutch and the Turkish Dutch participants, which indicates that as far as these self-feelings are concerned, it does not make a difference whether you belong to the majority or the minority.

There is always the question about what these experimental findings tell us about everyday life and the broader social context. It becomes more convincing if similar results are found in other experiments in other countries, which is indeed the case (e.g., Downie *et al.*, 2006; Yip, 2005; Yip & Fuligni, 2002). But that which can be manipulated in an experimental context remains a weak representation of the probing intensity of social reality. Therefore, we have also examined group identifications in the period immediately before (2001), during (2002) and after (2003) the rise of the Dutch far-right political leader Pim Fortuyn (Verkuyten & Zaremba, 2005). In that period there was a sharp turn in the political and public debate on multiculturalism. Emphasis shifted away from diversity to national unity and assimilation, and this merged with the national identity of the Dutch that would need to be protected from Islam. In 2002, it was indeed found that the native Dutch identified more strongly with the Netherlands than in 2001. For the Turkish Dutch these changes in the social and political climate were threatening to their identity, leading them, in response, to withdraw more into their own communities and to emphasize their ethnic identity. Indeed, in 2002 it appeared that the Turkish Dutch identified more strongly with their ethnic community than they had in 2001.

Multiculturalism and intergroup relations

Multiculturalism is a difficult and controversial issue that can be interpreted in different ways. Australian citizens have been found to see multicultural policy as beneficial for the country and as an impetus to greater social equality but at the same time to perceive disadvantages such as a threat to the status quo and to the unity and stability of the country (Ginges & Cairns, 2000). In the Netherlands, a positive social norm involving support for multiculturalism and a negative social norm referring to multiculturalism as a threat were found to co-exist (Breugelmans & Van de Vijver, 2004). Both social norms were predictors of multicultural attitudes.

Multiculturalism as a threat

In North American and European societies multicultural recognition typically offers a positive view of cultural maintenance by ethnic minority groups. Majority members, on the other hand, may see multiculturalism as a threat to their cultural dominance and group identity. An interview study among native Dutch participants mapped the social thought or main arguments used for justifying or criticizing the idea of multiculturalism (Verkuyten, 2004b). Issues of threat and anxiety were mentioned most often when arguing against a multicultural society and in favour of assimilation. Participants suggested that a multicultural society could pose a threat to natives and that assimilation of minorities provides a sense of security and control.

Majority members sometimes see multicultural recognition as threatening to their group because it requires them to relinquish some of their power and status (e.g., Correll *et al.*, 2008; Verkuyten, 2006). As a result, multiculturalism can contribute to a backlash against immigrants and minority groups. For example, when participants are exposed to multiculturalism, a stereotypical minority member is liked more than a counter-stereotypical member (Gutiérrez & Unzueta, 2010). This suggests that multiculturalism creates a preference for minority members who remain within the boundaries of their ethnicity. Furthermore, group identification has been found to be related to lower support for affirmative action when the focus was on losses for the White in-group but not when gains for the Black out-group were central (Lowery *et al.*, 2006).

Several studies in the United States have found that multicultural ideologies can increase prejudice and stereotyping of minority groups (Ryan *et al.*, 2007; Wolsko *et al.* 2000). These negative effects are particularly likely to occur in conflict situations (Correll *et al.*, 2008) and among high majority group identifiers who tend to respond to threats with prejudice and discrimination. For example, White Americans who are encouraged to think in terms of multicultural recognition show greater prejudice, especially when they identify strongly with their ethnicity and perceive threats to the value of their own group (Morrison *et al.*, 2010). Similarly, it has been shown that when the focus is on losses that the majority group will incur, the ethnic identification of White Americans is negatively related to their support for affirmative action (Lowery *et al.*, 2006). And three studies demonstrated that a salient multicultural ideology increases hostile treatment of threatening out-group interaction partners (Vorauer & Sasaki, 2011).

It is also likely that the more strongly majority members believe that immigrants and minorities want to maintain their original culture, the more threatened they feel, and that this threat, in turn, will reduce support for multiculturalism. In contrast, when majority group members believe that immigrants and minority members want to adopt the mainstream culture, they feel less threatened and are more likely to support multiculturalism. In the context of Great Britain, there is supporting evidence for these predictions in three studies (Tip *et al.*, 2012). These findings suggest that the majority group supports multiculturalism as long as they believe that minority members do not wish to segregate and maintain their original culture.

However, this does not necessarily mean that immigrants and minorities who want to assimilate to the mainstream are fully accepted. As discussed in chapter 5, those in the majority who support group-based dominance and inequality can become more prejudiced in a context of assimilation than in one of integration (Guimond *et al.*, 2010; Thomsen *et al.*, 2008). Assimilation implies the blurring of group boundaries, which can pose a threat to the existing group-based social hierarchies. In contrast, immigrants who adopt the mainstream culture but without giving up their ethnic culture (integration) are in a sense confirming the existing social hierarchy.

Positive implications of multicultural recognition

In the interview study mentioned (Verkuyten, 2004b), Dutch natives not only argued that multiculturalism can be threatening to their group, but they also said that a multicultural society is a good thing because it enriches society and allows one to learn about other ways of life and to improve and develop oneself ('it is important for your general development'). Multiculturalism was thought to 'open up your eyes', help one to develop an 'open attitude towards what you do not know', and to lead to more awareness of and sensitivity to the existence of different worldviews and, consequently, to a more nuanced view on one's own culture ('knowing that one's own culture is neither the only one nor the best one'). In addition, multiculturalism was believed to prevent discrimination and racism by stressing equality and stimulating people to be more tolerant and respectful towards others.

In line with this, social psychological research has found positive implications of multicultural recognition for intergroup relations (see Rattan & Ambady, 2013). Majority group members who endorse multicultural recognition tend to evaluate ethnic minorities more positively.[5] Furthermore, when experimentally encouraged to think in terms of multiculturalism, majority members exhibit lower levels of explicit and implicit prejudice against minority groups and show lower tendencies to discriminate (e.g., Kauff & Wagner, 2012; Richeson & Nussbaum, 2004; Wolsko *et al.*, 2000). The endorsement of multicultural recognition also predicts more positive attitudes towards controversial social policies, such as immigration and affirmative action, as well as citizenship engagement (Plaut, 2010).

Why is multiculturalism effective?

Proponents of multiculturalism always point at the positive implications for intergroup relations: that multiculturalism increases one's knowledge and perspective-taking ability, that it sets norms that go against stigmatization and intolerance, and that it leads to more mature identities.

Knowledge and perspective taking

In contrast to assimilation, multiculturalism prompts an outward focus away from the in-group and towards learning about and accepting ethnic out-groups. For example, within a multicultural experimental context White Canadians were found to be more other-focused and making more positive other-directed remarks during social interactions (Vorauer *et al.*, 2009). In a study among mainland Chinese residents, it was found that their negative attitude towards Hong Kong Chinese was related to perceived value incongruence (Guan *et al.*, 2011). The higher the value incongruence between mainland Chinese and Hong Kong Chinese, the more negatively the latter were evaluated. However, value incongruence was less strongly related to negative out-group evaluations among participants who endorsed multiculturalism, compared to those who did not. People with a more multicultural worldview appreciate diversity and support tolerance, making value incongruence less relevant for their out-group attitudes. For them, diversity offers, rather, the possibilities of learning about and from members of other groups.

Furthermore, in a health care organization it was found that Whites' multiculturalism is associated with higher minority engagement (Plaut *et al.*, 2009). The endorsement of multicultural recognition also has been found to be associated with lower levels of prejudice among majority members (e.g., Velasco González *et al.*, 2008; Ward & Masgoret, 2006). These findings support the argument that multicultural recognition can provide confidence, trust, and security among everyone living in plural societies (Berry, 2006). These positive associations and effects have been found independently of the level of group identification (Verkuyten, 2005a; Wolsko *et al.*, 2006).

A multicultural framework tends to increase perspective-taking with a more outward and responsive focus (see Plaut, 2010). Cultural diversity can lead to increased familiarity with other ways of thinking, feeling, and doing. This improves your creativity, broadens your horizon, and puts your own worldview into perspective. Being aware that others think very differently about not just everyday things but also important affairs of life allows you to take the perspective of others. And perspective-taking leads to a more positive attitude towards those others (Galinski & Moskowitz, 2000). Furthermore, experiences and knowledge contribute to increased understanding, and increased understanding prevents stereotyping. In six studies it was found that multicultural experience reduced the endorsement of negative stereotypes, racism, and discriminatory hiring decisions in relation to a range of minority groups in the United States and Israel (Tadmor *et al.*, 2012). The reason for these positive effects was that the exposure to multiculturalism lessened the need for cognitive closure – that is, the desire for firm and simple answers to questions. Other studies have found that experimental exposure to multicultural experience and immersing oneself in other cultures can have creative and performance advantages (Leung & Chiu, 2010; Leung *et al.*, 2008). Multicultural experience can lead to a process of cognitive 'unfreezing' in which existing assumptions and beliefs are questioned and alternatives considered. Greater cognitive flexibility seems especially likely when the experience – or cultural diversity more generally – challenges stereotypical expectations, and individuals are motivated and able to resolve the resulting stereotypical inconsistencies (Crisp & Turner, 2010). Stereotypically challenging diversity can stimulate more careful and elaborate thinking.

The idea that multicultural experience and knowledge have a positive effect on intergroup relations is central in the education context. In many countries and schools, curricula and educational practices aimed at learning about cultural differences and combating racism and discrimination have been proposed and implemented. Prejudice reduction is the most intensively studied aspect of multicultural education, and there is quite some evidence that multicultural education improves intergroup relations (see Stephan & Vogt, 2004; Zirkel, 2008). A basic assumption underlying most multicultural educational initiatives is that prejudice and out-group dislike result from ignorance about cultural others. Therefore, learning about cultural differences is considered of crucial importance (see Nagda *et al.*, 2004; Rosenthal & Levy, 2010).

Theoretically, learning about cultural differences may be effective in various ways. First, when counter-stereotypic information is acquired, negative out-group attitudes can be challenged. In addition, through learning, students can develop a better understanding of different cultural traditions, practices, and behaviours as well as a less ethnocentric worldview. Furthermore, there are not only differences between cultural groups but also many similarities, and learning about these similarities might stimulate the perception of cultural others being children or people 'just like us', which results in a more inclusive school identity (Houlette *et al.*, 2004; Levy *et al.*, 2005). Finally, by learning about negative historical and social experiences and circumstances of minority groups, students can develop more understanding and empathy and thereby greater acceptance of these groups (Hughes *et al.*, 2007).

Teaching children about other customs, traditions, and historical circumstances can increase their acceptance. Schools differ in the attention they pay to cultural diversity, and they also differ in the level of prejudice of their students. The question is whether the one is related to the other. By comparing a large number of classes one can statistically control for various school characteristics, such as denomination, number of students and ethnic composition. We have done this in four studies and focused on students' ethnic group evaluations and experiences with ethnic victimization and exclusion (see Verkuyten & Thijs, in press). The classroom context does, indeed, appear to play a significant role. Children from the same class are more alike in their evaluations and experiences than children from different classes. Furthermore, children are more positive about other ethnic groups in classes where more attention is paid to cultural diversity. More knowledge and understanding of other cultures seems to result in more positive attitudes towards ethnic out-groups. Children become more aware of cultural differences and may improve empathy towards ethnic out-groups (Chang & Le, 2010), which makes it less easy to make a simple distinction in favour of the in-group.

However, this awareness can also mean that one learns to interpret events and behaviours in stereotypical ethnic and cultural terms. It is not easy for multicultural education to stay away from re-confirming stereotypical group images whereby cultural differences are emphasized and linked to specific ethnic groups ('This is typical for Moroccans, this for Turks, and this for the Dutch'). This is one reason why some prefer to speak about 'intercultural' education in which the focus is on mutual interactions, dialogue, and exchanges that contribute to changing identities and cultures (Portera, 2008). This term has also found acceptance in the social welfare and health care sectors and suggests a more interactive and dynamic form of dealing with cultural differences (Rattansi, 2011).

So, multicultural education can have positive effects on intergroup relations. But the link that is found in these studies may also partly indicate just the opposite direction of influence. Tensions and conflicts between ethnic groups at school may be the reason to pay more attention to cultural diversity. Doubtless this also occurs. However, there is research that points to the causal importance of multicultural education (e.g., Hogan & Mallott, 2005; Nagda *et al.*, 2004). Nevertheless, the way in which this type of education is actually implemented in the educational system makes or breaks the anticipated effects. Moreover, it is not clear why exactly children become more tolerant. There is little understanding about what exactly happens in the day-to-day school reality and at the level of the individual development of the child.

Normative context

Multiculturalism is not just about knowledge and experiences, it usually also has a normative message: cultural differences should be acknowledged and recognized. It is argued that minority groups, just like everyone else, are entitled to their own culture and identity, not only in their private lives but also in public domains. Multiculturalists believe that newcomers should be supported in maintaining their own identity, and they reject assimilation with its focus on 'becoming like us'. According to some, multiculturalism is not so much about culture per se but, rather, about changing negative differences into positive differences: about the transformation of stigmatized identities to self-aware identities (Modood, 2007). Many Muslims want others to know they are Muslim, and they want to be accepted as such, just as homosexuals want others to know that they are gay and to be accepted as gay. It is about the public acceptance and recognition of ethnic, cultural, or religious identity and equality.

In one large-scale study, Dutch adolescents' attitudes towards Muslims living in the Netherlands were examined (Velasco Gónzalez *et al.*, 2008). Slightly more than half of the adolescents had explicit and strongly negative feelings towards Muslims. This percentage corresponds to national surveys in which Muslims are rejected by half of the Dutch natives.[6] One important reason is the perceived threat to Dutch identity and culture. But there was also a clear link with adolescents' attitude towards multiculturalism. Those who endorsed multiculturalism more strongly were much more positive about Muslims. This was not only because they perceived Muslims as less of a threat, but also because they viewed cultural diversity in itself as something of value. Similar results have been found in studies in other countries (Kauff & Wagner, 2012; Wolsko *et al.* 2006). The more one supports multiculturalism, the less threatened one feels and the more positive one's attitudes are towards ethnic minorities.

But there is again the question of cause and effect. It is very likely that natives who are more welcoming to minorities also are more in favour of multiculturalism. Yet the multiculturalism hypothesis emphasizes the inverse relationship. In a social context in which the normative importance of multiculturalism is propagated, out-groups will be accepted more, especially by the majority. In two experimental studies, I set out to examine whether this is the case among native Dutch and Turkish Dutch (Verkuyten, 2005a). The normative multicultural context was compared to a context in which assimilation was prioritized. Both studies yielded similar results: Dutch participants were more positive about ethnic minorities (Turkish, Moroccan, Surinamese, and Antillean Dutch) in the condition in which multicultural norms were salient, while in the assimilation condition they were more positive about the Dutch. In contrast, the Turkish Dutch were only more positive about their own group in the multicultural condition. Thus, multiculturalism appears to be a normative context in which majority members have more positive attitudes towards minorities, and minorities are more positive about their own community. This result is not an isolated finding but has also been confirmed in other experiments and other countries. In a study among White Americans, for example, it was examined whether a multicultural context affects both conscious and unconscious racial attitudes (Richeson & Nussbaum, 2004; see also Wolsko *et al.*, 2000). In the context in which the normative importance of multicultural recognition was highlighted, both these attitudes were found to be more positive.

Multicultural education does not only involve learning about cultural difference but also the transmission of social norms. It teaches about diversity, or what cultural groups and their experiences are like, but also aims to improve equality by prescribing how members of different groups should be treated. This prejudice reduction or anti-racism component of multiculturalism is central in most educational approaches. Students may conform to these norms for external reasons (e.g., social approval, punishments) and still be prejudiced and discriminate when significant others are not around (Monteiro *et al.*, 2009; Rutland *et al.* 2005). Yet conformity may eventually lead to norm internalization. As Allport (1954, p. 477) noted in his discussion of anti-discriminatory legislation: 'Law is intended only to control the outward expression of tolerance. But outward action, psychology knows, has an eventual effect upon inner habits of thought and feeling. And for this reason we list legislative action as one of the major methods of reducing, not only public discrimination, but private prejudice as well.' This means that in schools this normative aspect of multicultural education should be clearly and consistently expressed and endorsed.

Multicultural or anti-racism norms can also be internalized so that students adopt and personally endorse them. In addition, these norms can be expressed by classmates. Classmates are an important reference group for (early) adolescents, and students might adopt classmates' beliefs to guide their own evaluations (Aboud & Fenwick, 1999). For example, one study showed that the social dominance beliefs of peers have an impact on the homophobic attitudes of adolescents (Poteat *et al.*, 2007). In one of our studies we examined the impact of classmates' beliefs about multiculturalism on children's ethnic attitudes (Thijs & Verkuyten, 2013). The study was conducted among native Dutch early adolescents in 38 classes in 23 schools. We found that classmates' multicultural beliefs were positively related to Dutch children's evaluations of ethnic minority groups (Turks and Moroccans) via children's own multicultural beliefs. This finding suggests that children adopt these beliefs to guide their own ethnic evaluations. Another finding in line with this interpretation is that this influence was stronger for children who felt highly accepted by their peers, whereas the relation did not exist for children who felt weakly accepted. Well-accepted children are more easily influenced by their peers and more likely to personally endorse peer beliefs (Allen & Antonishak, 2008), and this is due to their stronger tendency to identify with their peer group (see Kiesner *et al.*, 2002). Group norms are more important for individuals with stronger group identification.

The important role of group norms for improving intergroup relations is not limited to classroom settings but is also found in experimental research (Jetten *et al.*, 1996) and in a yearlong field experiment in Rwanda after its recent history of genocide (Paluck, 2009). In this research, participants were randomly assigned to listening to different radio programmes: either a soap opera in which the fictional characters displayed positive social norms about intergroup relations, or one on health issues. The intervention was found to be effective in promoting trust, empathy, cooperation, and trauma healing. Importantly, the radio programme did not change listeners' personal beliefs but, rather, affected their perception of social norms. Media communicate what other people think, and the perception of views and beliefs shared by others functions as an important social norm for one's own feelings and behaviour.

A strong identity

The multiculturalism hypothesis is not only about the acceptance and recognition of cultural diversity, but also supposes an intermediate mechanism. This is well expressed in the quotes of Pierre Trudeau and the Canadian government presented earlier. Multiculturalism is assumed to lead to a positive and strong identity, which forms the basis for approaching others with an open mind. As the following quote illustrates, this reasoning is also used in the context of European integration:

> Own language, own culture, in short, identity and self-awareness are essential. From a self-confident position, we can play a pertinent role in the European Union.
>
> (Former Queen Beatrix of the Netherlands)

It is because of self-confidence, knowing who and what you are, that you can be open towards others. In chapter 3 we saw that self-doubt can cause people to withdraw into their own community, especially when this community is interpreted in essentialist terms. This reaction can also result from a sense of threat, exclusion, and stigmatization. Self-uncertainty and alienation are often associated with strong and exclusionary group boundaries (Hogg, 2007). And in chapter 4, ethnic development models were discussed that emphasize that a more mature or achieved identity is associated with a more open and positive attitude towards out-groups. A strong ethnic identity provides confidence and a secure basis on which to meet others. As a consequence, one feels less easily threatened, making it easier to view things from the perspectives of other ethnic groups and to seek contact with those who are different.

But where does this research stand next to the numerous historical and modern-day examples in which a strong and proud identity is associated with, for example, conflict, discrimination, radicalism, and racism? It goes without saying that various historical, political, economic, and social factors play a critical role in this. Psychologically, one might wonder whether behind a seemingly strong and positive identity there is not hidden a deeper feeling of uncertainty and negative self-feeling that drives prejudicial attitudes. Classic research into the authoritarian and dogmatic personality seems to suggest this. Recent research has a slightly different approach but points in the same direction. In this research, a distinction is made between a confident and a defensive sense of self. Individuals with a confident sense of self think positively about themselves on both the conscious and the more unconscious level. There is no deeper underlying doubt about who and what you are. This is the case, however, for individuals with a defensive sense of self. To the outside world you appear to have a strong and positive identity, but deep down inside you are unhappy and insecure about yourself. One way to deal with a defensive sense of self is to apply the well-known scapegoat mechanism by which outsiders are blamed, belittled, and excluded. Research has demonstrated that this is indeed the case (e.g., Jordan *et al.* 2005).[7] Individuals with a defensive sense of self react with more ethnic discrimination, especially when they feel threatened. Among individuals with a secure identity, little or no ethnic discriminatory behaviour is found. Some people can only feel confident and strong at the expense of others, while others do not need this for having these feelings. The multiculturalism hypothesis applies to the latter group, but perhaps the group of people with a more defensive sense of identity is quite substantial – both among the majority and ethnic minorities – which prevents multiculturalism from resulting in more positive intergroup relations.

Internal pressure and cholesterol

The term 'multiculturalism' has become negatively tainted especially in Europe, but, in contrast to assimilation, multicultural recognition appears to provide a more positive identity, greater acceptance of others, and it can contribute to higher creativity, innovation, and performance. It is therefore not surprising that the central idea of acceptance, recognition, and respect is replaced by names like 'diversity policy' (Vertovec & Wessendorf, 2010). Yet, from a social psychological perspective there are also limitations. Multiculturalism is no universal remedy, not even in the limited sense of multicultural recognition. What works in one particular national or local context does not necessarily work in another situation, and, in contrast to positive effects for some outcomes, there may be negative effects for others. There are also more principal objections. Multiculturalism concerns groups and group identities and therefore has implications for group processes, both within the own community as well as between groups. The former has to do with normative in-group pressures and the legitimacy of conservative forces, and the latter with the nature of cultural differences and the group differences that arise from this.

In-group norms

Multiculturalism is not just about relations between ethnic groups but also has important implications for relationships within ethnic communities. Group membership implies expectations for acceptance by and support from the own community, but also obligations and normative pressures. Minority groups typically try to maintain their group norms and values, and immigrant groups are often engaged in concerted efforts to preserve cultural continuity and ethnic cohesion (e.g., Bankston & Zhou, 1995). Furthermore, group norms influence the behaviour of individual group members through processes of social control and group identification (Tajfel & Turner, 1979). Individuals have a basic need to feel that they belong, and they tend to behave in ways that conform to the norms and demands of their in-group in order to secure acceptance as a group member (Klein *et al.*, 2007). Rejection and not receiving full recognition of one's group membership by in-group members is painful. It makes people uncertain about themselves and their position within their group. According to uncertainty-identity theory (Hogg, 2007), individuals are motivated to reduce this self-uncertainty, and they can try to do so by identifying more strongly with the groups they belong to, in particular with groups that are highly group-like (entitative) and distinctive. Religious groups are particularly effective because they provide a source of affiliation as well as clear norms for structuring beliefs and guiding behaviour (Hogg *et al.*, 2010). Furthermore, for most believers, and for Muslim immigrants in particular, religious identity is typically very important (chapter 4). When facing uncertainties about acceptance into an important in-group, people will try to present themselves as committed group members (Noel *et al.*, 1995). Therefore, in-group norms to maintain one's ethno-religious culture can make Muslim immigrants turn to their religion and strengthen their religious group identification.

In addition, distancing oneself from a relevant out-group is a way of confirming one's in-group membership (Klein *et al.*, 2007). In order to gain approval and recognition of one's group membership, immigrants can distance themselves from the host society and thereby show their loyalty to their ethnic community.

This might mean that in the presence of relatively strong in-group norms immigrants identify more strongly with their religious in-group and, via higher religious identification, distance themselves from the host society by showing lower national identification. This reasoning was supported in our research among Turkish Muslims in Germany and in the Netherlands. We found that perceived in-group norms were related to stronger religious group identification and via this identification to a lower sense of host national belonging (Martinovic & Verkuyten, 2012).

The communitarian perspective of multiculturalism emphasizes the importance of clear group boundaries and the maintenance of cultural groups which should be recognized and respected. One possible implication is that multiculturalism stimulates the positive acceptance of ethnic out-groups in the public sphere of work, school and civic life but not in the intimate private sphere of family and marriage. Ethnic endogamy is important for the continuation of the ethnic culture while inter-ethnic marriages reduce the possibilities of passing on ethnic cultural practices and beliefs to the next generation (Clark-Ibanez & Felmlee, 2004; Huijnk *et al*, 2010). Children born from inter-marriage blur ethnic group boundaries and in the long run raise questions about the nature of ethnic groups. Thus, one paradoxical effect of multiculturalism could be the acceptance of out-group members in public life together with the promotion of intra-ethnic marriages. The ideology of maintenance of cultural diversity and cultural recognition might not only result in the public acceptance of ethnic out-groups but also in the endorsement of ethnic endogamy. In the context of Mauritius we found evidence for this two-sidedness of multiculturalism (Ng Tseung-Wong & Verkuyten, 2013). Hindus, Muslims and Creoles reported relatively low public social distance (neighbourhood, school) towards ethnic out-groups but relatively high private social distance (marriage). Thus, multicultural ideology can promote positive feelings about interacting with members of ethnic out-groups in public life without necessarily being positive about ethnic out-groups in the private domain of marriage and family (Nave, 2000).

The communitarian perspective of multiculturalism further argues for the importance of a culture community for the development of personal autonomy. It is their own culture that would give people a meaningful life and provides a basis for being able to make personal choices. Membership of a culture community is said to be a prerequisite for personal growth and development. Thus, a particular group identity is placed first and foremost, and the assumed autonomy is related to the choices within the horizon of their own cultural community. But that horizon is always limited, and in a multicultural society one also has to learn to make choices between communities. Moreover, in daily life there are no clear-cut cultures in which children grow up. Societies are culturally diverse, and so are many people who are part of them.

Multiculturalism emphasizes one particular group identity, but not everyone feels at ease with this. There are people who identify with other groups or those who stress their individual talents and characteristics. For them, the groupthink of multiculturalism is rather threatening, and multicultural recognition has little to offer. Immigrants who emphasize their personal characteristics, qualities, and efforts appear not to be in favour of multiculturalism (Verkuyten & Martinovic, 2006). And, as we saw earlier, these immigrants are more likely to have positive self-feelings in a colourblind than in a multicultural context. Multiculturalism also has a tendency to legitimize one particular version of the presupposed group culture – often the version that is propagated in more traditional circles. Multicultural policies should be sensitive to these processes because these policies can legitimize in-group norms that distance people from society and that reinforce power dynamics, thus rendering the most disadvantaged group members (i.e., children and women) even more vulnerable. This 'paradox of multicultural vulnerability' (Sachar, 2000) raises difficult policy questions because it can mean that the integrity of ethnic minority groups is placed above the freedom and equality of the individuals within. For example, granting rights to separate schooling or exemptions from state regulations can imply in some circumstances the implicit support of children's oppression and their distancing from the host society (Reich, 2002). Furthermore, the emphasis on cultural maintenance and equality of cultures and the recognition of cultural diversity can legitimize the inequality of women (e.g., Okin, 1999). Multiculturalism has been criticized for supporting and justifying conservatism and repressive in-group practices (e.g., Barry, 2001). Multicultural policies recognize the importance of cultural groups for giving meaning to people's lives but should also emphasize cultural liberty, and this requires that individuals be as free to maintain their identities as they are to change them.[8] Stuart Hall summarizes this point as follows (in Rattansi, 2011, p. 1):

'Individual choice, however tarted up with a thin veneer of communitarianism, cannot supply the bonds of recognition, reciprocity and connection which give meaning to our lives as social beings … On the other hand we cannot enfranchise the claims of community cultures to norms over individuals without at the same time expanding – not only ideally but in practice – the right of individuals as bearers of rights to dissent from, exit and oppose if necessary their communities of origin.'

Diversity and diversity

Diversity is like cholesterol: there is a right type of diversity that makes the body healthy and strong, and there is a wrong type of diversity that leads to a heart attack (Haidt *et al.*, 2003). Some types of diversity are inspiring, challenging, and productive, while other kinds are disturbing, threatening, and disruptive. Diversity of views and ideas is good for a vibrant, innovative, and strong community, but that is much less the case for moral diversity. It is not so difficult to accept that some people would rather eat cowpea or couscous than pea soup or the local hot-pot stew. But the case is quite different if some people deny the equal position of men and women and reject homosexuality. Moral conflicts are difficult to reconcile. If I say that I stand for the equality of men and women but that others do not necessarily have to agree, it becomes a matter of personal preference. If I say that in our society we stand for gender equality but other societies may think differently about it, then it becomes a matter of social convention. But if I consider the equality of men and women a moral principle, I stand for gender equality everywhere, and require everyone else to do so too. If people from another group disagree, there is a problem – a problem that goes beyond differences in taste and conventions that can be solved with mutual understanding and accommodations. A moral principle has general validity. You can argue about its interpretation and applicability, but not about the principle itself. For instance, you can disagree about what freedom of expression really entails, how it relates to other moral principles like equality, and whether something is a matter of freedom of expression. But if you say that you are in favour of freedom of expression but are happy to live in a country where that is not guaranteed, it is not a moral principle but a matter of convention and tradition or of personal preference and taste. In a multicultural society, the discussion on different forms of diversity is important in at least two ways.[9]

First, there is often debate about whether something is a matter of principle or is a social convention. In the latter case one does not need to attach too much importance to it. For instance, take all the fuss about whether or not to shake hands with someone of the opposite sex: in several countries, there have been cases where this has led to some commotion. For some, the act of not shaking hands is a matter of principle, as it symbolizes the equality of men and women. For others it is only one of many ways to acknowledge another person as a fellow human being. This can also be done with a slight bow, a nod of the head, or placing your hand over your heart. It would be a fundamental right to greet and respect others in a different, culture-specific way. By making it a matter of moral principle, the discussion is polarized, and consequently it becomes more difficult to find a solution. Worries about different or changing conventions are often articulated as fears about moral principles.

That does not mean that there cannot be strong disagreements if something is made into a matter of social convention – especially if it is linked to national identity. In that case, shaking hands is presented as part of our identity: something that 'we' the Dutch do, that is how things simply are and should be in the Netherlands, and if you do not comply, you are rejecting the Netherlands, and you might as well leave. Another example is the Turkish Prime Minister Erdoğan, who made a moral issue out of assimilation. In a speech directed to Turkish Germans in early February 2008, he called assimilation a crime against humanity: that assimilation would boil down to the complete abandonment of the Turkish identity, and this would deny the fact that Turks will always remain Turks. In addition to the need to integrate, there should be, he claimed, a fundamental human right to retain one's own language, religion, and cultural practices. Such a right is supported by the European Convention for the protection of human rights and fundamental freedoms.

The second reason why a distinction in types of diversity is important is that in many European countries moral issues have become increasingly salient as a result of the presence of Muslim immigrants. In Europe, diversity has become equated with religious diversity. Religion is about eternal truths and moral doctrines, and for most (religious) believers the idea of making religious adjustments is considered blasphemy. Many majority members judge the male–female relationships and the parenting style within Muslim communities as morally reprehensible, and many Muslims reject the same 'liberal' practices of the natives. Both groups see the same differences, but they judge them by diametrically opposing standards. The result is that 'there are parallel barriers of prejudice: a desire of many Western Europeans to hold Muslims at a distance, combined with a desire of Muslims to keep their distance' (Sniderman & Hagendoorn, 2007, p. 26).

Intergroup tension is mainly centred on male–female relationships and sexuality. For many Muslims, any compromise in the area of gender and sexuality is often difficult to accept (Norris & Inglehart, 2004). And for many natives it is about the liberal values and the moral obligation to be loyal to the host society. The suspicion of a lack of loyalty and commitment is prevalent across European countries. Chancellor Angela Merkel responded to Prime Minister Erdoğan's speech by stating that integration does not mean 'that people have to abandon their own cultural background, but that their loyalty should however lie with the German state'. Among Muslim immigrants, there is a clear tension between a sometimes violent small minority who do not accept Western values and norms and distance themselves from the host society, and the moderate majority who try to find a place in society and to develop a sense of belonging. There are different groups of Muslim immigrants, and there are many different ways of being a Muslim, but there are also Muslims who live in Western Europe but do not want to be part of a Western, liberal country. They claim that their religious beliefs, rules, and practices are incompatible with liberal democratic principles and that they therefore do not consider themselves bound to those principles. A 'real or true' Islam is defined as being in opposition to the Western world, and Muslims must therefore keep their distance from the Western world.

Difference and cohesion

Multiculturalism is difficult and controversial. What exactly is meant by it often remains unclear, and nowadays the concept is increasingly being used in the sense of 'multicultural naïve individuals and toadies' who do not dare to set norms. Accusations of relativism, naïvety, and weakness tends to dominate in many current discussions. Social psychologists have mainly focused on multicultural recognition, which can have a range of positive effects. But from a social psychological point of view there are also dangers and disadvantages. Multiculturalism can lead to a situation in which certain group identities predominate and people view and judge themselves, as well as others, solely or mainly in light of their ethnic or religious identity. Multiculturalism can evolve into a one-sided focus on ethnic, cultural, and religious differences. This can lead to a sharpening of group boundaries, the creation of parallel worlds, and a limitation of individual freedoms, choices, and opportunities. In a situation in which intergroup relations are tense, multiculturalism does not appear to be a good strategy to avoid negative images and attitudes (Caprariello *et al.*, 2009). The native majority can easily start to perceive the focus on diversity as a threat to their own position, and concerns about this position are one of the main underlying factors that influence, for example, whether or not people support minority rights and diversity policy (Lowery *et al.*, 2006).

Multiculturalism is about the delicate balance between the recognition of differences and finding meaningful similarities, between differentiated treatment and equality, between group identities and individual rights. There are different types of diversity and different forms of multiculturalism that try to deal with diversity in a productive way. Some differences are relatively easy to accept and accommodate, but others go against moral beliefs and core principles and values. There are limits to pluralism, and multiculturalism cannot be an overt or disguised relativism within which all cultural differences are simply embraced. The fact that something is part of a tradition or culture is never a sufficient enough reason to accept and preserve it (Barry, 2001). Cultural diversity is not possible without cultural freedom: the freedom to make your own choices without being rejected or excluded. Others have proposed that the term 'multiculturalism' should be replaced with 'interculturalism' or even 'transculturalism'. (Rattansi, 2011; Taylor, 2012). This is not simply a matter of rhetoric: it is meant to offer an alternative story about a new way of interaction – a story that provides an interpretative account and frame of reference for policy decisions and everyday understandings. In comparison to multiculturalism, interculturalism puts more emphasis on the importance of integration in addition to acknowledging diversity.

Paying attention to differences also requires attention to similarities. The focus in multiculturalism on diversity and separate groups often implies that there is little concern for similarities and commonalities. But multiculturalism cannot exist without a shared identity. The countries in which multiculturalism is reasonably accepted, such as Canada, Australia, the United States, and Mauritius, are precisely those countries in which cultural diversity is, at least to some extent, part of the national self-image.

In Europe, government leaders have argued that by emphasizing differences at the expense of similarities multiculturalism would undermine national identities and feelings of belonging together, which are considered a prerequisite for solidarity, a unified society, and effective democracy. In addition, politicians and the media often claim that many immigrants have divided loyalties and a lack of attachment to the host society, which undermines a cohesive national identity. A shared sense of nationhood would be (part of) the solution to the lack of social cohesion and stability. To enhance the immigrants' national identification, policymakers have advocated, for example, language courses, tests on national history and culture, oaths of allegiance, and educational changes.

Proponents of multiculturalism argue that a society cannot ignore the demands of diversity. According to them, diversity has cultural and economic benefits, and minority groups need and deserve recognition and affirmation of their distinctiveness (Taylor, 1992). Ignoring these demands would provoke resistance, create suspicions, and threaten the very unity that assimilationists seek (Modood,

2007; Parekh, 2000). At the same time these proponents of multiculturalism argue that unity and a shared identity are equally important. A well-functioning society needs a sense of commitment and common belonging, making it important to foster a spirit of shared national identity. Without this, a society would degenerate into a collection of segregated cultural groups obsessed with their differences. It is argued that group distinctiveness should be affirmed within a context of common belonging. Cultural diversity requires an overarching framework in which everyone can feel at ease, comfortable, and involved. The quest for identity should therefore also be a quest for a shared feeling of 'we-ness', an inclusive identity that provides security and is emotionally appealing to all.

7   A shared sense of 'we'

> I chose to run for president at this moment in history because I believe deeply that we cannot solve the challenges of our time unless we solve them together, unless we perfect our union by understanding that we may have different stories but we hold common hopes, that we may not look the same and may not have come from the same place but we all want to move in the same direction towards a better future for our children and grandchildren.

This quote is from Barack Obama's famous 'Race Speech' (2008) in which he discusses racial diversity in the light of a common national identity. With the repeated use of 'we' he constructs an image of consensus and unity, in spite of diversity. As in many other of his speeches he highlights that America is socially and culturally very diverse but then subsequently attenuates these group differences by emphasizing shared responsibilities and values in an United States of America (Augoustinos & De Garis, 2012). His focus is on uniting together despite the existing differences. In many of his speeches he uses a discourse of national unity based on the ideological values of freedom, justice, equality, and prosperity that constitute the American Dream. In his emphasis on national unity, Obama discusses an issue that already ten years earlier was addressed by his Democratic predecessor, Bill Clinton, in a speech on diversity made at Portland State University on 13 June 1998. Clinton started his speech with saying, 'Today I want to talk about what may be the most important subject of all, how we can strengthen the bonds of our national community as we grow more racially and ethnically diverse.'

The continuing worldwide migration and the increased tensions after, for example, 9/11 and the bombings in London and Madrid have made this 'most important subject of all' even more important. Politicians in many countries have been arguing that there is an urgent need to create and strengthen common bonds and a broad 'we feeling' (chapter 1). It seems clear that a culturally diverse society needs some form of shared or inclusive identity. But that is easier said than done, and there is also the question whether this always will have a positive effect on relations between ethnic groups. There are many examples of fragmentation or schism occurring within a community or the bringing together of different groups under one umbrella leading to disagreement and conflict rather than acceptance and harmony. The fact that Sunnis and Shiites are both Muslims does not prevent serious conflicts from arising in, for example, Iraq or between Iraq and Iran, and the fact that different ethnic groups are all British does not means that they all get along. Why would a shared 'we-feeling' actually lead to better group relations? What is involved in a 'shared we', and why can it sometimes turn out very differently than anticipated? And here we must also keep in mind: what works in one situation does not necessarily work in another situation. An inclusive identity in the school or neighbourhood may contribute to mutual acceptance and tolerance, but that is not necessarily the case at the regional or national level.

In their report *The Binding School Culture* the Dutch Education Council (2007) addresses the question of ways of developing a school culture that binds different ethnic groups together. The basis for such a culture would lie in togetherness: everyone is part of *this* school, which is characterized in *this particular* way. In order to achieve this, schools appear to work in three distinct ways. The first is colour-blindness: where little or no attention is paid to the cultural or religious backgrounds of pupils. The future, not the origin, of the individual students is emphasized. The second way is to make the school known as a global community school, a mixed school that is a meeting-place of cultures. The idea here is that diversity should not be ignored but should, rather, be recognized and expressed within the unity of the school. Third, there are schools that consider their own (secular or educational) ideology or (Christian) religion as the means to bind and connect students. Diversity is considered from the perspective of the religious or educational identity of the school.

Through a colour-blind approach one aims to think and act in terms of individual pupils, not in terms of cultural groups and ethnic categories. Social psychologists call this the strategy of de-categorization. In the diversity approach, attention is focused on cultural differences together with what is shared, which is consistent with the dual categorization approach. In the third approach, group differences are considered from a common identity perspective. This resembles the social psychological strategy of re-categorization. In this chapter, I discuss each of these three strategies, but first I want to go into the importance of contacts for intergroup relations. In many sectors of society, people have caught on to the idea that the key to addressing prejudice and negative group relations lies in intergroup contact. For example, policies of school de-segregation and ethnically mixed school populations seek to improve mutual acceptance. The idea is simple: unknown means unloved, and if we intermingle ethnic groups in schools, organizations, institutions, neighbourhoods, and so on, people will get to know each other: bring people together and into contact with each other, and as a consequence ethnic and racial prejudices will gradually disappear. Through contact, the group boundaries with the related us-versus-them mentality, will be broken down.

Does mixing help?

> It has sometimes been held that merely by assembling people without regard
> for race, colour, religion, or national origin, we can thereby destroy stereotypes
> and develop friendly attitudes. The case is not so simple.

(Allport, 1954, p. 261)

This quote comes from one of the most multifaceted and influential books in the
field of social psychology. The author of the book is Gordon Allport, and it was
published in 1954, entitled *The Nature of Prejudice*. Allport was very interested
in social–psychological issues, but he was also a pioneer in the study of
personality. The commonly told story is that at the age of 22 he went to Vienna
to meet Freud. The encounter was very awkward because Freud just sat there
patiently waiting for Allport to say something. At some point the silence became
too much for Allport, and he started recounting that on the coach he had seen a
little boy who was very upset because he had to sit on a seat that had previously
been occupied by a dirty old man. For Freud, this was not merely a simple
observation, but the expression of a deeper concern, and he therefore asked,
'And were you that little boy?' This experience made Allport realize that at
times, psychology digs too deep, just as behaviourism remains too much on the
surface of human conduct.

Allport's book about prejudice and discrimination covers almost all conceivable
aspects and facets, backgrounds and causes, as well as approaches and solutions.
The wealth of his ideas and insights is great. The book has had an enormous
influence in social psychology. One of the issues that Allport discusses is the idea
that prejudices can be decreased by bringing people in contact with each other.
This was not a novel idea. Allport, however, formulated a number of optimum
conditions for such contact to work. The quote above comes from the beginning
of chapter 16, where Allport discusses the 'effect of contact'. The term 'contact
theory' suggests that contact is in itself sufficient to improve group relations. But,
as the quote indicates, that is, of course, far from always the case. Contact can
confirm existing stereotypes ('There you are: they *are* really like that') and
negative contact can evoke feelings of fear and threat that reinforce prejudice and
discrimination ('You see, they really *are* troublemakers, and I do not want them
in my nightclub'). Contact on its own is not enough, and schools or organizations
that think that 'mixing' alone is sufficient might be in for some bad news.

According to Allport, for contact to lead to better group relations, certain
conditions need to be met. The four most important ones are: (1) there needs to be
adequate opportunity for people to get to know each other; (2) the groups need to
have similar status positions in the situation that the contact occurs in; (3) the
situation needs to be one of cooperation and not competition; (4) the contact must
be supported by institutions and authorities. The first condition indicates that one-
off, casual, and relatively superficial contact is obviously not comparable to
regular, more profound, prolonged contact in which you are really able to get to
know another person. Casual contact will more easily lead to the confirmation of

stereotypes, and quality of the contact appears to be more important than quantity. A situation in which a group in a more superior position is in contact with an inferior group is therefore unlikely to contribute to the changing of prejudices. The 'blue eyes' and 'brown eyes' in the Jane Elliot class also found themselves in a contact situation. Contact will also have more positive effects in situations of cooperation rather than competition. Interethnic contacts also take place on sports and playing fields, but under those circumstances ethnic tensions and conflicts often occur. Finally, it is important that institutions and authorities (e.g., teachers, civil servants, and politicians) unambiguously endorse the importance of mutual contact.

The number of studies that has been conducted on the contact hypothesis is substantial. Every study has its own design, limitations, and setting in which it is carried out. There is experimental and field research, large-scale and small-scale research, there is research among adults and among adolescents and children, and there is research in different countries. If there is a great deal of research on a particular topic, it is possible to make a comparison or meta-analysis of all the findings. Tom Pettigrew and Linda Tropp have done this a number of times. One of their meta-analyses (2006) covers 515 studies involving more than 250,000 participants in nearly 40 countries. It appears that positive contact is associated with reduced prejudice. The association is not huge, but it is systematic and consistent. It is roughly equally strong among adults, adolescents, and children (Tropp & Prenevost, 2008). The results are similar in different countries and are valid for contact with diverse ethnic, cultural, and various other minority groups. Moreover, there is a positive effect even when Allport's conditions are not met. Yet contact yields better results in situations where these conditions are taken into account. Interethnic contact between pupils at school is associated, for example, with more harmonious group relationships, and this is especially the case if the contact is structured more-or-less according to Allport's optimal conditions. However, it should be noted that in everyday life these conditions rarely exist and are difficult to develop. For example, one can try to establish equal status positions in a particular context, but this might be undermined by the majority–minority distinction that exist at the level of society. Schools can strongly communicate and endorse the value of equality, but this does not make them immune from status differences in society.

The limits and downside of contact

So, there is empirical evidence supporting the idea that positive contact is associated with more harmonious group relations. Unknown means unloved, and getting to know each other can contribute to accepting each other. But how exactly does this work? To what extent does the positive effect generalize across time, context and groups? And is the effect of contact equally positive for majority and minority group members? These are questions that need to be addressed in order to understand the limits and possibilities of contact for improving interethnic relations. I want to discuss a number of issues.

Direction of influence

The contact hypothesis assumes that positive contact leads to less prejudice. But is it rather not the other way around? Tolerant people are more open to others and will more likely make an effort to seek and sustain contact with them. And intolerant people do not like others and therefore are less willing to participate in intergroup contact. This question of causality is frequently posed in contact research, but is also an example of a rather useless either/or dichotomy. Of course, it may be the case that one direction of the relationship is more important than the other, but this does not mean that the other direction does not exist or does not matter at all. A reciprocal relationship is most likely: for example, contact leads to less prejudice, which, in turn, encourages the extension and deepening of the contact, and so on. In any case, experimental and longitudinal studies show that contact can indeed reduce prejudice. In recent years several systematic studies have shown that positive contact leads to higher tolerance (e.g., Binder *et al.*, 2009; Brown *et al.*, 2007).

Majority and minority groups

There are indications that the positive effect of contact on prejudice is stronger and more consistent for majority members than for minorities. The most research by far has focused on majority members, and this is understandable because generally prejudices among the majority group have the strongest social and societal impact. But a multicultural society requires mutual acceptance from the minorities vis-à-vis the majority, as well as between minority groups. Negative stereotypes and prejudices are also found among minorities, which may result in discriminatory behaviour, such as in educational, organizational, and neighbour-hood settings in which minority groups sometimes dominate. The limited research among minorities shows that often there is little or no effect of contact (e.g., Binder *et al.*, 2009). This has been demonstrated for several minority groups in different countries. The reason behind this is not entirely clear. It may be that minorities in any case have knowledge of and are familiar with the majority group, making contact less effective for reducing negative attitudes. Another reason might be that minorities perceive a lack of equal status in their interactions with the majority. Minorities tend to be well aware of their group's lower status in society, and contact in unequal status relationships might reinforce rather than weaken existing stereotypes. Minorities may also experience more negative encounters or more subtle signs of derogation, such as being addressed in a patronizing tone or given disapproving and fearful looks. This on-going devaluation of their group may inhibit the potential for positive contact outcomes.

Even more limited than research on minority members' contact with the majority group are studies that examine intergroup attitudes and contact between minority groups. This is unfortunate because in our increasingly diverse societies, inter-minority relations are becoming more prevalent and important for understanding ethnic relations in regional, local and institutional settings. An early exception is the study by Tsukashima and Montero (1976), who showed that equal-status contact reduces prejudice of Blacks towards Jews. More recently, it was found that having Asian American roommates did not reduce prejudice among Black college students, whereas for Asian students having Black roommates was associated with more favourable attitudes towards Blacks (Van Laar *et al.*, 2005). A similar difference between Asian and Black students was found in another study (Bikmen, 2011). And in a large-scale study in the Netherlands among Turkish and Moroccan immigrants it was found that more contact with the Dutch majority group was not associated with less social distance towards this group. However, increased contact was associated with more positive minority attitudes. Turkish (or Moroccan) participants who had more contacts with Moroccans (Turks) indicated less social distance towards this minority group, and the same was found in relation to the minority group of Surinamese/ Antilleans (Hindriks *et al.*, 2013b). Thus, contact also seems to have a positive effect on the attitude towards other minority groups.

Generalization

If the intergroup contact is to fulfil its promise of more harmonious group relations, then the positive effects need to generalize to other group members and other minority groups. Some 40 years ago, in the southern states of America, many Whites had a Black housekeeper or gardener, but that did not necessarily mean that they were less racist. There is also the famous research of Minard (1952) that was carried out in a coal mine in West Virginia. Inside the mine, the White and Black workers were thrown into each other's company and indeed had good relationships, but outside the factory gates there was still a strict racial segregation. Generalizations of positive experiences in time, across situations, to the whole group, and to other minority groups is not self-evident. If I, as a native Dutch, get along well with my Surinamese colleague, that does not have to mean that I spend time with him outside work. And it also does not have to mean that I think more positively about Surinamese as a group. For me, this colleague may be the exception that confirms the rule. Moreover, it is even more unlikely that this particular positive contact will lead me to think more positively about other ethnic minority groups, such as Turkish and Moroccan immigrants.

The positive effects of contact do not necessarily generalize across situations, nor to the group in question, nor to other groups. But the fact that this need not happen does not mean that it cannot happen. For example, the so-called secondary transfer effect refers to the finding that positive contact with one particular out-group can lead to less prejudice against another out-group with which one does not have direct contact. One reason for this effect is the mechanism of attitude generalization that implies that attitudes towards one object generalize to other linked or similar objects (Walther, 2002). At the level of social groups, this means that the improved out-group attitude that results from contact with one minority group may lead to improved attitudes towards another minority group. Another reason is that contact with one particular out-group may lead to the realization that one's own norms, customs, and lifestyle are not the only ways to manage and look at the world. Limited knowledge and experience result in the in-group being seen as the centre of the world and its norms and customs providing the self-evident and invariant standards for judgement. Positive contact may broaden people's horizons by recognizing the value of other cultures and thereby put their own taken-for-granted cultural standards into perspective, making them less in-group-centric and more open to various other groups, including those they do not have contact with. There is some empirical evidence for this 'deprovincialization effect' of contact (Pettigrew, 1997; Verkuyten *et al.*, 2010).

In addition to the secondary transfer effect there is, among children as well as adults, evidence for the 'extended contact' effect. This refers to the finding that being aware of positive contacts between members of one's own group and another group can reduce prejudice (Pettigrew, 2009; Wright *et al.*, 1997). Thus, even if you do not have out-group contacts or friendships yourself, you may develop more favourable out-group attitudes as a result of the mere knowledge that your friends have these contacts and friendships. One reason for this is that it is uncomfortable to dislike the friend of your friend. This implies an unbalanced situation that typically involves feelings of dissonance that one tries to solve, for example by developing more positive attitudes towards the unknown out-group (Heider, 1958). A further reason is that your friend serves as a positive exemplar, and if more of your friends have out-group contacts, this can result in a friendship norm about tolerance of minority groups (De Tezanos-Pinto *et al.*, 2010). In general, people tend to be concerned about what their friends or in-group members would think about relationships with members of another group. A group norm for cross-ethnic friendships will make out-group attitudes more positive and reduce anxiety and worries that people might have about what significant others would think about these friendships.

Friendships and networks

Successful contact should permit the development of meaningful relationships between members of the groups concerned. Contact that has high 'acquaintance potential' (Cook, 1978, p. 97) is positively rewarding and can generalize to the out-group as a whole. The evidence for the importance of meaningful relationships for positive out-group attitudes is particularly strong with respect to friendships. Summarizing the research literature, Pettigrew and Tropp (2011, p. 119) conclude that 'these studies offer compelling evidence that cross-group friendships are especially effective in reducing prejudice and promoting a host of positive intergroup outcomes'. The best thing schools, organizations, institutions, and neighbourhoods can do is to create opportunities for friendships to emerge and develop. Friendship involves self-disclosure, empathy, and perspective-taking, and these are important psychological processes that are responsible for the positive effect of contact on prejudice. Furthermore, intimate contact does not only provide positive feelings and emotions, it also reduces negative feelings. Positive contact experiences can reduce uncertainty and anxiety to interact with other out-group members, which would normally lead one to shy away from contact. Research has clearly shown that contact leads to a reduction of such feelings and thus to less prejudice (see Pettigrew & Tropp, 2008).[1]

However, the effects of contact are not only due to affective processes. When people meet and interact, they also learn from one another. They discover that certain stereotypes are not true, they observe all kind of differences between people of the out-group, discover similarities between themselves and members of the out-group, and they learn to view characteristics of their own group in perspective to others. In a large-scale survey study among Dutch adolescents it was found that contact is associated with less negative attitudes towards Muslims (Velasco Gónzalez *et al.*, 2008). Adolescents with more intensive contact had fewer stereotypes about Muslims, and therefore their attitude was also more positive. However, contact had an effect on prejudice not only via stereotypes, but also directly. This has also been found in other studies and is usually interpreted in terms of 'exposure'. If people regularly come into contact with something, they will gradually come to accept it (Bornstein, 1989). Moreover, there is also the chance that they will start to influence one another and gradually become more alike. And people who resemble each other, generally like each other more and have the tendency to seek each other's company.

But the tendency for 'birds of a feather to flock together', can also impede the development of positive relationships. Contact between people evolves over time. You meet each other, discover commonalities, and you slowly begin to develop a bond. But if you barely know each other, you are more likely to go by differences that are considered socially meaningful. A multi-ethnic school, organization, or neighbourhood does not need to imply that there is close interethnic contact: often such contact is very superficial and casual. Numerical ratios only tell us about opportunities and chances for contact to occur, and little about what is actually happening. In multi-ethnic schools you often see that students with the same ethnic background choose to sit next to each other in class and spend time together during break times (Schofield & Eurich-Fulcer, 2001). Re-segregation takes place at de-segregated schools. The tendency to structure relationships along ethnic lines is particularly strong at the beginning of the school year and among first-form students. In these new situations students feel insecure; they have no idea where they stand and what they are in for. They are more likely to form bonds with members of their ethnic in-group and to mark their differences with other ethnic groups. The contact with ethnic others tends to be rather casual and aloof. The contact situation can lead to a sharpening of the differences and possibly even to competition. Some students will go against each other and can have a negative effect on other students. However, during the school year this may decrease as the students get to know each other. Other categorizations may come to dominate, such as music preferences, interests, and hobbies.

Social psychologists rarely carry out research on these developments over time. Even though longitudinal research looks into whether contact at Time 1 has a positive effect on prejudice at Time 2, it remains unclear how exactly contacts and relationships develop. The focus is on the underlying psychological processes and not on the social mechanisms that shape the gradual development of everyday relationships. The central question is on the effect of contact on stereotypes, prejudices, or desired social distance, while research into actual behaviour is much more rare. This is a clear limitation, as contact and experiences have an impact not only on mental life, but also on the development of relationships and social networks in schools, neighbourhoods, and cities. Research using a network perspective indicates, for example, that the social dynamics in peer and friendship networks are important for understanding when and why (extended) contact has positive or negative effects on prejudice (Munniksma *et al.*, in press; Stark, 2011).

Everyday life

The existing research on the contact hypothesis needs yet to be refined in another way. Allport's work is characterized by its broad theoretical insights and nuanced analysis. He emphasizes that prejudice and discrimination are the result of numerous factors and processes at various levels. In the preface of his book he states that 'plural causation is the primary lesson we wish to teach' (1954, p. xviii). In his chapter on the contact hypothesis there is a long list of factors that should be studied separately and in combination with each other. The existing empirical research, though, is more limited. There are numerous studies in which only the degree of contact is measured using ambiguous questions such as 'How many times in the past month have you been in contact with Mexicans (or Latinos, or Asians)?' The answers are then used in all sorts of complex statistical analyses to test whether contact does or does not help. But these results are not very informative, because the where, when, why, and how of the contact are ignored. This gives little insight into the underlying conditions and mechanisms that cause contact to result in either positive or negative outcomes in everyday life. Contact in one context does not have to be the same as in another. The meaning of the contact may vary greatly depending on the circumstances and also the way in which it is embedded in existing social and historical relations. The arrival of new Somali families in a predominantly White neighbourhood can be perceived as a threat rather than as an opportunity to break down ethnic boundaries through contact. Without an understanding of the background and meanings of everyday contact and how it develops, little can be said about how, why, and when it has a beneficial or a detrimental effect in social reality (see Dixon *et al.*, 2005). However, the positive impact that forms of contact can have on prejudice is also demonstrated in (experimental) field and intervention studies (e.g., Brenick *et al.*, 2007; Cole *et al.*, 2003).

Collective action

The contact research and the related policies can also be considered limited from the perspective of collective action and social justice. Contact research is typically based on the idea that social change requires a reduction in prejudice:[2] when people are brought into contact, they will abandon their faulty stereotypes and will like each other more, and this will lead to more tolerant and egalitarian societies. Yet societies can have structural inequalities and strong power differences between groups for which psychological changes are not the main solution. Contact can cure individual prejudice, but this is different from redressing societal inequality and conflict. This means that in some situations collective action for achieving social justice is a more appropriate model for social change. In these situations, change is predicated upon actions that aim to improve the rights, power, and influence of disadvantaged groups. This requires not only that people identify with their disadvantaged group but also that they recognize and feel angry about the social inequality, and that they consider change possible. Furthermore, collective action is facilitated when there are clear group boundaries and a generally negative moral characterization of the advantaged majority group (Wright & Baray, 2012).

Positive contact generally has the effect of improving intergroup attitudes. For minority members this may imply a lower perception of injustice and less readiness to engage in initiatives to expose inequalities and disadvantages and to demand change. Contact can lead to perceiving greater similarity between 'us' and 'them', a psychological blurring of group boundaries, and a more positive characterization of the advantaged majority group. Because of the positive contact, one comes to like and trust the advantaged, and it is difficult to rise up against friends. Research in Israel, India, South Africa, and the United States has demonstrated that positive contact is associated with more favourable attitudes towards the advantaged majority group but at the same time with reduced awareness of group inequality and decreased support for social change (e.g., Dixon *et al.,* 2007; Saguy *et al.,* 2009, 2011). For example, a longitudinal study found that over time closer friendship with Whites leads to lower perceptions of ethnic discrimination and less support for ethnic activism among African Americans and Latino Americans (Tropp *et al.,* 2012). And in an experimental research it was found that Latino students with higher levels of contact with the majority group were less likely to translate perceived commonality between Blacks and Latinos into political solidarity between minority group members (Glasford & Calcagno, 2012).

These findings indicate that contact can have other consequences and that the prejudice reduction model of social change has its limits. Promoting mutual contact can even be strategically used by the majority for undermining the political mobilization of minority groups. However, these consequences are more important in some situations (i.e. deeply divided and unjust societies) than in others and should not be overstated – for one thing, because, as mentioned earlier, the positive effect of contact is greater for advantaged majorities than for disadvantaged minorities. In addition, for the former it is not only associated with reduced prejudice but also with stronger support for affirmative action and other governmental policies to redress inequalities (Pettigrew & Tropp, 2011). Furthermore, contact among minorities can heighten the awareness that one's group is unjustly deprived. Contact allows them to learn about the world of the advantaged and to experience the systematic discrimination that their group faces.

This can lead to a greater willingness to engage in collective action – something that is especially important in deeply divided and unjust societies.

De-categorization

Everyone is different and unique, and people should perceive and evaluate each other as individuals. This conviction can be heard regularly, and there is clearly an element of truth in it. Positive contact may play a role here because it can lead to de-categorization. Through contact, people start to see each other as individuals rather than group members. This stimulates self-other comparisons whereby similarities and differences between you and me – rather than us and them – are compared. Individuation also stimulates the impression that the out-group is composed of members who are dissimilar.[3] And the more members of an out-group are perceived to be different from each other, the lower the tendency to associate specific characteristics with that group: increased variability implies a reduction of stereotyping (Miller, 2002). From a colour-blind perspective it is not group membership but, rather, personal traits and characteristics that should be the basis for approaching and evaluating others. With the emphasis on individual differences and personal qualities, the differences *within* groups become more clear, while the differences *between* groups fade into the background. You see each other primarily as individuals, also those who belong to your own group. This means, among other things, that in-group members no longer benefit from a self-evident preference for one's in-group. As a result of this, the previous positive differentiation in favour of the in-group is reduced.

Experimental research has shown that de-categorization can indeed lead to more harmonious relationships between groups (Ensari *et al.*, 2012; Miller, 2002). For example, in a number of studies conducted in France it was demonstrated that increasing the perceived variability of minority out-groups (Moroccans, Arabs, Chinese) reduces prejudice and discrimination towards its members (Brauer & Er-rafiy, 2011). Perceived variability makes the notion of group membership less meaningful and relevant. If there is much diversity within a group, it is of little help to use people's group membership as a basis for predicting their behaviour. The success of de-categorization may also derive from the fact that the focus is no longer on one particular identity. Repeated contact may facilitate the development of a more differentiated understanding of each other, where there is room not only for individual differences but also for other group memberships. People are always members of several categories and groups, and this means that the importance of the ethnic or religious background for understanding others can be lessened.[4]

An emphasis on individual characteristics and properties seems to be a useful strategy to improve intergroup relations. This is consistent with the liberal and meritocratic ideal of an education system and a society that give space to individual talent, regardless of one's background. No attention should be paid to people's cultural or religious background, because the talents and responsibilities of the individual student or citizen stand paramount. The only identity that matters is that of student or citizen. However, this ideal is not easy to realize in practice. For example, research shows that ethnic segregation occurs easily in multi-ethnic schools where the focus is on the individual student (Gaertner *et al.*, 1996). And in France the republican ideal of 'citoyen' goes hand in hand with ethnic and religious tensions. The same applies to countries like the United States, where the idea of individual freedom and responsibility prevails.

There is a tendency to treat people as individuals, but there is also a tendency to not do this. Muslim immigrants are told that they are personally responsible for what they do and achieve and that we, in the liberal Western world, perceive them as individuals and not as a member of a group. But, at the same time, Muslim individuals are held accountable for the entire Muslim community: 'Why do you not protest against these terrorist attacks that are committed in the name of your religion?' It is also true that in many situations people want to be seen and evaluated in terms of their personal characteristics and qualities. Who and what you are like as an individual is what makes you unique and special. You want people to be interested in your personal background, your personal life story, and your own perspective on things. And in many situations you also like to hear about someone else's personal story, reflecting his or her unique experiences and view on things. But it is likewise true that people also belong to various groups that play an important role in how they perceive themselves and their world. A colour-blind perspective is not appropriate for all situations, as people also want to be recognized and acknowledged in terms of their group membership. Your ethnic or religious identity can be central to your self-understanding and psychologically just as real for who you are and what you are like as the fact that you are an unique individual.

Moreover, in a colour-blind discourse one easily ignores the reality of discrimination. Colour-blindness can ensure equal opportunities for all, because the focus is on individual qualities. But, as research shows, it may also justify inequality by downplaying, or even denying, group disadvantages and deprivation (e.g., Levy *et al.*, 2005; Rattan & Ambady, 2013). The emphasis on individual opportunities and responsibilities can result in structural inequalities disappearing from view, both for the advantaged majority and for minorities.

Another limitation of the de-categorization strategy has to do with the generalization of the positive effect of contact. Everyone knows statements along the lines of 'Ali is my favourite colleague, but I do not like Turkish immigrants.' Positive interpersonal contact apparently does not always lead to favourable judgements of the group. And why should it, because Ali, after all, can be the exception to the rule. If contact occurs at the interpersonal level between individuals as individuals, it is not obvious that attitudes towards the group will change. That may happen if I perceive Ali not only as a good colleague, but also as a Turkish colleague. In that case his ethnic background plays a role in our personal contact, and my positive experiences can be transferred to Turkish people in general. There are several studies that confirm that this is how it works. An example is research conducted in the Netherlands (Van Oudenhoven *et al.*, 1996). In one experimental condition a native Dutch student and a Turkish student collaborated in a joint task, without any reference to the Turkish student's ethnic background. In the other condition, the task was the same, but the Turkish background was emphasized at the beginning and during the task. There was no difference in the judgements of the particular Turkish classmate between the two conditions, but in the second condition Dutch students were more positive about Turkish immigrants as a group. Thus for contact to have a positive effect on out-group attitudes, not only the individual but also his or her ethnic background needs to be salient. And the positive effect is stronger when the other is a relatively typical group member. If Ali is a very atypical Turkish immigrant (highly educated, Christian, and Westernized), then my positive contact with him will not easily generalize to Turkish immigrants as a group. Several studies have underscored the importance of typicality during contact (Liebkind & McAlister, 1999; Wright *et al.*, 1997).

Re-categorization

> ... and provided it is of a sort that leads to the perception of common interests and common humanity between members of the two groups.

This quote marks the end of Allport's chapter on contact (1954, p. 281). According to him, contact has particularly favourable effects when it is accompanied by a common interest or shared identity. One example of this is a study carried out in a multi-ethnic secondary school in the United States (Gaertner *et al.*, 1996). The students were asked to indicate how positive their contact is with students from other ethnic groups, and how strongly they perceive all the students in their school as belonging to *one* community. It turned out that positive contact was associated with a sense of being one community, and that this sentiment was, in turn, associated with more harmonious ethnic relations. As shown in Figure 7.1, we found a similar result in a secondary school in Rotterdam, for both ethnic minority and ethnic majority pupils.

In chapter 5, I discussed the summer camp study conducted by Sherif. In the third stage of this study, Sherif attempted to improve the relations between the two groups of boys. One way of doing this was by introducing shared activities and

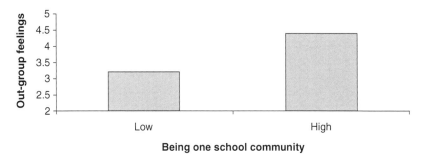

Figure 7.1 Ethnic out-group feelings and the – low vs. high – perception of being one school community

common goals whereby the two groups became interdependent. This resulted in improved relationships, and this effect has subsequently been found in cooperative learning groups in schools, including the well-known jigsaw technique (Aronson *et al.*, 1978; Slavin, 1983). There are several reasons why this happens, and one has to do with re-categorization. The original situation of two separate groups gradually changes into a situation in which a shared or common category comes first ('we boys from the summer camp').

When social identities are salient, the distinction between the in-group and a relevant out-group is readily available, and this affects people's thoughts, feelings, and actions. For example, positive information about one's own group and negative information about the out-group is remembered better. Furthermore, positive feelings and emotions such as sympathy, trust, and commitment are spontaneously associated with one's in-group, and people are more helpful towards someone who belongs to their group. Given these consequences, it is reasonable to assume that a shared or overarching identity can contribute to better intergroup relations. A new, inclusive sense of 'we' ensures that the previous out-group is incorporated and becomes one of 'us'. In this way, the former out-group benefits from the preference that usually exists for the in-group.

For more than 20 years John Dovidio and Samuel Gaertner have been examining the effects of re-categorization, or what they call the 'common in-group identity' model (Gaertner & Dovidio, 2000), which is visualized in the left circle of Figure 7.2. Their research includes survey, experimental and field studies, among adults and children, among different ethnic groups, and in various countries. The majority of the studies confirm the positive effects of re-categorization. An overarching or shared sense of 'we' (the 'C' of the left circle in Figure 7.2) improves intergroup relations. It is therefore not surprising that Obama emphasizes the importance of a common 'we' or that the municipality of Amsterdam has funded projects in the context of 'We, citizens of Amsterdam'. A shared identity provides a common point of reference and a moral framework with the related sentiments of commitment and responsibilities. Relationships are then embedded in a community and supported by a sense of belonging together. Research among children and adolescents demonstrates that ethnic

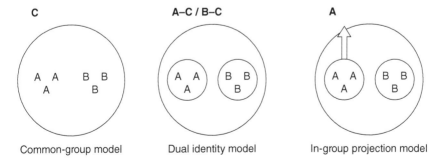

Figure 7.2 Three models of re-categorization

differences may disappear into the background when there is a shared concern, a shared interest, or joint activities. Research has also shown that identification with the neighbourhood or district where one lives can counter ethnic group contradistinctions (e.g., Back, 1996).

But, as mentioned earlier, if something works in one situation, it does not necessarily mean that it works in the same way in other situations. In a school, neighbourhood, or city, a shared local identity can overarch ethnic or religious differences. The local identity is an alternative categorization that often does not correspond to or run parallel with the ethnic and religious differences. This is different for identities that are hierarchically nested, such as Sunnis, Shiites, and Alevis, who are all Muslims, or the various ethnic groups that live in the same country, or the separate countries that together make up the European Union. There is research that shows that in these situations the introduction of an overarching identity may actually result in more resistance and a sharpening of group differences (see Wenzel *et al.*, 2007). A 'new we' is not so easy when, for example, there are important cultural or religious differences that are visible in appearance or behaviour. Furthermore, the overarching categorization can be perceived as being relatively more representative of one's own subgroup than of other subgroups. This is especially likely for majority group members who can more easily attribute their own cultural characteristics to the larger whole. Amélie Mummendey and her colleagues developed this idea in their 'in-group projection' model (see Wenzel *et al.*, 2007).[5]

In-group projection

A year after the fall of the Berlin Wall, in 1990, West and East Germany were reunited and once again known under the same name. In practice this meant that the East adapted to the West. The official political programme was aimed at changing the institutions, laws, and regulations to fit Western standards. Some have called this process the colonization of East Germany (Cooke, 2005). West Germany was the point of reference, and West Germans presented themselves as the 'real' Germans: what characterized West Germany and West Germans was considered to embody what Germany and being a German meant. Research showed that West Germans looked down upon the East, and that East Germans perceived themselves as second-class citizens and as inferior to West Germans. The new, unified Germany did not lead to more positive and harmonious relationships – quite the contrary.

The in-group projection model is shown in the right circle in Figure 7.2. Its starting point is that comparisons are always made against the background of what is shared. If I ask you to compare an apple with a train, you will probably look at me in surprise. Such a comparison is strange, as the two have nothing in common. But if I ask you to compare an apple with a banana, you start to think. Now we are dealing with fruit, and against that background it is a meaningful question. Characteristics of fruit, such as juiciness, firmness, and vitamins, can be used to make a comparison. And you would probably regard, say, an apple as a more typical fruit than a banana. What does this mean when it comes to perceiving social groups?

If two groups belong to a shared category, then the characteristics of that category will be used to assess the group differences and similarities. Furthermore, one group will be perceived as exemplifying or embodying that shared category more than the other. A shared national 'we' will be closer to the native population (ethnic Dutch or Germans) than to an ethnic minority group. Similarly, by defining itself as a Jewish state, Israel's national identity will be much closer to Jewish than to Palestinian citizens. Another example is the preamble of the constitution of Macedonia, which states that it is a 'historical fact that Macedonia is established as a national state *of* the Macedonian people, in which full equality as citizens and permanent co-existence with the Macedonian people is provided for Albanians, Turks, Vlachs, Romanics and other nationalities living in the Republic of Macedonia' (italics added). This definition places the Macedonian people in a privileged position compared to the different minority groups.

The most typical group will tend to project its own characteristics and qualities onto the larger category. This is indicated in Figure 7.2 by the arrow and the letter 'A', which goes from one subgroup to the shared category. A real, typical Dutchman is a native Dutch, a real, typical German is a native German, and a real, typical Macedonian is a native Macedonian. What is considered typical for the majority group is projected onto the society and is thereby normative for the shared identity. As a result, minority groups are considered not only different but also atypical. They are evaluated negatively precisely *because* they belong to the same overarching category. Within the shared identity, groups are judged by the same criteria and are expected to be similar, which in practice means like the majority population. And because 'they' (East Germans, minorities) deviate from the norm but are still part of the shared category (Germany, nation), the rejection is even stronger. Immigrants and minorities have to prove that they are full members of society. They must demonstrate that they deserve to be members of the imagined community, and because they apparently fail to do so they are rejected.

In a German study, people were asked about their attitudes towards Poles (see Wenzel *et al.*, 2007). In one experimental condition, this took place in the context of Europe and in the other condition in the context of Western Europe. Poland is part of Europe, but not of Western Europe. In turned out that attitudes towards Poles were more negative in the European condition than in the Western European condition. In the former condition Poles were compared to the common European 'we', which was not the case in the second condition. Moreover, only in the European condition were attitudes towards Poles increasingly negative, the more Germans were seen as embodying the European norm. The same results were found in another German study on attitudes towards the British. These attitudes were increasingly negative the more Germans were seen as the real Europeans in comparison to the British. Furthermore, Germans who considered their group as more typical for Germany were found to have, over time, more negative emotions and prejudices towards immigrants (Kessler *et al.*, 2010).

Another study showed the importance of 'normalization' (Verkuyten, 2001). The more the majority group norms, habits, and behaviour are described as natural, routine, and everyday, the more people from ethnic minorities are defined as 'abnormal'. Whatever is seen as being typical for the native majority group becomes the invisible norm against which events are evaluated and classified as normal or abnormal. Such a classification confirms the in-group identity and makes other groups subject to accusation and correction. Among native Dutch, national identification appears to be strongly associated with the expectation that everyone should act as normally as possible and thus behave in the same – assumed Dutch – way (Hagendoorn & Sniderman, 2004).

According to the in-group projection model, groups will try to portray themselves as the embodiment of the overarching identity. In doing so, in-group traits and characteristics are the point of reference. This is, for example, reflected in our research among groups of Turkish Dutch Muslims. Although Islam is a religion in which the Muslim world is united in the 'Ummah' or the 'Community of Believers', Muslim subgroups interpret Islam in different ways. The Sunnis and Alevis who participated in this study were asked to indicate the extent to which the followers of different Islamic subgroups are typical Muslims.

As can be seen in Figure 7.3, Sunnis consider themselves more as typical Muslims than Alevis, and for the Alevis it is the other way around. Note also that there is no disagreement about the Shiites. This indicates the importance of the intergroup situation in the Netherlands and Turkey, where there are hardly any Shiites.

For the Sunni participants, we could also examine their attitudes towards the Alevis and the Shiites (Lie & Verkuyten, 2012). In agreement with the in-group projection model, it was found that the more the Sunni in-group was considered to be the 'true' Muslims, the more positively the Sunnis were evaluated compared to the Alevis and the Shiites. Furthermore, the more Sunnis were engaged in their specific Muslim practices (e.g., mosque attendance, participation in Ramadan, daily prayers), the more these practices were seen as the appropriate religious behaviour of 'true' Muslims. Thus, the more Sunnis practise Islam, the more prototypical they think Sunnis are of Muslims, particularly in comparison to

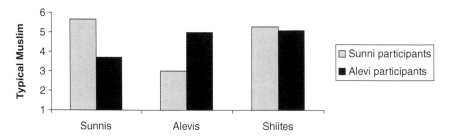

Figure 7.3 The degree to which Sunni and Alevi Muslims consider three Muslim subgroups as typical Muslims

Alevis, who have a different interpretation of Islam with different religious practices and customs. Instead of attending the mosque, as Sunnis and Shiites do, Alevis have congregational or assembly meetings in Cem houses led by a *dede* or *pir*, where men and women pray together. Furthermore, almost none of the Alevi practise ritual prayer five times a day, and neither do they participate in Ramadan or go on the *Hajj* to Mecca (Kaya, 2006). These pillars of Islam that define Muslim identity for Sunnis and Shiites are not Alevi practices. Among the Sunni participants, it was found that practising Islam did indeed increase bias towards Alevis, and this was due to considering the Sunnis as exemplifying or embodying Islam relatively more. Moreover, practising Islam did not affect the Sunni's evaluation of Shiites who perform the same religious practices that we examined.

It is, of course, not always possible to claim that your own group is representative or the embodiment of a shared identity. This is much easier in a school with 80% native pupils than in a school with 50 different nationalities, just as it is easier for White Americans in Fargo, North Dakota, and Missoula, Montana, than in Los Angeles or New York.[6] Minority members can sometimes claim a certain level of typicality for the shared category, and in multi-ethnic localities they might perceive their own group and natives as equally representative of the local identity. This has been found in research on urban neighbourhood identity that served as a common identity for native Dutch and ethnic minority inhabitants (Ufkes *et al.*, 2012). But for immigrants and minorities, it is hardly possible to put themselves forward as typical citizens of the country. If one is called Yilmaz or Yildirim, one is much less close to the heart of German identity than if one's name is Schulz or Schmidt. In such situations one can, though, disagree on the *relative* embodiment of the inclusive identity. After German reunification, West and East Germans agreed that the West Germans were to a greater extent the typical or 'real' Germans, but the West Germans subscribed to this view much more strongly than the East Germans did. Furthermore, an American study entitled 'American = White' showed that White Americans implicitly associate being American with being White, while this was much less the case among African Americans (Devos & Banaji, 2005).

The dual identity model

The in-group projection model indicates that there are several limitations to an overarching identity for improving intergroup relations. In some cases it may work out well, but in others it might not. A 'we-feeling' in a school, a neighbourhood, and at the city level seems more easy and positive than at the national level. Furthermore, the need for a distinctive and positive subgroup identity can make it unattractive to merge into a larger whole. This is especially true for minority groups and those who identify strongly with their group. Minorities may react rather negatively when attempts are made to put forward one shared identity. For them, this often comes down to assimilation: they feel that their ethnic or religious minority identity melts away and becomes lost in the larger whole. Gaertner and Dovidio (e.g., Dovidio *et al.*, 2009) recognize the limitations of their 'common in-group identity' model in which the focus is on a single and undivided 'we'. The resistance to such a model can be strong and may actually lead to worse relations.

An alternative is a dual identity model in which the separate group identities are affirmed within the context of a larger whole. This is the idea behind cultural diversity within the context of national unity: not a one-sided emphasis on unity and communality but also not one on diversity and difference. This model is represented in the middle circle of Figure 7.2 in which the shared category is identified with hyphenated labels. The idea is that intergroup relations will benefit if people are members of both their ethnic or religious group as well as the overarching community. In these situations, valuable group identities are recognized, while simultaneously allowing connections to develop with others that belong to the overarching identity. This is especially important if minorities feel that they are barely visible or poorly represented within the larger whole. Similarly, the European unification is particularly threatening to small countries that fear becoming unrecognizable and slowly vanishing into the European project. Those countries will be more likely to support a Europe based on the principle of 'unity in diversity'.

Several experimental studies confirm the dual identity model (e.g., González & Brown, 2003; Hornsey & Hogg, 2001). In those studies a comparison is often made between a context in which only separate group identities are salient, a context in which one common identity is stressed, and a context with dual identities. The dual strategy appears to work best for intergroup relationships, at least for minorities. They are most positive towards others when both their minority identity and the fact that they belong to the larger whole are taken into account. For example, Gaertner and Dovidio found that adolescents who perceived themselves both as ethnic minority group members and as Americans held the most positive attitudes towards various other groups.

It is also possible, however, that dual identity leads to more positive feelings towards the majority group but not towards fellow minorities. One possible reason for this is competition and a conflict of interest in which the gains of another minority group come at the expense of one's own minority group. Another reason is that societal stereotypes and prejudicial attitudes towards minorities might be transferred to minority group members who are seeking acceptance from the majority group. Lewin (1948) argues that members of minority groups can assimilate into the majority group, resulting in negative attitudes towards other minority groups. There is some empirical evidence for this transfer model for East Indians' attitudes towards African Americans (e.g., Philip *et al.*, 2010). In addition, the more Basque people identify with Spaniards, the more negatively they view Catalans as a subgroup that seeks autonomy (Martinovic *et al.*, 2011).

Yet several other studies found more evidence for the common in-group model, which predicts that higher dual identifiers are more positive towards various out-groups, than for the competition or transfer models, which predict a more negative evaluation of other minority groups but not of the majority group. A study among large representative samples of Moroccan and Turkish immigrants and controlling statistically for factors like age, education, generation, religion, and length of residence showed that stronger national identification was independently related to less social distance towards other ethnic minority groups (e.g., Surinamese, Antilleans) and towards the native Dutch majority (Hindriks *et al.*, 2013b). In addition, the effects for these different out-groups were similar in strength. Similar results were found in a study among Turkish Dutch Muslims (Verkuyten, 2007). Those who had both a strong Muslim as well as host national identification were more positive towards Christians and Hindustanis and less negative towards Jews and non-believers. In contrast, a strong Muslim identification without a sense of connectedness with the host society was associated with more negative feelings towards these religious out-groups. Hence, a simultaneous awareness of both a common national identity as well as an emphasis on one's Muslim identity – dual identity – was the best condition for relatively favourable feelings towards religious out-groups. Furthermore, in five experimental studies among Asians, Latinos, and African Americans it was found that discrimination against one's racial or ethnic in-group can trigger a shared disadvantaged minority identity that engenders more positive feelings and attitudes towards other minorities (Craig & Richeson, 2012).

Labels

Whereas minorities tend to emphasize group differences as well as similarities, the majority is usually more focused on similarities. This is particularly the case in situations with a large and traditional native population that is normative for the definition of the overarching national identity. But for the majority, a dual identity of minorities is, in any case, preferable to a one-sided emphasis on minority ethnicity or religion. At least, that is what you would expect. Hyphenated self-definitions like Turkish-Dutch or Moroccan-Dutch suggest lower social distance from society than a singular ethnic description as Turkish or Moroccan that might signal segregation. Hyphenated labels are common in the North American context (e.g. African-Americans, Mexican-Americans, Chinese-Canadian) but not in many European countries.

In chapter 11 of his *The Nature of Prejudice*, Allport (1954) discusses the importance of linguistic factors. He argues that social categorization involves labelling and that labels are 'nouns that cut slices'. He also points out that most groups can be labelled in various ways and that different labels have different connotations. In a newspaper interview in early 2008, the then Dutch Minister Ella Vogelaar said the following:[7]

> I belief that words have an important function in societal relations, they have a symbolic value. When you call someone a Turk, then you emphasize that he is not a Dutchman.

And after her forced resignation in November 2008 because of her alleged pro-immigrant statements, she wrote in a newspaper article:[8]

As long as the elite keeps talking in terms of *the* Moroccans, *the* Turks and *the* Antilleans … it is difficult for immigrants to identify with the Netherlands. Similar to America, we should recognize the dual identity of newcomers by consistently talking about the Moroccan, Turkish and Antillean Dutch.

This appeal is not a plea for political correctness, but for the proper use of actual designations. After all, the majority of these people have the Dutch nationality and were born in the Netherlands. They are simply Moroccan, Turkish or Antillean Dutch. And these labels are meaningful. In the Dutch media often single labels are used in relation to social and community problems, while dual terms are employed when it comes to outstanding achievements. There is talk about Moroccan troublemakers or Moroccan scum but of successful Moroccan Dutch soccer players and novelist. The former case has little to do with us (it is not 'our' scum), while in the second case it does involve us (they are 'our' soccer players and writers).

This appeal by Vogelaar and others[9] is consistent with the dual identity model. Labels like Moroccan Dutch and Turkish German emphasize that people are part simultaneously of their ethnic minority group and of the shared national category. That means that the use of these labels can be expected to lead to more positive attitudes than single ethnic labels that 'emphasize that one is not a Dutchman' (first quote above). Thus, the attitude towards ethnic minority groups can be expected to be more positive when these groups are identified with dual linguistic representations compared to single ethnic labels.

In a study among adolescents we found this to be the case (Verkuyten & Thijs, 2010). There were two conditions: half of the adolescents were asked to indicate their feelings towards Turks, Moroccans, Surinamese, and Antilleans (single designations), the other half was instructed to do the same with Turkish Dutch, Moroccan Dutch, Surinamese Dutch, and Antillean Dutch (dual designations). For all four groups there was a significant difference between the two conditions. As shown in Figure 7.4, it turned out that dual labels (e.g., Turkish Dutch) elicited more favourable feelings than single labels (e.g., Turks). This effect of labelling was found for ethnic minority groups that have a different position in the ethnic

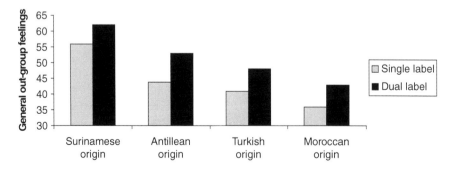

Figure 7.4 General out-group feelings by out-group labelling

hierarchy in the Netherlands (Hagendoorn, 1995). Thus, the dual labelling led to more positive feelings towards minority groups that, in general, are evaluated positively (Surinamese origin) or neutrally (Antilleans), but it also led to less negative feelings towards ethnic minorities that are at the bottom of the ethnic hierarchy (Turkish and Moroccan origin). This indicates that the labelling effect is not dependent on the type of minority out-group and whether this group is less or more accepted in society. This suggests that initiatives that promote a dual identity should be supported. They benefit from the favourable effects of a shared 'we-feeling', without being threatening to the separate ethnic or religious minority identities.

These findings show that labels do matter in an ethnically diverse society. They matter because words define categories, and each label has its own connotations. Minority members are sensitive to names given them, and majority members react differently towards ethnic minorities, depending on the labelling. Thus, an ethnically heterogeneous society should be sensitive to the way language is used. Group labelling is also an important issue for researchers and for the conclusions they draw and the findings they disseminate. For example, what should we conclude from Figure 7.4 about the attitude of Dutch adolescents towards people from Antillean or Turkish origin? Are these attitudes neutral and going in the direction of positive, or are they, rather, negative, indicating prejudice? The conclusion, and thereby the societal, educational, and policy implications, differs depending on the way that these groups are labelled. Thus, it is not only in everyday life that 'words have an important function in social relations' (first quote above), but also in research. The group label affects the level of prejudice found and is important for testing theoretical notions. Other research concurs with this conclusion, for example, by showing that the level of abstraction used to label a group (Chinese and Indians versus ethnic minorities) affects the attitude towards minority groups (Watt *et al.*, 2007).

Limits of the dual identity model

Although they are important, we should not expect too much of these kind of linguistic factors, and there are also limits and downsides to the dual identity model. If we know that a score below 50 represents negative feelings, then Figure 7.4 shows that feelings towards Turkish and Moroccan minorities are generally quite negative, also in the dual labelling condition. Furthermore, the findings of our study indicate that the difference in out-group feelings between the experimental conditions was significant for natives who endorsed multiculturalism but not for those who favoured assimilation. For the latter, both single- and dual-group labels are incompatible with an assimilation ideology that emphasizes a one-group representation in which majority group ('Dutch') and national identity (also 'Dutch') correspond. Thus, dual labels are not very helpful for improving the attitudes of assimilationists. For the former, multiculturalism seems to imply a dual identity representation in which group differences are recognized and ethnic minorities are included as equal members in the national category. This representation corresponds to the values that people who endorse multiculturalism tend to have for society (Modood, 2007; Parekh, 2000).

The dual identity model it is not always the best option. Not all research supports it, and according to Mummendey and colleagues a dual identity may be associated with a stronger tendency for in-group projection (Wenzel *et al.*, 2007). A Sunni Muslim will tend to view Sunnis as the true Muslims and therefore be more negative about Alevis and Shiites (Lie & Verkuyten, 2012). In a further study, German participants were asked about their opinion of Germans, Poles, and Europeans (see Wenzel *et al.*, 2007). Those who identified strongly with both Germans and Europeans viewed the Germans as the true representatives of Europe and as a result had a more negative attitude towards Poles.

Hence, there is research that supports the dual identity model and research that corresponds to the in-group projection model. This indicates that the validity of either model is dependent on additional factors. There are situations where subgroup identities occupy centre stage and the common identity is in the background: diversity in unity. We are all different and also belong to the same school, city, or nation. In these situations, in-group projection is likely. But there are also situations in which the common identity is paramount and the subgroup identities blend into the background: unity in diversity. We all belong to the same school, city, or nation, and within those communities there are differences. This situation can lead to more harmonious relations and mutual acceptance.

In the research mentioned earlier on urban neighbourhood identity (Ufkes *et al.*, 2012), it was found that for the native Dutch a stronger identification with the inclusive neighbourhood was related to lower prejudice, but only for those who considered the Dutch as not very typical or representative for the neighbourhood. In contrast, for ethnic minority inhabitants this positive association was found for those who perceived their minority group as typical or representative of the urban district. These findings demonstrate how a common identity and group typicality can work jointly and differently for majority and minority group members. A shared, inclusive identity will improve the ethnic out-group attitudes of majority members when they recognize that this identity is not only representing them. Conversely, minority members are more positive about out-groups when they have the feeling that they, too, are included and also representative of the shared neighbourhood.

Dimensions

Projection is likely to occur when the overarching identity is truly inclusive and relates to the same dimension of categorization, such as ethnicity and nationality. However, it is less likely when another categorization dimension is involved. This is the difference between local identities such as schools and neighbourhoods that in principle are not related to ethnicity, and the nested categories of ethnicity, nationality, and Europe. Depending on the numerical distribution, it is certainly possible that a particular group claims to be typical and, thus, normative for the school or neighbourhood. But this is more likely to happen at the national and

European level. If we think about the Dutch or German national identity, it is clear that native Dutch or Germans may put themselves forward as the true or typical inhabitants of the country. They set the tone and are the normative benchmark to which others are compared. There is little inclusive, shared 'we-feeling', because the properties and characteristics of the dominant group are projected onto the greater whole or even coincide completely with it. The dual identity model works particularly well when the individual groups are complementary to each other and need each other to maintain the greater whole, as in a mosaic or jigsaw puzzle in which every group contributes to the whole in its own way. If this is not the case, or if it is not perceived in this way, in-group projection by the majority might take place. Herein lies a major obstacle to a shared national 'we' feeling.

It is important that the shared identity is sufficiently open and complex so that any single group cannot put a claim to it, and that others can identify with it. The phenomenon of 'American = White' does not occur, for example, in New Zealand, where the symbolic position of the Maori has significantly changed in the last 30 years. Successive governments have emphasized that the Maori have shared equally in the creation of a national partnership. The Maori suffer many social disadvantages, and there are all kinds of negative stereotypes about them, but in the eyes of the public they are an intrinsic part of the imagined national community: 'New Zealand = bicultural' (Sibley & Liu, 2007). By no means did this happen overnight. This story of New Zeeland is transmitted and emphasized in the education system, the media, and in cultural and sporting events. This has established a clear symbolic significance of the Maori culture for the country as a whole.

Identity complexity

The dual identity model is advantageous for minority groups because it affirms their subgroup distinctiveness within a context of connection and shared belonging. However, for some minority groups this model is also limited, because it ignores religion. The European emphasis on Muslim immigrants has made the question of their national belonging more urgent. It is probably more difficult to feel that one is a Dutch or German Muslim than a Moroccan Dutch or a Turkish German. Furthermore, for Muslim immigrants, ethnicity and religion might overlap to a large extent. What it means to be a member of their ethnic minority group can intersect with what it means to be a Muslim. Research on social identity complexity (Roccas & Brewer, 2002; see chapter 4) suggests that the extent to which individuals subjectively combine or see their multiple identities as interrelated is associated with out-group attitudes. An inclusive or complex identity structure implies that an individual accepts and acknowledges his or her distinctive and separate group memberships. Alternatively, individuals with a relatively simplified structure (low identity complexity) perceive a strong overlap and interrelation among their identities, which depend on each other for meaning. Members of groups holding multiple disadvantaged statuses, in particular, would experience their social identities in close association and simultaneously (relative low identity complexity). One research study did indeed find lower identity complexity among Asian Australians compared to Anglo Australians, despite the fact that the objective identity overlap was actually greater for the latter than the former group (Brewer *et al.*, in press).

For Muslim immigrants in Western Europe there tends to be a relatively high degree of overlap between their meaningful and important ethnic and religious identities. What it means to be a Turk, Moroccan, Algerian, or Pakistani often intersects with what it means to be a Muslim: the one defines the other. When these identities are subjectively combined, there is a relatively simplified and exclusive identity structure that can be expected to be associated with a more negative attitude towards the host nation. The reason is that low social identity complexity means that multiple identities are embedded in a single in-group representation (Turkish Muslims), making a Dutch individual who is an out-group member on one dimension (not Turkish) also an out-group member on another dimension (not Muslim). This lack of cross-cutting identities increases the group distinctions and the motivation to favour one's own group and thereby strengthens the distancing from the host society (Crisp & Hewstone, 2006). In three studies in the Netherlands, we found that Muslim immigrants with a simple identity structure tended to distance themselves more from the host society than immigrants with a more complex structure (Verkuyten & Martinovic, 2012b). Furthermore, participants with simpler identity structures endorsed Dutch self-defining liberal practices less, showed less positive feelings towards the Dutch, and tended to have less positive stereotypes about them. These findings show that a dual identity in the form of a strong intersection between ethnicity and religion (low identity complexity) can have negative consequences for the integration of Muslim immigrants and for intergroup relations. Among majority members, low identity complexity has also been found to go together with lower acceptance of ethnic out-groups and lower support for multiculturalism and related social policies (Brewer & Pierce, 2005; Miller *et al.*, 2009).

Political action

There is another possible downside to the dual identity model.[10] This relates to the earlier discussion on the negative role of intergroup contact for social change and political mobilization of minority groups. From a social identity perspective, it has been proposed and found that a strongly developed and politicized sense of identification with a group or social movement is the best predictor for collective action (see Simon, 2004). For immigrants this means that a stronger ethnic or religious identity will be associated with stronger endorsement of minority group rights and higher normative (socially and legally accepted) political actions (see Phalet *et al.*, 2010; Verkuyten & Yildiz, 2010a).

Simon and Klandermans (2001, p. 326) point out, however, that a politicized identity is typically a dual identity, because minority members 'acknowledge or even stress their identity as a member of that society because only by virtue of their membership in this more inclusive group or community are they entitled to societal support for their claims'. Immigrants' dual identity functions as a politicized collective identity because of the combination of perceptions of injustice derived from identification with the ethnic minority group with feelings of entitlement derived from identification with the society. Thus, a dual identity would foster political involvement for one's minority group but without ignoring the requirements of the larger polity. This means that dual identity should stimulate conventional political actions (e.g. petitions, demonstrations) rather than radicalization or the use of non-normative means.

In support of this reasoning and using a sample of Turkish immigrants in Germany, Simon and Ruhs (2008) found that dual identification as both Turkish and German (e.g., 'I feel I belong to both the Turks and the Germans') was not related to political violence but showed a positive relationship to normative politicization. This relationship was established in both cross-sectional and longitudinal analyses. Similar findings were obtained in a study among Russian immigrants to Germany (Simon & Grabow, 2010) and among immigrant groups in the Netherlands and the United States (Klandermans *et al.*, 2008). The similarity of findings indicates that a dual identity can play a constructive role in the political integration of immigrants. It can foster political involvement and inhibit radicalization.

However, dual identity might also undermine political mobilization among minority groups. Dual identity implies a combined feeling of belonging to two communities, which can lead to perceiving greater similarity between the two, to a psychological blurring of group boundaries, and to a more positive characterization of the majority group. These are all important conditions that work against political mobilization as a minority group. A dual identity can discourage the maintenance of a strong religious group identity and thereby undermine the support for religious political mobilization. From a social justice perspective, the widespread public prejudice and distrust towards Muslims and their disadvantaged position in West European societies (see Helbig, 2012) makes support for Muslim minority rights and political engagement important. The political downside of a sense of dual identity is that it can discourage a strong religious group identification, which is pivotal for religious political mobilization and collective action support. In a study among Turkish Muslims in the Netherlands and Germany we found evidence of this political downside of dual identity (Martinovic & Verkuyten, 2013a). It turned out that stronger dual identity (Turkish Dutch/German) was associated with weaker Muslim group identification and thereby with lower support for the political organization of Islam, expressive rights of Muslims, and normative political actions to defend Islam. These findings support Wright and Lubensky's (2009, p. 297) claim that 'the dual identity model… is not encouraging the maintenance of a subordinate identity in service of collective action'.

Leadership

A shared 'we' can be formulated in different ways and by different people. In many of his speeches, Obama stresses that although the American people have different backgrounds and stories and come from very different places, they are held together by common efforts, hopes, and the shared ideals of the American Dream. He acknowledges the cultural and social diversity of America but downplays this diversity by emphasizing commonalities and shared values. The diversity as well as the shared American values are embodied by Obama himself. In his speeches he proactively works to depict himself as exemplifying the diversity of American society and personifying the American values (Augoustinos & De Garis, 2012). He presents his biracial heritage and his personal and family history as the living proof of what it means to be an American, and thereby himself as the one to lead the nation.

Political leaders can have a strong influence in how the public responds to immigration and cultural diversity. Many people are struggling with questions related to cultural diversity and ethnic minority policies. These issues are much debated in almost all Western societies, and not only far-right politicians but also mainstream political leaders can be influential. Politicians play a critical role in defining issues, problems, and solutions related to diversity and immigration and can therefore be expected to shape people's views.

According to the social identity perspective on leadership, individuals are primarily influenced by those who belong to their own group (Haslam *et al.*, 2011). Research has shown that people tend to agree and seek agreement with in-group members, and that they are more likely to trust, accept, and follow these members (see Haslam, 2001; Turner, 1991). Individuals who identify with a particular group will seek to find out what it means to be a group member and are motivated to conform to these meanings: identifiers seek 'information from others about the meanings associated with the group (e.g., what it means to be a Conservative) and about the implications of those meanings for situated practice (what, as a "good" Conservative, I am meant to do in the here and now)' (Haslam *et al.*, 2011, p. 55). Prominent group members are expected to know the values, beliefs, and priorities of the group and therefore define and confirm our understandings of the social world. Thus, according to the social identity perspective, people who identify with a group will use those who represent the group to seek out the associated meanings of the social identity and will act on the basis of these meanings.

Applying this reasoning to political parties leads to the expectation that partisans will follow their political leaders in order to determine their position on political issues. This ties in with research showing that most people do not have very strong political beliefs but, rather, 'are capable of warming to ideas of the left, right or center' (Jost, 2006, p. 658). This means that political leaders can play an important role in shaping people's understandings and reactions. Consequently, whether you do or do not endorses cultural diversity may depend on the leader of your political party making one or the other more salient and relevant.

Using two experiments embedded in a representative survey among the Dutch native population, we found that natives agreed more strongly with a pro *or* an anti-diversity statement when made by an own party politician compared to another party politician (Verkuyten & Maliepaard, in press).[11] This was found for people who identified with a large political party of the left (PvdA) and of the right (VVD). Thus, the politically mainstream both on the left and on the right were equally influenced by a politician from their own party. This finding is in agreement with the party-over-policy effect found by Cohen (2003) for the support of welfare policies among university students in the context of the United States. It suggests that partisanship has an important role to play in people's acceptance of political statements on diversity and affirmative action policies.

Another finding in support of this interpretation is that the greater influence of people's own party politician compared to another party's politician was independent of the content of the public statement. People agreed more with a leader of the party they identified with when this politician was either in favour of multiculturalism *or* of assimilation, and when affirmative action policies *or* general policies were proposed. Importantly, this indicates that – at least in the multi-party Dutch political system – people on the mainstream left can be moved in the direction of lower acceptance of diversity and minority policies and people on the mainstream right in the direction of greater acceptance. As argued by the social identity approach (Haslam *et al.*, 2011), the critical factor appears to be the group membership of the political leader who is saying it, rather than what is being said on these particular topics. The finding that people on the right can be made to support diversity and ethnic minority policies more might seem surprising, considering the fact that they tend to be more supportive of traditional culture and the status quo. However, conservative are also more likely to support conventional authority figures and strong leadership (Jost *et al.*, 2003a, 2003b) and are therefore likely to be influenced by their political party leader.

The important role of partisanship is also shown in the finding that there was no effect for 'political party leader' among people who did not identify with either the VVD or the PvdA. For them, both politicians are out-group party members, and they did not agree more with one or the other politician. In addition, people on the political left did not agree more with the left-wing PvdA politician compared to the right-wing VVD politician, and people on the right were not more in agreement with the latter compared to the former political leader. This further suggests that it is the politician's party membership rather than his or her (left/right) political orientation that influences people's views on cultural diversity and minority policies. In addition, the party over policy effect was found for males and females, younger and older participants, and those with a higher and lower education.[12] This indicates the generalizability of the effect.

It is important to note, however, that topics of cultural diversity and minority policies do not tend to be core self-defining features of, for example, libertarianism and conservatism, but vary in their ideological relevance across time and space (Jost, 2006). This might mean that party leaders will not be able to influence party members' attitudes in the direction of either higher or lower acceptance when core self-defining features are at stake, like attitudes towards social change versus tradition (Jost *et al.*, 2003a, 2003b). It also means that people politically on the far right will probably not be influenced in the direction of higher acceptance of ethnic minorities, because for them standpoints on immigration and cultural diversity are often self-defining political issues. We focused on the political mainstream because they receive most of the votes and are typically responsible for formulating and implementing diversity policies. Leaders of these parties can have quite some influence on the attitudes of political partisans on the mainstream political left and the right, independently of people's political orientation. Importantly, this influence can go in the direction of either higher or lower acceptance of cultural diversity and ethnic minority policies. This means that party members can be mobilized in opposite directions and that there is substantial room for politicians to pursue different strategies for mobilizing the public. This might be part of the reason why issues of immigration and integration are hotly debated in many Western countries. Moreover, the findings supports Allport's (1954) claim that it is critically important to examine processes of leadership for understanding people's attitudes towards immigrants and ethnic minorities and for prejudices more generally (see also Reicher, 2007).

Tolerance

> These movements form part of the wider struggle for recognition of identity and difference or, more accurately, of identity-related differences. Their demand for recognition goes far beyond the familiar plea for toleration, for the latter implies conceding the validity of society's disapproval and relying on its self-restraint.
>
> (Parekh, 2000, p. 1)

Cultural and religious diversity raises difficult questions, particularly when group positions are at stake and incompatible demands are involved. In general, and as illustrated in the quote above, a distinction can be made between approaches that focus on the recognition and active support of group differences and classical liberal approaches that emphasize the depoliticization of these differences and argue for the toleration of diversity (Barry, 2001).

The latter approaches claim that tolerance is sufficient for dealing adequately with diversity because it gives individual citizens the freedoms and rights to define and develop their own identities. It is argued that precisely because of the importance of culture and religion in people's lives, these should be neutralized as a political force in which group-specific claims are made. Proponents of cultural diversity argue, however, that 'mere' tolerance is not enough and that active support for cultural difference is needed. Toleration would be an act of generosity from the powerful who grudgingly agree to put up with minorities. In doing so the larger society's disapproval of minority identities and practices is implicitly affirmed. Or, in the words of Allport (1954, p. 425), 'To tolerate newcomers in a community is merely a negative act of decency.' For many minority members, the end result of tolerance is a poor substitute for the recognition and affirmation that they deserve and need. Furthermore, the discourse on tolerance is rhetorically powerful and can be used to justify intolerance of the dominant majority. Tolerance can be considered a (historical) national value that is threatened by the presence of 'them'. Majority members and populist politicians emphasize the self-defining meaning of national tolerance in order to criticize Muslim immigrants for their intolerance and their unwillingness to adapt (Verkuyten, in press). In portraying Muslim immigrants as transgressing 'our' tolerant way of life, they are positioned as moral outsiders to the national community.

The importance of tolerance

Yet the importance and benefits of tolerance for dealing with cultural and religious differences should not be underestimated. Its emphasis on civic identity and individuals' freedom to define and develop their own identities and ways of life offers crucial space for religious and cultural diversity. Furthermore, tolerance is important because it is around concrete practices that cultural and religious diversity is put to the test and ways of life collide. Should Muslim teachers be allowed to refuse to shake hands with children's parents of the opposite sex? Should all images of pigs be banned from pictures in public offices because these might offend Muslims' feelings? Should new mosques and minarets be allowed to be built and Islamic schools to be established? Should Islamic holidays be introduced as national public holidays in addition to Christian ones? Should it be allowed that civil servants wear a headscarf? Should all religious symbols be banned from public schools? These and many other questions are critical and indicate the importance of tolerance for dealing with diversity.

Tolerance is sometimes seen as the opposite of prejudice or even equivalent to openness and embracing diversity. Yet tolerance is, first and foremost, spoken about in the sense of tolerating someone doing something that you really do not agree with, or towards whom you actually hold prejudices. The main thing is that all people are given the right to live their lives according to their own discretion. Tolerance is thus a barrier against discrimination and exclusion and a condition for citizenship and democracy. It is the lowest level of peaceful coexistence between individuals and groups. And precisely because it is minimal, it is crucial. A diverse, equal, peaceful society does not require that we all like each other, but it does necessarily mean that people tolerate one another. Tolerance is the first step towards living together or the last barrier against exclusion and conflict (Vogt, 1997; Walzer, 1997). Tolerance does not concern superficial differences, but important matters that you really feel strongly about, that you do not agree with, but which you nevertheless put up with. It has to do with non-discrimination, non-exclusion, or non-rejection while actually being inclined and able to do so. Tolerance thus requires self-control – not because you are afraid, but because you regard diversity, equality, and social cohesion as important values in themselves.

Tolerance is not an easy matter because there are always limits. Not everything can and should be tolerated, especially not intolerance. Tolerance is not the same as relativism and should not be an excuse for letting things slide by. There are basic values and principles that are the foundations of a society. One's own freedom should not be at the expense of someone else's, and the right to religious freedom goes together with a duty to recognize and respect the beliefs of others.

Furthermore, gender equality, freedom of expression, free choice of a partner, and the right to apostasy cannot be violated without consequences. For the public debate, this implies that people should be able to critically question each other and that they need to set standards. And for upbringing and education, this means that youngsters must learn not only what *is* but also what is *not* to be tolerated and *why*. How do you responsibly and in an informed manner make a distinction between what should and what should not be tolerated? This is not an easy question and it is also far from evident what the best way is to teach and learn this.

Political tolerance

Political tolerance is probably a good starting point for teaching people the importance of tolerance. Political tolerance is anchored in the constitution and can be aligned with one's self-interest. The political system is meant to deal with conflicting interests, and it is relatively easy to show that in the long term, political tolerance is beneficial to everyone. Moreover, the idea of self-interest, together with recognizing the importance of the interests of others, only requires a low level of moral thinking.

Political tolerance is also a good starting point because it prevents ethnic and cultural identities from being immediately at stake. If that happens, endless accusations and justifications are often difficult to avoid, resulting in very little progress. Changes, mutual adjustments, and tolerance are often possible, on the condition that that which makes up the core of one's group identity is not brought into question as a matter of course (Kelman, 2001). Intolerance can be substantial when people believe that their culture and identity will fundamentally change (Zárate *et al.* 2012).[13] In a large-scale study among native Germans it was found that about three in four participants tolerated the wearing of a headscarf by Muslim women, and 72% supported the right of Muslims to build mosques in Germany. However, less than 6% agreed that important Islamic holidays should become national holidays in Germany (Van der Noll, 2012). A national holiday would make Islam part of the imagined national community, which is one bridge too far. Or, as the chairman of the German Christian Democratic Union said in an interview in 2012, 'Islam is not part of our German tradition and identity and therefore does not belong to Germany.'

It is also important for political tolerance that all groups have equal chances to take part in the public debate. Sometimes people get the impression that double standards are applied. If an imam calls homosexuals inferior people, this causes a public outcry and questions are asked in national parliament, but if a Protestant minister does the same, only eyebrows are raised. And if Muslims offend someone, there is the accusation of inciting hatred, but if Muslims are offended, this is justified by referring to freedom of expression. The feeling that double standards are applied in public debate, or at school, in the nightlife, by the police, or in the labour market is disastrous for mutual acceptance and social cohesion. People are very concerned about fair and just procedures (see Tyler *et al.*, 1997). They are much more likely to accept unfavourable decisions if they feel they have been treated fairly and with respect. And when this is the case, authorities are also appreciated in a more positive way. Fair procedures indicate that you belong to the moral community and that you are valued as a full member of that community. Applying double standards creates a feeling of unfairness and exclusion, making it hard to accept decisions and to trust authorities.

Three issues

There is quite some empirical research into the causes and development of tolerance (see Gibson, 2006; Vogt, 1997). There are researchers who address political tolerance, such as freedom of expression and demonstration and political participation. Others focus on tolerance in the moral domain, such as the acceptance of homosexuality, abortion, and parenting practices. The results of these studies are not nearly always straightforward and unequivocal. For example, age differences found by one researcher are not confirmed or are even contradicted by others. There are also few studies that focus on group identifications and compare tolerant judgements of people from different ethnic or religious groups. However, three things have become clear.

The first is that a strong difference may be found between the way in which people judge abstract principles in comparison to concrete cases or situations. It is one thing to agree with the ideal of freedom and equality, and something quite different to agree with the actual enactment of those ideals in specific practices. You can be in favour of freedom of speech, but the question is whether this also applies to a native councillor who refers to troublesome immigrant youth as 'Moroccan cunts' or to a minister who burns the Koran, and to an imam who dubs homosexuals as inferior people or to a spiritual leader inciting hatred. Principal considerations are interpreted and applied to the vicissitudes of daily life. Few people deny the importance of freedom or of equality, but the question is how these principles are interpreted in a given situation, and whether or not they are considered applicable in a particular case. The idea of equality may be limited to one's own group, and something that is a matter of freedom for one person may be a matter of unnecessary offence for another. Tolerance requires complex judgements in which moral, social-conventional, and personal considerations are weighed (Turiel, 2002). The conditions, consequences, and nature of the justification will have an effect on whether certain acts and activities will be tolerated.

A second and related point is that developmental and political science research has shown that tolerance is not a global construct. Tolerance depends on whom, what, and when people are asked to tolerate dissenting beliefs and practices (McClosky & Brill, 1983; Vogt, 1997). For example, there are indications that people are more tolerant towards actions that are based on a different factual view of the world ('They think it is like that') than on different moral beliefs ('They think that it is right and good') (e.g., Wainryb *et al.*, 1998). This has also been found in a study among Dutch adolescents' tolerant judgements of Muslims' political rights and dissenting beliefs and practices (Verkuyten & Slooter, 2007).

Adolescents took into account various aspects of what they were asked to tolerate and the sense in which they should be tolerant. The nature and the social implication of the behaviour and the underlying belief type all made a difference to the tolerant judgements. For example, the level of tolerance was lower when the social implications were greater (e.g., higher tolerance for headscarves than for Muslim schools), and participants were more tolerant of Muslim practices based on dissenting cultural beliefs than on dissenting moral beliefs.

Furthermore, accepting that people hold dissenting beliefs does not necessarily imply that one tolerates the public expression of these beliefs or the actual practices based on them (Vogt, 1997). These dimensions of tolerance can trigger different levels of acceptance. Research has shown that in general people are more tolerant of dissenting speech than practices. This higher acceptance of the public expression of dissenting beliefs is consistent with the idea of freedom of speech. It can be seen as stimulating debate that is important for the democratic process and as causing less direct harm or injustice than actual acts.

However, higher acceptance of public expressions of beliefs, compared to the actual practices based upon these beliefs, depends on the intergroup context. Specifically, Muslims expressing their views in order to try to persuade co-believers to engage in a dissenting practice can be perceived as a threat to the national culture by the majority group. One study (Gieling *et al.*, 2010) examined Dutch adolescents' perceptions of four concrete cases of specific practices that are not illegal but that were hotly debated in Dutch society: the wearing of a headscarf by Muslim women, the refusal to shake hands with males by a female Muslim teacher, the founding of separate Islamic schools, and the public expression of the view that homosexuals are inferior people by an imam. The focus was not only on the adolescents' tolerance of these practices but also on their acceptance of people trying to mobilize other Muslims. Participants were asked whether it should be allowed that these Muslims campaign in order to try to convince others to do the same thing. This social mobilization of Muslims is typically seen as threatening to Dutch identity and culture, and therefore the adolescents were expected to be less tolerant of Muslims campaigning for co-believers' support than of the actual practice itself. The findings clearly showed this to be the case. Campaigning for support and persuading others implies mobilizing Muslims, for example, to start wearing a headscarf, to stop shaking hands with people of the opposite sex, and to found more Islamic schools. Politicians and the media tend to present these practices as undermining the secular and Christian traditions of the Netherlands. Trying to persuade other Muslims to act similarly is seen as contributing to the 'Islamization of Dutch society' and therefore leads to lower acceptance compared to the act itself.

Third, tolerance is much more vulnerable than intolerance (Gibson, 2006). The asymmetry of (in)tolerance refers to the finding that it is easier to convince tolerant people to give up their tolerant attitudes than to persuade intolerant people to become more tolerant. In comparison with intolerance, tolerance is an attitude that is more demanding and often less easy to maintain (Gieling *et al.*, 2012). This has to do with the fact that there are always limits to tolerance and there are usually several basic values and principles at stake, which require complex decisions. Moreover, it is easier to maintain intolerance, because the negative attitude towards a group is in agreement with rejecting the practices of that group: you reject what you dislike. Being tolerant, on the other hand, is more difficult because it implies putting up with the actions and practices of a disliked group: you accept what you dislike. Thus those who have intolerant views are more likely to act on the basis of those beliefs than are people with tolerant views.

However, intolerance can have bases other than out-group dislike. A neutral or positive attitude does not have to imply an unconditional acceptance of actions and behaviours (Sniderman & Hagendoorn, 2007; Van der Noll *et al.*, 2010). A positive attitude towards Muslims, for example, does not have to mean that one accepts practices that go against operative public norms that govern civic relations between people (Parekh, 2000), such as civil servants wearing a *burqa* or a *niqab* or refusing to shake hands with citizens of the opposite sex. Consideration of social cohesion but also moral principles and humanistic values rather than prejudice can underlie the opposition to specific practices of minority groups.

8 Conclusion
A way forward

The debate on immigration and integration continues in many countries and in many spheres of life. The often heated nature of the debate indicates that a great deal is at stake: not only material and political interests but also identities and ways of life. Citizens, opinion makers, authorities, group representatives, and politicians are engaged in lively debates about what it means to be an immigrant, a minority member, a religious believer, a national, and a European. And there are numerous initiatives and debates about how to live with diversity, how to improve acceptance and tolerance, and how to develop and maintain a sense of unity and solidarity. These discussions and debates are very important for the functioning of the society (or neighbourhood, school, organization) and for shaping the future of the country. The academic world tries to make a contribution by theoretical reasoning and empirical research.

The contribution of social psychology

In comparison with some 15–20 years ago, the number of empirical studies has increased dramatically. A great deal has come to be known about the labour market position of immigrants and ethnic minority groups, about their educational achievements, about their mental and physical health, about processes of integration and acculturation, about interethnic contacts, about prejudice, racism and discrimination, and about ethnic, racial, religious, and (host) national identities. All this work has greatly advanced our understanding. Social psychologists also make a contribution, and in this book I have tried to show that social psychology has much to offer for a better understanding of questions of identity and cultural diversity.

Social psychology is not a homogenous discipline, however, and there are inevitable limitations to the contributions that social psychologists can make. The social psychological knowledge is rather fragmented, and many researchers increasingly have the tendency to dig deeper and deeper into the brain. The precision they hope to find there comes at the expense of the scope and relevance of their work for understanding the real multicultural world. It is of limited use to try to explain the richness and fibre of daily life out of basic mechanisms of the human brain.[1] Human action always takes place in a social context in which historical, cultural, political, and economic factors play a role. Psychological principles can work out quite differently depending on the circumstances. The fact that people look for a sense of security, or for a positive self-image, or for a sense of belonging does not, in itself, say anything about how they will act and behave. Similarly, the fact that people need to eat says nothing about what, when, and how they eat, and the fact that people have the inborn capacity to learn a language does not say anything about which language they will end up speaking. Also, the fact that many people have negative associations with ethnic minorities without even being aware of it says little about how and when exactly this will affect their behaviour and how this relates to social norms and moral beliefs (Devine, 1989; Tetlock & Mitchell, 2008). There are general psychological processes, but in order to be able to give explanations and make predictions, we have to consider specific features of society. Basic psychological processes are not the same as empirical regularities in the real world. The complexities and richness of ethnic identities and intergroup relations cannot be explained with a few assumptions about cognitive and motivational processes. Yet it is equally true that these processes cannot be missed and that psychology helps us to understand why particular features of society affect people's lives. The dynamics of inner life and ethnic self should not be ignored or defined as inaccessible and of little importance for understanding social reality. An analysis in terms of internal mechanism and processes cannot replace an analysis of the regularities at the level of social interactions, but a focus on these interactions does not replace an analysis of mental processes and psychological tendencies.

Social psychology has a great deal to offer, but there are at least two caveats. The first one is that it is important to consider other approaches and disciplines. In the last chapter in *The Nature of Prejudice*, Allport (1954, p. 514) writes,

> And we emphasize once again, as forcefully as possible, that a multiple approach is required … we saw that help comes from *historical, sociocultural,* and *situational* analysis, as well as from analysis in terms of *socialization, personality dynamics, phenomenology*, and finally, but not least important, in terms of actual *group differences*. To understand prejudice and its conditions the results of investigations at all these levels must be kept in mind. It is not easy to do so, but there is no other way.

There is indeed no other way, especially when one wants to understand the trials and tribulations of identities and the challenges of living with diversity (Verkuyten, 2005a).

Second, research findings cannot replace the always necessary normative and moral discussions. A debate on policy measures and priorities is impossible to resolve on purely scientific grounds. Let's assume that next year genetic scientists find indisputable proof that African Americans are naturally more intelligent than White Americans. What should we do with this? Should we implement group specific measures such as tax benefits that increase the number of African American children so that the country as a whole becomes smarter? Or should we try to compensate the Whites for their misfortune with extra provisions and special measures so that the country as a whole does not become more stupid? The decision one favours will depend on the importance attached to values of prosperity or equality, to meritocracy or egalitarianism. Research findings cannot replace moral and ideological debates, but they can provide adequate and necessary background information. Such information can be used, for example, to undermine the false arguments and rationalizations *both* against *and* in favour of diversity (of bigotry and political correctness), or to explain why something is a bad idea because it probably will not work, which is often easier than to recommend what will work. The practical value of theoretical insights should not be underestimated and systematic empirical analysis provides a counter to the often heated and self-interested commotion. I have tried to do the same in this book and despite the unavoidable limitations, I hope that I have presented sufficient food for further thought.

The ethnic and the minority aspect

Speaking of integration and integration problems of immigrants and ethnic minorities can nourish the idea that there is a foreign population that can be blamed for a whole list of things, including a lack of loyalty to the host society. These terms also suggest that culture, and cultural deficits in particular, are responsible for a range of problems. In debates, the emphasis is often on the 'ethnic' aspect of ethnic minorities whereby people are presented, implicitly or explicitly, as determined by their own culture. 'Their' culture would explain the lack of integration, school truancy, and even violence and criminal behaviour. References to culture are often used to blame 'them' and to make 'us' feel superior.

Cross-cultural research and ethnic studies have shown that to a certain extent it is possible to identify relatively enduring patterns of meaning that can play a role in a range of phenomena among and between ethnic groups. Ethnicity and culture should not be equated, but in people's mind and behaviour ethnic identity is typically associated with culture. Culture is in many ways important, but how, when, and why exactly is not always clear. Additionally, there is the interactive, changing, and conflicting character of culture and also its symbolic use.

In relation to ethnicity, Vermeulen (2001) makes a distinction between culture as a way of life and as a lifestyle. The notion of culture as a way of life refers to the body of beliefs, values, and knowledge at the level of the community that gradually develops in time, a way of life that is internalized by the individual but also changes in the acculturation process. In this sense we are all products of our culture, and we tend to perceive the world from the lens or point of view that this culture offers. 'Culture is what we carry with us, even when we want to get rid of it. And what we lose, even when we want to preserve it' (Vermeulen, 2001, p. 14). In contrast, culture as a lifestyle involves the use or creation of language, images, symbols, stories, and practices to distinguish oneself from others. Here, the focus is on the dynamic nature of culture as an on-going process in which people are not just culture-bearers, but they also appropriate and alter the meanings by which they live – culture as a tool for boundary drawing, for asserting and constructing difference and identity.

This process of drawing boundaries and constructing a distinctive and positive identity takes place in a context of status and power differences. Social psychologists and social scientists have convincingly argued and demonstrated that the 'minority' aspect of ethnic minorities is very important. How people understand themselves and others is linked to status and power differences. The way that society (or a neighbourhood, school, company) is structured and the ways in which this structure is ideologically justified or challenged deserves close attention. For example, many of the challenges and problems that Muslim immigrants face have to do with being in a minority position rather than with their religious culture. Muslim immigrants who find meaning and guidance in Islam attach importance to the public recognition of their religion. But many natives tend to be rather negative and reject the public recognition of Islam. They consider Islam as intolerable and threatening, while Muslims wish to publicly express their faith and identity. This may lead to tensions and conflicts, not so much because Muslims keep aloof and withdraw themselves from society, but precisely because they become visible and may organize themselves along religious lines. This raises the question about whose country this actually is, who is to decide, and what the nature of this country should be. Most immigrants try to find a place in the host society and to feel at home in it, while many natives often find it hard to provide this space and to let Muslims or minorities join with them to decide on matters that go beyond their own religious or ethnic community.

The quest for identity

Many people are drawn to identity issues. They are searching for a sense of who and what they are. The desire for a distinctive and secure ethnic, racial, religious, or national identity is strong. These identities can provide a sense of grip, of meaningful existence, of belonging, and of being of value. People want to know where they fit in and what that means, they want to feel at home, and they want to feel truly accepted for what they are. The search for identity is a process of trial and error, and the outcome depends on social, economic, political, and societal circumstances that provide opportunities and restrictions for a secure, meaningful, and positive sense of identity. The identity search takes place in a world that rapidly changes, with a speeding flow of information and people, making places increasingly culturally diverse.

Growing up in an ethnic and religious community is, for many people, of great importance and almost always leaves a trace or footprint behind. These experiences cannot simply be removed and exchanged for something else. For many, their ethnic, racial, or religious background is part of how they view the world. It defines what they are, and they want to be recognized and acknowledged as such. Yet people are not one-dimensional human beings but always belong to different categories and groups. It does happen that a particular social identity becomes dominant and taints all aspects of life, but this is the exception rather than the rule.

Generally people want to be addressed and approached in terms of a range of identities, depending on the circumstances.

Feeling that one is both

Most immigrants and ethnic minority members value the distinctive qualities of the group with which they identify.[2] At the same time, they are in the process of developing a commitment to the national community. There is not necessarily a trade-off between ethnic and national identification, and both can co-exist in the form of a dual identity. Politics of multiculturalism and politics of assimilation both share this assumption of a trade-off (Kundnani, 2007). The former tend to argue that any kind of commonality or shared identity dilutes ethnic minority identities, and the latter argues that any kind of ethnic identity undermines national solidarity.

However, a dual identity is a concept that can go beyond ethnic and national identities and their combinations. Apart from identifying themselves as Turkish, Indian, or Mexican on the one hand and as Dutch, British, or American on the other hand, immigrants and minorities can develop a fused sense of belonging, and identify more or less strongly as Turkish Dutch, Indian British, and Mexican American (see chapter 4). This type of dual identity is psychologically distinctive. People might not identify very strongly with the national category, but they might still define themselves as Turkish Dutch or Mexican American. Thus, the fact that in almost all countries immigrants compared to natives tend to have lower national identification (Elkins & Sides, 2007; Staerklé *et al.*, 2010) does not have to imply that they do not have a sense of national commitment and belonging. For immigrants and minorities, a dual identity affirms the distinctiveness of their minority group but within the context of attachment and connection with the society. Dual identification can lead to more positive evaluations of the majority group and of other minorities, and it can foster political involvement and inhibit radicalization (see chapter 7). So despite possible drawbacks (Baysu *et al.*, 2011 Martinovic & Verkuyten, 2013a), there are good reasons to develop integration and accommodation policies that strengthen minorities' and immigrants' national identification without denying their ethnic and/or religious identities. In doing so, it is important to consider the conditions for developing a harmonious dual identity.

Conditions for feeling both

Immigrants and minority members can find it difficult to reconcile the emotional and behavioural demands of multiple group belongings. This may result in the feeling of living *between* two cultures rather than *with* two cultures, and in not belonging to any fully. Apart from the psychological conflicts and dilemmas that people might face, it is also possible that they experience social disapproval and pressures from members of their ethnic or religious community for assimilating too much and from majority members for assimilating too little.

The possibility of a harmonious dual identity depends, further, on the way in which the national category is defined and understood. It is more difficult for immigrants and minority members to develop a sense of national belonging in societies in which an ethnic rather than a civic conception of the nation predominates. Political and public debates about the need to strengthen national unity and a sense of national identity are sometimes translated into specific measures such as tests on national history and culture, oaths of allegiance, and educational initiatives to enhance immigrants' national commitment. This can be useful when these measures are embedded in an 'open' conceptualization of what it means to be a national. These measures can contribute to an understanding of what nationals share and to feelings of inclusion, and they do not have to undermine ethnic and religious minority identities. However, when these measures are embedded in a discourse of ethnic nationalism, they tend to have assimilationist connotations and implications that are unattractive to most minority members. Rather than measures that help immigrants to 'become one of us', they can be considered measures to 'turn them into us'. Immigration and dual identities do not have to undermine national identity, but they do require a national identity that is amenable to cultural diversity.

Not only the content of national identity but also that of minority identity is important for the possibility of dual identities. For example, having a combination of ethnic and national identities is often easier than being at the same time a Muslim and a member of a West European nation. Muslims are often not accepted as co-nationals, and they sometimes do not want to belong. These issues are, of course, related, because people who feel accepted do more easily want to belong. Suspicions of disloyalty or a lack of commitment of immigrants – and Muslims in particular – show up everywhere in society and in many countries and can have a basis in reality. The national dis-identification of Muslim immigrants is sometimes substantial, and research has found that, for example, in Great Britain, Germany, and Spain the majority of Muslims consider themselves primarily as Muslims rather than citizens of their country (Pew Research Center, 2006). One important reason for this is that they feel rejected and discriminated against, which makes them turn away from the society in which they live. Discrimination is one of the most consistent and important conditions for social segregation in which one's minority identity is emphasized and the national category is rejected. Therefore, anti-discrimination policies are immensely important, not only because they improve people's opportunities, but also because they tell immigrants and minority members that they are equal members of society and that society itself is fair and has trustworthy institutions. The symbolic value of these policies should not be underestimated.

Another reason why dual identities are not always easy is that some Muslims argue that their religious tenets conflict with the principles of a liberal democracy and that they are therefore not bound by these principles. 'True' Islam is sometimes defined in contrast to Western practices and thinking, and a 'true' Muslim must distance him- or herself from the West. There is a conflict within Muslim groups between a minority that does not accept the norms of Western democracy and a moderate majority that does (Mirza *et al.*, 2007). More generally, immigrants' national identification is dependent not only on perceptions and experiences with exclusion and discrimination but also on in-group norms. Identification processes have important implications for the relations within groups and involve issues of in-group acceptance, obligations, and loyalties. As argued in chapter 6 in relation to the 'paradox of multicultural vulnerability' (Sachar, 2000), diversity policies can place the integrity of migrant groups above the freedom and equality of the individual. They can justify in-group norms that reject the host society and reinforce power dynamics that make children and women, as the most disadvantaged group members, even more vulnerable.

Religion is often essential and deeply ingrained in people's lives. Muslim group identification is very strong for a substantial segment of the Muslim immigrant population in Europe. This means that when studying the identification strategies of Muslim immigrants, ethnic, religious, and national identities should be examined simultaneously. The religious dimension further complicates the question of how to manage multiple identities and how to reconcile the differences and tensions they can bring with them. For example, Muslim immigrants tend to be more negative towards the majority group and society when there is a strong overlap between their ethnic and religious identity (chapter 7). It also raises additional policy questions. Discussions about diversity and integration policies often subsume the question of religion under that of cultural diversity or explicitly exclude religion from the politics of recognition (Taylor, 1992). Questions of diversity, however, are increasingly questions of religious diversity. Policies that try to accommodate and recognize religious differences are often difficult and politically sensitive because of the great importance that religion has for many people and the constitutional religious rights and traditions of the host societies. For example, in countries like Great Britain and the Netherlands the establishment of separate religious schools is endorsed by the government and by minority organizations. One important consequence of these policies and initiatives is that the opportunities for intergroup contact are reduced. This means that the beneficial effects of intergroup contact for improving a shared sense of belonging and for the development of positive intergroup relations are not possible. In contrast, in countries like Belgium, Germany, and France there are policy proposals and debates about prohibiting the wearing of the headscarf in schools as well as the use of languages other than the national language. One argument for this holds that policies of cultural diversity fuel segregation and conflicts within schools and also prevent the state from taking its responsibility to establish a shared national identity through the educational system. From the perspective of dual identities it can be concluded, however, that policymakers interested in stimulating immigrants' national identification would be well advised to create in schools opportunities for the enactment and recognition of minority identities. Research shows that forms of multicultural educational not only improve intergroup relations but can also contribute to a sense of belonging and national identification (chapter 6).

There are also country differences that can limit the effectiveness of dual identity policies for improving societal unity and solidarity. In nations built on immigration, such as the United States and Canada, it is conceivable that both the majority and minorities adopt a dual identity as the dominant White population is also of immigrant origin and ethnically diverse. All ethnic groups can therefore identify to some extent with their ethnic background and with the overarching American or Canadian national identity. In contrast, European countries that are home to many immigrants, such as Germany, the Netherlands, Belgium, and Sweden, have a historically established majority group that shares a common ethnic origin, which is at the same time their national identity. The linguistic representations of nationhood and of the native population often correspond: Dutch typically means ethnic Dutch, and German means ethnic German. While a Bosnian immigrant in Germany can feel both Bosnian and German at the same time, for a German person their ethnic and national identities are one and the same. Thus, the native population does not have a dual identity, and only immigrants and ethnic minority members can be defined in these terms. One implication is that for the majority group a focus on dual identities can be seen as emphasizing the position of immigrants rather than as contributing to the unity and cohesion of the society as a whole. They might consider immigrants with a dual identification more acceptable (chapter 7) but can still see them as weakening a cohesive national identity that undermines national solidarity. This means that policymakers interested in improving immigrants' sense of belonging should also consider the perspective of the majority group.

A way forward

I started this book with a quote from the now Queen Maxima, and I will end it with another quote from the same 2007 speech.

> One cannot place fences around the identity and loyalty of a human being.... Too often we still think in dividing lines. Also newcomers do that. Kind by kind. But the Netherlands is not a zoo. It is diversity and mixing that gives us strength.

Each identity definition is a temporary beacon in an ever-changing world. Identities are always re-defined, re-interpreted, and adapted in relation to the circumstances people find themselves in. They are not given things but, rather, tasks to fulfil, not set in stone but on-going projects of (re)interpretation – projects whereby people search for a place in an ever-changing world and one in which past, present, and future come together. This does not mean that there is no constant, or that everything changes just as quickly or just as easily. The importance of institutions and rules and regulations for society and the importance of an inner structure for the individual should not be underestimated. There are different trajectories of individual development that lead to a strong and confident sense of identity or, conversely, to self-uncertainty and negative self-feelings, with different implications for well-being, adjustments, and intergroup relations.

The demands of cultural diversity cannot be ignored. In plural societies, diversity is a fact of life, and assimilation creates insecurity and provokes resistance among immigrants and leads to more negative reactions towards immigrants and minorities among the native majority (chapter 6). Western countries of today, and European countries in particular, are no longer the countries of, say, 50 years ago. Any notion of a national or local community will need to recognize that immigrants and ethnic minorities are part of it. Cultural diversity will keep on increasing and identities are becoming more and more complex and less clearly defined. There is no future other than a common future, which should take shape within the basic principles of liberal democracy and the law. That should be the starting point for all, even if it is just to counteract mutual mistrust and to promote the idea of shared responsibility. Attention to the past is interesting and important, but ultimately the main concern is with the way in which a shared future is shaped, right here, right now. This includes a sense of unity and community that is inclusive and sufficiently complex and does not come at the expense of ethnic and religious bonds that are also important for people. Diversity is very difficult to accept when it implies that you have to change what you consider core elements of your identity (Kelman, 2001). It also includes a healthy dose of pragmatism, whereby one looks for forms of reasonable accommodation within legal boundaries and the social conventions that regulate everyday life.

A one-sided emphasis on cultural diversity is undesirable and unsustainable. Although differences do not always lead to tensions and conflicts, there is the real possibility that they will. Group differences may be associated with feelings of superiority and inferiority and can be understood in terms of opposing interests, opposing ways of life, opposing acculturation goals, and opposing rights and responsibilities. Differences require an overarching unity that everyone can identify and relate with. A culturally diverse community cannot exist without a shared sense of 'we', be it at the level of society, neighbourhood, institution, or organization. Such a feeling has to grow from below, out of what people do, experience, and envision together. Identities do not simply reflect the world as it is but can encourage people to work together towards a world they want to have. Particular identity constructions provide shared understandings and expectations that organize social and political action that can turn vision into reality (chapter 2). Authorities, opinion-makers, and political leaders can play a key role in this. They can shape a xenophobic climate or, on the contrary, one that values cultural diversity and inclusiveness. By proactively embracing and exemplifying cultural diversity, they can provide the societal conditions for trying to create more complex and inclusive categories of belonging.

Making diversity work takes time, patience, and hard labour. There is no golden solution, no sovereign formula or panacea that does the trick. The questions and challenges involved are many-sided, and what can work in one particular setting does not have to work in another. There are various models for dealing with diversity, such as multiculturalism, assimilation, and colour-blindness, but no single model is ideal in all societies and contexts and for all people. Multiculturalism, for example, can have beneficial effects in some counties (e.g., Canada) and some settings (e.g., education). Yet it might also have negative effects because it can go against the freedom of individual choice of minority members and lead to feelings of 'what about us?' among majority members. It is important to understand when and why people react positively or negatively to diversity. This makes it possible to create diversity messages, practices, and policies that focus on the difficult task of living together rather than on the identity of one group (minority) and thereby alienating the other (majority). Diversity practices and policies should explain very clearly and convincingly *why* they are necessary, *what* they try to achieve, and *how* exactly it will affect people's lives (De Jong & Verkuyten, 1990). And in order to prevent disappointment and cynicism from taking over, it should be made clear that there are no ultimate solutions. It is hard labour involving many small steps by many different people, but these steps can make a difference and together can give a cumulative push in the right direction.

Notes

Chapter 1

1 This quote is from a public statement by Paul Scheffer.
2 This quote is from a public statement by Mirjam Sterk.
3 This was meant as a legacy of Nicolas Sarkozy, but his successor Francois Hollande stopped the plan. Furthermore, during his presidency Sarkozy announced the abolition of the Ministery of Immigration and National Idenity, admitting that it had led to 'tensions and misunderstandings'.
4 E.g., *Applied Developmental Science,* 2011 (2, pp. 51-116).
5 'Trends in International Migration Stock', available on http://esa.un.org/migration
6 In Uberoi (2008, p. 417).
7 American Anthropological Association (1997, p. 20). *Response to OMB directive 15: race and ethnic standards for federal statistics and administrative reporting.* http://www.aaanet.org/gvt/ombdraft.htm.
8 There also are clear limits, however, to using a 'minority' or structural perspective (see Verkuyten, 2005c). One limitation is that there is a tendency to deal with issues of group status in a rather schematic manner: native people are the dominant majority group, and immigrants are the minority. At a national level this classification is adequate, and the doll studies described in chapter 3 show that children are already very much aware of status and power differences in society. Yet, local situations may differ from the national context. The broader social context is a different matter than the everyday living situation. It is certainly not easy to ignore or depart from that context, but in one's own family or neighbourhood, the significance of your background can be quite different. Relationships in the wider society do interfere in local situations, but they cannot be applied wholesale to, for example, the lives of people in many urban quarters or in desegregated schools. In these situations, status and power differences are actively defined and challenged, making a simple majority–minority model not always very adequate for understanding the dynamics of identities and group relations. This model has the danger of setting identities and group relations in stone and does not examine how status and power relations actually function and develop in particular settings. There are many settings in which particular immigrant or minority groups dominate and have a higher status than other minority groups, and where natives have become a relatively powerless numerical minority. Furthermore, the predominant concern with status and power leads to the presupposition that for ethnic minorities the relationship with the majority group is all that matters. This is a restricted and one-sided view of the ways that people from ethnic minority groups define and understand themselves (see chapter 3). For one thing, it ignores or underestimates the importance of continuity or the imagined history, culture, and homeland of many of these groups.
9 Statement on 14 October, 2008 of the then member of parliament for the Labour Party Hans Spekman in an interview with '*Vrij Nederland*'.

10 This example is taken from Hedström (2005).
11 This is a well-known statement made by the social psychologist Kurt Lewin.

Chapter 2

1 This example is taken from Stengs (2007).
2 Here I base myself on the work of Rob Wentholt; see also Wentholt & Verkuyten (1999).
3 In the literature, terms such as identity 'dimensions', 'elements', 'aspects', and 'components' are being used. Often it is not clear what exactly the difference between these terms is and whether this is important theoretically.
4 In *NRC-Handelsblad*, 8 December, 2007.

Chapter 3

1 The following discussion is partly based on Verkuyten (2011).
2 There is also empirical evidence for a conditional model in which the relationship between perceived discrimination and ethnic identification depends, for example, on minorities' interaction goals. Among different immigrant groups in Australia, France and Scotland it was found that only for those who are inclined to seek distance from the majority population, ethnic minority identification increases when discrimination is relatively high (Ramos *et al.* 2013). Further, because of different migration motives, refugees, compared to immigrant and minority groups, often have different interaction goals leading perceived discrimination not to be related to stronger minority identification (De Vroome *et al.* 2011).
3 In *'Tegenlicht'* (VPRO), 1 October 2007. The term 'integration paradox' comes from Buijs *et al.* (2006) in their research among Moroccan Dutch youth.
4 Quote from an interview with a transsexual in *NRC-Handelsblad*, 17 November 2012.
5 An exception is Barack Obama's 2008 speech entitled 'A more perfect union'. This speech later became known as the 'Race speech' because it was the first time that he explicitly attended to racial differences and his racial identity.
6 Klein *et al.* (2007) discuss this model further in relation to different audiences.

Chapter 4

1 Officially it was said that Szegedi had to leave the Jobbik Party not because he was Jewish but because he had tried to bribe people to keep his ancestry quiet.
2 The measure that Phinney developed is the 'Multigroup Ethnic Identity Measure' (Phinney, 1992). For a critical discussion, see Cokley (2007).
3 For the role of peers in (ethnic) identity development, see the special issue of the *Journal of Adolescence*, 2012 (35).
4 These findings are from secondary analyses of data that we collected.
5 For another example of research, see Hutnik and Street (2010).
6 In the Dutch TV documentary *'Insjallahm if God wants it'*, *Tegenlicht*, VPRO, 30 March 2009.
7 What also should not be underestimated is the difficulty of knowing to what extent radicalism and violence is really motivated by religion, and the difficulties in predicting which youth will become religiously radicalized. These are very difficult issues, despite the fact that security officials and scholars continue to look for simple explanations that will help to stop young people in time (Bramadat, 2012).
8 There was also the case of the endorsement of the right to demonstrate and protest, which was examined with the two scenarios: 'A group of Muslims wants to hold a

demonstration against the anti-Muslim feelings in the Netherlands. Is it okay when they burn the Dutch flag during the demonstration?' versus 'A group of extreme-right-wing people want to hold a demonstration against the presence of Turkish Muslims in the Netherlands. Is it okay when they burn the Turkish flag during the demonstration?' The two other cases were about the freedom to found separate and exclusive (Islamic versus Christian) primary schools and the freedom to reject females for important administrative functions in strict Islamic (versus Christian) organizations.

9 For critical evaluations and extensions of the acculturation framework, see, e.g., the special issue of the *International Journal of Intercultural Relations* (2009, 33).

10 This quote is from the '*Note on Integration*' of the Dutch main social democratic Labour Party the PvdA (2008).

11 There are also researchers who have proposed a tri-dimensional model of acculturation and adaptation (Ferguson *et al.*, 2012).

12 This was done by using cultural symbols and icons, as well as the Dutch and Greek language (see Verkuyten & Pouliasi, 2002, 2006).

13 Laya Cakir in an interview in '*NRC-Handelsblad*', 10 October 2007.

14 Most often mixed-race people are categorized in terms of the lowest status group, which tends to be the Black one. Yet it can also happen that being Black is more valued in a community than being White, as among 'half-blood' South Moluccans in the Netherlands (Verkuyten, 2005c).

Chapter 5

1 See, for example, Tajfel *et al.* (1971). An earlier, comparable study was conducted by Rabbie and Horwitz (1969) among Dutch children.

2 In these studies the '*Implicit Association Test*' is typically used (see Greenwald *et al.*, 1998).

3 This percentage is from data collected by Sniderman and Hagendoorn (2007).

4 Fortuyn said this in a special meeting with the board of the party to discuss whether he could continue as the party leader considering his controversial statements in the press. This meeting was filmed and later shown on television.

5 A very dramatic example is that of Anders Breivik, who, in the summer of 2011, killed 8 people with a bomb in Oslo and shot and killed 69 people on a small Norwegian island. At his trial, Breivik argued that he had acted out of self-defence because he wanted to defend Europe and Western civilization against the further immigration of Muslims. He stated that he was fighting a war against the multicultural elite and the Islamization of Europe. A similar rhetoric can be found among extreme right groups such as the English Defense League. These groups have shifted their negative focus from Blacks and Jews towards Muslims.

6 This does not, of course, mean that culture is always more important than economics. When there is economic decline, economic considerations can become more important because of feelings of zero-sum economic competition (see Esses *et al.*, 2010).

7 This example can also be found in Verkuyten (2005c).

8 See also Fritsche *et al.* (2011) for an analysis of the importance for intergroup conflict of a sense of group-based control (grip) in the face of symbolic and realistic threats.

9 I know of no research that has examined these possibilities empirically.

10 The analysis stems from an empirical investigation into the five steps of the development of collective hate proposed by Reicher *et al.* 2008.

Chapter 6

1 This description is based on Reysoo (1992).

2 The following discussion is partly based on Deaux and Verkuyten (2013).

3 For Canada, Berry and Kalin (1995); for Australia, Ho (1990); for the United States, Citrin *et al.* (2001); and for European countries, e.g., Piontkowski *et al.* (2000) and Zick *et al.* (2001).

4 Taylor (2012) has suggested that for the European context the term 'interculturalism' is more appropriate then 'multiculturalism' (see also Rattansi, 2011). The prefix 'multi' focuses more on the acknowledgment of diversity while 'inter' invokes more the facet of integration.

5 Additionally, in four studies among ethnic majority and minority members in the United States, Rosenthal and Levy (2012) found that greater endorsement of polyculturalism (viewing people of all racial and ethnic groups as deeply connected to one another through their interactions and mutual cultural influences) was associated with greater equality beliefs, willingness for intergroup contact, and endorsement of liberal immigration and affirmative action policies.

6 See, for example, Pew Research Center (2005). Islamic *Extremism: Common Concern for Muslim and Western Publics*. Retrieved from http://pewglobal.org/reports/display.php?ReportID=248.

7 See also, for example, Mikulincer and Shaver (2007) who focus on the importance of attachment security for intergroup tolerance.

8 This is the central argument of the *UN Development Report: Cultural liberty in today's diverse world* (United Nations, 2004).

9 The distinction between the moral, social conventional and personal domain is developed in social cognitive domain theory (Turiel, 2002).

Chapter 7

1 There is also some research on the prejudice reduction effect of 'imagined contact'. This involves a mental imagery exercise that in experimental research has been found to have a small positive effect on the attitude towards, for example, gay people, Muslims, and Mexican Mestizos (Crisp & Turner, 2009).

2 The prejudice reduction model of improving intergroup relations is also limited because existing interventions to reduce prejudice tend to have small or unknown effects (see Paluck & Green, 2009).

3 Ensari and colleagues (2012) argue that a distinction should be made between processes of individuation, de-categorization, and self-other comparisons.

4 This can be compared to so-called crossed-categorization research which examines social relations in situations where two dimensions of social categorization are salient at the same time, such as ethnicity and gender. This research shows that your attitude tends to be most positive when you share both characteristics with another person (same ethnicity and gender), followed by sharing one characteristic (ethnicity or gender), and that your attitude tends to be the least positive when you share no characteristics (see Crisp & Hewstone, 2006).

5 Wenzel *et al.* (2007) provide an overview of this research and some of the following examples are taken from this overview.

6 This is not to say that small town rural communities cannot be ethnically and culturally very diverse. The perhaps best known example that they can is Postville, Iowa (Bloom, 2000).

7 In *NRC-Handelsblad*.

8 In *NRC-Handelsblad*, 17 November, 2008.

9 For example, Kuitenbrouwer in *NRC-Handelsblad,* 20 November 2008.

10 There is also some evidence that among immigrants dual identity in combination with perceived discrimination is associated with poorer school performance (Baysu *et al.,* 2011).

11 These data have been collected and partly analysed by Sniderman and Hagendoorn (2007) in relation to the importance that people attach to conformity as a value. In contrast, our analysis focused on the role of partisanship and political orientation and examined both experiments that were used.
12 Sniderman and Hagendoorn (2007) have shown, however, that the effect depends on how strongly people endorse conformity values.
13 Research on 'cultural inertia' has found that Latinos' express greater prejudice against White Americans and more strongly endorse Latino culture politically when they believe that their culture will have to change (Quezada *et al.*, 2012; see also Zárate & Shaw, 2010).

Chapter 8

1 The language sometimes used in this kind of work is also interesting. Questions are phrased in terms of 'why does the brain want and like this?' rather than 'why do human beings want and like this?'.
2 Part of the following discussion is taken from Verkuyten and Martinovic (2012a).

References

Abbey, E. (2002). Ventriloquism: The central role of an immigrant's own group members in negotiating ambiguity in identity. *Culture and Psychology, 8*, 409–415.

Aboud, F.E., & Fenwick, V. (1999). Exploring and evaluating school-based interventions to reduce prejudice. *Journal of Social Issues, 55*, 767–786.

Agnew, R. (2001). Building on the foundation of a general strain theory: Specifying the types of strain most likely to lead to crime and delinquency. *Journal of Research in Crime and Delinquency, 38,* 319–361.

Alba, R. (2005). Bright vs. blurred boundaries: Second-generation assimilation and exclusion in France, Germany and the United States. *Ethnic and Racial Studies, 28*, 20–49.

Alexander, J. C. (2004). Toward a theory of cultural trauma. In J. C. Alexander, R. Eyerman, B. Giesen, N. J. Smelser & P. Sztompka (Eds.), *Cultural trauma and collective identity* (pp. 1–30). Berkeley, CA: University of California Press.

Allen, J. P., & Antonishak, J. (2008). Adolescent peer influences: Beyond the dark side. In M. J. Prinstein & K. A. Dodge (Eds.), *Understanding peer influence in children and adolescents*. New York: The Guilford Press.

Allport, G.W. (1954). *The nature of prejudice*. Reading, Mass: Addison-Wesley.

Altschul, I., Oyserman, D., & Bybee, D. (2006). Racial–ethnic identity in mid-adolescence: Content and change as predictors of academic achievement. *Child Development, 77*, 1155–1169.

Anderson, B. (1983). *Imagined communities*. London: Verso.

Andriessen, I., Nievers, E., & Dagevos, J. (2012). *Op achterstand: Discriminatie van niet-westerse migranten op de arbeidsmarkt (Behind: Labour market discrimination of non-Western immigrants)*. Den Haag: SCP.

Anisman, H., Ysseldyk, R., Haslam, S.A., & Matheson, K. (2012). Love thine enemy? Evidence that (ir)religious identification can promote outgroup tolerance under threat, *Group Processes and Intergroup Relations, 15*, 105–117.

Appelbaum, L.D. (2002). Who deserves help? Students' opinions about the deservingness of different groups living in Germany to receive aid. *Social Justice Research, 15*, 201–225.

Appiah, K.A. (2005). *The ethics of identity*. Princeton: Princeton University Press.

Appleby, R.S. (2000). *The ambivalence of the sacred: religion, violence and reconciliation*. Boston: Rowman & Littlefield.

Armistead, N. (Ed.) (1974). *Reconstructing social psychology*. Harmondsworth: Penguin.

Aronson, E., Blaney, N., Stephan, C., Sikes, J., & Snapp, M. (1978). *The jig-saw classroom*. London: Sage.

Arroyo, C.G., & Zigler, E. (1995). Racial identity, academic achievement, and the psychological well-being of economically disadvantaged adolescents. *Journal of Personality and Social Psychology, 69,* 903–914.

Ashmore, R.D., Deaux, K., & McLaughlin-Volpe, T. (2004). An organizing framework for collective identity: Articulation and significance of multidimensionality. *Psychological Bulletin, 130,* 80–114.

Atkinson, D., Morten, G., & Sue, D.W. (1990). *Counseling American minorities.* Dubuque, IA: William C. Brown.

Augoustinos, M., & De Garis, S. (2012). 'Too black or not black enough': Social identity complexity in the political rhetoric of Barack Obama. *European Journal of Social Psychology, 52,* 564–577.

Augoustinos, M., & Quinn, C. (2003). Social categorization and attitudinal evaluations: Illegal immigrants, refugees or asylum seekers? *New Review of Social Psychology, 2,* 29–37.

Back, L. (1996). *New ethnicities and urban culture: Racism and multiculturalism in young lives.* London: Routledge.

Badea, C., Jetten, J., Iyer, A., & Er-Rafiy, A. (2011). Negotiating dual identities: The impact of group-based rejection on identification and acculturation. *European Journal of Social Psychology, 41,* 586–596.

Banks, S.P. (1995). *Multicultural public relations.* London: Sage.

Bankston, C.L., & Zhou, M. (1995). Religious participation, ethnic identification, and adaptation of Vietnamese adolescents in an immigrant community. *The Sociological Quarterly, 36,* 523–534.

Barker, M. (1981). *The new racism.* London: Junction Books.

Baron, A.S., & Banaji, M.R. (2006). The development of implicit attitudes: Evidence of race evaluation from ages 6 and 10 and adulthood. *Psychological Science, 7,* 53–58.

Barreto, M., Spears, R., Ellemers, N., & Shahinper, K. (2003). Who wants to know? The effect of audience on identity expression among minority members. *British Journal of Social Psychology, 42,* 299–318.

Barry, B. (2001). *Culture and equality.* Cambridge: Polity Press.

Bar-Tal, D. (2004). The necessity of observing real life situations: Palestinian–Israeli violence as a laboratory for learning about social behaviour. *European Journal of Social Psychology, 34,* 677–702.

Barth, F. (1969). Introduction. In F. Barth (Ed.), *Ethnic groups and boundaries: The social organization of cultural difference.* London: Allen & Unwin.

Bastian, B. & Haslam, N. (2008). Immigration from the perspective of hosts and immigrants: Roles of psychological essentialism and social identity. *Asian Journal of Social Psychology, 11,* 127–140.

Baumeister, R.F. (2005). *The cultural animal: Human nature, meaning, and social life.* Oxford: Oxford University Press.

Baumeister, R.F., Brewer, L.E., Tice, D.M., & Twenge, J.M. (2007). Thwarting the need to belong: Understanding the interpersonal and inner effects of social exclusion. *Social and Personality Psychology Compass, 1,* 506–520.

Baumgartner, M.P. (1998). Moral life on the cultural frontier: Evidence from the experience of immigrants in modern America. *Sociological Focus, 31,* 155–179.

Baysu, G., Phalet, K., & Brown, R. (2011). Dual identity as a two-edged sword: Identity threat and minority school performance. *Social Psychology Quarterly, 74,* 121–143.

Benet-Martinez, V., Leu, J., Lee, F., & Morris, M.W. (2002). Negotiating biculturalism: Cultural frame switching in biculturals with oppositional versus compatible cultural identities. *Journal of Cross Cultural Psychology, 33*, 492–516.

Benson, P.L., Donahue, M.J., & Erickson, J.A. (1993). Adolescence and religion: A review of the empirical literature 1970–1986. *Annual review of religious research,* Vol. 1 (pp. 153–181). Greenwich, CT: J.A.I. Press.

Benwell, B., & Stokoe, E. (2006). *Discourse and identity.* Edinburgh: Edinburgh University Press.

Bergsieker, H.B., Shelton, J.N., & Richeson, J.A. (2010). To be liked versus respected: Divergent goals in interracial interactions. *Journal of Personality and Social Psychology, 99*, 248–264.

Berry, J.W. (2001). A psychology of immigration. *Journal of Social Issues, 57*, 615–631.

Berry, J.W. (2006). Mutual attitudes among immigrants and ethnocultural groups in Canada. *International Journal of Intercultural Relations, 30*, 719–734.

Berry, J.W., & Kalin, R. (1995). Multicultural and ethnic attitudes in Canada: An overview of the 1991 national survey. *Canadian Journal of Behavioural Sciences, 27*, 301–320.

Bertossi, C. (2011). National models of integration in Europe: A comparative and critical analysis. *American Behavioral Scientist, 55*, 1561–1580.

Bettencourt, B.A., Dorr, N., Charlton, K., & Hume, D.L. (2001). Status differences and in-group bias: A meta-analytical examination of the effects of status stability, status legitimacy, and group permeability. *Psychological Bulletin, 127*, 520–542.

Bhatia, S., & Ram, A. (2009). Theorizing identity in transnational and diaspora cultures: A critical approach to acculturation. *International Journal of Intercultural Relations, 33*, 140–149.

Bikmen, N. (2011). Asymmetrical effects of contact between minority groups: Asian and Black students in a small college. *Cultural Diversity and Ethnic Minority Psychology, 17*, 186–194.

Binder, J., Zagefka, H., Brown, R., Funke, F., Kessler, T., Mummendey, A., Maquil, A., Demoulin, S., & Leyens, J.-P. (2009). Does contact reduce prejudice or does prejudice reduce contact? A longitudinal test of the contact hypothesis among majority and minority groups in three European countries. *Journal of Personality and Social Psychology, 96*, 843–856.

Bizman, A., & Yinon, Y. (2001). Intergroup and interpersonal threats as determinants of prejudice: The moderating role of in-group identification. *Basic and Applied Social Psychology, 23,* 191–196.

Bloom, S.G. (2000). *Postville: A clash of cultures in heartland America.* New York: Harcourt.

Blumer, H. (1958). Race prejudice as a sense of group position. *The Pacific Sociological Review, 1*, 3–7.

Bobo, L.D. (1999). Prejudice as group position: Microfoundations of a sociological approach to racism and race relations. *Journal of Social Issues, 55,* 445–472.

Bornstein, R.F. (1989). Exposure and affect: Overview and meta-analysis of research, 1968–1987. *Psychological Bulletin, 106*, 265–289.

Bourhis, R.Y., Moïse, L.C., Perreault, S., & Senécal, S. (1997). Towards an interactive acculturation model: A social psychological approach. *International Journal of Psychology, 32,* 369–386.

Bramadat, P. (2012). *Radicalization, securitization and the simulacrum of youth.* Paper presented at the Society of Research on Adolescence, Vancouver, 9 March.

Brambilla, M., Sacchi, S., Rusconi, P., Cherubini, P., & Yzerbyt, V.Y. (2012). You want to give a good impression? Be honest! Moral traits dominate group impression formation. *British Journal of Social Psychology, 51*, 149–166.

Brand, E.S., Ruiz, R.A., & Padilla, A.M. (1974). Ethnic identification and preference: A review. *Psychological Bulletin, 81*, 860–890.

Branscombe, N.R., & Doosje, B. (Eds.) (2004). *Collective guilt: International perspectives.* Cambridge: Cambridge University Press.

Branscombe, N.R., & Wann, D.L. (1994). Collective self-esteem consequences of outgroup derogation when a valued social identity is on trial. *European Journal of Social Psychology, 24,* 641–657.

Brauer, M., & Er-rafiy, A. (2011). Increasing perceived variability reduces prejudice and discrimination, *Journal of Experimental Social Psychology, 47*, 871–881.

Brenick, A., Lee-Kim, J., Killen, M., Fox, N.A., Leavitt, L.A., & Raviv, A. (2007). Social judgments in Israeli and Arabic children: Findings from media-based intervention projects. In D. Lemish & M. Gotz (Eds.), *Children, media and war* (pp. 287–308). Cresskill, NJ: Hampton Press.

Breugelmans, S.M., & Van de Vijver, F.J.R. (2004). Antecedents and components of majority attitudes toward multiculturalism in the Netherlands. *Applied Psychology: An International Review, 53*, 400–422.

Brewer, M.B. (2001). Ingroup identification and intergroup conflict: When does ingroup love becomes outgroup hate? In R.D. Ashmore, L. Jussim & D. Wilder (Eds.), *Social identity, intergroup conflict and conflict reduction* (pp. 17–41). New York: Oxford University Press.

Brewer, M.B., & Brown, R. (1998). Intergroup relations. In D.T. Gilbert, S.T. Fiske, & G. Lindzey (Eds.), *The handbook of social psychology*. Boston: McGraw-Hill.

Brewer, M.B., Gonsalkorale, K., & Van Dommelen, A. (in press). Social identity complexity: Comparing majority and minority ethnic group members in a multicultural society. *Group Processes and Intergroup Relations*.

Brewer, M.B., & Pierce, K.P. (2005). Social identity complexity and outgroup tolerance. *Personality and Social Psychology Bulletin, 31*, 428–437.

Broermann, M. (2008). Language attitudes among minority youth in Finland and Germany. *International Journal of the Sociology of Language, 187/188*, 129–160.

Brown, R. (2010). *Prejudice: Its social psychology* (2nd ed.). Oxford: Wiley-Blackwell.

Brown, R., Eller, A., Leeds, S., & Stace, K. (2007). Intergroup contact and intergroup attitudes: A longitudinal study. *European Journal of Social Psychology, 37*, 692–703.

Brown, R. González, R., Zagefka, H., Manzi, J., & Cehajic, S. (2008). Nuestra culpa: Collective guilt and shame as predictors of reparation for historical wrongdoing. *Journal of Personality and Social Psychology, 94*, 75–90.

Brown, R., & Zagefka, H. (2011). The dynamics of acculturation: An intergroup perspective. *Advances in Experimental Social Psychology, 44*, 129–184.

Brubaker, R. (2004). *Ethnicity without groups.* Cambridge: Harvard University Press.

Brubaker, R., & Cooper, F. (2000). Beyond "identity". *Theory and Society, 29*, 1–47.

Buijs, F.J., Demant, F., & Hamdy, A. (2006). *Strijders van eigen bodem: radicale en democratische moslims in Nederland. (Fighters from the own soil: Radical and democratic Muslims in the Netherlands).* Amsterdam: Amsterdam University Press.

Buitelaar, M.W. (1998). Between ascription and assertion: The representation of social identity by women of Moroccan descent in the Netherlands. *Focaal, 32*, 29–50.

Buller, D.J. (2009). Four fallacies of pop evolutionary psychology. *Scientific American*, 74–81.

Buriel, R. (1987). Ethnic labeling and identity among Mexican Americans. In J.S. Phinney & M.J. Rotheram (Eds.), *Children's ethnic socialization: Pluralism and development* (pp. 134–152). Newbury Park: Sage.

Burke, P.J., & Stets, J.E. (2009). *Identity theory*. Oxford: Oxford University Press.

Burnet, J. (1995). Multiculturalism and racism in Canada. In J. Hjarno (Ed.), *Multiculturalism in the Nordic societies* (pp. 43–50). Copenhagen; TemaNord.

Butz, D.A., Plant, E.A., & Doerr, C.E. (2007). Liberty and justice for all? Implications of exposure to the U.S. flag for intergroup relations. *Personality and Social Psychology Bulletin, 33*, 396–408.

Campbell, D.T. (1958). Common fate, similarity, and other indices of the status of aggregates of persons as social entities. *Behavioral Science, 3*, 14–25.

Caprariello, P.A., Cuddy, A.J.C., & Fiske, S.T. (2009). Social structure shapes cultural stereotypes and emotions: A causal test of the stereotype content model. *Group Processes and Intergroup Relations, 12*, 147–155.

Ceuppens, B., & Geschiere, P. (2005). Autochthony: Local or global? New modes in the struggle over citizenship and belonging in Africa and Europe. *Annual Review of Anthropology, 34*, 385–407.

Chang, J., & Le, T.N. (2010). Multiculturalism as a dimension of school climate: The impact on the academic achievement of Asian American and Hispanic youth. *Cultural Diversity and Ethnic Minority Psychology, 16*, 485–492.

Chaudhury, S.R., & Miller., L. (2008). Religious identity formation among Bangladeshi American Muslim adolescents. *Journal of Adolescent Research, 23*, 383–410.

Chavous, T., Bernat, D., Schmeelk-Cone, K., Caldwell, C., Kohn-Wood, L., & Zimmerman, M. (2003). Racial identity and academic attainment among African American adolescents. *Child Development, 74*, 1076–1090.

Child, I. (1943). *Italian or American? The second generation in conflict*. New Haven, CT: Yale University Press.

Cieslik, A., & Verkuyten, M. (2006). National, ethnic and religious identities: Hybridity and the case of the Polish Tatars. *National Identities, 8*, 77–93.

Citrin, J., Sears, D.O., Muste, C., & Wong, C. (2001). Multiculturalism in American public opinion. *British Journal of Political Science, 31*, 247–275.

Clark, K.B., & Clark, M.P. (1947). Racial identification and preference in negro children. In T.M. Newcombe & E.K. Hartley (Eds.), *Readings in social psychology*. New York: Holt, Rinehart and Winston.

Clark-Ibanez, M., & Felmlee, D. (2004). Interethnic relationships: The role of social network diversity. *Journal of Marriage and Family, 66*, 293–305.

Clay, A. (2003). Keepin' it real: Black youth, hip hop culture, and Black identity. *American Behavioral Scientist, 46*, 1346–1358.

Cohen, A. (1969). *Custom and politics in urban Africa*. London: Routledge.

Cohen, G.L. (2003). Party over policy: The dominating impact of group influence on political beliefs. *Journal of Personality and Social Psychology, 85*, 808–822.

Cokley, K. (2007). Critical issues in the measurement of ethnic and racial identity: A referendum on the state of the field. *Journal of Counseling Psychology, 54*, 224–234.

Cole, C., Arafat, C., Tidhar, C., Zidan, W.T., Fox, N.A., Killen, M., Leavitt, L., Lesser, G., Richman, B.A., Ardila-Rey, A., & Yung, F. (2003). The educational impact of Rechov Sumsum/Shara'a Simsim, a television series for Israeli and Palestinian children. *International Journal of Behavioral Development, 27*, 409–422.

Cole, E.R. (2009). Intersectionality and research in psychology. *American Psychologist, 64*, 170–180.

Condor, S. (2006). Temporality and collectivity: Diversity, history, and the rhetorical construction of national identity. *British Journal of Social Psychology, 45*, 657–682.

Confer, J.C., Easton, J.A., Fleischman, D.S., Goetz, C.D., Lewis, D.M.G., Perilloux, C., & Buss, D.M. (2010). Evolutionary psychology: Controversies, questions, prospects, and limitations. *American Psychologist, 65,* 110–126.

Connor, W. (1993). Beyond reason: The nature of the ethnonational bond. *Ethnic and Racial Studies, 16*, 373–398.

Cook, S.W. (1978). Interpersonal and attitudinal outcomes in cooperating interracial groups. *Journal of Research and Development in Education, 12*, 97–113.

Cooke, P. (2005). *Representing East Germany since unification: From colonization to nostalgia.* Oxford: Berg.

Cooney, M. (2009). Ethnic conflict without ethnic groups: A study in pure sociology. *British Journal of Sociology, 60,* 473–492.

Cornell, S., & Hartmann, D. (1998). *Ethnicity and race: Making identities in a changing world.* London: Pine Forge.

Correll, J., Park, B., & Smith, J.A. (2008). Colorblind and multicultural prejudice reduction strategies in high-conflict situations. *Group Processes and Intergroup Relations, 11*, 471–491.

Cousins, S.D. (1989). Culture and self-perception in Japan and the United States. *Journal of Personality and Social Psychology, 56*, 124–131.

Craig, M.A., & Richeson, J.A. (2012). Coalition or derogation? How perceived discrimination influences intraminority intergroup relations. *Journal of Personality and Social Psychology, 102*, 757–777.

Crisp, R.J., & Hewstone, M. (Eds.) (2006). *Multiple social categorization: Processes, models and applications.* New York: Psychology Press.

Crisp, R.J., & Turner, R.N. (2009). Can imagined interactions produce positive perceptions? Reducing prejudice through simulated social contact. *American Psychologist, 64*, 231–240.

Crisp, R.J., & Turner, R.N. (2010). Cognitive adaptation to the experience of social and cultural diversity. *Psychological Bulletin, 137*, 242–266.

Crocetti, E., Rubini, M., Luyckx, K., & Meeus, W. (2008). Identity formation in early and middle adolescents from various ethnic groups: From three dimensions to five statuses. *Journal of Youth and Adolescence, 37*, 983–996.

Cronin, T.J., Levin, S., Branscombe, N.R., Van Laar, C., & Tropp, L.R. (in press). Ethnic identification in response to perceived discrimination protects well-being and promotes activism: A longitudinal study of Latino college students. *Group Processes and Intergroup Relations.*

Cross, W.E. (1991). *Shades of Black: Diversity in African–American identity.* Philadelphia: Temple University Press.

Crossley, M.L. (2000). *Introducing narrative psychology: Self, trauma and the construction of meaning.* Buckingham, UK: Open University Press.

Cuddy, A.J.C., Fiske, S., & Glick, P. (2008). Warmth and competence as universal dimensions of social perception: The Stereotype Content Model and the BIAS Map. *Advances in Experimental Social Psychology, 40*, 60–149.

Deaux, K. (2006). *To be an immigrant.* New York: Russell Sage Foundation.

Deaux, K., Bikmen, N., Gilkes, A., Ventuneac, A., Joseph, Y., Payne, Y.R. & Steele, C.M. (2007). Becoming American: Stereotype threat effects in Afro-Caribbean immigrant groups. *Social Psychology Quarterly, 70*, 384–404.

Deaux, K., & Verkuyten, M. (2013). The social psychology of multiculturalism: Identity and intergroup relations. In V. Benet-Martínez & Y-Y. Hong (Eds.), *The Oxford handbook of multicultural identity: Basic and applied psychological perspectives.* Oxford: Oxford University Press.

De Dreu, C.K.W., Greer, L.L., Van Kleef, G.A., Shalvi, S., & Handgraaf, M.J.J. (2011). Oxytocin promotes human ethnocentrism. *Proceedings of the National Academy of Sciences of the United States of America, 108,* 1262–1266.

Degner, J., & Wentura, D. (2010). Automatic prejudice in childhood and early adolescence. *Journal of Personality and Social Psychology, 98,* 356–374.

De Jong, W., & Verkuyten, M. (1990). Hoe, wat en waarom Positieve Actie: De gemeente Rotterdam als 'case study' (How, what and why positive action: The municipality of Rotterdam as a case study), *Migrantenstudies, 6,* 2–15.

De Koning, M. (2008). *Zoeken naar een 'zuivere' islam: Geloofsbeleving en identiteitsvorming van jonge Marokkaans-Nederlandse moslims (Searching for a pure Islam: Religion and identity formation of Young Moroccan Dutch Muslims).* Amsterdam: Bert Bakker.

Demant, F. (2006). *'Islam is inspanning': De beleving van de islam en de sekseverhoudingen bij Marokkaanse jongeren in Nederland (Islam is hard work: Islam and gender relations among Moroocan youth in the Netherlands).* Utrecht: Verwey-Jonker Instituut.

Derks, B., Van Laar, C., & Ellemers, N. (2007). The beneficial effects of social identity protection on the performance motivation of members of devalued groups. *Social Issues and Policy Review, 1,* 217–256.

De Tezanos-Pinto, P., Bratt, C., & Brown, R. (2010). What will the others think? In-group norms as a mediator of the effects of intergroup contact. *British Journal of Social Psychology, 49,* 507–523.

De Vroome, T., Coenders, M., Van Tubergen, F., & Verkuyten, M. (2011). Economic participation and national self-identification of refugees in the Netherlands. *International Migration Review, 45,* 615–638.

Devine, P.G. (1989). Stereotypes and prejudice: Their automatic and controlled components. *Journal of Personality and Social Psychology, 56,* 5–18.

DeVos, G.A. (1995). Ethnic pluralism: Conflict and accommodation. In L. Romanucci-Ross & G. DeVos (Eds.), *Ethnic identity: Creation, conflict, and accommodation* (pp. 15–47). Walnut Creek, CA: AltaMira.

Devos, T., & Banaji, M.R. (2005). American = white? *Journal of Personality and Social Psychology, 88,* 447–466.

Diekman, A.B., Eagly, A.H., Mladinic, A., & Ferreira, M.C. (2005). Dynamic stereotypes about women and men in Latin America and the United States. *Journal of Cross-Cultural Psychology, 36,* 209–226.

Dixon, J., Durrheim, K., & Tredoux, C. (2005). Beyond the optimal contact strategy: A reality check for the contact hypothesis. *American Psychologist, 60,* 687–711.

Dixon, J., Durrheim, T., & Tredoux, C. (2007). Intergroup contact and attitudes towards the principle and practice of racial equality. *Psychological Science, 18,* 867–872.

Doise, W., Deschamps, J-C., & Meyer, C. (1978). The accentuation of intracategory similarities. In H. Tajfel (Ed.), *Differentiation between social groups: Studies in the social psychology of intergroup relations.* London: Academic Press.

Doosje, B., Branscombe, N.R., Spears, R., & Manstead, A.S.R. (1998). Guilt by association: When one's group has a negative history. *Journal of Personality and Social Psychology, 75,* 872–886.

Dovidio, J.F., Gaertner, S.L., & Saguy, T. (2009). Commonality and the complexity of 'we': Social attitudes and social change. *Personality and Social Psychology Review, 13*, 3–20.

Downie, M., Mageau, G.A., Koestner, R., & Liodden, T. (2006). On the risk of being a cultural chameleon: Variations across social interactions. *Cultural Diversity and Ethnic Minority Psychology, 12*, 527–540.

Driver, E.D. (1969). Selfconceptions in India and the United States: A cross cultural validation of the Twenty Statements Test. *Sociological Quarterly, 10*, 341–354.

DuBois, W.E.B. (1982). *The souls of black folk.* New York: Signet Classics.

Duyvendak, J.W., & Scholten, P.W.A. (in press). Beyond national models of integration: The coproduction of integration policy frames in the Netherlands. *Journal of International Migration and Integration.*

Ebaugh, H.R.F. (1988). *Becoming an ex: The process of role exit.* Chicago: University of Chicago Press.

Eidelson, R.J., & Eidelson, J.I. (2003). Dangerous ideas: Five beliefs that propel groups toward conflict. *American Psychologist, 58*, 182–192.

Eisenberg, N.I., Lieberman, M.D., & Williams, K.D. (2003). Does rejection hurt? An fMRI study of social exclusion. *Science, 302*, 290–292.

Eisenlohr, P. (2006). *Little India: Diaspora, time and ethnolinguistic belonging in the Hindu Mauritius.* Los Angeles: University of California Press.

Elias, N., & Scotson, J.L. (1965). *The established and the outsiders.* London: Frank Cass.

Elkins, Z., & Sides, J. (2007). Can institutions build unity in multiethnic states? *American Political Science Review, 101*, 693–708.

Ellemers, N., Spears, R., & Doosje, B. (Eds.) (1999). *Social identity context, commitment, content.* Oxford: Blackwell.

Elms, A.C. (1975). The crisis and confidence in social psychology. *American Psychologist, 30*, 967–976.

Ely, R., & Thomas, D. (2001). Cultural diversity at work: The effects of diversity perspectives on work group processes and outcomes. *Administrative Science Quarterly, 46*, 229–273.

Ensari, N., Christian, J., Kuriyama, D.M., & Miller, N. (2012). The personalization model revisited: An experimental investigation of the role of five personalization-based strategies on prejudice reduction. *Group Processes and Intergroup Relations, 15*, 503–522.

Erickson, J.A. (1992). Adolescent religious development and commitment: A structural equation model of the role of family, peer group and educational influences. *Journal for the Scientific Study of Religion, 31*, 131–152.

Eriksen, T.H. (1993). *Ethnicity and nationalism: Anthropological perspectives.* London: Pluto.

Eriksen, T.H. (1994). Nationalism, Mauritian style: Cultural unity and ethnic diversity. *Comparative Studies in Society and History, 36*, 549–574.

Eriksen, T.H. (2004). Ethnicity, class, and the 1999 Mauritian riots. In S. May., T. Modood, & J.A. Squires (Eds.), *Ethnicity, nationalism and minority rights* (pp. 78–95). Cambridge University Press: Cambridge.

Erikson, E.H. (1966). The concept of identity in race relations: Notes and queries. *Daedalus, 95*, 145–177.

Erikson, E.H. (1968). *Identity: Youth and crisis.* New York: Norton & Company, Inc.

Esposito, J.L., & Mogahed, D. (2007). *Who speaks for Islam? What a billion Muslims really think.* New York: Gallup Press.

Esser, H. (2001). *Integration und Etnische Schichtung.* Mannheim: Arbeitspapiere, Mannheimer Zentrum für Europäische Sozialforschung.

Esses, V.M., Jackson, L.M., & Bennett-AbuAyyash, C. (2010). Intergroup competition. In J.F. Dovidio, M. Hewstone, P. Glick, & V.M. Esses (Eds.), *The Sage handbook of prejudice, stereotyping and discrimination* (pp. 225–240). London: Sage.

European Monitoring Centre on Racism and Xenophobia (2006). *Muslims in the European Union: Discrimination and Islamophobia.* Vienna: EUMC.

Every, D., & Augoustinos, M. (2008). Constructions of Australia in pro- and anti-asylum seeker political discourse. *Nations and Nationalism, 14,* 562–580.

Eyerman, R. (2004). Cultural trauma: Slavery and the formation of African American identity. In J.C. Alexander, R. Eyerman, B. Giesen, N.J. Smelser, & P. Sztompka (Eds.), *Cultural trauma and collective identity* (pp. 60–110). Berkeley, CA: University of California Press.

Falomir-Pichastor, J.M., Munoz-Rojas, D., Invernizzi, F., & Mugny, G. (2004). Perceived in-group threat as a factor moderating the influence of in-group norms on discrimination against foreigners. *European Journal of Social Psychology, 34,* 135–153.

Ferguson, G.M., Bornstein, M.H., & Pottinger, A.M. (2012). Tridimensional acculturation and adaptation among Jamaican adolescent-mother dyads in the United States. *Child Development, 83,* 1486–1493.

Fiske, S. (2012). Journey to the edges: Social structures and neural maps of inter-group processes. *British Journal of Social Psychology, 51,* 1–12.

Fleischmann, F. (2011). *Second-generation Muslims in European societies: Comparative perspectives on education and religion.* Utrecht: Ercomer.

Foote, N.N. (1951). Identification as a basis for a theory of motivation. *American Sociological Review,* 26, 14–21.

Francis, L.J., & Brown, L.B. (1991). The influence of home, church, and school prayer among 16-year-old adolescents in England. *Review of Religious Research, 33,* 112–122.

Fritsche, I., Jonas, E., & Kessler, T. (2011). Collective reactions to threat: Implications for intergroup conflict and for solving societal crises. *Social Issues and Policy Review, 5,* 101–136.

Fuligni, A.J. (1998). Authority, autonomy, and parent–adolescent conflict and cohesion: A study of adolescents from Mexican, Chinese, Filipino, and European backgrounds. *Developmental Psychology, 34,* 782–792.

Fuligni, A., Witkow, M.R., & Garcia, C. (2005). Ethnic identity and the academic adjustment of adolescents from Mexican, Chinese, and European backgrounds. *Developmental Psychology, 41,* 799–811.

Gaertner, S.L., & Dovidio, J.F. (2000). *Reducing intergroup bias: The common ingroup identity model.* Hove: Psychology Press.

Gaertner, S.L., Rust, M.C., Dovidio, J.F., Bachman, B.A., & Anastasio, P.A. (1996). The contact hypothesis: The role of a common in-group identity on reducing intergroup bias among majority and minority group members. In J.L. Nye & A.M. Brower (Eds.), *What's social about social cognition?* Newbury Park: Sage.

Galinski, A.D., & Moskowitz, G.B. (2000). Perspective-taking: decreasing stereotype expression, stereotype accessibility, and in-group favouritism. *Journal of Personality and Social Psychology, 78,* 708–724.

Gans, H.J. (1979). Symbolic ethnicity: The future of ethnic groups and cultures in America. *Ethnic and Racial Studies, 2,* 9–17.

Garcia, D.M., Reser, A.H., Amo, R.B., Redersdorff, S., & Branscombe, N.R. (2005). Perceivers' responses to in-group and out-group members who blame a negative outcome on discrimination. *Personality and Social Psychology Bulletin, 31*, 769–780.

Geschiere, P. (2009). *The perils of belonging: Autochthony, citizenship, and exclusion in Africa and Europe*. Chicago: University of Chicago Press.

Gibson, J.L. (2006). Enigmas of intolerance: Fifty years after Stouffer's communism, conformity, and civil liberties. *Perspectives on Politics, 4*, 21–34.

Gieling, M., Thijs, J., & Verkuyten, M. (2010). Tolerance of practices by Muslim actors: An integrative social-developmental perspective. *Child Development, 81,* 1384–1399.

Gieling, M., Thijs, J., & Verkuyten, M. (2011). Voluntary and involuntary immigrants and adolescents' endorsement of cultural maintenance. *International Journal of Intercultural Relations,* 35, 259–267.

Gieling, M., Thijs, J., & Verkuyten, M. (2012). Dutch adolescents' tolerance of practices by Muslim actors: The effect of issue framing. *Youth and Society, 44,* 348–365.

Gijsberts, M. (2005). Opvattingen van autochtonen en allochtonen over de multi-etnische samenleving (Views of autochtones and allochtones about the multi-ethnic society). In M. Gijsberts & J. Dagevos (Eds.) *Jaarrapport integratie 2005*. The Hague: SCP.

Gijsberts, M., & Lubbers, M. (2009). Wederzijdse beeldvorming (Mutual views). In M. Gijsberts & J. Dagevos (Eds.) *Jaarrapport Integratie 2009*. The Hague: SCP.

Gil-White, F. (2001). Are ethnic groups biological "species" to the human brain? Essentialism in our cognition of some social categories. *Current Anthropology, 42*, 515–554.

Ginges, J., & Cairns, D. (2000). Social representations of multiculturalism: A faceted analysis. *Journal of Applied Social Psychology, 30*, 1345–1370.

Glasford, D.E., & Calcagno, J. (2012). The conflict of harmony: Intergroup contact, commonality and political solidarity between minority groups. *Journal of Experimental Social Psychology, 48*, 323–328.

Goff, P.A., Eberhardt, J.L., Williams, M.J., & Jackson, M.C. (2008). Not yet human: Implicit knowledge, historical dehumanization, and contemporary consequences. *Journal of Personality and Social Psychology, 94*, 292–306.

Goffman, E. (1963). *Stigma: Notes on the management of spoiled identity*. New York: Touchstone.

Goldschmidt, W. (2006). *The bridge to humanity: How affect hunger trumps the selfish gene*. New York: Oxford University Press.

González, R., & Brown, R. (2003). Generalization of positive attitude as a function of subgroup and superordinate group identifications in intergroup contact. *European Journal of Social Psychology, 33*, 195–214.

Gordon, M.M. (1964). *Assimilation in American life: The role of race, religion and national origin*. Oxford: Oxford University Press.

Greenberg, J., Solomon, S., & Pyszcynski, T. (1997). Terror management theory of self-esteem and cultural worldviews: Empirical assessments and cultural refinements. In M.P. Zanna (Ed.), *Advances in experimental social psychology* (Vol. 29, pp. 61–139). Orlando, FL: Academic Press.

Greenwald, A.G., McGhee, D.E., & Schwartz, J.L.K. (1998). Measuring individual differences in implicit cognition: The implicit association test. *Journal of Personality and Social Psychology, 74*, 1464–1480.

Guan, Y., Verkuyten, M., Fung, H.H., Bond, M.H., Chan, C.C., & Chen, S.X. (2011). Outgroup value incongruence and intergroup attitude: The roles of multiculturalism and common identity. *International Journal of Intercultural Relations, 35*, 377–385.

Guimond, S., De Oliveira, P., Kamiesjki, R., & Sidanius, J. (2010). The trouble with assimilation: Social dominance and the emergence of hostility against immigrants. *International Journal of Intercultural Relations, 34*, 642–650.

Gutiérrez, A.S., & Unzueta, M.M. (2010). The effect of interethnic ideologies on the likability of stereotypic vs. counterstereotypic minority targets. *Journal of Experimental Social Psychology, 46*, 775–784.

Gutsell, J.N., & Inzlicht, M. (2012). Intergroup differences in the sharing of emotive states: Neural evidence of an empathy gap. *Social Cognitive Affective Neuroscience, 7*, 596–603.

Habermas, T., & DeSilveira, C. (2008). The development of global coherence in life narratives across adolescence: Temporal, causal, and thematic aspects. *Developmental Psychology, 44*, 707–721.

Hagendoorn, L. (1995). Intergroup bias in multiple group systems: The perception of ethnic hierarchies. In W. Stroebe & M. Hewstone (Eds.), *European Review of Social Psychology*, Vol. 6 (pp. 199–228). London: Wiley.

Hagendoorn, L., & Sniderman, P. (2004). Het conformisme effect: Sociale beïnvloeding van de houding ten opzichte van etnische minderheden (The conformity effect: Social pressure influencing the attitude towards ethnic minorities). *Mens en Maatschappij, 79*, 101–143.

Haidt, J., Rosenberg, E., & Hom, H. (2003). Differentiating diversities: Moral diversity is not like other kinds. *Journal of Applied Social Psychology, 33*, 1–36.

Hamilton, D.L. (2007). Understanding the complexities of group perception: Broadening the domain. *European Journal of Social Psychology, 37*, 1077–1101.

Hasan, R. (2010). *Multiculturalism: Some inconvenient truths*. London: Politico.

Haslam, S.A. (2001). *Psychology in organizations: The social identity approach*. London: Sage.

Haslam, S.A., Oakes, P.J., Reynolds, K.J., & Turner, J.C. (1999). Social identity salience and the emergence of stereotype consensus. *Personality and Social Psychology Bulletin, 25*, 809–818.

Haslam, S.A., Reicher, S., & Platow, J. (2011). *The new psychology of leadership: Identity, influence and power*. New York: Psychology Press.

Heath, A., & Roberts, J. (2008). *British identity: Its sources and possible implications for civic attitudes and behaviour*. Research report for Lord Goldsmith's Citizenship Review: University of Oxford.

Hedström, P. (2005). *Dissecting the social: On the principles of analytical sociology*. Cambridge: Cambridge University Press.

Hehman, E., Gaertner, S.L., Dovidio, J.F., Mania, E.W., Guerra, R., Wilson, D.C., & Friel, B.M. (2012). Group status drives majority and minority integration preferences. *Psychological Science, 23*, 46–52.

Heider, F. (1958). *The psychology of interpersonal relations*. New York: Wiley.

Helbig, M. (Ed.) (2012). *Islamophobia in the West: Measuring and explaining individual attitudes*. London: Routledge.

Helms, J.E. (Ed.) (1990). *Black and white racial identity: Theory, research and practice*. Westport, CT: Greenwood Press.

Helms, J.E. (2007). Some better practices for measuring racial and ethnic identity constructs. *Journal of Counseling Psychology, 54*, 235–246.

Herriot, P. (2007). *Religious fundamentalism and social identity*. London: Routledge.

Herriot, P. (2009). *Religious fundamentalism: Global, local, and personal*. London: Routledge.

Hindriks, P., Verkuyten, M., & Coenders, M. (2013a). *Fifth column beliefs in the Netherlands.* Utrecht: Ercomer.

Hindriks, P., Verkuyten, M., & Coenders, M. (2013b). *Inter-minority attitudes: The role of ethnic and national identification, contact and multiculturalism.* Utrecht: Ercomer.

Ho, R. (1990). Multiculturalism in Australia: A survey of attitudes. *Human Relations, 43*, 259–272.

Hodgson, D. (2002). Introduction: Comparative perspectives on the indigenous rights movement in Africa and the Americas. *American Anthropologist, 104*, 1037–1049.

Hogan, D.E., & Mallott, M. (2005). Changing racial prejudice through diversity education. *Journal of College Student Development, 46*, 115–125.

Hoge, D.R., Johnson, B., & Luidens, D.A. (1994). *Vanishing boundaries: The religion of mainline Protestant baby boomers.* Louisville, KY: Westminster Press.

Hogg, M. (2007). Uncertainty-identity theory. *Advances in Experimental Social Psychology, 39*, 69–126.

Hogg, M.A., Adelman, J.R., & Blagg, R.D. (2010). Religion in the face of uncertainty: An uncertainty-identity theory account of religiousness. *Personality and Social Psychology Review, 14*, 72–83.

Hollinger, D. (2000). *Postethnic America. Beyond multiculturalism.* New York: Harper Collins.

Hong, Y-y, Morris, M.W., Chiu, C-y, & Benet-Martínez, V. (2000). Multicultural minds: A dynamic constructivist approach to culture and cognition. *American Psychologist, 55*, 709–720.

Honneth, A. (1996). *The struggle for recognition: The moral grammar of social conflicts.* Oxford: Polity Press.

Hopkins, N., Regan, M., & Abell, J. (1997). On the context dependence of national stereotypes: Some Scottish data. *British Journal of Social Psychology*, 36, 553–563.

Hopkins, N., Reicher, S., Harrison, K., Cassidy, C., Bull, R., & Levine, M. (2007). Helping to improve the group stereotype: On the strategic dimension of prosocial behavior. *Personality and Social Psychology Bulletin, 33,* 776–788.

Hornsey, M.J., & Hogg, M.A. (2001). Subgroup relations: A comparison of mutual intergroup differentiation and common in-group identity models of prejudice reduction. *Personality and Social Psychology Bulletin, 26*, 242–256.

Hornsey, M.J., & Imani, A. (2004). Criticizing groups from the inside and the outside: An identity perspective on the intergroup sensitivity effect. *Personality and Social Psychology Bulletin, 30*, 365–383.

Horowitz, D.L. (2000). *Ethnic groups in conflict* (2nd ed.). Berkeley: University of California Press.

Houlette, M.A., Gaertner, S.L., Johnson, K.M., Banker, B.S., Riek, B.M., & Dovidio, J.F. (2004). Developing a more inclusive social identity: An elementary school intervention. *Journal of Social Issues, 60*, 35–55.

Hughes, D., Rodriguez, J., Smith, E.P., Johnson, D.J., Stevenson, H.C., & Spicer, P. (2006). Parents' ethnic–racial socialization practices: A review of research and directions for future study. *Developmental Psychology, 42*, 747–770.

Hughes, J.M., Bigler, R.S., & Levy, S.R. (2007). Consequences of learning about historical racism among European American and African American children. *Child Development, 78*, 1689–1705.

Huijnk, W. & Dagevos, J. (2012). *Dichter bij elkaar? De social-culturele positie van niet-Westerse migranten in Nederland (Closer together? The socio-cultural position of non-Western migrants in the Netherlands).* The Hague: SCP.

Huijnk. W., Verkuyten, M., & Coenders, M. (2010). Intermarriage attitude among ethnic minority and majority groups in the Netherlands: The role of family relations and immigrant characteristics. *Journal of Comparative Family Studies, 41*, 389–414.

Huntington, S. (2004). *Who are we? The challenges to America's national identity.* New York: Simon and Schuster.

Hurstfield, J. (1978). Internal colonialism: White, Black, and Chicano self-conceptions. *Ethnic and Racial Studies, 1,* 60–79.

Hutnik, N. (1991). *Ethnic minority identity.* Oxford: Clarendon.

Hutnik, N. & Street, R.C. (2010). Profiles of British Muslim identity: Adolescent girls in Birmingham. *Journal of Adolescence, 33*, 33–42.

Janmaat, J.G. (2006). Popular conceptions of nationhood in old and new European member states: partial support for the ethnic-civic framework. *Ethnic and Racial Studies, 29*, 50–78.

Jasinskaja-Lahti, I., Liebkind, K., & Solheim, E. (2009). To identify or not to identify? National disidentification as an alternative reaction to perceived ethnic discrimination. *Applied Psychology, 59*, 105–128.

Jasinskaja-Lahti, I., Mahonen, T.A., & Ketokivi, M. (2012). The dynamics of ethnic discrimination, identities and outgroup attitudes: A pre-post longitudinal study of ethnic migrants. *European Journal of Social Psychology, 42*, 904–914.

Jetten, J., Branscombe, N.R., Schmitt, M.T., & Spears, R. (2001). Rebel with a cause: Group identification as a response to perceived discrimination from the mainstream. *Personality and Social Psychology Bulletin, 27*, 1204–1213.

Jetten, J., Spears, R., & Manstead, A.S.R. (1996). Intergroup norms and intergroup discrimination: Distinctive self-categorization and social identity effects. *Journal of Personality and Social Psychology, 71*, 1222–1233.

Jetten, J., Spears, R., & Postmes, T. (2004). Intergroup distinctiveness and differentiation: A meta-analytic integration. *Journal of Personality and Social Psychology, 86*, 826–879.

Joppke, C. (2004). The retreat of multiculturalism in the liberal state: theory and policy. *British Journal of Sociology, 55*, 237–257.

Jordan, C.H., Spencer, S.J., & Zanna, M.P. (2005). Types of high self-esteem and prejudice: How implicit self-esteem relates to ethnic discrimination among high explicit self-esteem individuals. *Personality and Social Psychology Bulletin, 31*, 693–702.

Jost, J.T. (2006). The end of the end of ideology. *American Psychologist, 61*, 651–670.

Jost, J.T., Glaser, J., Kruglanski, A.W., & Sulloway, F. (2003a). Exceptions that prove the rule: Using a theory of motivated social cognition to account for ideological incongruities and political anomalies. *Psychological Bulletin, 129*, 383–393.

Jost, J.T., Glaser, J., Kruglanski, A.W., & Sulloway, F. (2003b). Political conservatism as motivated social cognition. *Psychological Bulletin, 129*, 339–375.

Kaiser, C.R., & Miller, C.T. (2001). Stop complaining! The social costs of making attributions to discrimination. *Personality and Social Psychology Bulletin, 27*, 254–263.

Kaiser, C.R., & Pratt-Hyatt, J.S. (2009). Distributing prejudice unequally: Do whites direct their prejudice toward strongly identified minorities? *Journal of Personality and Social Psychology, 96*, 432–445.

Kalev, A., Dobbin, F., & Kelly, E. (2006). Best practice or best guess? Assessing the efficacy of corporate affirmative action and diversity policies. *American Sociological Review, 71*, 589–617.

Kauff, M., & Wagner, U. (2012). Valuable therefore not threatening: The influence of diversity beliefs on discrimination against immigrants. *Social Psychological and Personality Science, 3*, 714–721.

Kaya, H. (2006). Verschillen in integratie Turken in Nederland (Differences in integration Turks in the Netherlands), *Demos, 22*, 45–48.

Kelman, H.C. (2001). The role of national identity in conflict resolution: Experiences from Israeli–Palestinian problem-solving workshops. In Ashmore, R.D., Jussim, L., & Wilder, D. (Eds,), *Social identity, intergroup conflict, and conflict resolution.* Oxford: Oxford University Press.

Kessel, B. (2000). *Suddenly Jewish: Jews raised as gentiles discover their Jewish roots.* Waltham, MA: Brandeis University Press.

Kessler, T., Mummendey, A., Funke, F., Brown, R., Binder, J., Zagefka, H., Leyens, J-P., Demoulin, S., & Maquil, A. (2010). We all live in Germany but . . . Ingroup projection, group-based emotions and prejudice against immigrants. *European Journal of Social Psychology, 40*, 985–997.

Kiang, L., Witkow, M., Baldelomar, O., & Fuligni, A. (2010). Change in ethnic identity across the high school years among adolescents with Latin American, Asian, and European backgrounds. *Journal of Youth and Adolescence, 39*, 683–693.

Kiesner, J, Cadinu, M., Poulin, F., & Bucci, M. (2002). Group identification in early adolescence: Its relation with peer adjustment and its moderator effect on peer influence. *Child Development, 73*, 196–208.

Kinket, B., & Verkuyten, M. (1997). Levels of ethnic self-identification and social context. *Social Psychology Quarterly, 60*, 338–354.

Klandermans, B., Van der Toorn, J., & Van Stekelenburg, J. (2008). Embeddedness and identity: How immigrants turn grievances into action. *American Sociological Review, 73*, 992–1012.

Klein, O., Spears, R. & Reicher, S. (2007). Social identity performance: Extending the strategic side of SIDE. *Personality and Social Psychology Review, 11*, 28–45.

Koning, E.A. (2011). Ethnic and civic dealings with newcomers: naturalization policies and practices in twenty-six countries. *Ethnic and Racial Studies, 34*, 1974–1995.

Koot, W., Tjon-A-Ten, V., & Uniken Venema, P. (1985). *Surinaamse kinderen op school (Surinamese children at school).* Muiderberg: Coutinho.

Kossman, E.H. (1996). Verdwijnt de Nederlandse identiteit? Beschouwingen over natie en cultuur (Does the Dutch Identity disappear? About nation and culture). In K. Koch & P. Scheffer (Eds.), *Her nut van Nederland: Opstellen over soevereiniteit en Identiteit* (pp. 59–68). Amsterdam: Bert Bakker.

Kuhn, M.H., & McPartland, T.S. (1954). An empirical investigation of self-attitudes. *American Sociological Review, 19*, 68–76.

Kundnani, A. (2007). Integrationism: The politics of anti-Muslim racism. *Race & Class, 48*, 24–44.

Kunovich, R.M. (2006). An exploration of the salience of Christianity for national identity in Europe. *Sociological Perspectives, 49*, 435–460.

Kuroiwa, Y., & Verkuyten, M. (2008). Narratives and the constitution of a common identity: The Karen in Burma. *Identities: Global Studies in Culture and Power, 15*, 391–412.

Kymlicka, W. (1995). *Multicultural citizenship.* Oxford, UK: Clarendon.

Kymlicka, W. (2010). The rise and fall of multiculturalism? New debates on inclusion and accommodation in diverse societies. In S. Vertovec & S. Wessendorf (Eds.), *The multiculturalism backlash: European discourses, policies and practices* (pp. 32–49). Oxford: Routledge.

Lay, C., & Nguyen, T. (1998). Acculturated-related and acculturation non-specific hassles: Vietnamese-Canadian students and psychological distress. *Canadian Journal of Behavioral Science, 30*, 172–181.

Lazar, A., & Lazar, M.M. (2004). The discourse of the New World Order: 'Out-casting' the double face of threat. *Discourse and Society, 15*, 223–242.

Leach, C.W., Ellemers, N., & Barreto, M. (2007). Group virtue: The importance of morality (vs competence and sociability) in the positive evaluation of in-groups. *Journal of Personality and Social Psychology, 93*, 234–249.

Leach, C.W., Iyer, A., & Pederson, A. (2006). Anger and guilt about ingroup advantage explain the willingness for political action. *Personality and Social Psychology Bulletin, 32*, 1232–1245.

Leach, C.W., & Smith, H.J. (2006). By whose standard? The affective implications of ethnic minorities' comparison to ethnic minority and majority referents. *European Journal of Social Psychology, 36*, 747–760.

Leach, C.W., van Zomeren, M., Zebel, S., Vliek, M.L.W., Pennekamp, S.F., Doosje, B., Ouwerkerk, J.W., & Spears, R. (2008). Group-level self-definition and self-investment: A hierarchical (multicomponent) model of in-group identification. *Journal of Personality and Social Psychology, 95*, 144–165.

Lechner, F.J. (2008). *The Netherlands: Globalization and national identity*: London: Routledge.

Lee, T.L., & Fiske, S. (2006). Not an outgroup, not yet an ingroup: Immigrants in the stereotype content model. *International Journal of Intercultural Relations, 20*, 751–768.

Leung, A., & Chiu, C. (2010). Multicultural experiences, idea receptiveness, and creativity. *Journal of Cross-Cultural Psychology, 41*, 723–741.

Leung, A., Maddux, W.W., Galinsky, A.D., & Chiu, C-y. (2008). Multicultural experience enhances creativity: The when and how. *American Psychologist, 63*, 169–181.

Levy, S.R., West, T.L., & Ramirez, L. (2005). Lay theories and intergroup relations: A social-developmental perspective. *European Review of Social Psychology, 16*, 189–220.

Lewin, K. (1948). *Resolving social conflicts: Selected papers on group dynamics*. New York: The Research Center for Group Dynamics, University of Michigan.

Lewis, P. (2007). *Young, British and Muslim*. London: Continuum.

Lie, J., & Verkuyten, M. (2012). Identity practices, ingroup projection, and the evaluation of subgroups: A study among Turkish-Dutch Sunnis. *Journal of Social Psychology, 152*, 510–523.

Liebkind, K. (2001). Acculturation. In R. Brown & S. Gaertner (Eds.), *Blackwell handbook of social psychology: Intergroup processes* (pp. 386–406). Oxford: Blackwell.

Liebkind, K., & McAlister, A. (1999). Extended contact through peer modeling to promote tolerance in Finland. *European Journal of Social Psychology, 29*, 765–780.

Lopez, A.B., Huynh, V.W., & Fuligni, A.J. (2011). A longitudinal study of religious identity and participation during adolescence. *Child Development, 82,* 1297–1309.

Lorasdagi, B.K. (2009). The headscarf and emancipation in the Netherlands. *Feminism & Psychology, 19*, 328–334.

Lowery, B.S., Unzueta, M.M., Knowles, E.D., & Goff, P.A. (2006). Concern for the in-group and opposition to affirmative action. *Journal of Personality and Social Psychology, 90*, 961–974.

Luyckx, K., Goosens, L., Soenens, B., Beyers, W., & Vansteenkiste, M. (2005). Identity statuses based upon four rather than two identity dimensions: Extending and refining Marcia's paradigm. *Journal of Youth and Adolescence, 34*, 605–618.

Macleod, A.E. (1991) *Accommodating protest: Working women, the new veiling, and change in Cairo.* Colombia: Colombia University Press.

Mahtani-Stewart, S., Bond, M.H., Ho, L.M., Zaman, R.M., & Anwar, M. (2000). Perceptions of parents and adolescent outcomes in Pakistan. *British Journal of Developmental Psychology, 18*, 335–352.

Maisonneuve, C., & Teste, B. (2007). Acculturation preferences of a host community: The effects of immigrant acculturation strategies on evaluations and impression formation. *International Journal of Intercultural Relations, 31*, 669–688

Major, B., Quinton, W.J., & McCoy, S.K. (2002). Antecedents and consequences of attributions to discrimination: Theoretical and empirical advances. In M.P. Zanna (Ed.), *Advances in experimental social psychology.* New York: Academic Press.

Maliepaard, M., Lubbers, M., & Gijsberts, M. (2010). Generational differences in ethnic and religious attachment and their interrelation: A study among Muslim minorities in the Netherlands. *Ethnic and Racial Studies, 33*, 451–472.

Mange, J., Young Chun, W., Sharvit, K., & Belanger, J.J. (2012). Thinking about Arabs and Muslims makes Americans shoot faster: Effects of category accessibility on aggressive responses in a shooter paradigm. *European Journal of Social Psychology, 42*, 552–556.

Marcia, J.E. (1966). Development and validation of ego-identity status. *Journal of Personality and Social Psychology, 3*, 551–558.

Margalit, A., & Halbertal, M. (1994). Liberalism and the right to culture. *Social Research, 61*, 491–513.

Marques, J.M., Abrams, D., Páez, D., & Hogg, M.A. (2001). Social categorization, social identification, and rejection of deviant group members. In M.A. Hogg & R.S. Tindale (Eds.), *Blackwell handbook of social psychology: Group processes* (pp. 400–424). Oxford: Blackwell.

Martin, T.F., White, J.M., & Perlman, D. (2003). Religious socialization: A test of the channelling hypothesis of parental influence on adolescent faith maturity. *Journal of Adolescent Research, 18*, 169–187.

Martinovic, B., & Verkuyten, M. (2012). Host national and religious identification among Turkish Muslims in Western Europe: The role of ingroup norms, perceived discrimination and value incompatibility. *European Journal of Social Psychology, 42*, 893–903.

Martinovic, B., & Verkuyten, M. (2013a). *Dual identity and political mobilization of Muslim immigrants.* Utrecht: Ercomer.

Martinovic, B., & Verkuyten, M. (2013b). *'We were here first, so we determine the rules of the game': Primordial autochthony and out-group rejection.* Utrecht: Ercomer.

Martinovic, B., Verkuyten, M. & Weesie, J. (2011). Group identity, ethnic separatism, and multiple out-groups: the Basque case. *Journal of Community and Applied Social Psychology, 21*, 28–40.

Mayall, B. (2001). Understanding childhoods: A London study. In L. Alanen & B. Mayall (Eds.), *Conceptualizing child-adult relations* (pp. 114–128). London: Routledge.

McAdams, D. (1993). *Stories we live by: Personal myths and the making of the self.* New York: Morrow.

McAdams, D., Bauer, J., Sakaeda, A., Anyidoho, N., Machado, M., Magrino-Failla, K., *et al.* (2006). Continuity and change in the life-story: A longitudinal study of autobiographical memories in emerging adulthood. *Journal of Personality, 74*, 1371–1400.

McClosky, H., & Brill, A. (1983). *Dimensions of tolerance: What Americans believe about civil liberties.* New York: Basic Books.

McGuire, W.J. (1973). The yin and yang of progress in social psychology: Seven koans. *Journal of Personality and Social Psychology, 26*, 446–456.

McKown, C., & Weinstein, R. (2003). The development and consequence of stereotype consciousness in middle childhood. *Child Development, 74*, 498–515.

McLaren, L.M. (2003). Anti-immigrant prejudice in Europe: Contact, threat perception, and preferences for the exclusion of migrants. *Social Forces, 81*, 908–936.

McPherson, M., Smith-Lovin, L., & Cook, J. M. (2001). Birds of a feather: Homophily and social networks. *Annual Review of Sociology*, 27, 415–444.

Meeus, J., Duriez, B., Vanbeselaere, N., & Boen, F. (2010). The role of national identity representation in the relation between in-group identification and out-group derogation: Ethnic versus civic representation. *British Journal of Social Psychology, 49*, 305–320.

Meeus, W. (2011). The study of adolescent identity formation 2000–2010: A review of longitudinal research. *Journal of Research on Adolescence, 21*, 75–94.

Michell, G. (2012). Revisiting truth and triviality: The external validity of research in the psychological laboratory. *Psychological Science, 7*, 109–117.

Midgley, M. (1979). *Beast and man: The roots of human nature*. London: Routledge.

Mikulincer, M., & Shaver, P.R. (2007). Boosting attachment security to promote mental health, prosocial values, and intergroup tolerance. *Psychological Inquiry, 18*, 139–156.

Miller, K.P., Brewer, M.B., & Arbuckle, N.L. (2009). Social identity complexity: Its correlates and antecedents. *Group Processes and Intergroup Relations, 12*, 79–94.

Miller, N. (2002). Personalization and the promise of contact theory. *Journal of Social Issues, 58*, 387–410.

Milliken, F.J., & Martins, L.L. (1996). Searching for common threads: Understanding the multiple effects of diversity in organizational groups. *Academy of Management Review, 21*, 402–433.

Milner, D. (1973). Racial identification and preference in 'black' British children. *European Journal of Social Psychology, 3*, 281–295.

Minard, R.D. (1952). Race relationships in the Pocahontas coal field. *Journal of Social Issues, 8*, 29–44.

Minescu, A. (2011). *Relative group position and intergroup attitudes in Russia.* Utrecht: ICS.

Mio, J.S., Barker-Hackett, L., & Tumambing, J. (2006). *Multicultural psychology: Understanding our diverse communities.* New York: McGraw-Hill.

Mirza, M., Senthilkumaran, D., & Ja'far, Z. (2007). *Living apart together: British Muslims and the paradox of multiculturalism.* London: Policy Exchange.

Mlicki, P., & Ellemers, N. (1996). Being different or being better? National stereotypes and identifications of Polish and Dutch students. *European Journal of Social Psychology, 26*, 97–114.

Modood, T. (2007). *Multiculturalism.* Cambridge: Polity Press.

Modood, T., Beishon, S., & Virdee, S. (1997). Changing ethnic identities in Britain. In Modood, T., Berthoud, R., Lakey, J., Nazroo, J., Smith, O., Virdee, S., & Beishon, S. (Eds.). *Ethnic minorities in Britain: Diversity and disadvantage.* London: Policy Studies Institute.

Moghaddam, F. (2008). *Multiculturalism and intergroup relations: Psychological implications for democracy in global context.* Washington: American Psychological Association.

Monteiro, M.B., de Franca, D.X., & Rodrigues, R. (2009). The development of intergroup bias in childhood: How social norms can shape children's racial behaviours. *International Journal of Psychology, 44*, 29–39.

Moors, A. (2009). Islamic fashion in Europe: Religious conviction, aesthetic style, and creative consumption. *Encounters, 1*, 175–201.

Moors, A. (2011). Colonial traces? The (post-)colonial governance of Islamic dress: Gender and the public presence of Islam. In M. Maussen, V. Bader, & A. Moors (Eds.), *The colonial and post-colonial governance of Islam* (pp. 135–155). Amsterdam: Amsterdam University Press.

Moran, A. (2011). Multiculturalism as nation-building in Australia: Inclusive national identity and the embrace of diversity. *Ethnic and Racial Studies, 34*, 2153–2173.

Morin, F., & Saladin d'Anglure, B. (1997). Ethnicity as a political tool for indigenous peoples. In C. Govers & H. Vermeulen (Eds.), *The politics of ethnic consciousness* (pp. 157–193). London: Macmillan.

Morrison, K.R., & Chung, A.H. (2011). "White" or "European American"? Self-identifying labels influence majority group members' interethnic attitudes. *Journal of Experimental Social Psychology, 47*, 165–170.

Morrison, K.R., Plaut, V.C., & Ybarra, O. (2010). Predicting whether multiculturalism positively or negatively influences White Americans' intergroup attitudes: The role of ethnic identification. *Personality and Social Psychology Bulletin, 36,* 1648–1661.

Moscovici, S., & Pérez, J.A. (2007). A study of minorities as victims. *European Journal of Social Psychology, 37*, 725–746.

Mullen, B., & Hu, L. (1989). Perceptions of ingroup and outgroup variability: A meta-analytic integration. *Basic and Applied Social Psychology, 10*, 233–252.

Mummendey, A., & Schreiber, H.J. (1983). Better or different? Positive social identity by discrimination against or differentiation from outgroups. *European Journal of Social Psychology, 13*, 389–397.

Munniksma, A., Stark, T., Verkuyten, M., Flache, A., & Veenstra, R. (in press). Extended intergroup friendships within social settings. *Group Processes and Intergroup Relations*.

Nagayoshi, K. (2011). Support of multiculturalism, but for whom? Effects of ethno-national identity on the endorsement of multiculturalism in Japan. *Journal of Ethnic and Migration Studies, 37,* 561–578.

Nagda, B.A., Kim, C., & Truelove, Y. (2004). Learning about difference, learning with others, learning to transgress. *Journal of Social Issues, 60*, 195–214.

Nave, A. (2000). Marriage and the maintenance of ethnic group boundaries: the case of Mauritius. *Ethnic and Racial Studies, 23*, 329–352.

Nekby, L., & Rödin, M. (2007). *Acculturation identity and labor market outcomes.* IZA Discussion paper No. 2826. Bonn: Institut zur Zukunft der Arbeit.

Nelson, D., Joseph, G.G., & Williams, J. (1993). *Multicultural mathematics.* Oxford: Oxford University Press.

Newman, B.J., Hartman, T.K., & Taber, C.S. (in press). Foreign language exposure, cultural threat, and opposition to immigration. *Political Psychology*.

Ng Tseung-Wong, C., & Verkuyten, M. (2010). Intergroup evaluations, Group indispensability and prototypical judgments: A study in Mauritius. *Group Processes and Intergroup Relations, 13*, 621–638.

Ng Tseung-Wong, C., & Verkuyten, M. (2013). 'We can't be lovers, only friends': The two-sidedness of multiculturalism. (manuscript under review).

Nguyen, A.T., & Benet-Martinez, V. (2013). Biculturalism and adjustment: A meta analysis. *Journal of Cross-Cultural Psychology, 44*, 122–159.

Nieguth, T. (1999). Beyond dichotomy: Concepts of the nation and the distribution of membership. *Nations and Nationalism, 5*, 155–173.

Noel, J.G., Wann, D.L., & Branscombe, N. (1995). Peripheral ingroup membership status and public negativity toward outgroups. *Journal of Personality and Social Psychology, 68*, 127–137.

Norris, P., & Inglehart, R. (2004). *Sacred and secular: Religion and politics worldwide.* Cambridge: Cambridge University Press.

Obdeijn, H., & Schrover, M. (2008). *Komen en gaan: Immigratie en emigratie in Nederland vanaf 1550 (Coming and going: Immigration and emigration in the Netherlands from 1550).* Amsterdam: Bert Bakker.

O'Brien, J. (2011). Spoiled group identities and backstage work: A theory of stigma management rehearsals. *American Sociological Quarterly, 74*, 291–309.

Ogbu, J.U. (1993). Differences in cultural frame of reference. *International Journal of Behavioral Development, 16*, 483–506.

Okin, S.M. (1999). *Is multiculturalism bad for women?* Princeton: Princeton University Press.

Ong, A., Phinney, J., & Dennis, J. (2006). Competence under challenge: Exploring the protective influence of parental support and ethnic identity in Latino college students. *Journal of Adolescence, 29*, 961–979.

Outten, H.R., Schmitt, M.T., Miller, D.A., & Garcia, A.L. (2011). Feeling threatened about the future: White's emotional reactions to anticipated ethnic demographic changes. *Personality and Social Psychology Bulletin, 38*, 14–25.

Paluck, E.L. (2009). Reducing intergroup prejudice and conflict using the media: A field experiment in Rwanda. *Journal of Personality and Social Psychology, 96*, 574–587.

Paluck, E.L., & Green, D.P. (2009). Prejudice reduction: What works? A review and assessment of research and practice. *Annual Review of Psychology, 60*, 339–369.

Parekh, B. (2000). *Rethinking multiculturalism: Cultural diversity and political theory.* London: MacMillan.

Pascoe, E.A., & Richman, L.S. (2009). Perceived discrimination and health: A meta-analytic review. *Psychological Bulletin, 135*, 531–554.

Peek, L. (2005). Becoming Muslim: The development of a religious identity. *Sociology of Religion, 66*, 215–242.

Pehrson, S., Brown, R., & Zagefka, H. (2009a). When does national identification lead to the rejection of immigrants? Cross-sectional and longitudinal evidence for the role of essentialist in-group definitions. *British Journal of Social Psychology, 48*, 61–76.

Pehrson, S., Vignoles, V., & Brown, R. (2009b). National identification and anti-immigrant prejudice: Individual and contextual effects of national definitions. *Social Psychology Quarterly, 72*, 24–38.

Perdue, C.W., Dividio, J.F., Gurtman, M.B., & Tyler, R.B. (1990). 'Us' and 'Them': Social categorization and the process of intergroup bias. *Journal of Personality and Social Psychology, 59*, 475–486.

Pereira, C., Vala, J., & Costa-Lopes, R. (2010). From prejudice to discrimination: The legitimizing role of perceived threat in discrimination against immigrants. *European Journal of Social Psychology, 40*, 1231–1250.

Pettigrew, T.F. (1997). Generalized intergroup contact effects on prejudice. *Personality and Social Psychology Bulletin, 23,* 173–185.

Pettigrew, T.F. (1998). Intergroup contact theory. *Annual Review Psychology, 49,* 65–85.

Pettigrew, T.F. (2009). Secondary transfer effect of contact: Do intergroup contact effects spread to noncontacted outgroups? *Social Psychology, 40,* 55–65.

Pettigrew, T.F., & Tropp, L. (2006). A meta-analytic test of intergroup contact theory. *Journal of Personality and Social Psychology, 90,* 751–783.

Pettigrew, T.F., & Tropp, L. (2008). How does intergroup contact reduce prejudice? Meta-analytic tests of three mediators. *European Journal of Social Psychology, 38,* 922–934.

Pettigrew, T.F., & Tropp, L.R. (2011). *When groups meet: The dynamics of intergroup contact.* New York: Psychology Press.

Pew Research Center (2005). *Islamic extremism: Common concern for Muslim and Western publics.* Washington: Pew Research Center.

Pew Research Center (2006). *Pew global attitudes project: 15 nation survey.* Washington: Pew Research Center.

Phalet, K., Baysu, G., & Verkuyten, M. (2010). Political mobilization of Dutch Muslims: Religious identity salience, goal framing, and normative constraints. *Journal of Social Issues, 66,* 759–780.

Phalet, K., Gijsberts, M. & Hagendoorn, L. (2008). Migration and religion: Testing the limits of secularisation among Turkish and Moroccan Muslims in the Netherlands 1998–2005. *Kölner Zeitschrift für Soziologie und Sozialpsychologie, 48,* 412–436.

Phalet, K., & Güngör, D. (2004). *Moslim in Nederland: religieuze dimensies, etnische relaties en burgerschap (Muslims in the Netherlands: religious dimensions, ethnic relations and civic identity).* The Hague: Social and Cultural Planning Office.

Philip, C.L., Mahalingam, R., & Sellers, R.M. (2010). Understanding East Indians' attitudes toward African Americans: Do mainstream prejudicial attitudes transfer to immigrants? *Journal of Ethnic and Migration Studies, 36,* 651–671.

Phinney, J.S. (1989). Stages of ethnic identity development in minority group adolescents. *Journal of Early Adolescence, 9,* 34–49.

Phinney, J.S. (1992). The multigroup ethnic identity measure: A new scale for use with adolescents and young adults from diverse groups. *Journal of Adolescent Research, 7,* 156–176.

Phinney, J.S., Berry, J.W., Vedder, P., & Liebkind, K. (2006). The acculturation experience: Attitudes, identities, and behaviors of immigrant youth. In J.W. Berry, J.S. Phinney, D.L. Sam & P. Vedder (Eds.), *Immigrant youth in cultural transition: Acculturation, identity, and adaptation across national contexts* (pp. 71–116). Mahwah, NJ: Lawrence Erlbaum.

Phinney, J.S., Jacoby, B., & Silva, C. (2007). Positive intergroup attitudes: The role of ethnic identity. *International Journal of Behavioral Development, 31,* 478–490.

Piontkowski, U., Florack, A., Hoelker, P., & Obdrzálek, P. (2000). Predicting acculturation attitudes of dominant and non-dominant groups. *International Journal of Intercultural Relations, 24,* 1–26.

Piontkowski, U., Rohmann, A., & Florack, A. (2002). Concordance of acculturation attitudes and perceived threat. *Group Processes and Intergroup Relations, 5,* 221–232.

Plaut, V.C. (2010). Diversity science: Why and how difference makes a difference. *Psychological Inquiry, 21,* 77–99.

Plaut, V.C., Garnett, F.G., Buffadi, L.E., & Sanchez-Burks, J. (2011). "What about me?": Perceptions of exclusion and white's reactions to multiculturalism. *Journal of Personality and Social Psychology, 101*, 337–353.

Plaut, V.C., Thomas, K.M., & Goren, M.J. (2009). Is multiculturalism or color blindness better for minorities? *Psychological Science, 20*, 444–446.

Portera, A. (2008). Intercultural education in Europe: Epistemological and semantic aspects. *Intercultural Education, 19*, 481–491.

Poteat, V. P., Espelage, D. L., & Green, H. D. (2007). The socialization of dominance: Peer group contextual effects on homophobic and dominance attitudes. *Journal of Personality and Social Psychology, 92*, 1040–1050.

Prins, B. (2002). Het lef om taboes te doorbreken: Nieuw realisme in het Nederlandse discours over multiculturalisme (Breaking taboos: New realism in the Dutch discourse on multiculturalism). *Migrantenstudies, 18*, 241–254.

Putnam, R. (2007). *E Pluribus Unum*: Diversity and community in the twenty-first century: The 2006 Johan Skytte Prize Lecture. *Scandinavian Political Studies, 30*, 137–174.

Quezada, S.A., Shaw, M.P., & Zárate, M.A. (2012). Cultural inertia: The relationship between ethnic identity and reactions to cultural change. *Social Psychology, 43*, 243–251.

Quillian, L. (1996). Prejudice as a response to perceived group threat: Population composition and anti-immigrant and racial prejudice in Europe. *American Sociological Review, 4*, 586–611.

Quinn, D.M., Kallen, R.W., & Spencer, S.J. (2010). Stereotype threat. In J.F. Dovidio, M. Hewstone, P. Glick & V.M. Esses (Eds.), *The Sage handbook of prejudice, stereotyping and discrimination* (pp. 379–394). London: Sage.

Quinn, K.A., Ross, E.M., & Esses, V.M. (2001). Attributions of responsibility and reactions to affirmative action: Affirmative action as help. *Personality and Social Psychology Bulletin, 27*, 321–331.

Quintana, S.M. (1998). Development of children's understanding of ethnicity and race. *Applied and Preventive Psychology: Current Scientific Perspectives, 7*, 27–45.

Quintana, S.M. (2007). Racial and ethnic identity: Developmental perspectives and research. *Journal of Counseling Psychology, 54*, 259–270.

Quintana, S.M., Castaneda-English, P., & Ybarra, V. (1999). Role of perspective-taking abilities and ethnic socialization in development of adolescent ethnic identity. *Journal of Research on Adolescence, 9*, 161–184.

Rabbie, J.M., & Horwitz, M. (1969). Arousal of ingroup-outgroup bias by chance win or loss. *Journal of Personality and Social Psychology, 13*, 269–277.

Ramos, M.R., Cassidy, C., Reicher, S., & Haslam, S.A. (2012). A longitudinal investigation of the rejection-identification hypothesis. *British Journal of Social Psychology, 51*, 642–661.

Ramos, M.R., Jetten, J., Zhang, A., Badea, C., Iyer, A., Cui, L., & Zhang, Y. (2013). Minority goals for interaction with the majority: Seeking distance from the majority and the effect of rejection on identification. *European Journal of Social Psychology, 43*, 72–83.

Rattan, A. & Ambady, N. (2013). Diversity ideologies and intergroup relations: An examination of colorblindness and multiculturalism. *European Journal of Social Psychology, 43*, 12–21.

Rattansi, A. (2011). *Multiculturalism: A short introduction*. Oxford: Oxford University Press.

Reeskens, T., & Hooghe, M. (2010). Beyond the civic-ethnic dichotomy: Investigating the structure of citizenship concepts across thirty-three countries. *Nations and Nationalism, 16*, 579–597.

Reich, B. (2002). *Bridging liberalism and multiculturalism in American education.* Chicago: University of Chicago Press.

Reicher, S. (2004). The context of social identity: Domination, resistance, and change. *Political Psychology, 25*, 921–945.

Reicher, S. (2007). Rethinking the paradigm of prejudice. *South African Journal of Psychology, 37*, 820–834.

Reicher, S., Cassidy, C., Wolpert, I., Hopkins, N., & Levina, M. (2006). Saving Bulgaria's Jews: An analysis of social identity and the mobilisation of social solidarity. *European Journal of Social Psychology, 36*, 49–72.

Reicher, S.D., Haslam, S.A., & Rath, R. (2008). Making a virtue of evil: A five-step social identity model of the development of collective hate. *Social and Personality Psychology Compass, 2/3*, 1313–1344.

Reyna, C., Henry, P.J., & Korfmacher, W. (2006). Examining the principles in principled conservatism: The role of responsibility stereotypes as cues for deservingness in racial policy decisions. *Journal of Personality and Social Psychology, 90*, 109–128.

Reysoo, F. (1992). Symbool en anti-symbool van culturele identiteit: De hoofddoekjes-affaire in Frankrijk (Symbol and anti-symbol of cultural identity: The headscarf controversy in France). *Focaal, 17/18*, 43–61.

Richeson, J.A., & Nussbaum, R.J. (2004). The impact of multiculturalism versus color-blindness on racial bias. *Journal of Experimental Social Psychology, 40*, 417–423.

Roald, A.S. (2001). *Women in Islam: The Western experience.* London: Routledge.

Roccas, S., & Brewer, M.B. (2002). Social identity complexity. *Personality and Social Psychology Review, 6*, 88–106.

Rogers, L.O., Zosuls, K.M., Halim, M.L., Ruble, D., Hughes, D., & Fuligni, A. (2012). Meaning making in middle childhood: An exploration of the meaning of ethnic identity. *Cultural Diversity and Ethnic Minority Psychology, 18*, 99–108.

Roosens, E. (1989). *Creating ethnicity: The process of ethnogenesis.* Newbury Park: Sage.

Rosenberg, M. (1979). *Conceiving the self.* New York: Basic Books.

Rosenthal, L., & Levy, S. (2010). The colorblind, multicultural, and polycultural ideological approaches to improving intergroup attitudes and relations. *Social Issues and Policy Review, 4*, 215–246.

Rosenthal, L., & Levy, S. (2012). The relation between polyculturalism and intergroup attitudes among racially and ethnically diverse adults. *Cultural Diversity and Ethnic Minority Psychology, 18*, 1–16.

Roy, O. (2007). *Secularism confronts Islam.* New York: Columbia University Press.

Rubin, M., & Hewstone, M. (2004). Social identity, system justification, and social dominance: Commentary on Reicher, Jost *et al.*, and Sidanius *et al. Political Psychology, 25*, 823–844.

Rudmin, F. (2003). Critical history of the acculturation psychology of assimilation, separation, integration, and marginalization. *Review of General Psychology, 7*, 3–37.

Ruggiero, K.M., & Taylor, D.M. (1997). Why minority members perceive or do not perceive the discrimination that confronts them: The role of self-esteem and perceived control. *Journal of Personality and Social Psychology, 72*, 373–389.

Rutland, A., Cameron, L., Milne, A., & McGeorge, P. (2005). Social norms and self-presentation: Children's implicit and explicit intergroup attitudes. *Child Development, 76*, 451–466.

Ryan, C.S., Hunt, J.S., Weible, J.A., Peterson, C.R., & Casas, J.F. (2007). Multicultural and colorblind ideology, stereotypes, and ethnocentrism among Black and White Americans. *Group Processes and Intergroup Relations, 10*, 617–637.

Sachar, A. (2000). On citizenship and multicultural vulnerability. *Political Theory, 28*, 64–89.

Saeed, A., Blain, N., & Forbes, D. (1999). New ethnic and national questions in Scotland: Post-British identities among Glasgow Pakistani teenagers. *Ethnic and Racial Studies, 22*, 821–844.

Saguy, T., Tausch, N., Dovidio, J.F., & Pratto, F. (2009). The irony of harmony: Intergroup contact can produce false expectations for equality. *Psychological Science, 29*, 114–1212.

Saguy, T., Tausch, N., Dovidio, J.F., Pratto, F., & Singh, P. (2011). Tension and harmony in intergroup relations. In P.R. Shaver & M. Mikulincer (Eds.), *Understanding and reducing aggression, violence, and their consequences* (pp. 333–348). Washington, DC: American Psychological Association.

Sahdra, B., & Ross, M. (2007). Group identification and historical memory. *Personality and Social Psychology Bulletin, 33*, 384–395.

Samaniego, R.Y., & Gonzales N.A. (1999). Multiple mediators of the effects of acculturation status on delinquency for Mexican American adolescents. *American Journal of Community Psychology, 27,* 189–210.

Sani, F. & Bennett, M. (2004). Developmental aspects of social identity. In M. Bennett & F. Sani (Eds.), *The development of the social self* (pp. 77–100). Hove: Psychology Press.

Sani, F., Bowe, M., Herrera, M., Manna, C., Cossa, T., Miao, X., & Zhou, Y. (2007). Perceived collective continuity: Seeing groups as entities that move through time. *European Journal of Social Psychology, 37*, 1118–1134.

Schalk-Soekar, S. (2007). *Multiculturalism: A stable concept with many ideological and political aspects*. Tilburg: Universiteit Tilburg.

Schaller, M. & Abeysinghe, A.M.N.D. (2006). Geographical frame of reference and dangerous intergroup attitudes: A double-minority study in Sri Lanka. *Political Psychology, 27*, 615–631.

Scheffer, P. 2000. *Het multiculturele drama* (The multicultural drama). NRC-Handelsblad, January 29.

Schmidt, G. (2004). Islamic identity formation among young Muslims: The case of Denmark, Sweden and the United States. *Journal of Muslim Affairs, 24*, 31–45.

Schofield, J.W., & Eurich-Fulcer, R. (2001). When and how school desegregation improves intergroup relations. In R. Brown & S. Gardner (Eds.), *Blackwell handbook of social psychology: Intergroup processes.* Oxford: Blackwell.

Schwartz, S.J., Unger, J.B., Zamboanga, B.L., & Szapocznik, J. (2010). Rethinking the concept of acculturation: Implications for theory and research. *American Psychologist. 65*, 237–251.

Seaton, E.K., Scottham, K.M., & Sellers, R.M. (2006). The status model of racial identity development in African American adolescents: Evidence of structure, trajectories, and well-being. *Child Development, 77*, 1416–1426.

Sellers, R.M., & Shelton, J.N. (2003). The role of racial identity in perceived racial discrimination. *Journal of Personality and Social Psychology, 84*, 1079–1092.

Selten, J-P., Cantor-Graae, E., & Kahn, R.S. (2007). Migration and schizophrenia. *Current Opinion in Psychiatry, 20*, 111–115.

Settles, I.H. (2006). Use of an intersectional framework to understand Black woman's racial and gender identities. *Sex Roles, 54,* 589–601.

Seul, J.R. (1999). 'Ours is the way of God': Religion, identity, and intergroup conflict. *Journal of Peace Research, 36,* 553–569.

Sherif, M., Harvey, O.J., White, B.J., Hood, W.R., & Sherif, C.W. (1961). *Intergroup conflict and cooperation: The Robbers cave experiments.* Norman, OK: University of Oklahoma.

Shih, M., Pittinsky, T.L., & Ambady, N. (1999). Stereotype susceptibility: Identity salience and shifts in quantitative performance. *Psychological Science, 10,* 80–83.

Shih, M., & Sanchez, D. (2005). Perspectives and research on the positive and negative effects of having multiple racial identities. *Psychological Bulletin, 131,* 569–591.

Shindeldecker, J. (2001). *Türkische Aleviten Heute (Turkish Alevi today).* Istanbul: Şahkulu Sultan Külliyesi Vakfı.

Shulman, S. (2002). Challenging the civic/ethnic and West/East dichotomies in the study of nationalism. *Comparative Political Studies, 35,* 554–585.

Sibley, C.G., & Liu, J.H. (2007). New Zealand = bicultural? Implicit and explicit associations between ethnicity and nationhood in the New Zealand context. *European Journal of Social Psychology, 37,* 1222–1243.

Sibley, C.G., Liu, J.H., Duckitt, J., & Khan, S.S. (2008). Social representations of history and the legitimation of social inequality: The form and function of historical negation. *European Journal of Social Psychology, 38,* 542–565.

Sidanius, J., & Pratto, F. (1999). *Social dominance: An intergroup theory of social hierarchy and oppression.* Cambridge: Cambridge University Press.

Simon, B. (1992). The perception of ingroup and outgroup homogeneity: Re-introduing the intergroup context. *European Review of Social Psychology, 3,* 1–30.

Simon, B. (2004). *Identity in modern society: A social psychological perspective.* Oxford: Blackwell.

Simon, B., & Brown, R. (1987). Perceived intragroup homogeneity in minority–majority contexts. *Journal of Personality and Social Psychology, 53,* 703–711.

Simon, B., & Grabow, O. (2010). The politicization of migrants: Further evidence that politicized collective identity is a dual identity. *Political Psychology, 31,* 717–738.

Simon, B., & Klandermans, B. (2001). Politicized collective identity: A social psychological analysis. *American Psychologist, 56,* 319–331.

Simon, B., & Ruhs, D. (2008). Identity and politicisation among Turkish migrants in Germany: The role of dual identification. *Journal of Personality and Social Psychology, 95,* 1354–1366.

Sirin, S.R., & Fine, M. (2008). *Muslim American youth: Understanding hyphenated identities through multiple methods.* New York: New York University Press.

Slavin, R.E. (1983). *Cooperative learning.* New York: Longman.

Smeekes, A. & Verkuyten, M. (2013). *When national history is disrupted: Cultural continuity and resistance to Muslim immigrants.* Utrecht: Ercomer.

Smeekes, A., Verkuyten, M., & Poppe, E. (2011). Mobilising opposition towards Muslim immigrants: National identification and the representation of national history. *British Journal of Social Psychology, 50,* 265–280.

Smeekes, A., Verkuyten, M., & Poppe, E. (2012). How a tolerant past affects the present: Historical tolerance and the acceptance of Muslim expressive rights. *Personality and Social Psychology Bulletin, 38,* 1410–1422.

Smith, T.B., & Silva, L. (2011). Ethnic identity and personal well-being of people of color: A meta-analysis. *Journal of Counseling Psychology, 58,* 42–60.

Smith, H.J., Pettigrew, T.F., Pippin, G.M., & Bialosiewicz, S. (2012). Relative deprivation: A theoretical and meta-analytic review. *Personality and Social Psychology Review, 16*, 203–232.

Snauwaert, B., Soenens, B., Vanbeselaere, N., & Boen, F. (2003). When integration does not necessarily imply integration: Different conceptualizations of acculturation orientations lead to different classifications. *Journal of Cross-Cultural Psychology, 34*, 231–239.

Sniderman, P.M., & Hagendoorn, L. (2007). *When ways of life collide: Multiculturalism and its discontents in the Netherlands*. Princeton, NJ: Princeton University Press.

Son Hing, L.S. & Zanna, M.P. (2010). Individual differences. In J.F. Dovidio, M. Hewstone, P. Glick, & V.M. Esses (Eds.), *The Sage handbook of prejudice, stereotyping and discrimination* (pp. 163–178). London: Sage.

Song, M. (2003). *Choosing ethnic identity*. Cambridge: Polity.

Spitzer, S., Couch, C., & Stratton, J. (1969). *The assessment of the self*. Iowa City: Sernoll.

Staerklé, C., Sidanius, J., Green, E.G.T., & Molina, L.E. (2010). Ethnic minority–majority asymmetry in national attitudes around the world: A multilevel analysis. *Political Psychology, 31*, 491–519.

Stangor, C., Van Allen, K.L., Swim, J.K., & Sechrist, G.B. (2002). Reporting discrimination in public and private contexts. *Journal of Personality and Social Psychology, 82*, 69–74.

Stark, T. (2011). *Integration in schools: A process perspective on students' interethnic attitudes and interpersonal relationships*. Groningen, The Netherlands: University of Groningen.

Steele, C.M. (1997). A threat in the air: How stereotypes shape intellectual identity and performance. *American Psychologist, 52*, 613–629.

Stengs, I. (2007). Commemorating victims of 'senseless violence': Negotiating ethnic inclusion and exclusion. In P.J. Margry & H. Roodenburg (Eds.), *Reframing Dutch culture: Between otherness and authenticity* (pp. 159–179). Aldershot: Ashgate.

Stephan, W.G., & Vogt, W.P. (Eds.) (2004). *Education programs for improving intergroup relations: Theory, research and practice*. New York: Teachers College Press.

Stevens, F.G., Plaut, V.C., & Sanchez-Burks, J. (2008). Unlocking the benefits of diversity: All-inclusive multiculturalism and positive organizational change. *Journal of Applied Behavioral Science, 44*, 116–133.

Stevens, G., Veen, V. & Vollebergh, W. (2009). *Marokkaanse jeugdelinquenten: Een klasse apart? (Moroccan youth delinquents: A separate class?)* The Hague, The Netherlands: Nicis.

Swann, W.B.Jr., Rentfrow, P.J., & Guinn, J.S. (2003). Self-verification: The search for coherence. In M.R. Leary & J.P. Tangney (Eds.) *Handbook of self and identity* (pp. 367–387). New York: Guildford Press.

Swim, J.K., & Miller, D.L. (1999). White guilt: Its antecedents and consequences for attitudes toward affirmative action. *Personality and Social Psychology Bulletin, 25*, 500–514.

Tadmor, C.T., Hong, T-y., Chao, M.M., Wiruchnipawan, F., & Wang, W. (2012). Multicultural experiences reduce intergroup bias through epistemic unfreezing. *Journal of Personality and Social Psychology, 103*, 750–772.

Tajfel, H. (1981). The social psychology of minorities. In H. Tajfel (Ed.), *Human groups and social categories: Studies in the social psychology of intergroup relations*. Cambridge, UK: Cambridge University Press.

Tajfel, H.C., Flament, C., Billig, M., & Bundy, R.P. (1971). Social categorization and intergroup behaviour. *European Journal of Social Psychology, 1*, 149–178.

Tajfel, H., & Turner, J. (1979). An integrative theory of intergroup conflict. In W.G. Austin & S. Worchel (Eds.), *The social psychology of intergroup relations*. Monterey, CA: Brooks/Cole.

Tajfel, H.C., & Wilkes, A.L. (1963). Classification and quantitative judgment. *British Journal of Psychology, 54*, 101–114.

Tarrant, M., Dazeley. S., & Cottom, T. (2009). Social categorization and empathy for outgroup members. *British Journal of Social Psychology, 48*, 427–446.

Tausch, N., Tam, T., Hewstone, M., Kenworthy, J., & Cairns, E. (2007). Individual-level and group-level mediators of contact effects in Northern Ireland: The moderating role of social identification. *British Journal of Social Psychology, 46*, 541–556.

Taylor, C. (1992). The politics of recognition. In A. Gutmann (Ed.), *Multiculturalism: Examining the politics of recognition*. Princeton, NJ: Princeton University Press.

Taylor, C. (2012). Interculturalism or multiculturalism? *Philosophy and Social Criticism, 38*, 413–423.

Taylor, D.M., Wright, S.C., Moghaddam, F.M., & Lalonde, R.N. (1990). The personal/group discrimination discrepancy: Perceiving my group, but not myself, to be a target of discrimination. *Personality and Social Psychology Bulletin, 16*, 254–262.

Taylor, D.M., Wright, S.C., & Porter, L.E. (1993). Dimensions of perceived discrimination: The personal/group discrimination discrepancy. In M.P. Zanna & J.M. Olson (Eds.), *The psychology of prejudice: The Ontario symposium*, Vol. 7. Hillsdale, NJ: Erlbaum, pp. 233–256.

Ten Teije, I., Coenders, M., & Verkuyten, M. (in press). The paradox of integration: Immigrants and their attitude towards the native population. *Social Psychology*.

Tetlock, P.E., & Mitchell, G. (2008). Calibrating prejudice in milliseconds. *Social Psychology Quarterly, 71*, 12–16.

Thijs, J., & Verkuyten, M. (2013). Multiculturalism in the classroom: Ethnic attitudes and classmates' beliefs. *International Journal of Intercultural Relations, 37*, 176–187.

Thomsen, L., Green, E.G.T., & Sidanius, J. (2008). We will hunt them down: How social dominance orientation and right-wing authoritarianism fuel ethnic persecution of immigrants in fundamentally different ways. *Journal of Experimental Social Psychology, 44*, 1455–1464.

Tip, L.K., Zagefka, H., González, R., Brown, R., Cinnirella, M., & Na, X. (2012). Is support for multiculturalism threatened by . . . threat itself? *International Journal of Intercultural Relations, 36*, 22–30.

Titzmann, P., & Silbereisen, R.K. (2012). Acculturation or development? Autonomy expectations among ethnic German immigrant adolescents and their native German age-mates. *Child Development, 83*, 1640–1654.

Trojanow, I. (2008). *De wereldverzamelaar*. Breda: De Geus.

Tropp, L.R., Hawi, D.R., Van Laar, C., & Levin, S. (2012). Cross-ethnic friendships, perceived discrimination, and their effects on ethnic activism over time: A longitudinal investigation of three ethnic minority groups. *British Journal of Social Psychology, 51*, 257–272.

Tropp, L.R., & Prenevost, M.A. (2008). The role of intergroup contact in predicting children's interethnic attitudes: Evidence from meta-analytic and field studies. In S.R. Levy & M. Killen (Eds.), *Intergroup Attitudes and Relations in Childhood Through Adulthood*. New York: Oxford University Press.

Tsukashima, R.T., & Montero, D. (1976). The contact hypothesis: Social and economic contact and generational changes in the study of Black anti-Semitism. *Social Forces, 55*, 149–165.

Turiel, E. (2002). *The culture of morality*. Cambridge: Cambridge University Press.

Turner, J.C. (1982). Towards a cognitive redefinition of the social group. In H. Tajfel (Ed.), *Social identity and intergroup relations* (pp. 15–40). Cambridge: Cambridge University Press.

Turner, J.C. (1991). *Social influence*. Milton Keynes: Open University Press.

Turner, J.C., Hogg, M.A., Oakes, P.J., Reicher, S.D., & Wetherell, M. (1987). *Rediscovering the social group: A self-categorization theory*. Oxford: Blackwell.

Turner, J.C., & Reynolds, K.J. (2001). The social identity perspective in intergroup relations: Theories, themes, and controversies. In R. Brown & S. Gaertner (Eds.), *Blackwell handbook of social psychology, Vol. 4: Intergroup processes*. Oxford: Blackwell.

Turner, T. (1993). Anthropology and multiculturalism: What is anthropology that multiculturalists should be mindful of it? *Cultural Anthropology, 8*, 411–429.

Tyler, T.R., Boeckmann, R., Smith, H., & Huo, Y. (1997). *Social justice in a diverse society*. Boulder, CO: Westview Press.

Uberoi, V. (2008). Do policies of multiculturalism change national identities? *The Political Quarterly, 79*, 404–417.

Ufkes, E.G., Otten, S., Van der Zee, K.I., Giebels, E., & Dovidio, J.F. (2012). Urban district identity as a common ingroup identity: The different role of ingroup prototypicality for minority and majority groups. *European Journal of Social Psychology, 42*, 706–717.

United Nations (2004). *Human development report: Cultural diversity in today's diverse world*. New York: United Nations Development Program.

Unkelbach, C., Forgas, J.P., & Denson, T.F. (2008). The turban effect: The influence of Muslim headgear and induced affect on aggressive responses in the shooter bias paradigm. *Journal of Experimental Social Psychology, 44*, 1409–1413.

Updegraff, K., Umana-Taylor, A., McHale, S.M., Wheeler, L.A., & Perez-Brena, N. (2012). Mexican-origin youth's cultural orientations and adjustment: Changes from early to late adolescence. *Child Development, 83*, 1655–1671.

Vaes, J., Leyens, J-P., Paladino, M.P., & Miranda, M.P. (2012). We are human, they are not: Driving forces behind outgroup dehumanization and the humanization of the ingroup. *European Review of Social Psychology, 23*, 64–106.

Vala, J. (2008). Black immigrants in Portugal: Luso-Tropicalism and prejudice. *Journal of Social Issues, 64*, 287–302.

Van Bavel, J.J., Packer, D.J., & Cunningham, W.A. (2008). The neural substrates of in-group bias: A functional magnetic resonance imagining investigation. *Psychological Science, 19*, 130–138.

Van Bruinessen, M. (1996). Kurds, Turks, and Alevi revival in Turkey. *Middle East Report, 200*, 7–10.

Van den Berghe, P. (1981). *The ethnic phenomenon*. New York: Elsevier Press.

Van der Noll, J. (2012). *Beneath the surface of intolerance: Studies on the acceptance of Muslims in Western Europe*. Bremen: International Graduate School of Social Sciences.

Van der Noll, J., Verkuyten, M., & Poppe, E. (2010). Political tolerance and prejudice: Differential reactions toward Muslims in the Netherlands. *Basic and Applied Social Psychology, 32*, 46–56.

Van Doorn, M., Scheepers, P. & Dagevos, J. (in press). Explaining the integration paradox among small immigrant groups in the Netherlands. *International Migration and Integration.*

Van Laar, C., Levin, S., Sinclair, S., & Sidanius, J. (2005). The effect of university roommate contact on ethnic attitudes and behavior. *Journal of Experimental Social Psychology, 41*, 329–345.

Van Oudenhoven, J.P., Groenewoud, T., & Hewstone, M. (1996). Cooperation, ethnic salience and generalization of interethnic attitudes. *European Journal of Social Psychology, 26*, 649–661.

Van Oudenhoven, J.P., Prins, K.S., & Buunk, B.P. (1998). Attitudes of minority and majority members towards adaptation of immigrants. *European Journal of Social Psychology, 28*, 995–1013.

Vasta, E. (2007). From ethnic minorities to ethnic majority policy: Multiculturalism and the shift to assimilationism in the Netherlands. *Ethnic and Racial Studies, 30*, 713–740.

Vega, W.A., Gil, A.G., Warheit, G.J., Zimmerman, R.S., & Apospori E. (1993). Acculturation and delinquent behaviour among Cunam American adolescents: Towards an empirical model. *American Journal of Community Psychology, 21,* 113–125.

Velasco González, K., Verkuyten, M., Weesie, J., & Poppe, E. (2008). Prejudice towards Muslims in the Netherlands: Testing the Integrated threat theory. *British Journal of Social Psychology, 47*, 667–685.

Veling, W., Susser, E., Van Os, J., Mackenbach, J.P., Selten, J-P., & Hoek, H.W. (2008). Ethnic density of neighborhoods and incidence of psychotic disorders among immigrants. *American Journal of Psychiatry, 165*, 66–73.

Verkuyten, M. (1997a). Discourses of ethnic minority identity. *British Journal of Social Psychology*, 36, 565–586.

Verkuyten, M. (1997b). *'Redelijk racisme': Gesprekken over allochtonen in oude stadswijken ('Reasonable racism': talking about ethnic minorities in the inner city)*. Amsterdam: Amsterdam University Press.

Verkuyten, M. (2001). 'Abnormalization' of ethnic minorities in conversation. *British Journal of Social Psychology, 40*, 257–278.

Verkuyten, M. (2003). Discourses about ethnic group (de-)essentialism: Oppressive and progressive aspects. *British Journal of Social Psychology, 42*, 371–391.

Verkuyten, M. (2004a). Emotional reactions to and support for immigrant policies: Attributed responsibilities to categories of asylum seekers, *Social Justice Research*, 17, 293–314.

Verkuyten, M. (2004b). Everyday ways of thinking about multiculturalism. *Ethnicities, 4*, 53–74.

Verkuyten, M. (2005a). Ethnic group identification and group evaluation among minority and majority groups: Testing the multiculturalism hypothesis. *Journal of Personality and Social Psychology, 88,* 121–138.

Verkuyten, M. (2005b). Immigration discourses and their impact on multiculturalism: A discursive and experimental study. *British Journal of Social Psychology*, 44, 223–241.

Verkuyten, M. (2005c). *The social psychology of ethnic identity*. Hove: Psychology Press.

Verkuyten, M. (2006). Multicultural recognition and ethnic minority rights: A social identity perspective. In W. Stroebe & M. Hewstone (Eds.), *European review of social psychology*. London: Psychology Press.

Verkuyten, M. (2007). Religious group identification and inter-religious relations: A study among Turkish-Dutch Muslims. *Group Processes and Intergroup Relations, 10*, 341–357.

Verkuyten, M. (2009a). Self-esteem and multiculturalism: An examination among ethnic minority and majority groups. *Journal of Research in Personality, 43*, 419–427.

Verkuyten, M. (2009b). Support for multiculturalism and minority rights: The role of national identification and outgroup threat. *Social Justice Research, 22*, 31–49.

Verkuyten, M. (2010). Assimilation ideology and situational wellbeing among ethnic minorities. *Journal of Experimental Social Psychology, 46*, 269–275.

Verkuyten, M. (2011). Ethnic discrimination and ethnic minority identity: A social psychological perspective. In S. Bonjour, A. Rea & D. Jacobs (Eds). *The others in Europe* (pp.127–136). Brussels: Editions de l'Université de Bruxelles

Verkuyten, M. (in press). Justifying discrimination of Muslim immigrants: Outgroup ideology and the five-step social identity model. *British Journal of Social Psychology*.

Verkuyten, M., & Brug, P. (2004). Multiculturalism and ethnic group status: The role of ethnic identification, group essentialism and protestant ethic. *European Journal of Social Psychology*, 34, 647–661.

Verkuyten, M., & De Wolf, A. (2002). Ethnic minority identity and group context: Self-descriptions, acculturation attitudes and group evaluations in an intra- and intergroup situation. *European Journal of Social Psychology, 32*, 781–800.

Verkuyten, M., & Maliepaard, M. (in press). A further test of the ' party over policy' effect: Political leadership and ethnic minority policies. *Basic and Applied Social Psychology*.

Verkuyten, M., & Martinovic, B. (2006). Understanding multicultural attitudes: The role of group status, identification, friendships, and justifying ideologies. *International Journal of Intercultural Relations, 30*, 1–18.

Verkuyten, M., & Martinovic, B. (2012a). Immigrants' national identification: Meanings, determinants and consequences. *Social Issues and Policy Review, 6*, 82–112.

Verkuyten, M., & Martinovic, B. (2012b). Social identity complexity and immigrants' attitude towards the host nation: The intersection of ethnic and religious group identification. *Personality and Social Psychology Bulletin, 38*, 1165–1177.

Verkuyten, M., Masson, K., & Elffers, H. (1995). Racial categorization and preference among older children in the Netherlands, *European Journal of Social Psychology, 25*, 637–656.

Verkuyten, M., & Pouliasi, K. (2002). Biculturalism among older children: Cultural frame switching, attributions, self-identification, and attitudes. *Journal of Cross Cultural Psychology, 33*, 596–609.

Verkuyten, M., & Pouliasi, K. (2006). Biculturalism and group identification: The mediating role of identification in cultural frame switching. *Journal of Cross Cultural Psychology, 37*, 312–326.

Verkuyten, M., & Reijerse, A. (2008). Intergroup structure and identity management among ethnic minority and majority groups: The interactive effects of perceived stability, legitimacy and permeability. *European Journal of Social Psychology, 31*, 106–121.

Verkuyten, M., & Slooter, L. (2007). Tolerance of Muslim beliefs and practices: Age related differences and context effects. *International Journal of Behavioral Development*, 31, 467–477.

Verkuyten, M., & Thijs, J. (2002). Racist victimization among children in the Netherlands: The effect of ethnic group and school. *Ethnic and Racial Studies, 25*, 310–331.

Verkuyten, M., & Thijs, J. (2004). Global and ethnic self-esteem in school context: Minority and majority groups in the Netherlands. *Social Indicators Research, 67*, 253–281.

Verkuyten, M., & Thijs, J. (2010). Ethnic minority labeling, multiculturalism and the attitude of majority group members. *Journal of Language and Social Psychology, 29*, 467–477.

Verkuyten, M., & Thijs, J. (in press). Multicultural education and inter-ethnic attitudes: An intergroup perspective. *European Psychologist*.

Verkuyten, M., Thijs, J., & Bekhuis, H. (2010). Intergroup contact and ingroup reappraisal: Examining the deprovincialization thesis. *Social Psychology Quarterly, 73*, 398–416.

Verkuyten, M., Thijs, J., & Stevens, G. (2012). Multiple identities and religious transmission: A study among Moroccan-Dutch Muslim adolescents and their parents. *Child Development, 83*, 1577–1590.

Verkuyten, M., & Yildiz, A.A. (2006). The endorsement of minority rights: The role of group position, national context, and ideological beliefs. *Political Psychology, 27*, 527–548.

Verkuyten, M., & Yildiz, A. (2007). National (dis)identification and ethnic and religious identity: A study among Turkish-Dutch Muslims. *Personality and Social Psychology Bulletin, 33*, 1448–1462.

Verkuyten, M., & Yildiz, A. (2009). Muslim immigrants and religious group feelings: Self-identification and attitudes among Sunni and Alevi Turkish-Dutch. *Ethnic and Racial Studies, 32*, 1121–1142,

Verkuyten, M., & Yildiz, A.A. (2010a). Religious identity consolidation and mobilisation among Turkish Dutch Muslims. *European Journal of Social Psychology, 40*, 436–447.

Verkuyten, M., & Yildiz, A.A. (2010b). Orthodoxie en integratie van Turks Nederlandse Moslims (*Orthodoxy and integration of Turkish Dutch Muslims*). *Mens en Maatschappij, 85*, 5–26.

Verkuyten, M., & Zaremba, K. (2005). Inter-ethnic relations in a changing political context. *Social Psychology Quarterly, 68*, 375–386.

Vermeulen, H. (2001). *Etnisch-culturele diversiteit als 'feit' en norm (Ethnic-cultural diversity as 'fact' and norm)*. Amsterdam: Vossius.

Vermeulen, H., & Govers, C. (1997). From political mobilization to the politics of consciousness. In C. Govers & H. Vermeulen (Eds.), *The politics of ethnic consciousness* (pp. 1–30). London: MacMillan.

Vermeulen, H., & Slijper, B. (2003). *Multiculturalisme in Canada, Australië en de Verenigde Staten: Ideologie en beleid, 1950–2000 (Multiculturalism in Canada, Australia and the United States: Ideology and Policy, 1950–2000)*. Amsterdam: Aksant.

Vertovec, S. (1998). Multi-multiculturalisms. In M. Martiniello (Ed.), *Multicultural policies and the state: A comparison of two European societies* (pp. 25–38). Utrecht: Ercomer.

Vertovec, S., & Wessendorf, S. (2010). Introduction: Assessing the backlash against multiculturalism in Europe. In S. Vertovec & S. Wessendorf (Eds.), *The multiculturalism backlash: European discourses, policies and practices* (pp. 1–31). Oxon: Routledge.

Vignoles, V.L. (2011). Identity motives. In K. Luyckx, S.J. Schwartz, & V.L. Vignoles (Eds.), *Handbook of identity theory and research* (pp. 403–432). New York: Springer.

Vink, M. (2007). Dutch multiculturalism: Beyond the pillarization myth. *Political Studies Review, 5*, 337–350.

Voas, D., & Fleischmann, F. (2012). Islam moves West: religious change in the first and second generations. *Annual Review of Sociology, 38*, 525–545.

Vogt, W.P. (1997). *Tolerance and education: Learning to live with diversity and difference*. London: Sage.

Volkan, V. (1999). Psychoanalysis and diplomacy: Part 1, Individual and large group identity. *Journal of Applied Psychoanalytic Studies, 1*, 29–55.

Vorauer, J.D., & Sasaki, S.J. (2011). In the worst rather than the best of times: Effects of salient intergroup ideology in threatening intergroup interactions. *Journal of Personality and Social Psychology, 101*, 307–320.

Vorauer, J.D., Gagnon, A., & Sasaki, S.J. (2009). Salient intergroup ideology and intergroup interaction. *Psychological Science, 20*, 838–845.

Vorhoff, K. (2003). The past in the future: Discourses on the Alevis in contemporary Turkey. In P. J. White & J. Jongerden (Eds.), *Turkey's Alevi Enigma: A Comprehensive Overview* (pp. 93–109). Leiden: Brill.

Wagner, U., Christ, O., & Heitmeyer, W. (2010). Anti-immigrant bias. In J.F. Dovidio, M. Hewstone, P. Glick., & V.M. Esses (Eds.), *The Sage handbook of prejudice, stereotyping and discrimination* (pp. 361–376). London: Sage.

Wainryb, C., Shaw, L.A., & Maianu, C. (1998). Tolerance and intolerance: Children's and adolescents' judgments of dissenting beliefs, speech, persons, and conduct. *Child Development, 69*, 1541–1555.

Wakefield, J.R.H., Hopkins, N., Cockburn, C., Shek, K.M., Muirhead, A., & Reicher, S. (2011). The impact of adopting civic conceptions of national belonging for others' treatment. *Personality and Social Psychology Bulletin, 37*, 1599–1610.

Walters, D., Phythian, K., & Anisef, P. (2007). The acculturation of Canadian immigrants: Determinants of ethnic identification with the host society. *Canadian Review of Sociology and Anthropology, 44*, 37–64.

Walther, E. (2002). Guilt by mere association: Evaluative conditioning and the spreading attitude effect. *Journal of Personality and Social Psychology, 82*, 919–934.

Walzer, M. (1997). *On toleration*. New Haven: Yale University Press.

Wandert, T., Ochsmann, R., Brug, P., Chybicka, A., Lacassagne, M-F., & Verkuyten, M. (2009). Black German identities: Validating the multidimensional inventory of Black identity. *Journal of Black Psychology, 35*, 456–484.

Ward, C., & Masgoret, A. (2006). An integrative model of attitudes toward immigrants. *International Journal of Intercultural Relations, 30*, 671–682.

Waters, M.C. (1990). *Ethnic options*. Berkeley, CA: University of California Press.

Watson, W.E., Johnson, L., Kumar, K., & Critelli, J. (1998). Process gain and process loss: Comparing interpersonal processes and performance of culturally diverse and non-diverse teams across time. *International Journal of Intercultural Relations, 30*, 671–682.

Watt, S.E., Maio, G.R., Rees, K., & Hewstone, M. (2007). Functions of attitudes towards ethnic groups: Effects of level of abstraction. *Journal of Experimental Social Psychology, 43*, 441–449.

Wentholt, R., & Verkuyten, M. (1999). *Meanings of the term identity: That, who, what and how you are*. Utrecht, The Netherlands: Ercomer.

Wenzel, M., Mummendey, A., & Waldzus, S. (2007). Superordinate identities and intergroup conflict: The ingroup projection model. *European Review of Social Psychology, 18*, 331–372.

White, J.B., & Langer, E.J. (1999). Horizontal hostility: Relations between similar minority groups. *Journal of Social Issues, 55*, 537–559.

268   *References*

White, J.B., Schmitt, M.T., & Langer, E.J. (2006). Horizontal hostility: Multiple minority groups and differentiation from the mainstream. *Group Processes and Intergroup Relations, 9*, 339–358.

Whitesell, N., Mitchell, C., Kaufman, C., & Spicer, P. (2006). Developmental trajectories of personal and collective self-esteem among American Indian adolescents. *Child Development, 77*, 1487–1503.

Wiley, S. (in press). Rejection–identification among Latino immigrants in the United States. *International Journal of Intercultural Relations.*

Williams, K.D. (2001). *Ostracism: The power of silence*. London: Guildford.

Williams, R.H., & Vashi, G. (2007). Hijab and American Muslim women: Creating the space for autonomous selves. *Sociology of Religion, 68*, 269–287.

Wolsko, C., Park, B., & Judd, C. (2006). Considering the tower of Babel: Correlates of assimilation and multiculturalism among ethnic minority and majority groups in the United States. *Social Justice Research, 19*, 277–306.

Wolsko, C., Park, B., Judd, C.M., & Wittenbrink, B. (2000). Framing interethnic ideology: Effects of multicultural and color-blind perspectives on judgements of groups and individuals. *Journal of Personality and Social Psychology, 78*, 635–654.

Wong, C.A., Eccles, J., & Sameroff, A. (2003). The influence of ethnic discrimination and ethnic identification on African American adolescents: school and socioemotional adjustment. *Journal of Personality,71*, 1197–1232.

Wood, C., & Finlay, W.M.L. (2008). British National Party representations of Muslims in the month after the London bombings: Homogeneity, threat, and the conspiracy tradition. *British Journal of Social Psychology, 47*, 707–726.

Wright, S.C., Aron, A., McLaughlin-Volpe, T., & Ropp, S.A. (1997). The extended contact effect: Knowledge of cross-group friendships and prejudice. *Journal of Personality and Social Psychology, 73*, 73–90.

Wright, S.C., & Baray, G. (2012). Models of social change in social psychology: Collective action or prejudice reduction? Conflict or harmony?. In J. Dixon & M. Levine (Eds.), *Beyond prejudice: Extending the social psychology of conflict, inequality and social change* (pp. 225–247). Cambridge, UK: Cambridge University Press.

Wright, S.C., & Lubensky, M.E. (2009). The struggle for social equality: Collective action versus prejudice reduction. In S. Demoulin, J-P. Leyens & J.F. Dovidio (Eds.), *Intergroup misunderstandings: Impact of divergent social realities* (pp. 291–310). London: Psychology Press.

Wright, S.C., Taylor, D.M., & Moghaddam, F.M. (1990). Responding to membership in a disadvantaged group: From acceptance to collective protest. *Journal of Personality and Social Psychology, 58*, 994–1003.

WRR (2007). *Identificatie met Nederland (Identification with the Netherlands)*. Wetenschappelijke Raad voor het Regeringsbeleid [Scientific Council of Government Policy] Amsterdam: Amsterdam University Press.

Yildiz, A.A., & Verkuyten, M. (2011). Inclusive victimhood: Social identity and the politicization of collective trauma among Turkey's Alevis in Western Europe. *Peace and Conflict: Journal of Peace Psychology,17*, 243–269.

Yildiz, A.A. & Verkuyten, M. (2012). Conceptualizing Euro-Islam: Managing the societal demand for religious reform. *Identities: Global Studies in Culture and Power, 19*, 360–376.

Yildiz, A.A., & Verkuyten, M. (2013). 'We are not terrorists': Turkish Muslim organizations and the construction of a moral identity. *Ethnicities, 13*, 268–283.

Yip, T. (2005). Sources of situational variation in ethnic identity and psychological well-being: A palm pilot study of Chinese American students. *Personality and Social Psychology Bulletin, 31*, 1603–1616.

Yip, T., & Fuligni, A.J. (2002). Daily variation in ethnic identity, ethnic behaviours, and psychological well-being among American adolescents of Chinese descent. *Child Development, 73*, 1557–1572.

Ysseldyk, R., Matheson, K., & Anisman, H. (2010). Religiosity as identity: Toward an understanding of religion from a social identity perspective. *Personality and Social Psychology Review, 14*, 60–71.

Yzerbyt, V., Castano, E., Leyens, J-P., & Paladino, M-P. (2000). The primacy of the ingroup: The interplay of entativity and identification. *European Review of Social Psychology, 11*, 257–295.

Yzerbyt, V., Provost, V., & Corneille, O. (2005). Not competent but warm . . . really? Compensatory stereotypes in the French-speaking world. *Group Processes and Intergroup Relations, 8*, 291–308.

Zagefka, H., & Brown, R. (2002). The relationship between acculturation strategies, relative fit and intergroup relations: Immigrant-majority relations in Germany. *European Journal of Social Psychology, 32*, 171–188.

Zagefka, H., Tip, L.K., Gonzalez, R., Brown, R., & Cinnirella, M. (2012). Predictors of majority members' acculturation preferences: Experimental evidence. *Journal of Experimental Social Psychology, 48*, 654–659.

Zárate, M.A., & Shaw, M.P. (2010). The role of cultural inertia in reactions to immigration on the U.S./Mexico border. *Journal of Social Issues, 66*, 45–57.

Zárate, M.A., Shaw, M.P., Marquez, J.A., & Biagas, D. (2012). Cultural inertia: The effects of cultural change on intergroup relations and the self-concept. *Journal of Experimental Social Psychology, 48*, 634–645.

Zick, A., Wagner, U., van Dick, R., & Petzel, T. (2001). Acculturation and prejudice in Germany: Majority and minority perspectives. *Journal of Social Issues, 57*, 541–557.

Zimmermann, L., Zimmermann, K.F., & Constant, A. (2007). Ethnic self-identification of first-generation immigrants. *International Migration Review, 41*, 769–781.

Zirkel, S. (2008). The influence of multicultural educational practices on student outcomes and intergroup relations. *Teachers College Record, 110*, 1147–1181.

Zolberg, A.R., & Long, L.W. (1999). Why Islam is like Spanish: Cultural incorporation in Europe and the United States. *Politics and Society, 27*, 5–38.

Zomeren, van M., Postmes, T., & Spears, R. (2008). Toward an integrative social identity model of collective action: A quantitative research synthesis of three socio-psychological perspectives. *Psychological Bulletin, 134*, 504–535.

Index

Romanians, in France, study among 104
Romanics 203
Roosens, E. 10, 12
Rosenberg, M. 35, 50, 51, 64
Royal Dutch Indian Army (KNIL) 27, 43
Ruhs, D. 213
Rwanda 129, 179

Sarkozy, N. 6
Scheffer, P. 159
Schily, O. 159
scientific and policy relevance of identity
    concept, 27–66
Scientific Council for Government Policy
    (WRR) 1, 2, 49, 108
Scotland 97, 134
Scotson, J.L. 150
secondary transfer effect 193, 194
self: concept of, and concept of 'identity'
    and, distinction between 34; sense of:
    see sense of self
self-categorization 54–6
self-definitions, psychological dynamics of
    57
self-feeling 34, 180; and identity 35
self-verification 68; feedback loop in 85–6;
    of social identity 81–2
sense of self 30, 35, 41, 80, 113, 170, 180;
    individual development of 88–94;
    secure and confident 96; and social
    identity 39
Sherif, M. 116, 117, 143, 200
Shiites 4, 189, 202, 204, 205, 210
Sikhs in USA 81
Simon, B. 73, 127, 212, 213
Singalese 150
Sioux Indians (South Dakota) 90
situational dependency of ethnic identity,
    67–86
situational threat, stereotype threat as 41
Sivas massacre (1993) 45, 46
slavery 43, 44, 129, 154
Slovakia 163
Sniderman, P. 124, 137, 144, 155, 185,
    204, 221
social cohesion 1, 5, 129, 160, 167, 186,
    217, 218, 221; and immigration and
    cultural diversity 3; and stability 169
social dominance theory 164

social identities 35–7; comparisons and
    distinctions between 79–80; power of
    113; situational changes in 77–8
social identity (*passim*): conduct
    appropriate to 56–7; dimensions 53–8;
    distinctive and positive, human need for
    122; evaluation of 55; experimental
    manipulation of 114–16; negative 72;
    positive 42, 72, 73, 76, 121, 122; and
    sense of self 39; sense of 38–41
social identity complexity 111, 211, 212
social identity theory 72, 117–20, 122,
    142, 164, 167
social inequality 167, 197
social integration 105, 106, 146, 147, 161
social mobility, individual, integration
    paradox of 74–5
social psychological assumptions of
    multiculturalism 161–2
social psychology 12–18, 24, 25, 95, 115,
    119, 120, 162, 170, 190; contribution of
    26 (to solving problems in a
    multicultural society 222–4); crisis in
    17–19; and ethnicity 15–17
social validation: and ethnic discrimination
    67–86; of identity 81; of social identity
    81–6
solidarity: and identity, countries' search
    for 1–27; national 3, 6, 226, 229; search
    for 1–27; social 2, 12
Somalia 27; refugees and asylum seekers
    from, arrival of in Netherlands 27
Sorbs in Germany 82
South Africa 33, 166, 197
South Moluccans 80; immigration of, to
    Netherlands 27; in Netherlands 43, 111
Spain 6, 7, 227; Jews in, in fifteenth
    century 87; settlement of Muslims
    originating from former colonies in 6,
    7, 227
Sri Lanka, Singalese and Tamils in 150
stereotype(s) 17, 39, 72, 126, 128, 190,
    191, 195, 206; effect of contact on 196;
    group 12; negative 16, 20, 41, 75, 81,
    85, 90, 93, 95, 97, 125, 175, 192, 211;
    of immigrant groups 137–8; out-group
    137; positive 212; social 41; threat,
    research on 40, 41, 81
stereotyping 126, 128, 153, 173, 175, 198